BUYING A HOME IN BRITAIN

by

David Hampshire

SURVIVAL BOOKS • LONDON • ENGLAND

First published 2000

All rights reserved. No part of this publication may be reproduced, stored in a
retrieval system or recorded by any means, without prior written permission from the
publisher.

Copyright © Survival Books 2000

Survival Books Limited, Suite C, Third Floor
Standbrook House, 2-5 Old Bond Street
London W1X 3TB, United Kingdom
☎ +44-207-493 4244, Fax +44-207-491 0605
E-mail: info@survivalbooks.net
Internet: www.survivalbooks.net

British Library Cataloguing in Publication Data.
A CIP record for this book is available from the British Library.
ISBN 1 901130 15 0

Printed and bound in Spain by Estudios Gráficos Zure, SA, Carretera Lutxana-Asua,
24A, 48950 Erandio Goikoa (Bizkaia), Spain.

ACKNOWLEDGEMENTS

M y sincere thanks to all those who contributed to the successful publication of this book, in particular the many people who took the time and trouble to read and comment on the draft versions, including Joanna Styles, Karen Verheul (proof-reader), John Verheul, Debbie Joyce, Pat and Ron Scarborough and everyone else who contributed in any way and who I have omitted to mention. Also a special thank you to Jim Watson for the superb cover, illustrations, cartoons and maps.

By the same publisher:

The Alien's Guide to France
Buying a Home Abroad
Buying a Home in Florida
Buying a Home in France
Buying a Home in Ireland
Buying a Home in Italy
Buying a Home in Portugal
Buying a Home in Spain
Living and Working in America
Living and Working in Australia
Living and Working in Britain
Living and Working in Canada
Living and Working in France
Living and Working in London
Living and Working in New Zealand
Living and Working in Spain
Living and Working in Switzerland

What Readers and Reviewers Have Said About Survival Books

When you buy a model plane for your child, a video recorder, or some new computer gizmo, you get with it a leaflet or booklet pleading 'Read Me First', or bearing large friendly letters or bold type saying 'IMPORTANT – follow the instructions carefully'. This book should be similarly supplied to all those entering France with anything more durable than a 5-day return ticket. It is worth reading even if you are just visiting briefly, or if you have lived here for years and feel totally knowledgeable and secure. But if you need to find out how France works then it is indispensable. Native French people probably have a less thorough understanding of how their country functions. – Where it is most essential, the book is most up to the minute.

Living France

We would like to congratulate you on this work: it is really super! We hand it out to our expatriates and they read it with great interest and pleasure.

ICI (Switzerland) AG

Rarely has a 'survival guide' contained such useful advice – This book dispels doubts for first-time travellers, yet is also useful for seasoned globetrotters – In a word, if you're planning to move to the USA or go there for a long-term stay, then buy this book both for general reading and as a ready-reference.

American Citizens Abroad

It is everything you always wanted to ask but didn't for fear of the contemptuous put down – The best English-language guide – Its pages are stuffed with practical information on everyday subjects and are designed to complement the traditional guidebook.

Swiss News

A complete revelation to me – I found it both enlightening and interesting, not to mention amusing.

Carole Clark

Let's say it at once. David Hampshire's *Living and Working in France* is the best handbook ever produced for visitors and foreign residents in this country; indeed, my discussion with locals showed that it has much to teach even those born and bred in *l'Hexagone*. – It is Hampshire's meticulous detail which lifts his work way beyond the range of other books with similar titles. Often you think of a supplementary question and search for the answer in vain. With Hampshire this is rarely the case. – He writes with great clarity (and gives French equivalents of all key terms), a touch of humour and a ready eye for the odd (and often illuminating) fact. – This book is absolutely indispensable.

The Riviera Reporter

The ultimate reference book – Every conceivable subject imaginable is exhaustively explained in simple terms – An excellent introduction to fully enjoy all that this fine country has to offer and save time and money in the process.

American Club of Zurich

What Readers and Reviewers Have Said About Survival Books

What a great work, wealth of useful information, well-balanced wording and accuracy in details. My compliments!

Thomas Müller

This handbook has all the practical information one needs to set up home in the UK – The sheer volume of information is almost daunting – Highly recommended for anyone moving to the UK.

American Citizens Abroad

A very good book which has answered so many questions and even some I hadn't thought of – I would certainly recommend it.

Brian Fairman

A mine of information – I may have avoided some embarrassments and frights if I had read it prior to my first Swiss encounters – Deserves an honoured place on any newcomer's bookshelf.

English Teachers Association, Switzerland

Covers just about all the things you want to know on the subject – In answer to the desert island question about *the one* how-to book on France, this book would be it – Almost 500 pages of solid accurate reading – This book is about enjoyment as much as survival.

The Recorder

It's so funny – I love it and definitely need a copy of my own – Thanks very much for having written such a humorous and helpful book.

Heidi Guiliani

A must for all foreigners coming to Switzerland.

Antoinette O'Donoghue

A comprehensive guide to all things French, written in a highly readable and amusing style, for anyone planning to live, work or retire in France.

The Times

A concise, thorough account of the DO's and DON'Ts for a foreigner in Switzerland – Crammed with useful information and lightened with humorous quips which make the facts more readable.

American Citizens Abroad

Covers every conceivable question that may be asked concerning everyday life – I know of no other book that could take the place of this one.

France in Print

Hats off to Living and Working in Switzerland!

Ronnie Almeida

CONTENTS

4. FINDING YOUR DREAM HOME   129

5. ARRIVAL & SETTLING IN   215

6. APPENDICES 225

INDEX 247

SUGGESTIONS 251

ORDER FORMS 254

IMPORTANT NOTE

Readers should note that the laws and regulations regarding buying property in Britain *aren't* the same as in other countries and are also liable to change periodically. **I cannot recommend too strongly that you check with an official and reliable source (not always the same) and take expert legal advice before paying any money or signing any legal documents. Don't, however, believe everything you're told or read, even, dare I say it, herein!**

To help you obtain further information and verify data with official sources, useful addresses and references to other sources of information have been included in all chapters and in appendices A and B. Important points have been emphasised throughout the book **in bold print**, some of which it would be expensive or foolish to disregard. **Ignore them at your peril or cost.** Unless specifically stated, the reference to any company, organisation, product or publication in this book *doesn't* constitute an endorsement or recommendation. Any reference to any place or person (living or dead) is purely coincidental!

AUTHOR'S NOTES

- The term Britain, as used in this book, embraces Great Britain (the island comprising England, Wales and Scotland) and Northern Ireland. Its official name is the United Kingdom (UK) of Great Britain and Northern Ireland. Northern Ireland is made up of the former province of Ulster, which remained part of the UK when the Irish Free State was established in 1921. *Buying a Home in Ireland* is covered in our sister publication of the same name by Joe Laredo. The British Isles is the geographical term for the group of islands that includes Great Britain, Ireland and many smaller islands surrounding Britain. When referring to the Irish Republic (Eire) I have used the name Ireland. Although Britain is officially referred to as the United Kingdom, I have generally kept to the shorter term Britain except when using official names or titles.

- Frequent references are made throughout this book to the European Union (EU), which comprises Austria, Belgium, Denmark, Finland, France, Germany, Greece, Ireland, Italy, Luxembourg, the Netherlands, Portugal, Spain, Sweden and the United Kingdom. The European Economic Area (EEA) includes the EU countries plus Iceland, Liechtenstein and Norway.

- Unless otherwise stated, all prices quoted are in pounds (£) sterling and include VAT at 17.5 per cent. Prices should be taken as estimates only, although they were mostly correct at the time of publication.

- His/he/him/man/men (etc.) also mean her/she/her/woman/women (no offence ladies!). This is done simply to make life easier for both the reader and (in particular) the author, and **isn't** intended to be sexist.

- Warnings and important points are shown in **bold** type.

- Lists of **Useful Addresses** and **Further Reading** are contained in **Appendices A** and **B** respectively. Most associations, organisations and publications mentioned in the book are listed in **Appendix A**.

- For those unfamiliar with the Imperial system of weights and measures, metric conversion tables are included in **Appendix C**. Most measurements in this book are shown in metric and imperial.

- A list of property, mortgage and other terms used in this book is included in a **Glossary** in **Appendix D**.

- A **Map of Britain** showing the regions is included on page 132 and a map showing the major cities and geographical features is on page 6.

INTRODUCTION

If you're planning to buy a home in Britain or even just thinking about it — this is **THE BOOK** for you! Whether you want an apartment, townhouse, cottage, executive house or a mansion, a holiday or a permanent home, this book will help make your dreams come true. The aim of *Buying a Home in Britain* is to provide you with the information necessary to help you choose the most favourable location and most appropriate home **to satisfy your individual requirements.** Most important of all, it's intended to help you avoid the pitfalls and risks associated with buying a home in Britain, which for most people is one of the largest financial transactions they will make during their lifetimes.

You may already own a home in another country; however, buying a home in Britain (or any foreign country) is a different matter altogether. One of the most common mistakes many people make when buying a home in Britain is to assume that the laws and purchase procedures are the same as in their home country (which is unlikely to be the case). Buying property in Britain is, however, generally very safe, particularly when compared with certain other European countries. Nevertheless, if you don't follow the rules provided for your protection, a purchase can result in serious financial loss, as some people have discovered to their cost.

Before buying a home in Britain you need to ask yourself *exactly* why you want to buy a home there? Is your primary concern a good long-term investment or do you wish to work or retire there? Where and what can you afford to buy? Do you plan to let your home to offset the running costs? What about capital gains and inheritance taxes? *Buying a Home in Britain* will help you answer these and many other questions. It won't, however, tell you where and what to buy, or whether having made your decision you will be happy – that part is up to you!

For many people, buying a home in Britain has previously been a case of pot luck. However, with a copy of *Buying a Home in Britain* to hand you'll have a wealth of priceless information at your fingertips. Information derived from a variety of sources, both official and unofficial, not least the hard won personal experiences of the author, his friends, colleagues and acquaintances. This book doesn't, however, contain all the answers (most of us don't even know the right questions to ask). What it *will* do is reduce the risk of making an expensive mistake that you may regret later and help you make informed decisions and calculated judgements, instead of costly mistakes and uneducated guesses (forewarned is forearmed!). **Most important of all, it will help you save money and will repay your investment many times over.**

The recession in the early '90s caused an upheaval in world property markets, during which many so-called 'gilt-edged' property investments went to the wall. However, property remains one of the best long-term investments (particularly in London and the south-east of England) and it's certainly one of the most pleasurable. Buying a home in Britain is a wonderful way to make new friends, broaden your horizons and revitalise your life – and in rural areas provides a welcome bolt-hole to recuperate from the stresses and strains of modern life. I trust this book will help you avoid the pitfalls and smooth your way to many happy years in your new home in Britain, secure in the knowledge that you have made the right decision.

Good Luck!   **David Hampshire**
                                                        October 1999

1.

WHY BRITAIN?

Britain is one of the most cosmopolitan countries in Europe, with a diversity that's unmatched in many other countries; from bustling cities to picturesque villages, remote islands (where the way of life has barely changed in centuries) to modern 'new' towns, designed and built in the latter part of the 20th century. It's a country of huge variety with something for everyone: fine beaches for water sport enthusiasts; beautiful unspoilt countryside for the greens; a wealth of magnificent ancient cities and towns for history enthusiasts; vibrant night-life for the jet set; fine wines and cuisine from all corners of the globe for gourmets; a profusion of culture, art and serious music for art lovers; and tranquillity for the stressed. Few other countries in the world offer such a captivating mixture of history and tradition, culture and art, liberty and energy. As when buying a home anywhere, you aren't buying simply a home, but a lifestyle.

There are many excellent reasons for buying a home in Britain, although it's important not to be under any illusions about what you can expect from a home there. The first and most important question you need to ask yourself is *exactly* why do you want to buy a home in Britain? For example, are you seeking a holiday or a retirement home? If you're seeking a second home, will it be mainly used for long weekends or lengthier stays? Do you plan to let it to offset some of the mortgage and running costs? How important is the property income? Are you primarily looking for a sound investment or do you plan to work or start a business in Britain? Often buyers have a variety of reasons for buying a home in Britain, for example many people buy a holiday home with a view to living there permanently or semi-permanently when they retire. If this is the case, there are many more factors to take into account than if you're 'simply' buying a holiday home that you will occupy for a few weeks a year only (when it may be wiser not to buy at all!). If, on the other hand, you plan to work or start a business in Britain, you will be faced with a whole different set of criteria.

Can you really afford to buy a home in Britain? What about the future? Is your income secure and protected against inflation and currency fluctuations? In the '80s, many people purchased holiday homes by taking out second mortgages on their family homes and stretching their financial resources to the limits. Not surprisingly, when the recession struck in the early '90s, many people had their homes repossessed or were forced to sell at a huge loss when they were unable to maintain the mortgage payments. Buying a home in Britain can be an excellent investment, although in recent years many people have had their fingers burnt in Britain's volatile property market.

Property prices in Britain vary considerably depending on the location and while some regions such as Greater London and the south-east are booming, others (such as the north-east) are in sharp decline. Note that although prices rise faster than average in popular towns and regions, this is reflected in much higher than average prices and in many areas first-time buyers are finding it almost impossible to get a foot on the property ladder. However, for those with the resources, buying a property in many regions of Britain is an excellent investment and it's possible to double your money in less than five years. Nevertheless, you shouldn't expect to make a fast buck when buying property in Britain, but should look upon it as an investment in your family's future happiness, rather than merely in financial terms.

As in all countries, there are both advantages and disadvantages to buying a home in Britain, although for most people the benefits outweigh the drawbacks. Among the many advantages of buying a home in Britain are relatively good value for money (providing you avoid the most expensive areas); excellent build quality and fixtures and fittings; a vast range of designs and architectural styles; stable or buoyant property market in most areas; excellent investment potential in many areas; strong government and general lack of bureaucracy (compared with most other European countries); safe and straightforward purchase procedure (providing you aren't reckless); lack of corruption and integrity of (most) estate agents; low purchase fees (the lowest in Europe) and relatively low taxes; relatively easy and inexpensive to get to (at least for most western Europeans) and good communications; good rental possibilities in most areas; the availability of good local tradesmen and services; the friendliness of British people (particularly in rural areas); the timeless grandeur of Britain on your doorstep; and, last but not least, an excellent quality of life.

There are of course a few drawbacks, not least the risk of paying too much for a home and being unable to sell and recoup your investment; the possibility of over-stretching your finances (e.g. by taking on too large a mortgage) and being unable to maintain the payments; the possibility of gazumping; the relatively high crime rate in some areas; the threat of floods and storms in some regions; overcrowding in popular tourist areas; high traffic congestion and pollution in many towns and cities; the relatively high running costs of a home compared with some other countries; a high and increasing cost of living, particularly in London and the south-east; the expense of getting to and from Britain if you own a holiday home there and don't live in a nearby country or a country with good air connections and, last but not least, Britain's generally poor and unpredictable weather.

Unless you know exactly what you're looking for and where, it's advisable to rent a property for a period until you're more familiar with an area. As when making any major financial decision, it isn't advisable to be in too much of a hurry. Some people make expensive (even catastrophic) errors when buying homes in Britain, usually because they do insufficient research and are in too much of a hurry, often setting themselves ridiculous deadlines. Not surprisingly, most people wouldn't dream of acting so rashly when buying a property in their home country! It isn't uncommon for buyers to regret their decision after some time and wish they had purchased a different type of property in a different region (or even in a different country).

Before deciding to buy a home in Britain, it's advisable to do extensive research and read a number of books especially written for those planning to live or work there (like this one!) and study specialist property magazines and newspapers (such as those listed in **Appendix A**) and visit exhibitions such as the Ideal Home Exhibition staged at London's Earls Court Exhibition Centre in March. **Bear in mind that the cost of investing in a few books or magazines (and other research) is tiny compared with the expense of making a big mistake.** Finally, don't believe everything you read (even herein)!

This chapter provides information about permits and visas, retirement, working, buying a business, communications (e.g. telephone), getting to Britain and getting around, particularly by car.

DO YOU NEED A PERMIT OR VISA?

Before making any plans to buy a home in Britain, you must check whether you'll need a visa or residence permit and ensure that you'll be permitted to use the property when you wish and for whatever purpose you have in mind. While foreigners are freely permitted to buy property in Britain, most aren't permitted to remain longer than six months a year without becoming a resident. If there's a possibility that you or any family members may want to live permanently or work in Britain, you should enquire whether it will be possible before making any plans to buy a home there. If you were born in a European Union (EU) or European Economic Area (EEA) country (Austria, Belgium, Denmark, Finland, France, Germany, Greece, Iceland, Ireland, Italy, Liechtenstein, Luxembourg, Netherlands, Norway, Portugal, Spain, Sweden and the UK) or can show that at least one of your parents or grandparents was born in Britain, you're free to live in Britain without restrictions, providing you're able to support yourself (and any dependants) without state assistance.

Before making any plans to travel to Britain, you *must* ensure that you have the appropriate entry clearance (e.g. a visa) and permission, as without the correct documentation you will be refused permission to enter the country. **If you're in any doubt as to whether you require clearance to enter Britain, enquire at a British Embassy, High Commission or other British Diplomatic Mission overseas (collectively known as British Diplomatic Posts) before making plans to travel.** Note that in some countries, entry clearance can take some time to be granted due to the high number of applications to be processed.

Nationals of some non-Commonwealth and non-EEA countries who have been given permission to remain in Britain for more than six months or who have been allowed to work for more than three months, are required to register with the police (see page 219). When applicable, this condition is stamped in your passport, either on entry or by the Immigration and Nationality Directorate (IND) of the Home Office when granting an extension of stay. The Home Office (called the Interior Ministry in many countries) has the final decision on all matters relating to immigration.

The latest information about immigration, permits and visas can be obtained from the Immigration and Nationality Department (which publishes leaflets and booklets regarding all immigration categories), local law centres, Citizens Advice Bureaux and community relations councils. At the time of writing, the immigration service had introduced a new Integrated Casework Directorate and a restricted service was also being operated by the Public Enquiry Office in London. All applications for permits or visas should be sent to the Immigration and Nationality Directorate (IND), Block C, Whitgift Centre, Croydon CR9 2AR (Internet: www.homeoffice.gov.uk/ind/hpg.htm). The appropriate telephone number depends on the type of enquiry: general enquiries about immigration rules and procedures (☎ 0870-606 7766); requests for immigration application forms (☎ 0870-241 0645); and enquires about individual cases already under consideration (☎ 0870-608 1592).

Visitors

Nationals of certain countries, officially called 'visa nationals', require a visa (an official stamp in their passport) to enter Britain, irrespective of the purpose of their visit, e.g. holiday, residence or employment. **If you need a visa and arrive without one, you will be sent back to your home country at your own expense.** Visitors' visas are issued for a maximum stay of six months and are never extended beyond this period. If you want to stay longer you must leave and apply for a new visa. Visa nationals aren't permitted to change their status.

In 1999, nationals of the following countries *required* a visa to enter Britain: Afghanistan, Albania, Algeria, Angola, Armenia, Azerbaijan, Bangladesh, Belarus, Benin, Bhutan, Bosnia-Herzegovina, Bulgaria, Burkina, Burma (Myanmar), Burundi,

Cambodia, Cameroon, Cape Verde, Central African Republic, Chad, China, Comoros, Congo, Cuba, Djibouti, Egypt, Equatorial Guinea, Ethiopia, Gabon, Georgia, Ghana, Guinea, Guinea-Bissau, Haiti, India, Indonesia, Iran, Iraq, Jordan, Kazakhstan, Kirgizstan, Korea (North), Laos, Lebanon, Liberia, Libya, Madagascar, Mali, Mauritania, Moldova, Mongolia, Morocco, Mozambique, Nepal, Nigeria, Oman, Pakistan, Philippines, Romania, Russia, Rwanda, Sao Tome e Principe, Saudi Arabia, Senegal, Somalia, Sri Lanka, Sudan, Syria, Taiwan, Tajikistan, Thailand, Togo, Tunisia, Turkey, Turkmenistan, Uganda, Ukraine, Uzbekistan, Vietnam, Yemen and Zaire. With the exception of Croatia and Slovenia, nationals of the territories of the former Yugoslavia also require a visa.

Non-EEA nationals can visit Britain for a period of up to six months, although there's nothing to stop anyone leaving Britain for a few days after remaining for six months, and then returning for another six months (providing you're able to satisfy the immigration officer that you're a bona fide visitor). However, if an immigration officer thinks that you're spending more time in Britain than in your country of origin (or residence) or are really living in Britain, entry will be refused. If applicable, you still need entry clearance to enter Britain. The passports of visitors who aren't entitled to work in Britain are stamped with 'employment prohibited', which is strictly enforced.

Visitors may be required to convince immigration officers that they will stay for a limited period only and won't attempt to find work in Britain. You may be asked to show proof that you can support yourself financially during your stay or that you have relatives or friends who can support you, and to show a return ticket or the money to buy one. Visitors are usually given permission to stay for six months, even when planning a short visit only. If you're given permission to stay for less than six months on entry, you can apply to extend your stay up to a maximum of six months in total. If you want to establish temporary residence for longer than six months and believe you're eligible under the immigration rules, you should apply at a British Diplomatic Post *before* coming to Britain.

Frequent visitors (e.g. business people) can apply for a multiple-entry visitor's visa valid for two years. A non-EEA national may transact business during a visit, but may not take paid or unpaid employment or self-employment, or engage in business or any professional activity. Visitors have no right of appeal against refusal of entry clearance and refusal of leave to enter, although they can make a second application after receiving an explanation about why an application was refused.

RETIREMENT

Pensioners who are EEA nationals have the right of residence in any EEA country, providing they can prove they have sufficient income so as not to become a burden on the host country and have private health insurance (if they're ineligible for cover under the National Health Service). An application for a residence permit must be made before an EEA national has spent six months in Britain. Non-EEA nationals who wish to live but not work in Britain require entry clearance in the form of a Letter of Consent before arrival in Britain. To qualify you must be aged at least 60 and have under your control and disposal in the UK an income of not less than £25,000 a year. You must also be able to show that you're able to support and accommodate yourself and your dependants indefinitely without working and without recourse to public funds. Your presence must be in the best interests of Britain (whatever that means) or you must have close ties with Britain, e.g. close relatives, children attending school or periods of previous residence in Britain. If you're prohibited from working in Britain, this also applies to members of your family and any dependants. Persons of independent means are usually admitted for an initial period of one year and qualify for settlement (permanent residence) after four years continuous residence.

WORKING

If there's a possibility that you or any family members may wish to work in Britain, you must ensure that it will be possible before buying a home. If you don't qualify to live and work in Britain by birthright, family relationship or as a national of a European Economic Area (EEA) country, obtaining a work permit may be difficult or impossible. If you're a national of an EEA member country, you don't require official approval to live or work in Britain, although you still require a residence permit. A work permit must be obtained by an employer for a named worker and is always issued for a specific job for a specified period. Permits are issued providing no other person who's already allowed to live and work in Britain can be found to do the job, which must be proven by providing copies of advertisements and explaining why any applicants (who don't require a work permit) weren't suitable.

Vacancies must be advertised in the local, national and European press, as well as in any appropriate trade and professional journals. The salary and conditions of employment offered must be equal to those prevailing for similar jobs; the qualifications and experience must be exactly what's required; and they must usually have been acquired outside Britain. Employees should usually be aged between 23 and 54 (inclusive) for most occupations and applicants are normally expected to have an adequate knowledge of English. The lower age limit doesn't apply to sportsmen and sportswomen, and neither limit applies to artists and entertainers.

An employer must apply for a work permit at least eight weeks before he expects the prospective employee to start work in Britain by completing form OW1, available with explanatory leaflet OW5 from Jobcentres. After completion, the form must be sent with documentary evidence of the applicant's qualifications and experience (including original references), the job description and evidence of advertising (plus full details of any replies received), to the Department of Education and Employment, Overseas Labour Section (W5), Moorfoot, Sheffield S1 4PQ (☎ 0114-840224) for overseas workers living abroad.

Before moving to Britain to work, you should dispassionately examine your motives and credentials. What kind of work can you realistically expect to find in Britain? What are your qualifications and experience? Are they recognised in Britain? How good is your English? Unless your English is fluent, you won't be competing on equal terms with Britons (you won't anyway, but that's a different matter!). Most British employers aren't interested in employing anyone without, at the very least, an adequate working knowledge of English. Are there any jobs in your profession or trade in the area where you wish to live? The answers to these and many other questions can be quite disheartening, but it's better to ask them *before* moving to Britain rather than afterwards. While hoping for the best, you should plan for the worst case scenario and have a contingency plan and sufficient funds to last until you're established.

Many people turn to self-employment (see below) or start a business to make a living, although this path is strewn with pitfalls for the newcomer. Many foreigners don't do sufficient homework before moving to Britain. Note that it's difficult for non-EEA nationals to obtain a residence permit to work as self-employed in Britain.

SELF-EMPLOYMENT & STARTING A BUSINESS

Anyone who's a British citizen, an EEA-national or a permanent resident, can work as self-employed in Britain, which includes partnerships, co-operatives, franchises, commission-only jobs and private businesses. Unlike most other EU countries, there are few restrictions and little red tape for anyone wanting to start a business or work as self-employed in Britain (although you must still conform to EU regulations). One of the government's main initiatives for reducing the number of unemployed has been to encourage people to start their own businesses.

The number of self-employed has risen dramatically in the last decade and totals some 3.5 million (around 15 per cent of the workforce), the highest in the European Union. Much of the reduction in unemployment in recent years has been as a result of self-employment or jobs created by small companies. Redundancy (and the difficulty in finding full-time employment) is often the spur for over 45's to start their own business. Those aged 45 to 55 account for some 20 per cent of new business start-ups, although many are hollow 'consultancies', where professionals eke out a living on commission, and over 20 per cent of all men over 45 are now self-employed. **However, self-employment isn't a panacea for unemployment.** Over half of the self-employed work from home and a further third work in construction or retailing.

Research: For many people, starting a business is one of the quickest routes to bankruptcy known to mankind. In fact, many people who open businesses would be better off investing in lottery tickets – at least they would then have a chance of getting a return on their investment! **Most experts reckon that if you're going to work for yourself you must be prepared to fail.** The key to starting or buying a successful business is exhaustive research, research and yet more research (plus innovation, value for money and service). It's absolutely essential to check out the level of competition in a given area, as a saturation of trades and services is common in many areas.

Finance & Cash Flow: Most people are far too optimistic about the prospects of a new business and over-estimate income levels (it often takes years to make a profit). Be realistic or even pessimistic when estimating your income and overestimate the costs and underestimate the revenue (then reduce it by up to 50 per cent!). While hoping for the best, you should plan for the worst and have sufficient funds to last until you're established. New projects are rarely, if ever, completed within budget. Make sure you have sufficient working capital and that you can survive until a business takes off. British banks are extremely wary of lending to new businesses, especially businesses run by foreigners (would you trust a foreigner?). If you wish to borrow money to buy property or for a business venture in Britain, you should carefully consider where and in what currency to raise finance. Under-capitalisation is one of the main reasons for small business failures, which isn't helped by the routine late payment of bills.

Payment: Late payment of bills is the scourge of small businesses in Britain. The average small firm waits up to 80 days for an invoice to be paid (big companies get paid an average of 35 days earlier), one of the longest periods in the EU. Not surprisingly many small businesses are bankrupted by late payers. Under new legislation, small companies have the right to claim interest on the late payment of bills, although most companies dare not for fear of losing business.

Loans & Overdrafts: British banks are reluctant to lend to small businesses without security and were blamed by many businessmen for prolonging the recession and bankrupting sound businesses by calling in loans and withdrawing overdraft facilities at a moment's notice. British banks probably have the worst record of refusing loans to sound businesses in the western world. During the recession in the '90s, relations between small businesses and banks reached an all-time low and although they have since improved, they are still terrible.

Information & Professional Advice: A wealth of free advice and information for budding entrepreneurs is available from government agencies, local councils and the private sector. Many books are published on self-employment and starting your own business including *Starting Your Own Business* and *Which? Guide to Earning Money From Home*, both published by Which? Books. Libraries are an excellent source of information about starting a business. The Employment Service publishes a 'Jobhunt' booklet entitled *Be Your Own Boss* and a magazine entitled *Home Run* (☎ 0208-846 9244) is published for homeworkers.

A number of local authority agencies and government departments provide free professional advice and assistance on starting and running a business, including finance and borrowing; marketing and selling; setting up and naming a company; bookkeeping and tax; premises and employment; advertising and promotion; patents and copyright; equipment and computing. These include the government run Small Firms Service and Business Enterprise or Business Advice Centres, financed by county councils. To find your local business enterprise or advice office, consult your local phone book or Yellow Pages.

The Small Firms Service (or the Scottish or Welsh Development Agencies in Scotland and Wales) provides information, signposting (to put you in touch with the right people), confidential counselling and business development services. The last two services are provided in consultation with business counsellors. The Small Firms Service produces an information pack entitled *Working for Yourself*. If you wish to start a business in the London area, a comprehensive booklet about enterprise aid entitled *Getting Started*, is available from the London Enterprise Agency (LEntA), 4 Snow Hill, London EC1A 2BS (☎ 0207-236 3000).

Grants, Low-Interest Loans and Training: There are a number of schemes designed to assist people (particularly young people) in starting a business including Livewire, Enterprise Training, the Enterprise Allowance Scheme, the Prince's Youth Business Trust and the London Enterprise Agency. Local, county and borough councils offer a variety of low-interest loans and grants, e.g. London LINK (Local Investment Networking Company). The government also provides a number of financial incentives and training schemes for those who wish to go it alone. Many county youth and community services run self-employment projects for young people, e.g. those aged 16 to 25. Ask your local Careers Centre for information.

Buying A Business: Businesses and franchises are advertised for sale each week in *Dalton's Weekly*, *Exchange & Mart*, and weekly and Sunday newspapers (e.g. the *Sunday Times*). There are also franchise magazines such as *What Franchise*. However, you should be wary of franchises, many of which take years to make a profit (often the only ones who get rich are the franchise companies).

Miscellaneous: If you're self-employed, you must pay your own income tax and National Insurance (social security) contributions. To work as a self-employed sub-contractor in the building trade, you must have a sub-contractor's tax certificate card, without which an employer must deduct 25 per cent for standard tax and National Insurance contributions. The Inland Revenue publish many leaflets for the self-employed that come under the general title of *Tax and Your Business* including *Starting Your Own Business* (CWL1). Note that anyone who's self-employed and whose taxable turnover exceeds £50,000 a year, must register for Value Added Tax (see page 108). Depending on the type of work you're engaged in, you may need to adhere to local regulations (e.g. noise, safety and hygiene) and you may need to take out insurance against accidents at work or against damage to a third party's property.

Postscript: Whatever people may tell you, starting your own business isn't easy (otherwise most of us would be doing it). It requires a lot of hard work (self-employed people work an average of ten hours more a week than employees), usually a sizeable amount of cash (many businesses fail because of lack of capital), good organisation (e.g. bookkeeping and planning) and a measure of luck – although generally the harder you work, the more 'luck' you will have!

KEEPING IN TOUCH

Telephone

The telephone system in Britain is dominated by British Telecom (BT), created with a 25-year licence (to print money) in 1984 when the state-owned telephone system was privatised. In 1991, the government ended the duopoly of BT and Mercury, and opened up the telecommunications market to national and international competition (although BT still has a monopoly on local calls in most areas). Britain is at the forefront of telecommunications technology and other European countries lag behind when it comes to telecoms liberalisation (although most countries have now privatised their former public monopolies). Over 100 companies are licensed to operate telecoms services in Britain and the market is very competitive for most services, therefore it's important to shop around and compare rates in order to save money.

Users can choose between BT, cable companies, radio-based networks and a large number of indirect operators. In recent years cable (TV and phone) companies have proliferated and now cover some 11 million homes. To find out which cable phone company operates in your area ☎ 0990-111777. Radio-based companies include Ionica, Atlantic Telecom and Scottish Telecom, all of which operate in restricted areas but are planning to increase their coverage. With indirect companies you need to dial a code before each number you call or call a free number to obtain a dialling code.

The major companies include ACC Telecom*, AT&T*, Atlantic Telecom, BT*, Cable & Wireless*, The Cable Corporation, CableTel, ComTel, Eurobell, First Telecom*, Ionica, Kingston, Scottish Telecom, Telewest and Yorkshire Cable (* = national operators). In 1998, Ionica, Eurobell and Kingston offered the largest savings for most users, but are available in certain parts of the country only. ACC Telecom is among the cheapest national indirect companies and Scottish Telecom provides the cheapest direct service. The savings depend on how large your monthly bill is, when you make most calls and what sort of calls you make (e.g. local, national or international). Connection costs range from free up to around £30. Also shop around the Internet, e.g. www.toll.co.uk, which provides tariff calculators for both terrestrial and mobile phone services.

Installation: Before moving into a new home, check whether there's a telephone line and that the number of lines or telephone points is adequate (most new homes already have phone lines and points in a number of rooms). If a property has a cable system or other phone network (see above), you could decide not to have a BT phone line installed. If you move into an old house or apartment (where you aren't the first resident) a telephone line will probably already be installed, although there won't be a phone. If you're moving into a house or apartment without a phone line, e.g. a new house, you may need to apply to BT for a line to be installed.

BT's target for residential line installation is four working days, depending on the area and the particular exchange. The installation of a new line (to an address where there wasn't previously a service) is £99 and to take over an existing line costs £9.99 or is free of charge if you move house and take over a working phone line on the *same day* as the existing customer moves out. If a property has an old-style phone point (which cannot be unplugged), it should be replaced with a new-style linebox or master socket. This can be done only by BT and it's illegal to do it yourself or get anyone other than a BT engineer to do it. Once you have a BT linebox or master socket, you can install as many additional sockets as you like, but you shouldn't connect more than four telephones to one telephone line. You can install additional sockets yourself by buying DIY kits from BT or a DIY shop, or BT can install them for you (although their labour charges are astronomical). BT sell a wide range of extension kits, sockets and cords.

Using the Telephone: Using the telephone in Britain is much the same as in any other country, with a few British eccentricities thrown in for good measure. When dialling a number within your own exchange area, dial the number only, e.g. if you live in Toy Town and wish to dial another subscriber in Toy Town. When dialling anywhere else the area code must be dialled before the subscriber's number. When telephone numbers are printed, they may be shown as any of the following: Toy Town 1234, 01567-1234 or Toy Town (01567) 1234, the recommended method. One problem when the area name isn't shown is that you may not know whether a number is in the local area or at the other end of Britain (although you can always ask the operator). When dialling a number in Britain from overseas, you dial the international access code of the country from which you're calling (e.g. 00), followed by Britain's international code (44), the area code *without* the first 0 (e.g. 1567 for Toy Town) and the subscriber's number. For Toy Town 1234, you would dial 00-44-1567-1234.

Free numbers, called freefone by BT, have a prefix of 0800 (BT), 0500 (Mercury) or 0321 (Vodaphone). They are usually provided by businesses who are trying to sell you something or having sold you something, provide a free telephone support service. Some companies have a freefone name rather than a number, in which case you can phone the operator (100) and ask for the freefone name. Numbers with the prefix 0345 (BT), 0645 (Mercury) and 0845 (various operators) are charged at the local rate, irrespective of where you're calling from. Numbers with the prefix 0990 (BT), 05415 (Mercury) and 0870 (various operators) are charged at the national rate even when you're calling locally. At the moment it's difficult to know what kind of phone (or even a pager) you're calling and what it's costing. In future a number's prefix will tell you what type of number it is; for example 00 (international dialling), 01/02 (national area codes), 03 to 06 (these are reserved for future use), 07 (mobiles, pagers and personal numbers), 08 (freefone and special rate services) and 09 (premium rate services).

The use of premium rate information and entertainment numbers has increased considerably in recent years and includes numbers with the prefixes 03311, 03313, 03314, 0336, 0338, 0880, 08364, 0839, 0881, 0891, 08941, 08942, 08943, 08944, 0895, 0897, 08975, 0898, 09301, 09305, 09309 and 0991. The rate for premium rate numbers, which must be shown when they are listed or quoted, is a minimum of 39p at cheap rate and 49p at all other times, e.g. 0839 numbers. Calls to 0897 numbers cost £1.49 per minute at all times. Call rates for numbers with the above prefixes are listed in a BT leaflet *UK call prices*. They are huge money-spinners for the companies and are beloved by TV and radio competitions, which although the prizes may look attractive, are nothing compared to the revenue generated by the phone lines. **If you use these numbers frequently you can go bankrupt!**

Standard telephone tones (the strange noises phones make when they aren't connected to a subscriber) are provided to indicate the progress of calls. Note that tones in Britain may be completely different from those used in other countries. There's sometimes a pause before you hear a tone, so hold on for a few seconds before replacing the receiver to allow the equipment time to connect your call. To listen to typical examples of tones ☎ freefone 0800-789456. In Britain you dial 100 for the operator, 155 for the international operator, 192 for domestic directory enquiries and 153 for international directory enquiries. The emergency number is 999.

Extra Services: BT network or select services are available to subscribers with a tone phone connected to a digital exchange, which includes most BT customers. If you subscribe to Mercury or Energis you can still use most network services and most cable companies offer similar services. Network services include call barring, caller display, call diversion, call minder, call return, call waiting, reminder call, ring back, ring me free and three-way calling. Services can be ordered individually or as part of a package and cost from around £3 to £7 a quarter or, in some cases, you can choose to pay on a 'per call' basis. For more information or to order network services ☎ freefone 0800-334422.

Costs: BT remains by far the largest telephone company in Britain and therefore its call rates are listed here for comparison purposes. They are NOT meant as an endorsement of BT, which charges some of the highest rates in Britain. BT charges for all calls, including local calls, for which there's no standard flat-rate charge or a number of free calls. BT levy a quarterly line rental fee of £26.77 for a residential line (there's a £1 reduction when your is bill paid by direct debit) or £12.72 for those who come under the Light User Scheme. VAT (at 17.5 per cent) is levied on line rental and all calls, and is included in all rates shown unless otherwise noted. For a large percentage of BT's customers, the line rental fee accounts for over half their bill.

BT have three charge rates for self-dialled, domestic calls from ordinary lines (not payphones or mobile phones), depending on the time and day. **Daytime Rate** is in operation from 0800 to 1800, Mondays to Fridays; **Evening and Nightime Rate** is from 1800 to 0800, Mondays to Fridays; and **Weekend Rate** from midnight Friday until midnight Sunday. Note, however that BT charges a minimum of 5p for all calls, therefore your cheap weekend local call will need to be five minutes in length to take advantage of the 1p a minute rate. Some companies (e.g. One.Tel) offer national calls for 2½p per minute at all times and are therefore cheaper at all times for anything other than local calls.

Tariff/Cost Per Minute (1999)

* Type of Call	Daytime	Evening/Night	Weekend
Local	4p	1.5p	1p
Regional	8p	4p	3p
National	8p	4.2p	3p

* Local calls are calls within your local call area, regional calls are up to 56km (35mi), and national calls over 56km.

BT and other telephone companies offer a range of tariffs and discount schemes, although it's difficult to compare their value for money and most offer relatively small savings.

International Calls: BT charges for dialled international calls from ordinary lines are based on charge bands (1 to 16), which are shown in phone books with international dialling information. In 1999, BT's lowest weekend rates were 39.11p per minute to Australia, 23.12p to France and Germany, 17.76p to Ireland, 54.29p to Japan, 67.47p to South Africa and 20.86p to the USA. These can be reduced by 25 per cent with BT's Friends & Family option using a BT Chargecard, which costs an additional £24 a year. International charges are listed in a BT leaflet entitled *International call prices*. **Note that rates are much higher during the daytime from Mondays to Fridays. Using an alternative company to BT, e.g. an indirect access company (see below), can result in huge savings.**

Indirect Access Companies: The cheapest companies for international calls are usually indirect access companies (previously termed 'callback' companies as you needed to ring a number and receive a call back to obtain a line). Nowadays you simply dial a freefone number to connect to the company's own lines or dial a code before dialling a number. They may offer low rates for national long-distance and international calls. Some charge a subscription fee. Calls are charged at a flat rate 24 hours a day, seven days a week. Some companies allow you to make calls from any tone phone (even abroad), while others restrict you to a single (e.g. home or office) number. Calls may be paid for with a credit card, either in advance when you must buy a number of units, or by direct debit each month. Alternatively you may be billed monthly in arrears.

Low cost companies have devastated BT's share of the international market in recent years, particularly transatlantic calls, which isn't surprising when you consider the savings that can be made. For example in mid-1999 One.Tel (☎ 0800-634 1860) charged a flat rate of 3p per minute to the USA, 5p to Australia and Canada, 6p to Ireland and New Zealand, 7p to France and Germany, 8p to Japan and 18p to South Africa (these rates aren't applicable to mobile phones or payphones). Compare these rates with BT's above – isn't competition wonderful! Most other indirect access companies such as Alpha Telecom (☎ freefone 0800-279 0000), AXS Telecom (☎ freefone 0800-358 2223), Callmate (☎ freefone 0800-376 3000), First telecom (☎ freefone 0800-458 5858), Primus (☎ freefone 0800-036 0003) and Swiftcall (☎ freefone 0800-769 0200) have similar rates to One.Tel. It's possible to buy a box that you connect between your phone and wall socket that automatically routes long-distance and international calls via the cheapest carrier. For example Telecom Plus' Service Plus service costs £23.50 to join plus £1.76 per month, in addition to call costs and the cost of the switching box.

Home Country Direct: Many European countries subscribe to a Home Country Direct service that allows you to call a special number giving you direct and free access to an operator in the country you're calling. The operator will connect you to the number required and will also accept credit card and reverse charge calls. The number to dial is shown in phone books in the International code section. You should be extremely wary of making international reverse charge calls to Britain using BT's UK Direct scheme, as you will pay at least double the cost of using a local payphone. For information about countries served by the Home Country Direct service call international directory enquiries on 153.

Bills: You're billed each quarter (three months) by BT for your line rental, phone rental (if applicable) and calls, when you're sent a blue *Telephone Account* plus a 'Statement'. If applicable, the telephone connection fee is included in your first bill. BT provides free itemised bills to all customers on demand, which include the number called, the date and time, the duration and the call cost. Customers can choose to have all calls itemised or some only. BT phone bills can be paid by budget account (to spread bills evenly over 12 months); quarterly direct debit; by post using the envelope provided; at your bank (complete the form provided) or a post office; and at a BT phone shop. The best way for most people to pay their phone bill is monthly via a budget account or quarterly from an interest-bearing bank or building society account. With quarterly direct debit, your account is debited 14 days after you receive the bill. Other phone companies may bill you monthly, bimonthly or quarterly.

Payphones: Most payphones (public telephones) permit International Direct Dialling (IDD) and international calls can also be made via the operator. Payphones in Britain were traditionally located in the famous red telephone boxes, which have been replaced in the last decade or so by sterile 'vandal-proof' steel and glass booths containing push-button payphones. Many payphones aren't enclosed and some offer little protection from the elements and surrounding noise (although if they remain in working order, most people will be happy). New payphones are easier to use than the old ones, for example handsets are set at a lower, more convenient height for those in wheelchairs and they're fitted with an 'inductive coupler' for wearers of post-aural hearing aids. They also have a wider entrance to provide access for the disabled and wheelchair users. There are also private 'call shops' in major cities where you can buy a pre-paid calling card and make calls in comfort.

Payphones in Britain are operated by British Telecom and IPM, and accept coins (BT only), Phonecards (BT and IPM) and credit cards (BT and IPM). Cards are replacing cash in payphones and various new payment cards have been introduced in recent years. Since installing new payphones in the last decade, BT claims that over 95 per cent (almost 100,000) are in working order at any one time. Public payphones are widely available in all cities and towns in Britain, in public streets; inside and outside post offices and railway stations; and in hotels, pubs, restaurants, shops and other private and public buildings. If you're driving, finding a payphone is usually easy, but finding somewhere to park is a different matter altogether!

Charges for dialled inland calls from payphones are calculated in units of 10p which is the minimum charge. This means the cost of a call from a payphone is double the minimum cost (5p) from a private phone using BT. Operator connected calls from payphones are roughly double the cost of dialled calls and should be avoided if at all possible. Most payphones are push-button operated and accept all coins except for 1p and 5p (i.e. 10p to £2). You'll need at least £1 to make an international call or a Phonecard with at least ten units left on it (see below). Note, however, that payphones should be avoided at all costs when making international calls as the rates are prohibitively high.

Mobile Phones: Britain has among the highest number of mobile phone users in Europe (over ten million in 1998), which is expected to double by 2006. In addition to being a necessity for travelling business people, a car telephone is a vital status symbol for yuppies and the young. Some car manufacturers fit phones in their cars as standard equipment, particularly to attract women drivers (a mobile phone is useful in an emergency). On the negative side, mobile phones are now so widespread that many businesses (e.g. restaurants, cinemas, theatres, concert halls, etc.) ban them and some even use mobile phone jammers that can detect and jam every handset within 100m. In recent years there has been widespread publicity about a possible health risk to users from the microwave radiation emitted by mobile phones.

There are four digital mobile phone companies in Britain: Cellnet, Vodafone, One-2-One and Orange, all of which cover most of Britain (maps showing the areas covered are available). There's little discernible difference between the two major companies, Cellnet and Vodafone, although you should check out the reception in your local area, particularly if you live or work in a remote rural area. Some companies (particularly Vodafone) have been criticised for their poor reception in many areas of the country (and even worse customer service). Subscribers can buy a GSM phone that can be used in many countries world-wide including much of western Europe, Australia, Hong Kong, South Africa and parts of the Middle East. You must have a contract with a 'roaming' agreement if you wish to use your mobile phone abroad and should check the countries your service provider has contracts with.

Fax: There has been a huge increase in the use of fax (facsimile) machines in the last few decades in Britain, helped by lower prices of both fax machines and calls. Fax machines can be purchased from BT and a wide variety of other companies and shops. Shop around for the best price. Before bringing a fax machine to Britain, check that it will work there or that it can be modified. Note, however, that getting a fax machine repaired in Britain may be impossible unless the same machine is sold there. Mobile phone and portable computer users can use a portable fax, which allows fax transmissions to be made from virtually anywhere in Britain. BT business communication centres provide 'faxbureau' facilities as does the Royal Mail and many private businesses. The Royal Mail also provides a fax/courier service called 'Faxmail', where messages are delivered the same day to most British addresses and to many destinations world-wide.

Mail Services

There's a post office in most towns in Britain, offering over 100 different services, which (in addition to the usual post office services provided in most countries) include a number of unique services. The term 'post office' is used in Britain as a general term for three separate businesses: the Royal Mail, Post Office Counters Limited and Parcelforce (formerly Royal Mail Parcels). Girobank plc, the former post office banking division, still operates from post offices, but is now owned by Alliance & Leicester Giro.

Inland mail refers to all mail to addresses in Great Britain, Northern Ireland, the Channel Islands and the Isle of Man. Of some 19,000 post offices in Britain, only around 600 are operated directly by the post office. The remainder are franchise offices or sub post offices run on an agency basis by sub-postmasters (which don't offer all the services provided by a main post office). There are plans to partly privatise the post office (the government has already been accused of back-door privatisation with the transfer of many post offices from the high street to supermarkets, stationery stores, newsagents and other shops).

In addition to postal services, the post office also acts as an agent for a number of government departments and local authorities (councils), for example, the sale of television licences (exclusive to post offices), national insurance stamps and road tax. You can also pay many bills at a post office including electricity, gas, water, telephone, cable, store cards, mail-order bills, council tax, rent payments and housing association rents. The post office is also the largest chain of outlets for national lottery tickets and a distribution centre for social security leaflets. It provides bureaux de change facilities in most branches (although you may need to order foreign currency) and provides an expensive international money transfer service in conjunction with Western Union International.

The post office (founded in 1635) is the last bastion of the old state sector and like all nationalised companies it's over-staffed and inefficient in some areas. Despite this, it provides one of best postal services in the world, delivering some 75 million letters and packets every day to around 26 million addresses. Services have improved considerably in recent years and it's now one of the world's most modern and automated post offices, offering a vast range of services compared with most foreign post offices. The Royal Mail even has an office in New York (offering a cheaper and faster international service than the US postal service) from where it ships mail in bulk to London and forwards it to other international destinations. However, overseas rivals are also muscling in on Royal Mail services and a number of overseas groups handle mail in Britain.

Post office business hours in Britain are usually from 0900 to 1730, Mondays to Fridays, and from 0900 to 1230 on Saturdays. In small towns and villages there are sub post offices (usually part of a general store) that provide many of the services provided by a main post office. Sub post offices usually close for an hour at lunchtime, e.g. 1300 to 1400, Mondays to Fridays, and may also close on one afternoon a week, usually Wednesday. Main post offices in major towns don't close at lunchtime. There are post offices at major international airports, some of which are open on Sundays and public holidays, and in major cities some post offices have extended opening hours, e.g. the Trafalgar Square branch in London.

Letter Post: The post office provides a choice of first and second class domestic mail delivery (further evidence of the British preoccupation with class). The target for the delivery of first class mail is the next working day after collection and the third working day after collection for second class. Some 95 per cent of first class mail is delivered the next day, although some letters fail to arrive until weeks after posting (probably those that are delivered by rail). It's unnecessary to mark mail as first or second class, as any item that's posted with less than first class postage is automatically sent second class.

Airmail letters to Europe take an average of from 2½ days to Denmark, Norway and Switzerland and up to seven days to Italy and some other countries (which provides a good indication of the relative efficiency or otherwise of European postal services). Airmail to other destinations usually takes four to seven days. Surface mail takes up to two weeks to Europe and up to 12 weeks outside Europe. Underpaid airmail items may be sent by surface mail or will incur a surcharge. Leaflets are published in September listing the latest mail posting dates for Christmas for international mail (forces, surface and airmail).

International letters, small packets and printed papers (both airmail and surface) are limited to a maximum of 2kg and up to 5kg for books and pamphlets. Second class mail mustn't exceed 750g (£1.45), although there's no limit for first class mail. This means that parcels weighing between 750g and 1kg must be sent by first class mail. Parcel mail standard service costs £2.70 for up 1kg, which is more expensive than first class mail (£2.50 for 1kg). Inland postage rates have been frozen for three years and the cost of sending a 2nd class letter was actually reduced from 20p to 19p in April 1999 (a 1st class letter costs 26p). To ensure delivery the next day, first class mail should be posted by 1700 for the local area (e.g. a letter posted in the south-east of England to any address in the same region) or by 1300 for other parts of Britain excluding Northern Scotland.

Private sector couriers are able to handle only time-sensitive and valuable mail, subject to a minimum fee of £1. The courier industry, particularly in London and other major cities, is growing by some 20 per cent a year and Britain is a major centre for international air courier traffic. Major companies include Federal Express, DHL, UPS and TNT, plus the post office Parcelforce service. The post office produces a wealth of brochures about postal rates and special services, including a *Mini Mailguide* containing information about all Royal Mail products and services. It also has a telephone helpline (☎ 0345-223344) and an Internet site (www.royalmail.co. uk).

GETTING THERE

Although it isn't so important if you're planning to live permanently in Britain and stay put, one of the major considerations when buying a holiday home is the cost of getting to and from Britain. How long will it take you to get to a home in Britain, taking into account journeys to and from airports, ports and railway stations? How frequent are flights, ferries or trains at the time(s) of year when you plan to travel? Are direct flights or trains available? Is it feasible to travel by car? What is the cost of travel from your home country to the region where you're planning to buy a home in Britain? Are off-season discounts or inexpensive charter flights available? If a long journey is involved, you should bear in mind that it may take you a day or two to recover, e.g. from jet-lag after a long flight. Obviously the travelling time and cost of travel to a home in Britain will be more critical if you're planning to spend frequent long weekends there, rather than lengthier stays.

By Air: There's a total of over 140 licensed civil airports in Britain, including many international airports, the most important of which are London-Heathrow, London-Gatwick, Manchester, Glasgow, Birmingham, Luton, Edinburgh, Belfast, Aberdeen, Newcastle, East Midlands and London-Stanstead (all handling over one million passengers a year). Many regional airports also operate a limited number of international flights (excluding flights to Ireland, which are widespread) including

Bristol, Cardiff, Humberside, Leeds-Bradford, London-City, Lydd, Norwich, Southend and Teeside. Regional airports often have bargain fares to popular European destinations. A number of smaller airports operate scheduled domestic flights to both regional and international airports.

London's Heathrow airport is the world's busiest international airport, handling over 50 million passengers a year (terminal one alone handles 20 million passengers a year), which is expected to increase to over 80 million by 2016. Heathrow has four terminals (and is planning a fifth) and handles mostly scheduled flights. London's Gatwick airport is the world's second busiest international airport after Heathrow, handling over 25 million passengers a year. Gatwick has one runway only (although an additional runway is under consideration) and just two terminals, and is used extensively by charter airlines. Both Heathrow and Gatwick have excellent bus and rail connections to central London, the provinces and other British airports. Heathrow can also be reached by tube and via the high-speed Heathrow Express direct rail connection from Paddington station taking just 15 minutes.

Air fares to and from Britain are the most competitive in Europe and among the most competitive in the world. Competition between BA and Virgin (and American carriers) on Atlantic routes helps stimulate competition. BA and Virgin routinely match each others prices and usually knock a further £1 off (so they can claim that they're cheaper). BA triggered a price war in summer 1998 when it put two million cut-price tickets on the market (fares to 80 World-wide destinations were slashed by up to £500) and Ryanair (an Irish airline based in Dublin but operating widely in Britain) gave away 500,000 tickets in a 'buy one get one free' promotion on certain routes. Stiff competition from US airlines has also shaken up the transatlantic fare structure. The low 'shoulder' period between Christmas and Easter is best for Transatlantic bargains (prices rise sharply again in the spring), when fares are cut by up to 50 per cent.

Deregulation in 1997 led to a spate of new low-cost airlines such as Debonair, Easyjet, Go (owned by BA) and Virgin Express, which have hit the profits of the major airlines and cemented Britain's position as Europe's low-cost, air travel hub. These airlines offer a no-frills service (some even operate without tickets) and undercut other airlines by charging for seats only. Meals and entertainment must be paid for separately. The biggest problem facing airlines trying to gain access to a new route is the allocation of takeoff and landing slots during peak times, which are jealously guarded by all national airlines (which is why new airlines must operate from less popular airports). **Bear in mind when buying tickets that flights are usually much cheaper from travel agents than direct from airlines.**

By Train: The opening of the Channel tunnel in 1994 gave Britain a direct rail connection with the continental rail system, with the introduction of the Eurostar train service between London and Brussels and Paris. This threatens to drag Britain's railways screaming and kicking into the 21st century, although passengers will have to wait for high-speed trains on British soil. Since the start of Eurostar services an estimated 25 per cent of business travellers have switched from air to rail for journeys between London and Brussels and Paris. Airlines have tried to play down the affect that Eurostar has had on their business, although for many travellers Eurostar is cheaper overall when you take into account the cost of getting to and from airports. However, many analysts believe that Eurostar must undercut airlines and ferries significantly if it's to increase its share of travellers further.

Eurostar trains run from London Waterloo International to Paris and Brussels at speeds of up to 185mph (on the continent!), taking around three hours to Paris. Meals in first class are complementary (i.e. you have already paid for them in the price of your ticket), although the food leaves much to be desired. There are a range of special fares (including discovery special, weekend return, apex weekend, pass holder (for holders of international rail passes), senior return, youths (under 26) and groups. In September 1999 the cost of a Standard Plus return to Paris was £249, although special deals were available from £79 (weekend day return). For reservations ☎ 0990-186186 or 01233-617575.

By Sea: Regular car and passenger ferry services to Britain operate all year round from ports in Belgium, France, Germany, Holland, Iceland, Ireland, Spain and various Scandinavian countries. The proportion of passengers travelling to and from Britain by sea has reduced considerably since the early '60s due to the reduced cost of air travel and competition from Eurotunnel (see below). The major ferry companies operating international services are P&O (which also operates as P&O Stena Line on some routes) and Brittany ferries, which dominates the routes in the western Channel (Caen, Cherbourg, Roscoff and St. Malo) with around 40 per cent of the market. Hoverspeed operates a hovercraft service from Dover to Calais and catamaran (Seacat) services on the same route plus Folkestone to Boulogne and Dover to Ostend. A larger Hoverspeed superseacat service operates from Newhaven to Dieppe.

Some ferry services operate during the summer months only, e.g. May to September, and the frequency of services varies from dozens a day on the busiest Dover-Calais route during the summer peak period, to one a week on longer routes. Services are less frequent during the winter months, when bad weather can also cause cancellations. Most Channel ferry services employ large super ferries with a capacity of up to 1,800 to 2,000 passengers and 700 cars. Ferries carry all vehicles, while hovercraft take all vehicles except large trucks and buses. All operators except Hoverspeed offer night services, which may be cheaper. Berths, single cabins and pullman seats are usually available, and most ships have a restaurant, self-service cafeteria, a children's play area and shops. Generally the longer the route, the better and wider the range of facilities provided, which often makes it worthwhile considering alternative routes to the Dover-Calais crossing. Although Dover-Calais is the shortest route and offers the most crossings, longer passages are generally less crowded and more relaxing, and fares may also be lower.

Le Shuttle: Eurotunnel started operating their shuttle car train service from Folkestone (access to the Eurotunnel terminal is via the M20 motorway, junction 11a) to Coquelles, near Calais, in 1995. The shuttle provides a 15-minute service during peak periods, taking just 35 minutes. One of the advantages (in addition to the short travel time) of Le Shuttle is that you can remain in your car isolated from drunken soccer fans and screaming kids. Fares are similar to ferries, e.g. a peak (summer) club class return costs around £340 and an off-peak (January to March) return £170, for a vehicle and all passengers. It's advisable to book in advance (☎ 0990-353535), although if you arrive earlier than planned you will be able to travel on an earlier train if there's space. Don't expect to get a place in summer on the 'turn up and go' service, particularly on Fridays, Saturdays and Sundays. Demand is lighter on services from France to Britain, when bookings may be unnecessary. Trains carry all 'vehicles' including cycles, motorcycles, cars, trucks, buses, caravans and motorhomes.

By Road: International bus services to and from Britain are provided by a number of companies including Eurolines, Supabus, Hoverspeed and Transline services, with regular buses to around 200 destinations in Europe and Ireland. Most international services operate to/from London Victoria Coach Station, with domestic nation-wide connections, although some operate directly from the provinces. Many people prefer to drive to Britain, which saves you the expense of renting a car on arrival.

GETTING AROUND BY PUBLIC TRANSPORT

Public transport services in Britain vary from region to region and town to town. In some areas services are excellent and good value for money, while in others they are infrequent, slow and expensive. Britain has no unified general transport policy, particularly a long-term strategy that balances the needs of the public transport user against those of the motorist. Consequently, Britain has one of the most congested and ill-planned transport systems in Europe (exacerbated by the disastrous rail privatisation, which has driven even more people onto the roads). However, it isn't *always* essential to own a car in Britain, particularly if you live in a large town or a city with adequate public transport (where parking is impossible in any case). On the other hand, if you live in a remote village or a town away from the main train and bus routes, it's usually essential to have your own transport. Public transport is cheaper if you're able to take advantage of the wide range of discount, combination (e.g. rail, bus and underground), season and off-peak tickets available.

Britain's transport 'system' is heavily weighted in favour of road transport and the level of public transport subsidies in Britain is among the lowest in Europe. Despite more people using public transport in London than in any other European city (London has the world's largest rail and tube network), it has the most expensive public transport of any capital city in Europe, with fares around four times those of Rome and some 15 (fifteen) times more expensive than Budapest. The percentage of travellers in Britain using public transport is, not surprisingly, very low, with some 90 per cent of all journeys made by car.

The poor services and high cost of public transport has made a huge contribution to the heavy road congestion, with traffic levels in the south-east and other heavily populated areas approaching saturation point. Apart from the environmental damage caused by the ever increasing number of cars on British roads, road congestion costs British business, billions of pounds a year, which, when added to the cost of road accidents, suggests a huge commercial benefit would be reaped from improved public transport. Many cities and counties promote the use of public transport instead of private cars, although trying to encourage people to travel by public transport has met with little success. One of the biggest problems facing Britain is that it's much cheaper to run a car than it is to use the railways. Most analysts believe the reverse must be true if Britain isn't to suffer almost permanent gridlock in its major cities in the next millennium.

Rising levels of traffic pollution are choking Britain's cities, where asthma and other bronchial complaints (which are aggravated by exhaust pollution) have increased hugely in recent years. Many experts believe the only answer is to pedestrianise town centres and severely limit traffic in town and cities (which is done in many European countries), while at the same time investing heavily in electric (pollution-free) public transport systems. Although Britain killed off its trams (which in mainland Europe still perform an excellent role midway between a bus and a train) many years ago, a number of cities are building new metro, light rail transit and supertram systems, and banning cars from city centres.

Bus: In Britain there are two main types of bus service: town and city services and long-distance, usually referred to as coaches. Each region of Britain has its own local bus companies providing local town and country services. In large towns and cities, most bus services start and terminate at a central bus station, but it can be confusing trying to find the right connection. If you need assistance ask at the bus station information office. Most bus companies provide free timetables and route maps, and many local district and county councils publish a comprehensive booklet of timetables and maps (possibly for a small fee) for all bus services operating within their boundaries. In many cities a night bus service is in operation. Timetables are also posted at major bus stops.

The deregulation of bus services in 1986 allowed any bus company to operate on any route, and led to cut-throat competition and many companies going out of business. In the last few years the large operators have swallowed up many of their competitors (amid numerous claims of dirty tricks) and on many routes have established a monopoly or near monopoly. Stagecoach are the biggest bus company with around 25 per cent of the market, followed by FirstBus (Badgerline and GRT) and British Bus. The largest seven bus companies own some three-quarters of the industry. National long-distance bus services are listed in *Getting About Britain* distributed by the BTA (☎ 0208-846 9000, Internet: www.visitbritain.com).

Long-distance Buses: A number of companies provide long-distance bus services in Britain. The major operator is National Express (NE), which provides a nation-wide service in England, Wales and Scotland (where services are operated in conjunction with its sister company, Caledonian Express Stagecoach). Some local bus companies operate express bus services (which make a limited number of stops) within their area, e.g. London Transport's Green Line Coach service. Bus companies also operate sightseeing trips throughout Britain. National Express serves over 1,400 major towns and cities nation-wide daily (with the exception of Christmas Day) and carries over 11 million passengers more than a billion miles a year. It operates a fast and reasonably priced hourly service to the most popular destinations which is much cheaper than train travel (what isn't?). Express buses are the cheapest form of long-distance travel within Britain and although journeys take up to twice as long as trains, fares are often 50 per cent lower. National Express coaches arrive and depart from Victoria coach station (☎ 0207-730 3499 for information) in London, which is a 10-minute walk from Victoria railway station.

Rail: The railway network in Britain is one of the most extensive in Europe with over 17,500km (11,000mi) of lines, some 2,500 passenger stations and around 15,000 trains a day. Britain pioneered railways and the Stockton and Darlington Railway (1825) was the first public passenger, steam-powered railway in the world. In 1938 Britain set a world steam record of 126.5mph (203kph), although it now lags far behind its international competitors (incredibly trains on some routes were actually faster 100 years ago!). In an effort to reduce government subsidies and as part of its privatisation doctrine, one of the Conservative government's last acts in office was to privatise British Rail. The privatisation was completed in 1997 and passenger services are now operated by some 25 separate private companies. Other privatised companies include Railtrack, which is responsible for the tracks and infrastructure; rolling stock companies that lease locomotives and passenger carriages; freight service providers; infrastructure maintenance companies; and track renewal companies.

Since privatisation railway services in Britain have gone from bad to worse and resulted in higher fares, fewer services, poor connections, increased train cancellations, late trains (punctuality is one of the biggest problems), too few seats (overcrowding is widespread), narrower seats, closed ticket offices, unhelpful staff or a lack of staff, poor or no catering on trains, and a paucity of accurate information. Not surprisingly there's widespread public dissatisfaction, which resulted in almost one million complaints in 1998! In fact most observers believe that privatised rail services are even worse than official figures reveal and that Britain has the worst and most expensive railway in Europe. Note that in the last few years Britain's railways have been changing at an incredible pace and some of the information contained in this chapter will inevitably be out of date by the time you read it.

Trains in Britain are expensive and even if you're able to take advantage of special tickets, excursion fares, family reductions and holiday package deals, they are still usually dearer than buses over long distances. The harsh reality (accepted by every other western European country) is that it's impossible to run a comprehensive, quality rail service at a price people are willing to pay (or can afford) without huge public subsidies. Although services are expected to improve in the long term thanks to new investment programmes, most analysts believe that without increased state subsidies (or re-nationalisation) the only certain thing about Britain's rail service is that fares will continue to increase and services will be slashed.

Most trains consist of first (shown by a '1' on windows) and standard class carriages. Services categorised as suburban or local are trains that stop at most stations along their route, many provided by modern Sprinter and Super Sprinter class trains, with push-button operated or automatic doors. Long distance trains are termed express and InterCity, and stop at major towns only. Express services are provided by new 158 (158kph/98mph) class trains in some areas. InterCity 125 trains, so named after their maximum speed of 125mph (201kph), are the world's fastest diesel trains and operate on most InterCity services. New InterCity 225 (225kph/140mph) trains have been introduced on major routes.

All InterCity 125 and 225 trains are air-conditioned, have a buffet car in standard class and a restaurant car in first class, although the food has been criticised for its poor quality and high cost. During rush hours (before 0930 and from 1600 to 1900) trains are frequent on most routes, although it's best to avoid travelling during rush hours, when trains are packed. Although travelling by train may not always compare favourably on paper with air travel, it's often quicker when you add the time required to get to and from town centres and airports. Many towns and cities are served by half-hourly or hourly services.

Railway operators offer a bewildering range of tickets depending on a variety of considerations, such as the day and time of day you're travelling, when you will be returning and how often you travel. Railway companies operate diverse services ranging from local rural lines to major cross-country routes, many offering few standard services and tickets. Therefore with the exception of national InterCity services, some rail passes and tickets may be available in certain regions only, although most companies provide similar services. Ticket staff are supposed to provide you with the cheapest ticket available for your journey, although overcharging is commonplace (but less widespread than previously). Always double or treble check ticket prices before buying a ticket for a long-distance journey involving a number of railway companies.

Air: Domestic flights are available from Aberdeen, Belfast, Birmingham, Bristol, Cardiff, East Midlands, Edinburgh, Glasgow, Humberside, Leeds-Bradford, London-City, London-Heathrow, London-Gatwick, London-Stanstead, Luton, Lydd, Manchester, Newcastle, Norwich, Southend, Teeside and dozens of smaller airports. Domestic air services are provided by many airlines, including Air UK, British Airways, British Midland, Brymon Airways, Capital Airlines, Dan-Air Services, GB Airways (a BA franchise partner) and Jersey European Airways, most of which offer reduced off-peak and standby fares.

Ferries: Within Britain (and the British Isles) there are regular ferry services to the Isle of Wight, i.e. Portsmouth to Fishbourne and Ryde, Southsea to Ryde and from Lymington to Yarmouth. Car ferry services operate from Heysham, Fleetwood and Liverpool to Douglas (Isle of Man). From Douglas there are regular services to Belfast and Dublin. Services operate from the west of Scotland to the Western Isles and to the Orkney and Shetland islands from the north and east of Scotland. There are also ferry services to the Channel Islands from Poole, Torquay and Weymouth throughout the year. Services to Ireland operate between Stranraer-Larne, Fishguard-Rosslare, Holyhead-Dun Loghaire (for Dublin) and Swansea-Cork.

Taxis: Taxis are usually plentiful in Britain except when it's raining, you have lots of luggage or you're late for an appointment. There are two kinds of taxis in Britain, licensed taxis or cabs (abbr. of cabriolet) and private hire cars or minicabs. All taxis must be licensed by the local municipal or borough council and have a registered license number. Minicabs don't always need to be licensed, although most are. The main difference from the passenger's point of view, is that taxis can be hailed in the street and minicabs can be booked only by phone. In addition to taxi services, many taxi and minicab companies operate private hire (e.g. weddings, sightseeing), chauffeur and courier services, and provide contract and account services, e.g. to take children to and from school. Many taxi and minicab companies provide a 24-hour service with radio controlled cars.

Taxis aren't particularly expensive in Britain and are cheaper than in many other European countries. London taxis (officially called Hackney Carriages) cover an area of around 1,580km² (610mi²) and each cab has a license number plate and the driver (cabby) wears a badge bearing his driver number. There's a minimum charge of around £1.40 for roughly the first 500m or two minutes and around 30p for each additional 250m or minute (a lot of time is spent stuck in traffic). There are extra charges for additional passengers, baggage, and surcharges for evenings between 2000 and midnight, nights, weekends and public holidays. The fare from London-Heathrow airport (served by London cabs) to central London is around £30. There are also business class cabs in London with more luxurious seats, soundproofing and a telephone (and higher rates than standard cabs). In rural areas taxis charge around £2.50 a mile (1.6km). Taxi drivers expect a tip of around 10 per cent of the fare, although it isn't obligatory.

DRIVING

Like motorists in all countries, the British have their own idiosyncrasies and customs. In general, Britons have a reputation for being good and considerate drivers, and most take their driving seriously. Most drivers are courteous and, unlike many other

Europeans, are usually happy to give way to a driver waiting to enter the flow of traffic or change lanes. However, tempers are rising on Britain's overcrowded streets and road rage ('invented' in California), where drivers blow their tops and attack or drive into other motorists, is becoming more common. It's often provoked by tailgating, headlight flashing, obscene gestures, obstruction and verbal abuse, so be careful how you behave when driving in Britain. Although British drivers are generally law abiding (except with regard to speed limits), a recent survey found that millions would drive on the wrong side of the law if they thought they could get away with it.

A phenomenon known as 'motorway madness', where motorway driving turns normal people into lunatics, is widespread in Britain, where many drivers are afraid of motorways and have little idea how to drive on them. Common faults include poor lane discipline, undertakers (motorists who overtake on the inside), driving too fast in poor conditions (e.g. fog and heavy rain), and driving much to close to the vehicle in front. One thing most foreigners immediately notice when driving in Britain is the speed at which most people drive, which is often 50 per cent above the prevailing speed limit (unless you're on the M25, in which case you will be stationary). The exception to this rule is the ubiquitous 'Sunday driver', so-called because he rarely drives on any other day of the week and is never actually going anywhere, but just enjoying the scenery (hence his maximum 20mph speed). You'll also notice that many motorists are reluctant to use their lights in poor visibility or until it's completely dark at night, and even then may use only parking lights in areas with street lighting. Sometimes it's just as well that people fail to use their headlights as many are badly adjusted and dazzle oncoming drivers (it's hard to believe they are ever checked during the annual serviceability test).

Take it easy when driving in winter. Although heavy snow is rare, particularly in the south, Britain has a lot of fog and ice, which make driving extremely hazardous (it also gets dark at around 1600 or even earlier in the north). Black ice is also common and is the most dangerous sort because it cannot be seen. When road conditions are bad, allow two to three times longer than usual to reach your destination (or better still take a train).

One of the biggest problems when motoring in towns and most residential areas in Britain, is the vast number of cars parked (legally or illegally) on roads. You'll often find that you must stop because your side of the road is completely blocked or because oncoming traffic isn't keeping over to its side of the road to allow you sufficient room to pass. Parked cars are also particularly hazardous when pulling out of busy junctions (many more of which should have roundabouts).

Despite their idiosyncrasies, British drivers are above average (average is bad) and more polite than most other drivers in Europe. Don't be discouraged by the tailgaters and road hogs as driving in Britain is less stressful than in many countries (apart from the jams). Most people who come from countries where traffic drives on the right quickly become used to driving on the 'wrong' side of the road. Just take it easy at first and bear in mind that there may be other motorists around just as confused as you are.

British Roads

There are some 362,000km (225,000mi) of roads in Britain, including around 3,100km (1,950mi) of motorways. In general the quality of British roads are excellent, although some main roads and motorways are in a poor condition due to

being constantly chewed up by juggernauts and the heavy volume of traffic. Britain has a smaller motorway network than many other western European countries and has no toll motorways, although trials are underway and tolls may be introduced within the next few years. It's practically impossible to introduce toll booths as used on the continent and vehicles would be fitted with a 'transponder' which communicates with toll-charging gantries installed on motorways. Motorists will receive a monthly bill. Tolls are expected to create havoc on other roads as motorists desert motorways for A and B roads.

Motorway travel in Britain is generally fast, although it's often slowed to a crawl by road works and the ubiquitous contra-flow, where two-way traffic occupies a single carriage. Motorways are generally accident free, except in fog and poor visibility, when multiple-vehicle accidents are frequent due to motorists driving too fast and too close (the police believe the general standard of motorway driving in Britain is abysmal). However, despite their high traffic density, motorways are Britain's safest roads, accounting for just 3 per cent of all casualties or 11 injuries per 100 million miles, compared with over 100 injuries per 100 million miles in towns and around 35 in rural areas. By the year 2020 traffic on motorways is set to rise by between 50 and 100 per cent.

Emergency SOS telephones are located on motorways, where arrows on marker posts at the roadside indicate the direction of the nearest telephone. The hard shoulder on motorways is for emergencies only and you mustn't stop there simply to have a rest (for which you can be fined). Note also that the hard shoulder is a dangerous place to stop and many fatal accidents involve vehicles stopped there.

Importing a Car

If you plan to import a motor vehicle or motorcycle into Britain, either temporarily or permanently, first make sure that you're aware of the latest regulations. Obtain a copy of Notice 3 (*Bringing your Belongings and Private Motor Vehicle to the United Kingdom From Outside the European Union*) or PI1 (*Permanent Import of Motor Vehicles into Great Britain*) from Her Majesty's Customs and Excise, CDE5 Southbank, Dorset House, Stamford Street, London SE1 9PY, United Kingdom (☎ 0207-620 1313). You must complete customs form C104F if you're importing your private vehicle for no more than six months in a 12-month period. If you're setting up home in Britain you must complete form C104A. Forms are available from shipping agents or from the above address. Information is also available from motoring organisations. The regulations also apply to the importation of boats and aircraft.

You should check whether you will be able to register and licence a particular vehicle in Britain and whether it can, if necessary, be modified to comply with British standards of construction, i.e. receive National Type Approval. Check with the manufacturer's export department, the British importers or the vehicle licensing authority in Britain that the vehicle you're planning to import meets the latest regulations. For further information obtain a copy of leaflet P11 from HM Customs and Excise at the above address. If you wish to import a car (except as a visitor), inform the customs staff on arrival in Britain. Whether you're required to pay import duty and car tax depends on how long you have owned the car and how long you have lived abroad. Duty is 10 per cent on cars, 8.6 per cent on motorcycles below 250cc and 7.8 per cent on motorcycles above 250cc, plus VAT at 17.5 per cent. There's a reduced rate of duty for vehicles imported from some countries.

Buying or Selling a Car

Cars are dearer in Britain than in many other European countries, although you can obtain a discount off the list (book) price of most new cars. Shop around and compare prices, discounts and incentives from a number of dealers. There has been a slump in sales to private buyers (rather than fleet sales) in recent years, which means that buyers can usually get a good deal. Free insurance, servicing and petrol are just some of the incentives on offer. You can often get a good bargain by buying an old model that has been, or is due to be, replaced by a new model. When new registration numbers are issued (twice annually) is a good time to buy a new car with the previous year's registration number, which may be sold for £thousands below list price. One way to get a good price without haggling is to contact a company such as Woolwich Motorbase (☎ 0870-607 2727), which buys in bulk and deals directly with manufacturers.

New car prices in Britain are, according to most consumer organisations and the British government, a rip-off. British drivers pay up to 60 per cent more than their European counterparts for *exactly* the same cars, with most costing 30 to 40 per cent more in Britain than on the continent (you can make even larger savings on servicing!). A government report in 1998 found that 60 out of 74 best-selling cars were more expensive in Britain than Europe (cars are even cheaper in the USA), which has led to an investigation into car prices by the Office of Fair Trading. One survey sited examples such as the Ford Mondeo, which was found to be 58.5 per cent more expensive in Britain than Spain and a Nissan model selling for £9,000 in the Netherlands costing £15,000 around the corner from the British factory where it's made! Spurious arguments concerning equipment levels, exchange rates, higher taxes, etc. account for only a tiny fraction of the difference in UK and continental prices.

Huge savings can be made by buying on the continent, although manufacturers try to prevent British buyers from doing so by refusing to provide dealers with right-hand-drive models (although this is illegal). British car dealers and manufacturers deliberately provide misleading and false information to discourage buyers from buying abroad, although the procedure is straightforward and simple, and any drawbacks are more than offset by the vast savings. The biggest savings can usually be made in Belgium and the Netherlands, although it depends on the make and model of car that you're buying. One of the easiest ways to buy a car abroad is in conjunction with Broadspeed (☎ 0207-413 9940/9950) and Stena Line (☎ 01233-646881 for reservations) travelling on the Harwich–Hook of Holland route. Broadspeed provide a complete buying package with buyers negotiating directly with Dutch dealers. Dutch prices include over 50 per cent tax, which makes the

Netherlands one of the cheapest countries in Europe in which to purchase a car for export. All British buyers need to pay is UK VAT at 17.5 per cent.

You can get a guide to the value of most second-hand cars from motoring magazines such as *What Car?*, *Motorists Guide*, *Parker's Car Price Guide* and *Used Car Prices & Information*, all of which are published monthly. Always do your own research in your area by comparing prices at dealers, in local papers (and free car magazines) and in the national press, e.g. *Exchange & Mart*, *Loot* and the *Thames Valley Trader*. Many private sellers are willing to take a considerable drop and dealers will also usually haggle over the price. The average annual mileage for a car in Britain is around 12,000 (19,311km) a year and cars with high mileage (e.g. 20,000mi/32,186km a year) can usually be bought for substantially less than the average price. A new innovation in recent years has been car 'supermarkets' (e.g. CarLand, ☎ freefone 0800-783 3366, Internet: www.carland.com) selling nearly-new or recent used models, mainly ex-fleet or ex-lease.

Car sales are covered by the Misrepresentation of Goods Act 1967, which means that a seller cannot lawfully make false claims. If you buy from a dealer, you're additionally covered by the Sale of Goods Act 1979, which says a car must be of 'merchantable' quality and good for the purpose intended. *Which?* magazine (see **Appendix A**) publish an annual *Which? Car* edition containing independent information on best buys, performance, comfort, convenience, reliability, trouble spots, running costs, safety, recalls, and new and second-hand prices. New and used car reports are available via the AA's telephone and fax information service (to order a free directory ☎ 01256-493747).

Driving Licences

The minimum age for driving in Britain is 17 for a motor car (up to 3.5 tonnes laden) or motorcycle over 50cc, and 16 for a motorcycle (moped) up to 50cc, an invalid carriage and certain other vehicles. For commercial vehicles up to 7.5 tonnes laden, the minimum age is 18 and for heavy goods vehicles (HGV) it's 21. Driving licences are issued for certain categories of vehicles, e.g. category A is for a motorcycle, B is for a car, C is for a truck and D is for a bus. Holders of a full foreign driving licence or an international driving permit may drive in Britain for one year.

As of July 1996, all EU (pink) driving licences (i.e. with a multi-lingual cover) have been recognised in all EU countries irrespective of the length of your stay. If you hold a licence issued in Australia, Barbados, the British Virgin Islands, Cyprus, Gibraltar, Hong Kong, Japan, Kenya, Malta, New Zealand, Singapore, Switzerland or Zimbabwe, you can obtain a British driving licence in your first year in Britain without taking a driving test. **If you don't apply during your first year, you aren't permitted to drive after this period until you have passed a driving test.** If you hold a licence issued by a country that isn't listed above, you must take a driving test during your first year in Britain. If you don't pass the driving test during your first year in Britain, you must apply for a provisional licence and drive under restricted conditions (i.e. with a qualified driver) until you have passed your test.

Some foreign licences (for example licences printed in Arabic or Japanese) must be translated into English or an international driving permit must be obtained before arrival. To apply for a British driving licence, you must obtain an application form (D1) and form D100 (which explains what you need to know about driver licensing) from any post office. An eye test certificate isn't required, although you must be able to read a number plate at 67 feet (20.5m) in daylight, with glasses or contact lenses, if necessary (you *will* be tested). Unlike most foreign driving licences, a British licence doesn't contain a photograph.

Car Insurance

All motor vehicles plus trailers and semi-trailers must be insured for third party liability when entering Britain. However, it isn't mandatory for cars insured in most European countries to have an international insurance 'green' card. Vehicles insured in EU countries, the Czech Republic, Hungary, Liechtenstein, Norway, Slovakia and Switzerland are automatically covered for third party liability in Britain. The following categories of car insurance are available in Britain:

Third party: The minimum cover required by law, which includes all public and private roads. In addition to the legal minimum, it includes cover for injury to other people caused by your passengers. Not all insurance companies offer third party car insurance.

Third party, fire and theft (TPF&F): Known in some countries as part comprehensive, TPF&F includes (in addition to third party cover) loss or damage caused to your car and anything fitted to it by fire, lightning, explosion, theft or attempted theft. It usually includes broken glass.

Comprehensive: Covers all the risks listed under the two categories above plus damage to your own car, theft of contents (usually limited to £100 or £150), broken glass (e.g. windscreen replacement), personal accident benefits and medical expenses (e.g. £100 or £200). It also usually includes damage due to natural hazards, e.g. storm damage. Extra cover may be included free or for an additional fee and may include the cost of hiring a car if yours is involved in an accident or stolen, legal assistance, no-claims discount protection, and extra cover for a car stereo or phone. Comprehensive insurance may also cover you against loss when your car is in a garage for service or repair. Check a policy for any restrictions, for example if your car isn't garaged and locked overnight you may not be covered against theft. Most lenders usually insist on comprehensive insurance for leasing, contract hire, hire purchase and loan agreements.

British motor insurance doesn't include a free green card (that extends comprehensive or TPF&F cover to the countries listed above), which is usually available for a maximum period (e.g. three months a year) and is expensive. It isn't necessary to have a green card when driving in Western Europe, but without one you're covered only for the legal minimum third party insurance required by law.

There's a competitive motor insurance market in Britain, which has been intensified in recent years by the proliferation of direct marketing and direct response insurance companies who are often able to offer cheaper insurance by cutting out the commission paid to traditional insurance brokers. However, there's no longer much difference between premiums offered by direct-selling companies and traditional brokers. Car insurance is also offered by banks, motoring organisations, manufacturers (expensive) and a range of other companies.

Car Crime

Over 500,000 cars are stolen annually in Britain (one every minute), which has the highest (per capita) number of stolen cars in Europe. Car crime is a huge and profitable business in Britain, costing £billions a year and representing around a third of all reported crime. It's estimated that some 70 per cent of stolen cars are broken up and sold for spares, while the rest are given a false identity and sold (many are exported to the Middle and Far East). One car in ten becomes a victim of 'autocrime' in England and Wales, and if you regularly park your car in a city street, you have a one in four chance of having it or its contents stolen. Having your car stolen means more than just taking a taxi home. It may mean weeks of delay sorting out insurance, extra time and expense travelling to work, possible loss of personal (maybe irreplaceable) possessions and loss of your insurance no-claims discount. It may also involve hiring a solicitor or going to court to re-claim your car after it has been sold by the thief (if a car is stolen and sold, it can be a nightmare getting it back).

If you drive a new or valuable car it's wise to have it fitted with an alarm, an engine immobiliser (preferably of the rolling code variety with a transponder arming key) or other anti-theft device, and to also use a visible deterrent such as a steering or gear change lock. This is particularly important if you own a car that's desirable to car thieves, which includes most new sports and executive cars, which are often stolen by professional crooks to order (although the most vulnerable cars are GTI hatchbacks which are often stolen and wrecked by joyriders – a British phenomenon). A reflection of the high rate of stolen cars in Britain is that it's standard practice for many new cars to be fitted with dead locks and sophisticated alarm systems (some cars such as the Jaguar XJ are, according to experts, virtually theft-proof). Professional thieves now steal cars by towing them or removing them on trailers rather than crack security devices. Needless to say, if you're driving anything other than a worthless wreck, you should have theft insurance (which includes your stereo and belongings).

Don't take unnecessary risks and always lock your car, engage your steering lock and completely close all windows (but don't leave children or pets in an unventilated car or at any time in hot weather). Never leave you keys in the ignition, not even when filling up at a petrol station or in your driveway. Put any valuables (including clothes) in the boot or out of sight and don't leave your vehicle documents in the car or any form of identification. If possible avoid parking in commuter and long-term car parks (e.g. at airports and railway stations), which are favourite hunting grounds for car thieves. When parking overnight or when it's dark, park in a well-lit area, which helps deter car thieves.

Car theft has spawned a huge car security business in the (losing) battle to prevent or deter car thieves. These include a multitude of car alarms, engine immobilisers, steering and gear stick locks, personal wheel clamps, window etching with the car registration number, locking wheel nuts and petrol caps, and removable/coded stereo systems (a favourite target of thieves). A good security system won't prevent someone breaking into your car (which usually takes a professional a matter of seconds) or prevent it being stolen (which takes a few minutes more), bit it will make it more difficult and may prompt a thief to look for an easier target. If you plan to buy an expensive stereo system, buy one with a removable unit or control panel/fascia (which you can pop in a pocket), but never forget to remove it, even when stopping for a few minutes (although thieves sometimes steal the back box, leaving you with a useless facia). For complete peace of mind, particularly in London, you're better off using public transport.

The best security for a valuable car is a tracking device that's triggered by concealed motion detectors. The vehicle's movements are tracked by radio or satellite and the police are automatically notified and recover over 90 per cent of vehicles. Some systems can immobilise a vehicle while it's on the move (which might not be such a good idea!). Tracking systems include Securicor Trakbak (around £600 plus £150 installation and £120 annual membership) and Tracker Network (note that some systems are more accurate than others). Many insurance companies offer a discount on comprehensive insurance (e.g. 20 per cent) when you have a tracking system fitted.

General Road Rules

The following general road rules and tips may help you adjust to driving in Britain and avoid an accident:

- Among the many strange habits of the British is that of driving on the left-hand side of the road (if everyone else drove on the left, the British would drive on the right!). You may find this a bit strange if you come from a country which drives on the right, however, it saves a lot of confusion if you do likewise. It's helpful to have a reminder (e.g. 'think left!') on your car's dashboard. Take extra care when pulling out of junctions, one-way streets and at roundabouts. Remember to look first to the *right* when crossing the road and drivers of left-hand cars should note that headlights should be dipped to the left when driving at night.

  If you're unused to driving on the left, you should be prepared for some disorientation or even terror, although most people have few problems adjusting to it. However, some people have a real fear of driving on the 'wrong' side of the road. If this applies to you, the International Drivers Service (☎ 0208-570 9190) specialises in teaching foreigners how to survive on British roads. The road system, narrow roads, parking, density and speed of traffic is also completely alien to many foreigners, particularly Americans.

- All motorists are advised to carry a warning triangle, although it isn't mandatory. If you have an accident or a breakdown, you should signal this by switching on your hazard warning lights. If you have a warning triangle it must be placed at the edge of the road, at least 50 metres behind the car on secondary roads and at least 150 metres on motorways.

- In Britain there's no priority to the right (or left) on any roads, as there is in many European countries. At all crossroads and junctions in Britain, there's either an octagonal stop sign (solid white line on road) or a triangular give way sign (dotted white line on road), where a secondary road meets a major road. Stop or give way may also be painted on the road surface. You must stop completely at a stop sign (all four wheels must come to rest) before pulling out onto a major road, even if you can see that no traffic is approaching. At a give way sign, you aren't required to stop, but must give priority to traffic already on the major road.

- The different types of traffic signs in Britain can usually be distinguished by their shape and colour as follows:
  - warning signs are mostly triangular with **red** borders;
  - signs within circles with a **red** border are mostly prohibitive;
  - signs within **blue** circles but no red border give positive instructions;
  - direction signs are mostly rectangular and are distinguished by their background colour: **blue** for motorway signs, **green** for primary routes and **white** for secondary routes. Local direction signs often have blue borders with a white background. Signs with brown backgrounds are used to direct motorists to

tourist attractions. All signs are shown in a booklet entitled *Know Your Traffic Signs*.

- On roundabouts (traffic circles), vehicles on the roundabout (coming from your right) have priority and not those entering it. There are many roundabouts in Britain, which although they are a bit of a free-for-all, speed up traffic considerably and are usually preferable to traffic lights, particularly outside rush hours (although some busy roundabouts also have traffic lights). Some roundabouts have a filter lane which is reserved for traffic turning left. Traffic flows clockwise round roundabouts and not anti-clockwise as in countries where traffic drives on the right. You should signal as you approach the exit you wish to take. In addition to large roundabouts, there are also mini-roundabouts, indicated by a round blue sign. The British think roundabouts are marvellous (we spend most of our time going round in circles), although they aren't so popular in countries where traffic drives on the right. Roundabouts are particularly useful for making a U-turn when you discover that you're travelling in the wrong direction. The biggest roundabout in the world is the M25 motorway, affectionately known as the magic roundabout.

- Speed humps, known as 'sleeping policemen', are becoming a common sight on Britain's roads, particularly in residential areas, near schools, on private roads, in university grounds and in car parks. They are designed to slow traffic (or wreck your suspension) and are sometimes indicated by warning signs – if you fail to slow down it's possible to turn your car over!

- On country roads, sharp bends are shown by signs and the severity (tightness) of a bend is indicated by white arrows on a black background (or vice versa); the more arrows the tighter the bend (so SLOW down).

- The wearing of seat belts is **compulsory** for all front and rear seat passengers (over one year of age) and children under 14 in rear seats must use seat belts or child restraints when fitted (although it makes sense to wear rear seat belts at all times irrespective of age). Seat belts or restraints must be appropriate for the age and weight of a child, as follows:

  - **under 1 year old (weighing less than 10kg):** a front or rear-facing baby seat with a built-in three-point harness in either the front (but not when the front seat is fitted with an airbag) or rear of a car;

  - **1 to 4 years old (under 18kg):** a rear-facing Renault Argonaute-style seat or a front-facing restraint with a built-in (e.g. five point) harness;

  - **3½ to 7 years old (15 to 25kg):** lap table (for use when only a lap belt is available);

  - **3 to 12 years old (15 to 36kg):** a three-point adult belt with a booster seat with head restraint.

Special harnesses and belts are also available for the handicapped. Note that all belts, seats, harnesses and restraints **must be correctly fitted and adjusted, without which they may be useless.** Some child car seats have fatal flaws and many cars have seat belt straps that are too short for rear-facing baby seats. It's estimated that some two-thirds of child seats are wrongly fitted. The Royal Automobile Club (☎ freefone 0800-550055) produce a safety video entitled

There's No Excuse!. If all available restraints in a car are in use, children may travel unrestrained (although this is extremely unwise).

It's estimated that seat belts would prevent 75 per cent of the deaths and 90 per cent of the injuries to those involved in accidents who weren't wearing belts. Note, however, that lap belts fitted in the centre rear seat of many cars are dangerous and should be changed. In addition to the risk of death or injury, you can be fined £50 for ignoring the seat belt laws. The vast majority of British people wear seat belts, due in no small part to a shocking (but effective) advertising campaign in the '80s called 'Clunk Click, Every Trip'. Note that it's the driver's responsibility to ensure that passengers are properly fastened. If you're exempt from wearing a seat belt for medical reasons, an exemption certificate is required from your doctor. The ultimate protection is supposed to be afforded by airbags, although a number of deaths have been blamed on them in recent years.

- Don't drive in lanes reserved for buses and taxis, unless necessary to avoid a stationary vehicle or obstruction, and give priority to authorised users. Bus lanes are indicated by road markings and signs indicating the period of operation, which is usually during rush hours only (although some lanes are in use 24 hours a day), and which vehicles are permitted to use them. Bus drivers get irate if you illegally drive in their lane and you can be fined for doing so.

- Headlights must be used at night on all roads where there's no street lighting, where street lamps are over 185 metres (200 yards) apart and on roads where street lamps aren't lit. You must use your headlamps or front fog lamps at any time when visibility is generally reduced to less than 100 metres. In Britain it's legal to drive on parking (side) lights on roads with street lighting (although they do little to help you see or be seen). Note that headlight flashing has a different meaning in different countries. In some countries it means "after you", while in others it means "get out of my way". It can even mean "I'm driving a new car and haven't yet worked out what all the switches are for". In Britain headlamp flashing has no legal status apart from warning another driver of your presence, although it's usually used to give priority to another vehicle, e.g. when a car is waiting to exit from a junction. Hazard warning lights (all indicators operating simultaneously) are used to warn other drivers of an obstruction, e.g. an accident or a traffic jam on a motorway (using them when stopping illegally has no legal significance unless you have broken down).

- Front fog or spot lights must be fitted in pairs at a regulation height. Rear fog lamps should be used only when visibility is seriously reduced, i.e. to less than 100 metres, and shouldn't be used when it's just dark or raining. Unfortunately many British drivers don't know what fog lamps are for and use them when visibility is good, but don't use them (or any lights) in fog.

- The sequence of British traffic lights is red, red + amber (yellow), green, amber and back to red. Red + amber is a warning to get ready to go but you mustn't start moving until the light changes to green. Amber means stop at the stop line and you may proceed only if the amber light appears after you have crossed the stop line or when stopping might cause an accident. A green filter light may be shown in addition to the full lamp signals, which means you may drive in the direction shown by the arrow, irrespective of other lights showing.

You may notice that many traffic lights have an uncanny habit of changing to green when you approach them, particularly during off-peak hours. This isn't magic or due to your magnetic personality. Around half of Britain's traffic signals are vehicle-actuated, where sensors between 40 and 150 metres from the lights (depending on the speed limit) are set into the road and change the light to green unless other traffic already has priority. Signals stay at green for a minimum of seven seconds, although it can be as long as one minute.

- At many traffic lights, cameras are installed to detect motorists driving through red lights (you receive notification around one month later and must *prove* that you weren't driving the vehicle to avoid prosecution). In Britain, traffic lights are placed on the left side of the road at junctions and may also be duplicated opposite. You won't have to play hunt the traffic lights as on the continent of Europe, where lights and road signs may be placed on the left, right, opposite side of the road or up in the air, and may present a multitude of confusing signals.

- Always approach pedestrian crossings with caution and don't park or overtake another vehicle on the approach to a crossing marked by a double line of studs or zig-zag lines. At pelican (pedestrian) crossings, a flashing amber light follows the red light, to warn you to give way to pedestrians before proceeding. **Note that pedestrians have the legal right of way once they have stepped onto a crossing without traffic lights and you must STOP. Motorists who don't stop are liable to heavy penalties.** Where a road crosses a public footpath, e.g. when entering or emerging from property or a car park bordering a road, you *must* give way to pedestrians.

- Britain lacks a rule of the road which compels slow moving vehicles (such as tractors or cars towing caravans) to pull over to allow other traffic to overtake. The AA states that a driver towing a caravan who sees more than six vehicles following him, should pull over and let them pass, but it isn't compulsory. Worse still, timid drivers who never overtake anything unless it's stationary, bunch up behind slow moving vehicles, thus ensuring that nobody can overtake without having to pass a whole stream of traffic (or forcing a gap).

- Fines can be exacted for a wide range of motoring offences, although on-the-spot fines *aren't* imposed in Britain. Convictions for most motoring offences means an 'endorsement' of your licence, which results in penalty points being imposed. Serious offences such as dangerous or drunken driving involving injury or death to others can result in a prison sentence.

- Many motorists seem to have an aversion to driving in the left-hand lane on a three-lane motorway, which in effect reduces the motorway to two lanes. It's illegal to overtake on an inside lane unless traffic is being channelled in a different direction. Motorists must indicate before overtaking *and* when moving back into an inside lane after overtaking, e.g. on a dual carriageway or motorway. Learner drivers, pedestrians, cyclists and mopeds aren't permitted on motorways.

- White lines mark the separation of traffic lanes. A solid single line or two solid lines means no overtaking in either direction. A solid line to the left of the centre line, i.e. on your side of the road, means that overtaking is prohibited in your direction. You may overtake only when there's a single broken line in the middle of the road or double lines with a broken line on your side of the road. If you drive a left-hand drive car, take extra care when overtaking (the most dangerous manoeuvre in motoring) and when turning right. It's wise to have a special 'overtaking mirror' fitted to your car.

● The edges of motorways and A-roads are often marked with a white line with a ribbed surface, which warns you through tyre sound and vibration when you drive too close to the edge of the road. The edges of motorways are also marked with reflective studs (cat's eyes).

● In Britain there are three main kinds of railway level crossings: automatic half-barrier level crossings, automatic open crossings and open level crossings without gates or barriers. Always approach a railway level crossing slowly and **STOP**:

 – as soon as the amber light is on and the audible alarm sounds followed by flashing red warning lights (half-barrier level crossings and automatic open crossings)

 – as soon as the barrier or half-barrier starts to fall (if applicable) or the gates start to close

 – in any case when a train approaches.

Many automatic and manual crossings have a telephone that can be used to contact the signalman in an emergency or to ask for advice or information. In remote areas, open level crossings have no gates, barriers, attendant or traffic lights. Some level crossings have gates, but no attendant or red lights. If there's a telephone, contact the signalman to check that it's okay to cross, otherwise providing a train isn't coming, open the gates wide and cross as quickly as possible. Close the gates after crossing. **Crossings without gates must be approached with extreme caution (including pedestrian railway crossings).** Even a car that's built like a tank won't look so smart after a scrap with a 70-tonne locomotive.

● Be particularly wary of cyclists, moped riders and motorcyclists. It isn't always easy to see them, particularly when they are hidden by the blind spots of a car or when cyclists are riding at night without lights. **When overtaking, ALWAYS give them a wide . . . WIDE berth.** If you knock them off their bikes, you may have a difficult time convincing the police that it wasn't your fault; far better to avoid them (and the police). Drive slowly near schools and be wary of children getting on or off buses.

● A 'GB' nationality plate (sticker) must be affixed to the rear of a British registered car when motoring abroad. Drivers of foreign registered cars in Britain must have the appropriate nationality plate affixed to the rear of their car (not an assortment). Note that yellow headlights are illegal in Britain (except for visitors) and should be converted.

● If you need spectacles or contact lenses to read a number plate 79.4mm high at a distance of 20.5m (67ft) in good daylight, then you must always wear them when motoring. It's advisable to carry a spare pair of glasses or contact lenses in your car.

● The police routinely prosecute motorists for using a mobile phone while driving (classed as 'inconsiderate driving'), although in itself it isn't illegal. It's one of the most common and hazardous driving habits in Britain and has resulted in numerous accidents, many fatal, and has been calculated to increase the risk of an accident by some 400 per cent (even hands-free phones are little safer, as they all distract the driver's attention).

• A booklet published by the Department of Transport entitled *The Highway Code*
(The Stationery office) contains advice for all road users, including motorists,
motorcyclists and pedestrians. It's available for 99p from bookshops and British
motoring organisations and is essential reading. Although *The Highway Code*
shows many road signs commonly used in Britain, a comprehensive explanation is
given in a booklet entitled *Know Your Traffic Signs*, available at most bookshops
for £1.20. A free booklet entitled *On the Road in Great Britain* (in English,
French, German, Italian and Spanish) is published by the Department of Transport
and is available from British motoring organisations, travel agents and government
offices.

Car Hire

There are four multinational car hire (or 'car rental') companies in Britain (Avis,
Budget, Europcar and Hertz), plus a number of large independents, e.g. British Car
Rental, Godfrey Davis, Kenning Car Rental, Practical and Swan National. All have
offices in towns throughout the country and at most major international airports
(open from around 0630 to 2300). Most major companies provide one-way hire,
which means you can hire a car at one branch and leave it at another (for an extra
charge). When hiring from a national company, check whether you're being quoted
the national or local rate (which is cheaper). The national rate is usually charged
when hiring in major cities or at airports and should be avoided unless someone else
is paying. Always check what's included in the rental charge as what appears to be an
expensive quote could turn out to be the cheapest.

Cars can also be rented from many garages and local car hire offices in most
towns, which often charge much lower rates than the nationals. Look in local
newspapers and under 'Car rentals' in the Yellow Pages. Shop around for the best
buy, as the car hire business is extremely competitive. However, you should beware
of cowboy hire companies who offer 'hire cars from hell'. Some cars offered by local
companies, particularly in tourist areas, are unroadworthy and could put your life at
risk. Be particularly careful if hiring an older car (cars from major hire companies
aren't more than three years old and are usually less than one year old) as it could be
in a dangerous condition. If you're offered an old car or a car with high mileage, it's
probably wise to reject it (unless the company is in the business of renting cheap
wrecks). If you hire a car in an unroadworthy condition, you're responsible if you're
stopped by the police or cause an accident.

All national hire companies offer fly-drive deals on flights to or within Britain,
which must be booked in advance. You can also hire a car from major railway
stations and leave it at another station or delivery point. Providing you book 24-hours
in advance, a car can be waiting to meet you at the station at any time of day or night.
Cars can also be hired on the spot from some stations from Hertz and other hire
companies. Note that Hertz (and other companies) charge their highest rate for
fly-drive and executive connection services. Special rates are available when
combined with British Rail InterCity weekend or longer trips. Rental costs vary
considerably between rental companies, particularly over longer periods (weekly and
monthly rates are lower). Rates are usually inclusive of unlimited mileage, collision
damage waiver insurance, personal accident, baggage insurance and VAT. Rental
cars usually mustn't be driven outside Britain unless prior arrangement is made with
the rental company and continental insurance (a green card) obtained.

Rental cars from national companies can often be ordered with a portable phone, child restraints or a roof rack, for which some companies charge a fee. All rental cars from national companies are covered for roadside breakdown assistance from a British motoring organisation. You can also hire a 4-wheel-drive car, estate, minibus, prestige luxury car or a sports car, and a choice of manual or automatic gearbox is often available. Minibuses are also for hire (e.g. from Hertz) and are accessible to wheelchairs. Performance cars can be hired from a number of specialist hire companies, although if you want to test drive a car for a few days with a view to buying one, you may get a better deal from a garage. Some companies also hire cars with hand controls for registered disabled drivers.

To hire a car in Britain you require a full British, European or international driving licence, which must have been held for a minimum of one year (or two years if aged under 23). If you hold a British licence with an endorsement for driving without due care and attention (or worse), you may be refused car hire, although an endorsement for speeding is usually permitted. You may be asked for some form of identification in addition to your driving licence. The minimum age is usually between 18 and 23, although those aged 18 to 21 must normally provide their own fully comprehensive insurance or purchase collision damage waiver (CDW) insurance at a special (high) rate. Drivers aged under 21 are usually restricted in their choice of cars and some hire companies insist on a higher minimum age (e.g. 25) for some categories of cars.

You must usually be aged 23 to 25 to hire a minibus or motor caravan (the maximum age for hiring a car may be 70 or 75). A minimum deposit of £50 to £75 (or equal to the total hire charge) is usually required if you don't pay by credit card (national car rental companies also have their own credit cards) and may be much higher if you don't take out CDW insurance. Cheques must be supported by a guarantee card. When paying by credit card, check that you aren't charged for erroneous extras or for something for which you've already paid, e.g. petrol. In fact paying by credit card usually means that you give the hire company a 'continuous authority' (or blank cheque) to debit your card account.

Vans and pick-ups are available from major rental companies by the hour, half-day or day, or from smaller local companies (which once again, are cheaper). You can also hire a motor caravan, a caravan or trailer, or a minibus, from a number of companies (prices vary with the season). In addition to self-drive car hire, in many cities you can hire a car with a chauffeur for business or sightseeing. The British Tourist Authority publish an annual *Vehicle Hire* directory.

2.

FURTHER
CONSIDERATIONS

This chapter contains important considerations for most people planning to buy a home in Britain, particularly those planning to live there permanently or semi-permanently. It includes information about the climate, geography, health, insurance, shopping, pets, television and radio, learning English, crime, public holidays and time difference.

CLIMATE

Britain has a generally mild and temperate climate, although it's extremely changeable and usually damp at any time of year. Because of the prevailing south-westerly winds, the weather is variable and is affected by depressions moving eastwards across the Atlantic Ocean (which make British weather reports depressing). This maritime influence means that the west of the country tends to have wetter, but also milder weather than the east. The amount of rainfall also increases with altitude and the mountainous areas of the north and west have more rain (1,600mm or 60 inches annually) than the lowlands of the south and east, where the average is 800mm (30in). Rain is fairly evenly distributed throughout the year (i.e. it rains most of the time) in all areas. For many, spring is the most pleasant time of year, although early spring is often very wet, particularly in Scotland.

In winter, temperatures are higher in the south and west than in the east, and winters are often harsh in Scotland and on high ground in Wales and northern England, where snow is usual. December and February are traditionally the severest months, when it's often cold, wet and windy. When it snows the whole country comes to a grinding halt (except for the kids, who love it) and people complain that the authorities are unprepared. Although temperatures drop below freezing in winter, particularly at night, it's rarely below freezing during the day, although the average temperature is a cold 4°C (39°F).

The most unpleasant features of British winters are freezing fog and black ice, both of which make driving hazardous. The 'pea-soup' fog which was usually the result of smog and pollution, and which many foreigners still associate with Britain, is generally a thing of the past. The warmest areas in summer are the south and inland areas, where temperatures are often around 26°C (75°F) and occasionally rise above 30°C (86°F), although the average temperature is 15°C to 18°C (60°F to 65°F). Fine autumn weather is often preceded by early morning fog, which may last until midday. Early autumn is often mild, particularly in Scotland. Average daily temperatures are: winter 4°C (39°F), spring 9°C (48°F), summer 16°C (61°F) and autumn 10°C (50°F).

The worst aspect of British weather is the frequent drizzle (light rain) and the almost permanent grey skies, particularly in winter. British winter weather has given rise to a condition known as seasonal affective disorder (SAD), which is brought on by the dark dull days of winter and causes lethargy, fatigue and low spirits. However, there's some good news. British winters are becoming milder and in recent years they have been nothing like as severe as in earlier decades, although whether this is a permanent change is unclear.

In fact, British weather is becoming warmer all round, with recent years experiencing some of the driest summers since records began in 1659. To add a little spice to the usual diet of cold and rain, in the last decade Britain has been afflicted with gales and torrential rain (including the infamous storms of 1987 and 1990), which caused severe damage and flooding in many areas. Tornadoes do occur in Britain, but are extremely rare. There's much debate among weather experts and scientists as to whether the climatic changes (not just in Britain, but world-wide) are a result of global warming or just a temporary change. If present trends continue, some scientists predict that temperatures will increase considerably in the next century and the south-west region could become frost-free.

Weather forecasts in Britain appear designed to be deliberately evasive, as if the meteorologists are continually hedging their bets, and forecasts often include both scattered showers and sunny periods at the very least. Meteorologists usually find it particularly difficult to forecast abrupt changes or extremes of weather (which are common in Britain). A new style of weather report in recent years introduced percentage forecasting, such as a 70 per cent chance of rain, a 50 per cent likelihood of frost overnight and a 10 per cent probability of sunny periods (and a 100 per cent chance that it'll all be wrong!). The Meteorological Office sells its long-term weather predictions to industry, agriculture and tourism, who, if they have any sense, would insist on a guarantee (the Met Office has been accused of fiddling its success-rate figures).

The weather forecast is available by telephone from Weathercall, which divides Britain into 27 areas, each with a separate (0891) telephone number. To obtain a free Weathercall card, phone 0207-236 3500. Similar services are provided by Weatherwatch (from the Automobile Association, ☎ 01256-493747 for a directory) and WeatherCheck (☎ 09001-333111). The weather forecast is also available via the television teletext services, in daily newspapers, on the Internet, and on TV and radio (usually after the news). Warnings of dangerous weather conditions affecting motoring, e.g. fog and ice, are broadcast regularly on all BBC national and local radio stations.

The most detailed weather forecasts are broadcast on BBC Radio 2 and BBC Radio 4 (which also broadcasts weather forecasts for shipping). Many newspapers also include temperatures and the weather outlook in European and world capitals, European holiday centres, and in winter, the weather and snow conditions in major ski resorts. During early summer, when pollens are released in large quantities, the pollen count is given on radio and TV weather forecasts and in daily newspapers. In summer, the maximum exposure time for the fair-skinned is also included in TV weather forecasts on hot days. If you suffer from insomnia, *The Story of Weather* by Bill Giles (Stationery Office) should provide an instant cure.

GEOGRAPHY

The title of this book may cause some confusion, particularly as there are occasional references to the United Kingdom, England, Scotland, Wales, Ireland and Northern Ireland. The term Britain (as used in this book) comprises Great Britain, the island which includes England, Wales and Scotland, and Northern Ireland, the full name of which is the 'United Kingdom (UK) of Great Britain and Northern Ireland'. The British Isles is the geographical term for the group of islands, which includes Great Britain, Ireland and many smaller islands surrounding Britain.

Britain covers an area of 242,432km² (93,600mi²) and is about the same size as New Zealand or Uganda and almost half the size of France. It's some 1,000km (600mi) from the south coast to the northernmost point of Scotland and under 500km (around 300mi) across in the widest part. Nowhere in Britain is more than 120km (75mi) from the sea and the coastline, which is strikingly varied and one of the most beautiful in the world. Britain has a varied landscape and most of England is fairly flat and low lying (particularly East Anglia), with the exception of the north and south-west, while much of Scotland and Wales is mountainous. If the worst predictions of global warming become a reality, many coastal regions of Britain will be flooded in the next century or two as the sea level rises. The highest mountains are Ben Nevis in Scotland at 1,343m (4,406ft) and Snowdon in Wales at 1,085m (3,560ft). The country can roughly be divided into a highland region in the north and west, and a lowland region in the east, approximately delimited by the mouths of the River Exe (Exeter) in the south-west and the River Tees (Teeside) in the north-east. Britain has around 1,931km² (1,200mi²) of inland waters, the most famous and largest area being the Lake District in the north-west of England.

HEALTH

One of the most important aspects of living in Britain (or anywhere else for that matter) is maintaining good health. Britain is famous for its National Health Service (NHS), which provides 'free' health care to all British citizens and most foreign residents. The standard of training, dedication and medical skills of British doctors and nursing staff is among the highest in the world, and British medical science is in the vanguard of many of the world's major medical advances (many pioneering operations are performed in Britain). Emergency medical services in Britain are generally excellent. Many foreigners visit Britain each year for private medical treatment and Harley Street (London) is internationally recognised as having some of the world's pre-eminent (and most expensive) specialists, encompassing every conceivable ailment. However, Britain spends only around 7 per cent of its GDP on health care compared with almost 10 per cent in France and Germany and over 14 per cent in the USA.

The pride of the British welfare system is the National Health Service (NHS), established in 1948 to ensure that everyone had equal access to medical care. The NHS includes services provided by family doctors, specialists, hospitals, dentists, chemists, opticians, community health services (e.g. the district nursing and health visitor services), the ambulance service, and maternity and child health care. Originally all NHS medical treatment was free, the service being funded entirely from general taxation and National Insurance contributions. However, as the cost of treatment and medicines have increased, part of the cost has been passed onto patients via supplementary charges. While hospital treatment, the ambulance service and consultations with doctors remain free, many patients must now pay fixed charges for prescriptions, dental treatment, sight tests and NHS glasses, although charges are usually well below the actual cost. Family doctors, called General Practitioners (GPs), still make free house calls and community health workers and district nurses visit people at home who are convalescent, bedridden or have new-born babies

If you don't qualify for health care under the public health service, it's essential to have private health insurance (in fact, you may not qualify for a residence permit without it). This is often advisable in any case if you can afford it, due to the inadequacy of public health services in many areas and long waiting lists for specialist appointments and non-urgent operations. Visitors to Britain should have holiday health insurance (see page 66) if they aren't covered by a reciprocal arrangement.

Medicines and drugs are obtained from a chemist (or pharmacy) in Britain, most of which provide free advice regarding minor ailments and suggest appropriate medicines. There are three categories of drugs and medicines in Britain: those that can be prescribed only by a doctor (via an official form called a prescription) and purchased from a chemist; medicines that can be sold only under the supervision of a pharmacist; and general-sale list medicines (such as aspirin and paracetamol) that can be sold in outlets such as supermarkets. Some drugs and medicines requiring a doctor's prescription in Britain are sold freely in other countries, although other drugs are freely available in Britain that are controlled in other countries (an increasing number of previously restricted drugs are now available over the counter).

It's possible to have medication sent from abroad, when no import duty or value added tax is usually payable. If you're visiting a holiday home in Britain for a limited period, you should take sufficient medication to cover your stay. In an emergency a local doctor will write a prescription that can be filled at a local pharmacy or a hospital may refill a prescription from its own pharmacy. It's also advisable to take some of your favourite non-prescription drugs (e.g. aspirins, cold and flu remedies, lotions, etc.) with you, as they may be difficult or impossible to obtain in Britain or may be much more expensive. If applicable, you should also take a spare pair of spectacles, contact lenses, dentures or a hearing aid.

The infant mortality rate in Britain is around six per 1,000 births (an all-time low), while the average life expectancy is around 74 for men and 79 for women. The main causes of death are circulatory diseases (including heart attacks and strokes) and cancer. Nearly half of all British men and more than a quarter of the women who die between the ages of 45 and 55, do so as a result of heart and circulatory disease, in which Britain is a world leader (due mainly to poor diet and lack of exercise). However, the total number of smokers is reducing, although it remains the greatest preventable cause of illness and death in Britain, and is responsible for over 100,000 deaths and 30 million lost working days annually. Around 30 per cent of Britons smoke, including many more women (particularly young women) than men.

Alcohol abuse is an increasing problem, although drunkenness (lager louts) is more of a social problem than a serious health problem (unlike alcoholism). According to the Mental Health Foundation, around six million people in Britain (one in ten) suffer from mental illness (including most politicians!). Stress is an increasing problem and an estimated 250 million working hours are lost annually due to stress-related absences (more people are also turning to anti-depressants to cope with life).

Air pollution caused by sunshine and high temperatures (they do occur occasionally) is an increasing concern in Britain, not just in the cities but in rural areas, where asthmatics, bronchitis sufferers and the elderly are particularly at risk. Levels of air pollution are already well above safe health limits on hot days and in cities signs of asthma are found in some 20 per cent of children. Hay fever sufferers can obtain the daily pollen count between March and July from weather broadcasts and daily newspapers. Britain has a relatively high incidence of skin cancer due to over-exposure to the sun (although this occurs more often abroad) and the maximum exposure time for the fair-skinned is included in TV weather forecasts on hot days.

Health (and health insurance) is an important issue for anyone retiring to Britain. Many people are ill-prepared for old age and the possibility of health problems. Residential and nursing homes are also an important part of the private health sector (although not all are private). Long-term health care is an increasing problem in

Britain, where many people are forced to pay for the cost of a nursing home with their savings and homes. Local authority social services and voluntary organisations provide invaluable help and advice to the most vulnerable members of the community, including the elderly, disabled and children in need of care.

If you're planning to take up residence in Britain, even for part of the year only, it's wise to have a health check (medical or screening, eyes, teeth, etc.) before your arrival, particularly if you have a record of poor health or are elderly. If you're already taking regular medication, you should bear in mind that the brand names of drugs and medicines vary from country to country, and should ask your doctor for the generic name. If you wish to match medication prescribed abroad, you will need a prescription with the medication's trade name, the manufacturer's name, the chemical name and the dosage. Most drugs have an equivalent in other countries, although particular brands may be difficult or impossible to obtain in Britain.

There are no special health risks in Britain and no immunisations are required unless you arrive from an area infected with yellow fever. You can safely drink the water (unless there's a sign to the contrary), although it sometimes tastes awful. Many people prefer bottled water when not drinking wine (red wine is also beneficial to your health – **providing it's consumed in moderation!**) and various other alcoholic beverages.

INSURANCE

An important aspect of owning a home in Britain is insurance, not only for your home and its contents, but also for your family when visiting Britain. If you live in Britain permanently you will require additional insurance. It's unnecessary to spend half your income insuring yourself against every eventuality from the common cold to being sued for your last penny, but it's important to insure against any event that could precipitate a major financial disaster, such as a serious accident or your house being demolished by a storm. The cost of being uninsured or under-insured can be astronomical.

As with anything connected with finance, it's important to shop around when buying insurance. Simply collecting a few brochures from insurance agents or companies or making a few telephone calls can save you a lot of money. One of the best sources of independent information is *Which?* magazine (see page 71). Bear in mind that not all insurance companies are equally reliable or have the same financial stability, and it may be better to insure with a large international company with a good reputation than with a small company, even if this means paying a higher premium. Read all insurance policies carefully and make sure that you understand the terms and the cover provided before signing them. Some insurance companies will do almost anything to avoid paying claims and will use any available legal loophole, therefore it pays to deal only with reputable companies (not that this provides a foolproof guarantee). Policies often contain traps and legal loopholes in the small print and it's sometimes advisable to obtain legal advice before signing a contract.

In all matters regarding insurance, you're responsible for ensuring that you and your family are legally insured in Britain. Regrettably you cannot insure yourself against being uninsured or sue your insurance agent for giving you bad advice! Bear in mind that if you wish to make a claim on an insurance policy, you may be required to report an incident to the police within 24 hours (this may also be a legal requirement). The law in Britain may differ considerably from that in your home country or your previous country of residence, and you should *never* assume that it's the same. If you're unsure of your rights, it's advisable to obtain legal advice for anything other than a minor claim.

This section contains information about health insurance, household insurance, and holiday and travel insurance. See also **Car Insurance** on page 41.

Health Insurance

If you're visiting, living or working in Britain, it's extremely risky not to have health insurance for your family, as if you're uninsured or under-insured you could be faced with some very high medical bills. When deciding on the type and extent of health insurance, make sure that it covers *all* your family's present and future health requirements in Britain <u>before</u> you receive a large bill. A health insurance policy should cover you for *all* essential health care whatever the reason, including accidents (e.g. sports accidents) and injuries, whether they occur in your home, at your place of work or when travelling. Don't take anything for granted, but check in advance that you're covered.

Long-stay visitors should have travel or long stay health insurance or an international health policy (see **Health Insurance for Visitors** on page 59). If your stay in Britain is limited, you may be covered by a reciprocal agreement between your home country and Britain. When travelling in Britain, you should carry proof of your health insurance with you.

Health Insurance for Residents

If you're planning to take up residence in Britain and will be contributing to social security, you and your family will be entitled to subsidised or free medical treatment. The National Health Service (NHS) provides free or subsidised medical treatment to all British subjects with the right of abode in Britain and to anyone who, at the time of treatment, has been a resident for the previous year (although there are exemptions for certain people). Anyone living or working in Britain who isn't eligible for treatment under the NHS should take out a private health insurance policy (also referred to as private medical insurance or PMI).

Nationals of countries with reciprocal health agreements with Britain also receive free or subsidised medical treatment, including EU nationals and citizens of Anguilla, Australia, Austria, Barbados, British Virgin Islands, Bulgaria, Channel Islands, Czech Republic, Falkland Islands, Gibraltar, Hong Kong, Hungary, Iceland, Isle of Man, Malta, Montserrat, New Zealand, Norway, Poland, Romania, Russia, Slovak Republic, St. Helena, Turks and Caicos Islands, and states comprising the former Yugoslavia. Exemption from charges for nationals of the above countries is generally limited to emergency or urgent treatment (e.g. for a communicable disease) required during a visit to Britain. Anyone who doesn't qualify under one of the above categories, must pay for all medical treatment received, although minor medical and dental emergencies may be treated free of charge, e.g. urgent treatment at a hospital 'emergency' department as a result of an accident (or patients admitted to hospital for no longer than one night).

Anyone who has paid regular social security contributions in another European Union (EU) country for two full years prior to coming to Britain (e.g. to look for a job) is entitled to public health cover for a limited period from the date of the last contribution made in their home country. Social security form E106 must be obtained from the social security authorities in your home country and given to your local social security office in Britain. Similarly, pensioners and those in receipt of invalidity benefits must obtain form E121 from their home country's social security administration.

You will be registered as a member of social security and be given a social security card, a list of local medical practitioners and hospitals, and general information about services and charges. If you're receiving an invalidity pension or other social security benefits on the grounds of ill-health, you should establish exactly how living in Britain will affect those benefits. In some countries there are reciprocal agreements regarding invalidity rights, but you must confirm that they apply in your case. Citizens of European Economic Area (EEA) countries are able to make payments in their home country entitling them to use public health services in Britain and other EEA countries.

Private Health Insurance: If you aren't covered by the NHS you should take out private health insurance, as medical treatment in Britain can be very expensive with the cost of an operation and hospitalisation running into £thousands. The number of people with private health insurance in Britain increased from around 1.5 million in 1966 to some 6.5 million in 1998 (around 12 per cent of the population), half of whose premiums are paid by employers. The remainder are spilt between those who pay their own premiums and those who share them with their employers. Private health care is restricted mainly to the middle to upper income brackets. The best advertisement for private health insurance is the eternal NHS waiting lists for non-emergency operations. NHS waiting lists for all types of treatment (including operations) totalled over one million people in 1998. One in every five operations in Britain is performed privately.

Private health insurance isn't usually intended to replace NHS treatment, but to complement it. Most health insurance policies fall into two main categories: those providing immediate private specialist or hospital treatment (e.g. BUPA, PPP and WPA) and so-called 'budget' or 'waiting-list' policies, where you're treated as a private patient only when waiting lists exceed a certain period. Under waiting-list policies, if you cannot obtain an appointment with an NHS specialist or an NHS hospital admission within a certain period (e.g. six weeks), you can do so as a private patient.

Most health insurance policies have an annual limit on the amount they will pay out for each policyholder, which may be anywhere between £5,000 and £1 million. They usually include consultations with specialists; hospital accommodation and nursing; operations or other treatment (e.g. physiotherapy, radiotherapy or chemotherapy); physician's, surgeon's and anaesthetist's fees; all drugs, X-rays and dressings while in hospital; home nursing; and a daily cash allowance when hospitalised under the NHS.

You cannot take out private health care to cover or obtain treatment for an existing or previous medical condition (depending on how serious and how long ago it was) and there's usually a qualifying period of around three months before you can make a claim. For example, if you need a hernia operation, for which there are currently long NHS waiting lists, you cannot obtain private health cover to jump the queue. Your only solution, other than waiting your turn under the NHS, is to have private treatment and pay for it yourself (a hernia operation costs around £2,000 and a hip replacement up to £7,000). In fact, if you have serious health problems you will need to pay extra for insurance or may be refused cover altogether.

The cost of private health insurance depends on your age and the state of your health. There are maximum age limits for taking out health insurance with some insurers, e.g. 65 for BUPA, although age limits may be higher if you're willing to accept some restrictions. Some companies have special policies for those aged over 50 or 55. There are generally no restrictions on continuing membership, irrespective of age. Treatment of any medical condition for which you have already received medical attention or was aware existed in the five years prior to the start date of the policy, may not be covered. However, existing health problems are usually covered after two years membership, when no further medical attention has been required. Some group policies do, however, include cover for existing or previous health problems. Other exclusions are listed in the policy rules.

The cost of health insurance has increased at double the rate of inflation in recent years. One of the reasons is that BUPA and PPP have a stranglehold on private health care in Britain (they also own many hospitals) and other companies find it difficult to gain a foothold in the market. The cost varies considerably depending on the insurance company and whether you have fully comprehensive health insurance or a 'waiting-list' policy. The cost of insurance also depends on the hospital in which you're treated (the more expensive hospitals cost around twice as much as the cheapest). Note that should you choose to have treatment outside the hospitals covered by your insurance policy (which may be severely limited), you may have to pay the whole cost of treatment yourself!

Standard policies may offer three scales (usually designated A, B and C) of hospital treatment which may include London NHS teaching hospitals (A, high scale), provincial NHS teaching hospitals (B, medium scale) and provincial non-teaching hospitals (C, low scale). Accommodation is usually in a private room, but in some hospitals it may be in a twin or four-bedded ward. Premiums range from a few pounds a week for a budget plan offering limited benefits (e.g. HSA) up to £hundreds a month for a comprehensive policy with a major insurance company. Comprehensive top-of-the-range cover costs from £40 a month for a single person and from around £100 for a family (some companies offer lower premiums but have a compulsory annual excess of £500 or £1,000).

Health Insurance for Visitors

Visitors spending short periods in Britain (e.g. up to a month) should have a travel health insurance policy (see page 66), particularly if they aren't covered by an international health policy. If you plan to spend up to six months in Britain you should either take out a travel policy, a special long stay policy or an international health policy. Premiums vary considerably and it's important to shop around. Most international health policies include repatriation or evacuation (although it may be optional), which may also include shipment (by air) of the body of a person who dies abroad to his home country for burial. An international policy also allows you to choose to have non-urgent medical treatment in the country of your choice.

Most international insurance companies offer health policies for different areas, e.g. Europe, world-wide excluding North America, and world-wide including North America. Most companies offer different levels of cover, for example basic, standard, comprehensive and prestige. There's always a limit on the total annual medical costs, which should be at least £250,000 (although many companies provide cover of up to £1 million) and some companies also limit the charges for specific treatment or care such as specialists' fees, operations and hospital accommodation. A medical examination isn't usually required for international health policies, although pre-existing health problems are excluded for a period, e.g. two years.

Claims are usually settled in all major currencies and large claims are usually settled directly by insurance companies (although your choice of hospitals may be limited). Always check whether an insurance company will settle large medical bills directly, as if you're required to pay bills and claim reimbursement from an insurance company, it can take several months before you receive your money (some companies are slow to pay). It isn't usually necessary to translate bills into English or another language, although you should check a company's policy. Most international health insurance companies provide emergency telephone assistance.

The cost of international health insurance varies considerably depending on your age and the extent of cover. Note that with most international insurance policies, you must enrol before you reach a certain age, e.g. between 60 and 80, to be guaranteed continuous cover in your old age. Premiums can sometimes be paid monthly, quarterly or annually, although some companies insist on payment annually in advance. When comparing policies, carefully check the extent of cover and exactly what's included and excluded from a policy (often indicated only in the *very* small print), in addition to premiums and excess charges. In some countries, premium increases are limited by law, although this may apply only to residents in the country where a company is registered, and not to overseas policyholders. Although there may be significant differences in premiums, generally you get what you pay for and can tailor premiums to your requirements. The most important questions to ask yourself are does the policy provide the cover required and is it good value for money? If you're in good health and are able to pay for your own out-patient treatment, such as visits to your family doctor and prescriptions, then the best value is usually a policy covering specialist and hospital treatment only.

Buildings Insurance

For most people, buying a home is the biggest financial investment they will ever make. When buying a home, you're usually responsible for insuring it before you even move in. If you take out a mortgage to buy a property, your lender will usually insist that your home (including most permanent structures on your property) has buildings insurance from the time you exchange contracts and are legally the owner. If you buy the leasehold of an apartment, your buildings insurance will be arranged by the owner of the freehold. Even when it isn't required by a lender, you would be extremely unwise not to have buildings insurance.

Buildings insurance usually includes loss or damage caused by fire; theft; riot or malicious acts; water leakage from pipes or tanks; oil leakage from central heating systems; flood, storm and lightning; explosion or aircraft impact; vehicles or animals; earthquake, subsidence, landslip or heave; falling trees or aerials; and cover for temporary homelessness, e.g. up to £5,000. It usually includes all permanent fixtures and fittings such as baths, toilets, fitted kitchens, bedroom cupboards and interior decoration, i.e. anything that cannot reasonably be removed and taken with you when moving house. Some insurance companies also provide optional cover to include trees and shrubs damaged maliciously or by storms. Note that there may be an excess, e.g. from £25 or £50, for some claims, which is intended to deter people from making small claims. Buildings insurance should be renewed annually and insurance companies are continually updating their policies, so you must take care that a policy still provides the cover required when you receive a renewal notice.

Lenders fix the initial level of cover when you first apply for a mortgage and often offer to arrange the insurance for you, but you're usually free to make your own arrangements. Some lenders require you to buy the expensive building and contents insurance (typically 30 per cent above identical cover available elsewhere but can be double or triple the price) from them and may refuse to give you a quotation until a valuation (which you pay for) has been done. These should be avoided. Note that if you change your buildings insurance from your lender to another insurer, you may be charged a transfer fee (e.g. £25) and an 'administration' fee to encourage you *not* to change. If you arrange your own buildings insurance, your lender will insist that the level of cover is sufficient. Most people take the easy option and arrange insurance through their mortgage lender, which is generally the most expensive option, e.g. many insurance companies guarantee to cut buildings insurance costs for the majority of homeowners insured through banks and building societies.

The amount for which your home must be insured isn't the current market value, but the cost of rebuilding it should it be totally destroyed. This varies depending on the type of property and the area, for example an inexpensive terraced house in the north of England could cost twice its market value to rebuild whereas a more expensive detached property in the south of England, may cost a lot less than its market value to rebuild, due to the high value of the land. There's generally no deduction for wear and tear and the cost of redecoration is usually met in full. Note that buildings insurance doesn't cover structural faults that existed when you took out the policy, which is why it's important to have a full structural survey done when buying a property.

Many people pay far too much for their buildings insurance because many insurance companies have greatly over-estimated the cost of rebuilding (in contrast, many better-off homeowners don't have sufficient insurance). In many cases building costs were calculated using the Royal Institute of Chartered Surveyors (RICS) Rebuilding Costs Index rather than the correct Tender Price Index, which takes into account actual building prices. If you're in doubt, check how the rebuilding cost of your home was calculated and whether it's correct. Shop around a number of companies and agents and compare rates (you can do this on the Internet via www.find.co.uk/insurance/, www.intersure.co.uk, www.screentrade.com and www. swinton.co.uk).

Most lenders provide index-linked buildings insurance, where premiums are linked to inflation and building costs (premiums are usually added to your monthly mortgage payments). It is, however, your responsibility to ensure that your level of cover is adequate, particularly if you carry out improvements or extensions which substantially increase the value of your home. All lenders provide information and free advice. If your level of cover is too low, an insurance company is within its rights to reduce the amount it pays out when a claim is made, in which case you may find you cannot afford to have your house rebuilt or repaired should disaster strike.

The cost of buildings insurance varies depending on the insurer, the type of building and the area, and is calculated per £1,000 of insurance, e.g. from £1 per £1,000 of cover per year in an inexpensive area to between £2 to £4 (or over £4 in London) in more expensive areas. Therefore insurance on a property costing

£100,000 to rebuild usually costs from £100 to £400 a year. In recent years increased competition, particularly from direct insurers, has reduced premiums. Shop around as many people can reduce their premium by half (but don't believe the advertising blurb, as some companies that claim to save you money actually charge more). Insurance for 'non-standard' homes such as those with thatched roofs, timber construction, holiday homes, old period properties and listed buildings is usually much higher. The highest level of cover usually includes damage to glass (e.g. windows and patio doors) and porcelain (e.g. baths, washbasins and WCs), although you may have to pay extra for accidental damage, e.g. when your son blasts a cricket ball through the patio window. Always ask your insurer what *isn't* covered and what it will cost to include it (if required).

Premiums can usually be paid monthly (although there may be an extra charge) or annually. Some home insurance policies charge an excess (e.g. £50) for each claim, while others have an excess for certain claims only, e.g. subsidence or landslip (when your house disappears into a hole in the ground or over a cliff), which is usually £1,000 or £2,000. Owners of houses vulnerable to subsidence (e.g. those built on clay) and those living in flood-prone areas are likely to pay much higher premiums. However, it's estimated that over a million people pay too much for their insurance cover because their insurers have wrongly assumed that they are at risk from subsidence (even when your home isn't at risk from subsidence, it's difficult to find a policy that excludes it).

Many insurance companies provide emergency telephone numbers for policyholders requiring urgent advice. Should you need to make emergency repairs, e.g. to weather-proof a roof after a storm or other natural disaster, most insurance companies allow work up to a certain limit (e.g. £1,000) to be carried out without an estimate or approval from the insurance company, but check first. If you let your house (or part of it) or you intend leaving it unoccupied for a period of 30 days or longer, you must usually inform your insurance company. A booklet entitled *Buildings Insurance for Home Owners*, including a valuation table, is available from the Association of British Insurers (56 Gresham Street, London EC2V 7HQ, ☎ 0207-600 3333). British insurance companies are covered by the Policyholders' Protection Act (PPA), which guarantees that in the unlikely event of an insurance company going bust, 90 per cent of the value of any outstanding claims will be met.

Buildings insurance is often combined with home contents insurance (see below), when it may be termed household insurance, although it may be cheaper to buy buildings and home contents insurance separately.

Home Contents Insurance

Home contents insurance is advisable for anyone who doesn't live in an empty house. Burglary and house-breaking is a major problem in Britain (particularly in cities) and there's a burglary every minute somewhere. Although there's a lot you can do to prevent someone breaking into your home, it's often impossible or prohibitively expensive to make your home completely burglar-proof without turning it into a fortress. However, you can ensure you have adequate contents insurance and that your most precious possessions are locked in a safe or safety deposit box. Around one in four homes in Britain have no home contents insurance.

Types of Policy: A basic home contents policy covers your belongings against the same sort of 'natural disasters' as buildings insurance (see page 60). You can optionally insure against accidental damage and all risks. A basic contents policy doesn't usually include such items as credit cards (and their fraudulent use), cash, musical instruments, jewellery (and other valuables), antiques, paintings, sports equipment and bicycles, for which you normally need to take out extra cover. You can usually insure your property for its second-hand value (indemnity) or its full replacement value (new for old), which covers everything except clothes and linen (for which wear and tear is assessed) at the new cost price. Replacement value is the most popular form of contents insurance in Britain. In the case of replacement value, it's best to take out an index-linked policy, where the level of cover is automatically increased by a percentage or fixed amount each year.

A basic policy doesn't usually include accidental damage caused by you or members of your family to your own property (e.g. 'accidentally' putting your foot through the TV during a political party broadcast) or your home freezer contents (in the event of a breakdown or power failure). A basic policy may include replacement locks, garden contents, personal liability insurance (see below), loss of oil and metered water, and temporary accommodation. If they aren't included, these can usually be covered optionally. Some policies include legal expenses cover (e.g. up to £50,000) for disputes with neighbours, shops, suppliers, employers and anyone who provides you with a service (e.g. a plumber or builder). Most contents policies include public liability cover of up to £1 million. Items such as computers and mobile phones may need to be listed as named items on your policy, and computers and other equipment used for business aren't usually covered (or may be covered only for a prohibitive extra premium). If you have friends or lodgers in your home, their personal property won't usually be covered by your policy.

Premiums: Premiums are dependent largely on where you live and your insurer. All insurance companies assess the risk by location based on your postcode. **Check before buying a home as the difference between low and high-risk areas can be as much as 500 per cent!** The difference between premiums charged by companies for the same property can also vary by as much as 200 per cent. Annual premiums are usually calculated per £1,000 of cover and range from around £2 to £3 in a low-risk area to between £10 and £15 in a high-risk area. Although many homeowners in high-risk areas would be willing to forego theft insurance, insurance companies are unwilling to offer this, because premiums would be substantially reduced if theft was omitted (theft is a convenient excuse to load premiums). Your premiums will also be higher if you live in a flood-prone area.

As with buildings insurance it's important to shop around for the lowest premiums, which vary considerably depending on the insurer (premiums have fallen in recent years due to intense competition). If you're already insured, you may find that you can save money by changing insurers, particularly if you're insured through a bank or building society, which are usually the most expensive. However, watch out for penalties when switching insurers.

Combining your home contents insurance with your buildings insurance (see page 60) can save you money (most insurers offer a 5 to 10 per cent discount), although it may be cheaper to buy each separately. However, it can be advantageous to have your buildings and contents insurance with the same insurer, as this avoids disputes over which company should pay for which item, as could arise if you have a fire or flood affecting both your home and its contents. Those aged over 50 or 55 (and possibly first-time homeowners) are offered discounts or special rates by some companies (e.g. Saga, who specialise in insurance for people over 50). Some companies also provide special policies for students in college accommodation or lodgings (ask an insurance broker).

Security: Most insurers offer no-claims discounts or discounts for homes with burglar alarms, high security locks, neighbourhood watch schemes and smoke detectors. In high-risk areas, good security is a condition of insurance. Beware of the small print in policies, particularly those regarding security, which insurers often use to avoid paying claims. You will forfeit all rights under your policy if you leave doors or windows open (or the keys under a mat or flowerpot!), particularly if you have claimed a discount due to your 'Fort Knox' security. If there are no signs of forced entry, e.g. a broken window, you may be unable to claim for a theft. You should inform your insurer of any changes that may affect your policy, e.g. a storm blows away a wall of your house (a common occurrence in recent years). If you're going to leave your house empty for a long period, e.g. a month or longer, you should inform your insurer. In future, insurers plan to give houses a burglary rating and set the premium accordingly.

Sum-insured or bedroom-rated? There are two ways to insure you possessions: 'sum-insured' (where you calculate the cover you need and the insurer works out the premium based on the cover required) and 'bedroom-rated' policies (where you pay a set premium based on the number of bedrooms). Take care that you don't under-insure your house contents (including anything rented such as a TV or video recorder) and that you periodically reassess their value and adjust your premium accordingly (half of all homeowners are thought to underestimate the value of their home contents). Your contents should include everything that isn't part of the fixtures and fittings and which you could take with you if you were moving house. If you under-insure your contents, your claim may be reduced by the percentage by which you're under-insured. It's common for those with valuable belongings to inadvertently under-insure them (don't forget antiques, designer clothes, jewellery, art, collections, etc.).

With a bedroom-rated policy the insurance company cannot scale down a claim because of under-insurance, however, you're usually better off calculating the value of the contents to be insured. Some companies have economy (e.g. for struggling authors), standard and deluxe rates for contents valued, for example, from £10,000 to £40,000. You can take out a special policy if you have high-value contents, which may be cheaper than a standard contents policy. However, this usually requires a valuation costing around £300 and therefore isn't worthwhile unless your home contents are worth over £50,000. **Always list all previous burglaries on the proposal form, even if nothing was stolen.**

World-wide Cover: An 'all risks' (also termed a world-wide or extra cover policy) is offered by most insurance companies as an extension to a home contents policy. With this type of policy your personal possessions (such as jewellery, watches and cameras) are covered against accidental loss or damage outside your home, anywhere in the world. Usually each item valued above a minimum sum, e.g. £250 to £1,000, must be declared in writing (it's wise to take photographs of your valuables and to keep a record of the make and serial numbers of valuable items). The cost is between £10 and £30 a year for each £1,000 covered, depending on where you live.

Claims: Some insurers provide a 24-hour emergency helpline for policyholders and emergency assistance for repairs for domestic emergencies, such as a blocked drain or electrical failure, up to a maximum limit (e.g. £200) for each claim. Take care when completing a claims form as insurers have tightened up on claims and few people receive a full settlement. Many insurers have an excess of from £25 to £75 on claims. Bear in mind that if you make a claim, you must usually wait months for it to be settled. Generally the larger the claim, the longer you need to wait for your money, although in an emergency most companies will make an interim payment. If you aren't satisfied with the amount offered, don't accept it and try to negotiate a higher figure. If you still cannot reach agreement on the amount, you can contact the insurance ombudsman for independent arbitration.

Holiday Homes: Premiums are generally higher for holiday homes due to their high vulnerability (particularly to burglaries) and are usually based on the number of days a year a property is inhabited and the interval between periods of occupancy. Cover for theft, storm, flood and malicious damage may be suspended when a property is left empty for more than three weeks at a time. It's possible to negotiate cover for periods of absence for a hefty surcharge, although valuable items are usually excluded. If you're absent from your property for long periods, e.g. more than 60 days a year, you may also be required to pay an excess on a claim arising from an occurrence that takes place during your absence (and theft may be excluded). You should read all small print in policies. **Note that, where applicable, it's important to ensure that a policy specifies a holiday home and not a principal home.**

In areas with a high risk of theft (e.g. most major cities and holiday areas), you may be required to fit extra locks and other security measures. Some companies may not insure holiday homes in high-risk areas. It's unwise to leave valuable or irreplaceable items in a holiday home or a home that will be vacant for long periods. Note that some insurance companies will do their utmost to find a loophole, which makes you negligent and relieves them of their liability. Always carefully check that the details listed in a policy are correct, otherwise your policy could be void.

Mortgage Protection Insurance

It's possible to take out mortgage protection insurance (MPI – also called mortgage payment protection insurance/MPPI and mortgage repayments insurance/MRI) to pay your mortgage in the event that you fall ill, have an accident or are made redundant. If you're unable to pay your mortgage, government help is limited to the mortgage interest on mortgages of £100,000 or under (or the first £100,000 of a higher mortgage) and nothing at all is paid for the first nine months. The benefit is also means-tested and it's estimated that 80 per cent of borrowers wouldn't qualify. Currently around 30 per cent of borrowers have MPI, although the government has indicated that it could be made compulsory if voluntary take-up doesn't increase. Policies usually exclude the self-employed and contract workers, and you must usually have been in continuous employment for three to six months before purchasing being accepted. You unable to make a claim until a policy has been running for at least three months.

The cost is usually between £5 and £7 per month for each £100 per month of cover required, e.g. if you want to receive a payment of £500 a month your premium will be from £25 to £35 a month (generally the more you pay, the more extensive the cover). Some lenders provide free mortgage protection insurance. All policies have a 30 to 90-day waiting period before paying out and most policies meet your mortgage payments for a maximum of 12 months only. As it stands, MPI is of limited value to most homeowners as policies contain numerous flaws and many claims are rejected due to hidden clauses. Policies are frequently mis-sold and insurers regularly bend the rules to avoid paying claims. Not surprisingly, some experts advise that many mortgage protection policies aren't worth the paper they're printed on (payments involving redundancy are fraught with problems). You should have a policy checked by your legal adviser for hidden loopholes and make sure it covers what it says it does or what you want it to cover.

Holiday & Travel Insurance

Holiday and travel insurance is recommended for all who don't wish to risk having their holiday or travel spoilt by financial problems or to arrive home broke. As you know, anything can and often does go wrong with a holiday, sometimes before you even get on the aeroplane (particularly if you *don't* have insurance). Travel insurance is available from many sources including travel agents, insurance brokers, tour operators, banks, building societies, post offices, motoring organisations and railway companies. Around 85 per cent of Britons take out holiday or travel insurance.

Level of Cover: Before taking out travel insurance, carefully consider the level of cover required and compare policies. Most policies include loss of deposit or holiday cancellation (usually limited from £2,500 to £5,000); missed flight; departure delay at both the start *and* end of a holiday (a common occurrence); delayed baggage; personal effects; lost baggage (e.g. £1,500); medical expenses (up to £2 million) and accidents (including evacuation home if necessary); personal money (e.g. £250 to £500); personal liability (£1 or £2 million); legal expenses; and a tour operator going bust.

You should also insure against missing your flight due to an accident or transport breakdown, as almost 50 per cent of travel insurance claims are for cancellation (you should also be covered for transport delays at the end of your holiday, e.g. the flight home). With some policies, the amount you can claim for personal belongings may be limited to around £200 per item, which will be insufficient to cover your Rolex watch or SLR auto-focus camera. If you have a world-wide home contents policy (see page 62), you will automatically be covered for the full cost of all listed items anywhere. However, note that your insurance company won't pay out if you're negligent, e.g. you leave your camera in a taxi or on a beach.

Medical Expenses: Medical expenses are an important aspect of travel insurance and it isn't advisable to rely on reciprocal health arrangements (such as provided by form E111 in European Union countries). When you pay for your travel costs with some credit cards, your family (e.g. including children under the age of 25), are provided with free travel accident insurance up to a specified amount, e.g. £150,000. **Don't rely on this insurance, as it usually covers death or serious injury only.** In fact you shouldn't rely on travel insurance provided by charge and credit card companies, house contents policies or private medical insurance, none of which provide the necessary cover. The minimum medical insurance recommended by experts is £250,000 for Europe and £1 million for North America and the rest of the world. Personal liability should be at least £1 million for Europe and £2 million for the rest of the world. **Note that most travel and holiday insurance policies, don't provide the minimum level of cover that most people need.** Always check any exclusion clauses in contracts by obtaining a copy of the full policy document, as all relevant information *isn't* included in insurance leaflets.

Exclusions: Health or accident insurance included in travel insurance policies usually contains exclusions, e.g. dangerous sports (mountaineering, hang-gliding and scuba-diving) or even riding a motorbike. Check the small print and find out exactly what terms such as 'hazardous pursuits' include or exclude. Skiing and other winter sports should be specifically covered and *listed* in a travel insurance policy. Special winter sports policies are available, which are usually more expensive than normal holiday insurance (higher cover is required for North America than for Europe). Skiing or winter holiday insurance costs from around £25 to £80 a week, for basically the same package of £1 million medical expenses, £1 million personal liability, £300 to £400 for skis and £1,000 personal effects.

Cost: The cost of travel insurance varies considerably, depending on your destination. Many companies have different rates for different areas, e.g. Britain, Europe, North America and world-wide (excluding North America). Premiums for British travel are around £7.50 per person for two weeks, European destinations are usually £15 to 20 for two weeks, and North America (where medical treatment costs an arm and a leg) and a few other destinations costs £35 to £50 for three weeks. The cheapest policies offer reduced cover and may be inadequate for most people. Premiums may also be increased for those aged over 65 or 70. Generally the longer the period covered, the cheaper the daily cost, although the maximum period is usually limited, e.g. six months. With some policies an excess (e.g. £25) is levied for each claim made. Compulsory (expensive) travel insurance, which was previously included in holiday package deals, is now illegal (although many travel agents may still try to pressure you into buying expensive travel insurance).

Annual Policies: For people who travel abroad frequently, whether for business or pleasure, an annual travel policy is often excellent value, costing from around £100 to £250 a year for world-wide cover for an unlimited number of trips. However, carefully check exactly what it includes (some exclude winter sports) and read the small print (some insist that travel is by air). Most annual policies don't cover you for travel in Britain and there's a maximum limit on the length of a trip of from one to six months. Some companies offer 'tailor-made' insurance for independent travellers for any period from a few days to one year.

Claims: Although travel insurance companies will gladly take your money, they aren't so keen to pay claims and you may have to persevere before they pay up. Fraudulent claims against travel insurance are common, so unless you can produce evidence to support your claim the insurers may think you're trying to cheat them. Always be persistent and make a claim irrespective of any small print, as this is often unreasonable and therefore invalid in law. **All insurance companies require you to report any loss (or any incident for which you intend to make a claim) to the local police or carriers within 24 hours and to obtain a report. Failure to do this will mean that a claim usually won't be considered.**

SHOPPING

The choice, quality and variety of goods on sale in British shops is excellent, particularly in London, which is one of the great shopping cities of the world. Not only is Britain in the words of Napoleon, 'a nation of shopkeepers', but it's a country of compulsive shoppers, which is the number one 'leisure' activity (after watching TV). In Britain you often hear references made to the 'High Street' (e.g. high street stores and high street banks), which isn't usually a reference to the name of a street (although many towns *do* have a High Street), but a collective term for any business commonly found in most towns. Shops in most towns and cities vary from huge department stores, selling just about everything (e.g. Harrods and Selfridges in London), to small high-class specialist shops in Georgian or Victorian-style arcades. The traditional high street has a number of small shops which usually include a butcher, baker, greengrocer, grocer or general store, newsagents, chemist (pharmacy), bank, post office and the inevitable pub (or two).

In larger towns, shops may include a fishmonger (fresh fish shop), ironmonger (hardware, household wares), launderette (laundromat), off-licence (alcoholic beverages), turf accountant (betting shop), fried fish and chip shop, dry cleaners, hairdresser, bookshop, health food shop, ladies' and men's fashions, shoe shops, take-away restaurants, banks and building societies. Many larger towns also have one or more supermarkets and department stores, and most country towns have a market on at least one day a week. In most towns (outside the main shopping centre) there are 'corner shops', which are general stores or mini-supermarkets selling a wide range of food and household products. Prices in small village and town shops are necessarily higher than in supermarkets, although many have a reasonably priced Happy Shopper, Spar or VG store.

Shopping Hours: Shopping hours in Britain are usually from around 0900 or 0930 to 1730 or 1800, Mondays to Saturdays. New Sunday shopping laws were introduced in 1995 in England and Wales allowing large stores to open for six hours on Sundays, although smaller shops aren't affected. However, Sunday shopping has become very popular in the last few years and many shops open in large towns and are very busy. Most large stores and supermarkets also open on public holidays. In smaller towns, shops and businesses may close for lunch (usually 1200 to 1300 or 1300 to 1400). Most towns have late night shopping until around 2000 or 2100 one evening a week, e.g. Wednesdays, Thursdays or Fridays. Shops also stay open later during the weeks before Christmas. The majority of people shop on Saturdays and Sundays, which are best avoided if you can shop during the week.

Small privately owned grocery stores and supermarkets in cities, towns and sometimes even villages, are often open until between 2000 and 2200 and also at weekends, which is usually the only way they can make a living and compete with supermarkets. There are even 24-hour convenience stores in some towns. Many supermarkets and superstores open from 0800 until 2000 from Mondays to Saturdays and 1000 to 1600 (or 1100 to 1700) on Sundays. All shops are closed on Christmas Day (25th December) and many on New Year's Day (1st January); however, an increasing number of stores open on Boxing Day (26th December), when many start their 'new year' sales.

Food & Supermarkets: The quality and variety of food in British supermarkets (which sell over 75 per cent of Britain's food) has increased in leaps and bounds in the last few decades, and is now among the best in the world. They excel in many areas including freshness, efficiency of supply, hygiene, quality standards, safety, convenience, variety (from around the world) and the ambience of the shopping environment, which is designed to maximise the temptation and impulse to buy and relieve you of your hard-earned cash. The major supermarkets have also branched out into other fields such as banking and financial services in recent years.

However, there's a high price to pay for these services. British supermarkets are among the most expensive in the world and British shoppers pay up to 40 per cent more for their food than those in many other western European countries and North America (of the major countries only Scandinavia, Switzerland and Japan have higher food prices). The EU Common Agricultural Policy (CAP) also helps push up the cost of food in EU countries. British supermarkets have huge mark-ups on many foods (up to 60 per cent) and have been accused of profiteering in recent years, which has resulted in an investigation by the Office of Fair Trading. Savings (e.g. by bulk buying or when commodity prices fall) are rarely, if ever, passed onto the consumer. For example meat prices bear no relation to the price paid to producers; in 1998 supermarkets were charging around £1 for a single lamb chop while farmers received 'a few pence' for a whole lamb! Not surprisingly, British supermarkets are the most profitable in the world.

The major supermarket chains in Britain (not all are national) include Asda, Co-op, Iceland, Kwik Save, Morrisons, Safeway, Sainsbury's, Somerfield, Tesco and Waitrose. Some department and chain stores are also famous for their food halls, including Harrods, Selfridges and Fortnum and Mason in London, and Marks and Spencer (the clothing and home furnishings chain store). Marks and Spencer offer a smaller range of foods than a supermarket but are renowned for their high quality (and high prices), particularly their excellent range of convenience (prepared) meals in which they were pioneers (supermarkets were quick to copy them).

Many foreign foods can be found in local supermarkets if you look hard enough, but don't overlook the many delicious local foods on offer. Supermarkets are usually good for fresh fruit and vegetables, due to the high turnover of stock (although fresh produce isn't always fresh and may have been stored for up to a year in special 'bunkers' to prevent it rotting). Many supermarkets bake their own bread on the premises and most have fresh fish, meat and dairy counters. Although most supermarkets offer a wide range of frozen products, most large towns also have a freezer shop (e.g. Iceland), which generally offers a wider choice and lower prices when you buy in bulk. There are many foreign food shops, delicatessens and gourmet shops in Britain's major cities. Food markets, which may include farmers' markets where farmers sell their produce direct to the public, are common in most towns and are after the cheapest place to buy fresh produce, meat and other foodstuffs.

There's generally no bargaining or bartering in Britain, although if you intend to spend a lot of money or buy something expensive (e.g. hi-fi, TV, computer or furniture) you should shop around and shouldn't be shy about asking for a discount (except in most department stores, chain stores and supermarkets, where prices are usually fixed). The poor trading climate in recent years has forced many shops to haggle over prices and it's possible to pick up some excellent bargains, particularly when paying cash. Many shops will also meet any genuine advertised price.

VAT (see page 108) at 17.5 per cent is usually included in the price of most goods with the exception of food, books and children's clothes, and the advertised price is usually the price you pay (there are no hidden extras). Some items such as computers and electronic goods may be advertised exclusive of VAT, as these items are often purchased by businesses, which can reclaim VAT. Always shop around before buying, and when comparing prices remember to add VAT if it isn't included. Note that the chain store Dixons has a stranglehold on the home electronics trade (they also own Curry's and PC World) and charge high prices (the company has even been criticised by manufacturers for overcharging). It's cheaper to buy a computer from a direct-marketing company such as Compaq, Dell or Gateway. PCs cost up to a third more in Britain than in the USA and even many European buyers can buy computers for up to 40 per cent less than in Britain. When comparing prices make sure that you're comparing similar goods or services, as it's easy to 'save' money by purchasing inferior products. Most shops accept major credit cards, although in some stores they accept debit cards or their own account cards only.

Most shops hold sales at various times of the year, the largest of which are held in January and July, when bargains abound, particularly in the main cities (many newspapers publish sales' guides). Sales are also held in spring and autumn (most shops will hold a sale at the drop of a hat). Some stores seem to have a permanent sale, although retailers aren't permitted to advertise goods as reduced when they have never been advertised or sold at the stated price. Goods may, however, have been advertised at a higher price for a short time simply to get around the law. Beware of bogus bargains.

In addition to sales, you can also shop at hundreds of factory shops around Britain, where prices are much lower than at retailers, particularly if products are flawed in some way (called 'seconds'). Ask your friends and neighbours if there are any factory shops in your area and look out for them on your travels. Factory malls (another American import) have sprung up in recent years, many specialising in fashion 'seconds' and end-of-line goods from top names such as Aquascutum, Jaeger and Ralph Lauren. Prices are typically at least 30 per cent below normal retail prices. For information see *The Official Great British Factory Shop Guide* by Gillian Cutress and Rolf Stricker.

Most retailers offer club or loyalty cards offering a discount (typically 10 per cent) to cardholders. Some retailers participate in an 'air miles' scheme, while others have clubs or belong to a discount card scheme offering member's discounts. Coupons in national and local newspapers and leaflets also provide discounts. In many towns there are shops run by charitable organisations, e.g. Oxfam, Helping Hand, Imperial Cancer Research and Sue Ryder, selling both new and second-hand items (a great place to find bargains).

Shopping guides are available in many areas from tourist information centres. Comprehensive guides for those who live in the London area include the *Time Out Guide to Shopping & Services in London*, listing over 2,000 shops, and *The Serious Shoppers Guide to London* by Beth Reiber (Prentice Hall Press). Stable Publishing (☎ 01476-870870) publish a series of Alternative Shopping Guides for various regions. The *Which? Buying Guide* contains a rundown on the best buys featured in the monthly *Which?* magazine (see **Appendix A**) and is highly recommended. Many stores, particularly department and chain stores, provide free catalogues at Christmas and other times of the year. If you're looking for a particular item or anything unusual, you will find that the Yellow Pages will save you a lot of time and trouble (and shoe leather).

If you have any questions about your rights as a consumer, contact your local trading standards or consumer protection department, consumer advice centre or Citizens Advice Bureau. Most retailers, particularly department and chain stores, will exchange goods or give a refund without question (although the British rarely complain or return goods), but smaller stores aren't so enthusiastic. Another invaluable book is *Fair Deal* (Stationery Office), which is a guide to shoppers' rights and family budgeting published by the Office of Fair Trading.

Britain officially converted to metrication on 1st October 1995 and all retailers must now price goods in kilogrammes, litres and metres, despite the fact that many Britons haven't got a clue whether a pound (454 grammes) weighs more or less than a kilogramme (1,000 grammes). However, British measures such as pounds, pints and feet can be used alongside metrication and many stores display conversion tables.

For those who aren't used to buying goods with British measures and sizes, a list of comparative weights and measures are included in **Appendix C**.

Before buying any major goods or services it's wise to consult *Which?* magazine published by the Consumers' Association (Castlemead, Gascoyne Way, Hertford SG14 1LH, ☎ 01992-822800, Internet: www.which.net). All goods and services are tested independently by the Consumers' Association including financial services (e.g. insurance, banking, pensions and investment); cars; leisure; food and health; household and domestic appliances; and items of public interest. Dangerous products are highlighted, best buys are recommended and, most importantly, you're told how to obtain your legal rights when things go wrong. A subscription to *Which?* magazine costs around £60 a year, although it's available in the reference section of public libraries.

Furniture & Furnishings

Furniture is usually good value for money in Britain and top quality furniture is often cheaper than in many other European countries. There's a huge choice of both traditional and contemporary designs in every price range, although as with most things, you generally get what you pay for. Exclusive modern designs from Italy, Denmark and many other countries are available (usually with matching exclusive prices), although imports also include reasonably priced quality leather suites and a wide range of cane furniture from the Far East. Among the largest furniture chain stores in Britain are Courts, Perrings, Heal's and Trends, all of which offer a wide range of top quality British furniture from manufacturers such as Ercol, G-Plan, Parker Knoll and Topley.

Oak is the most common wood used for traditional British quality furniture and pine is also popular, which can be bought stained or unstained. Note that when ordering furniture, you may need to wait weeks or months for delivery, so you should try to find a store which has what you want in stock or which will give you a guaranteed delivery date (after which you can cancel and receive a full refund). A number of manufacturers sell direct to the public, although you shouldn't assume that this will result in huge savings, and should compare prices and quality before buying. There are also stores specialising in beds, leather, reproduction and antique furniture, and many companies manufacture and install fitted bedrooms and kitchens. Note that fitted kitchens are an extremely competitive business in Britain and you should be wary of cowboy companies who are specialists in shoddy workmanship.

If you want reasonably priced, good quality, modern furniture, there are a number of companies selling furniture for home assembly (which helps keep down prices), e.g. MFI, Habitat and Ikea (Sweden), the latter being the world's only global furniture chain (note, however, that the price of Ikea furniture varies depending on the country and most items are much cheaper in, for example, France, than in Britain). Assembly instructions are generally easy to follow (although some people think Rubik's cube is easier) and some companies print instructions in a number of languages (Double Dutch is the favourite).

All large furniture retailers publish catalogues that may be distributed with free local newspapers. Some stores offer you £50 or £100 for your old lounge suite when you buy a new one from them, although a suite in reasonable condition is likely to be worth much more and you should sell it privately. Always shop around for the best price and quality available and don't be taken in by bogus offers. Furniture and home furnishings are very competitive businesses in Britain and you can often reduce the price by some judicious haggling, particularly if you're spending a large amount. Another way to save money is to wait for the sales, when many items are sold at reductions of up to 50 per cent. If you cannot wait and don't want to (or cannot afford) to pay cash, look for an interest-free credit deal.

Check the advertisements in local newspapers and national home and design magazines such as *House & Garden*, *Country Homes & Interiors* and *Ideal Home* (see **Appendix A** for a list). Advertisements in free colour and 'home' or 'style' magazines provided with the Saturday and Sunday editions of national newspapers such as *The Times/Sunday Times*, *The Telegraph/Sunday Telegraph* and the (Sunday) *Observer*. Many advertisers sell direct to the public and pass the savings on to the buyer, although you should *always* compare prices with local stores. You may also be able to find a few bargains on the Internet (see page 74).

The kind of furniture you buy for your British home will depend on a number of factors including the style and size of your home, whether it's a permanent or holiday home, your budget, and not least, your personal taste. If you intend to furnish a holiday home with antiques or expensive modern furniture, bear in mind that you will need adequate security and insurance. If you own a holiday home in Britain, it may be worthwhile shipping surplus items of furniture you have in your home abroad (unless you live in Australia!). If you intend to move permanently to Britain in a number of years and already have a house full of good furniture abroad, there's little point in buying expensive furniture in Britain.

There are numerous do-it-yourself 'warehouses' in Britain selling everything for the home including DIY supplies, furniture, bathrooms, kitchens, decorating and lighting, plus services such as tool rental and wood cutting. There are also salvage and second-hand companies selling old doors, window frames, fireplaces, tiles and other materials that are invaluable when restoring an old home or wishing to add a 'lived-in' feel to a modern home. Furniture can also be rented from a number of companies if you rent an unfurnished home for a limited period and don't want to buy furniture. There's a good market for second-hand furniture (including antiques) in Britain – check the ads. in local newspapers and specialist newspapers such as *Dalton's Weekly*, *Exchange & Mart* and *Loot* (see **Appendix A**).

Household Goods

Household goods in Britain are generally of good quality with a large choice. Prices compare favourably with most other European countries and bargains can be found at supermarkets and hypermarkets. Large household appliances such as cookers and refrigerators are usually provided in rented accommodation and may also be fitted in new homes. Many owners include fitted kitchen appliances such as a cooker, refrigerator, dishwasher and washing machine when selling a house or apartment, or may offer to sell them separately. If you wish to bring large appliances with you, such as a refrigerator, washing machine or dishwasher, note that the standard British unit width isn't the same as in other countries. Check the size and the latest British safety regulations before shipping these items to Britain or buying them abroad, as they may need expensive modifications. There's a wide range of household appliances in Britain, from both British and foreign manufacturers, and some stores (e.g. Harrods in London) also sell American refrigerators, in which you can store a year's supply of dairy products for a family of 14 (and a few pets). Note that some appliances such as refrigerators cost twice as much to run as others.

If you already own small household appliances, it's worthwhile bringing them to Britain as usually all that's required is a change of plug, but check first. If you're coming from a country with a 110/115V electricity supply (e.g. the USA) then you will need a lot of expensive transformers (see page 195). Don't bring a television to Britain from the continent or the USA as it won't work (see page 77). Smaller appliances such as vacuum cleaners, grills, toasters and electric irons aren't expensive in Britain and are usually of excellent quality. If you want to buy a ceramic or halogen hob, bear in mind that it may be necessary to replace all your saucepans. Before buying household appliances, whether large or small, check the test reports and surveys in *Which?* magazine (see **Appendix A**) at your local library.

Stores such as Comet, Power Warehouse and warehouse clubs such as Costco and Cargo offer among the best prices for household goods. You can buy household goods at low prices from Value Direct (☎ 01295-755015, Internet: www.value-direct.co.uk/wol), who claim to offer the lowest prices in Britain and back their claim with a guarantee, and Home Electrical Direct (www.hed.co.uk). A one-year guarantee is normally provided, which can usually be extended by a further two or four years. However, although extended warranties may provide additional peace of mind, they are usually a waste of money and should be avoided. If you need kitchen measuring equipment and cannot cope with decimal measures, you will need to bring your own measuring scales, jugs, cups (US and British recipe cups aren't the same size) and thermometers (see also **Appendix C**). Note also that British pillows and duvets aren't the same size or shape as in many other countries.

Shopping Abroad

Shopping abroad for most British people consists of a day trip to Calais or Boulogne, and a visit to a French hypermarket (similar to a British superstore). Considerable savings can be made on a wide variety of goods including food (e.g. cheese, ground coffee, chocolate, cooked meats and paté), alcohol (beer, wine and spirits), toys, houseware (e.g. hardware, glassware and kitchenware) and clothing (if you take your car you can also save on servicing!). Don't forget your passports or identity cards, car papers, foreign currency and credit cards. Many French stores accept sterling, but usually give you a worse exchange rate than a bank. It's usually best to use a credit card when shopping abroad and on board ferries, as you receive a better exchange rate (and can delay payment). Note that in towns much frequented by British shoppers and tourists, the price of some goods may be slightly higher than in inland towns.

From 1st January 1993, there have been no cross-border shopping restrictions within the European Union for goods purchased duty and tax paid, providing all goods are for personal consumption or use and not for resale. Although there are no restrictions, there are 'indicative levels' for certain items, above which goods may be classified as commercial quantities. For example, persons entering Britain aged 17 or over may import the following amounts of alcohol and tobacco:

- 10 litres of spirits (over 22° proof);

- 20 litres of fortified wine such as port or sherry (under 22° proof);

- 90 litres of wine (or 120 x 0.75 litre bottles/10 cases) of which a maximum of 60 litres may be sparkling wine;
- 110 litres of beer;
- 800 cigarettes, 400 cigarillos, 200 cigars and 1kg of smoking tobacco.

There's no limit on perfume or toilet water. If you exceed the above amounts you may need to convince the customs authorities that you aren't planning to sell the goods. There are huge fines for anyone who sells duty-paid alcohol and tobacco, which is classed as smuggling. Hand-rolling tobacco is one of the smugglers' favourites, as it costs around five times as much in Britain as in France. Beer is also popular and costs less than half the British price in France.

The vast cross-Channel shopping business is made possible by cheap off-season ferry trips costing as little as £10 return for a car and £1 for foot passengers! Most special offers are available during off-peak periods only and are usually offered via coupons provided in daily newspapers. Cross-Channel shopping has led to a number of British companies opening outlets in Calais including Sainsbury's, Tesco, Victoria Wine and The Wine Society. If you don't fancy a trip to France, you can buy wine direct from vineyards and breweries in Austria, France, Germany, Italy and Spain (and beer direct from Belgium) via intermediaries such as Classic Wines & Beers (Crossways, Mount Pleasant, Wareham, Dorset BH20 4HG, ☎ 01929-553912), which is legal. Savings of up to 40 or 50 per cent can be made on British high street prices.

Alcohol and tobacco are favourite tax targets of the Chancellor of the Exchequer in Britain, although if too many people hit the Calais trail he may be forced to rethink his taxation policies. The estimated revenue loss to the British government of cross-Channel shopping for alcohol and tobacco is around £500 million (over £1 billion at retail cost). Cross-Channel shopping has also had a huge impact on pubs and off-licences in the south-east of England (over 150 million litres of wine are personally imported into Britain annually).

Internet Shopping: Shopping via the Internet is the fastest-growing form of retailing and although it's still in its infancy, UK sales are forecast to be over £3 billion a year by 2003. Shopping on the Internet is *very* secure (secure servers, with addresses beginning https:// rather than http://, are almost impossible to crack) and in most cases safer than shopping by phone or mail-order. There are literally thousands of shopping sites on the Internet including Taxi (www.mytaxi.co.uk), which contains the Internet addresses of 2,500 world-wide retail and information sites, www. enterprisecity.co.uk, www.iwanttoshop.com, www.shopguide.co.uk. and www.virgin .net (which has a good directory of British shopping sites). One company called Priceline (www.priceline.com) even allows you to name your own price when buying such things as airline tickets, hotel rooms, cars and mortgages (if Priceline can find a company willing to accept the offer it's passed on).

With Internet shopping the world is literally your oyster and savings can be made on a wide range of goods including CDs, clothes, sports equipment, electronic gadgets, cameras and film, jewellery, books, CDs, wine, computers and computer software, and services such as insurance, pensions and mortgages. Huge savings can also be made on holidays and travel. Small high-price, high-tech items (e.g. cameras, watches and portable and hand-held computers) can usually be purchased cheaper somewhere in Europe or (particularly) in the USA (for cameras try www.aaacamera. com), with delivery by courier within as little as three days.

Buying Overseas: When buying goods overseas ensure that you're dealing with a bona fide company and that the goods will work in Britain (if applicable). If possible, *always* pay by credit card when buying by mail-order or over the Internet, as when you buy goods costing between £100 and £30,000 the credit card issuer is jointly liable with the supplier. Note, however, that many card companies claim that the law doesn't cover overseas purchases, although many issuers will consider claims up to the value of the goods purchased (and they *could* also be liable in law for consequential loss). When you buy expensive goods abroad, always have them insured for their full value while in transit.

VAT & Duty: When buying overseas, take into account shipping costs, duty and VAT. There's no duty or tax on goods purchased within the European Union or on goods from most other countries worth £18 or less (or £36 if a gift). Don't buy alcohol or cigarettes abroad as the duty is usually too high to make it pay. When VAT or duty is payable on a parcel, the payment is usually collected by the post office or courier company on delivery.

Duty-Free Allowances

Duty-free shopping within the EU ended on the 30th June 1999, although it's still available when travelling further afield. Although many people will miss their duty-free booze, many so-called duty-free 'bargains' were up to one-third cheaper in British shops including some alcohol, perfumes, cameras and clothes. As an indication of the huge profits made by 'duty-free' shops, most still sell goods at the old 'duty-free' prices and absorb the tax themselves. Duty-free allowances for those aged 17 or over travelling to Britain from a non-EU country are shown below:

- two litres of still table wine;

- one litre of alcohol over 22° volume or 38.8 per cent proof (e.g. spirits and strong liquors) **OR** two litres not over 22° volume (e.g. low strength liquors or fortified or sparkling wines);

- 200 cigarettes **OR** 100 cigarillos **OR** 50 cigars **OR** 250 grammes of tobacco;

- 60cc/ml (50gr or 2fl oz) of perfume;

- 250cc/ml (8fl oz) of toilet water;

- other goods (including gifts, souvenirs, beer and cider) to the value of £75.

PETS

Britain is generally regarded abroad as a nation of animal lovers and has some 14 million pet owners (including seven million dog owners). This is attested to by the number of bequests received by the Royal Society for the Prevention of Cruelty to Animals (RSPCA), which far exceed the amount left to the Royal Society for the Prevention of Cruelty to Children (RSPCC). The British are almost uniquely sentimental about animals, even those reared for food, and protests over the exports of calves for veal (which are raised in small crates) and other livestock has caused headline news in recent years. Britons are also prominent in international animal protection organisations that attempt to ban cruel sports and practices in which animals are mistreated (such as bullfighting).

Quarantine: Britain has the toughest quarantine regulations in the world in order to guard against the importation of rabies and other animal diseases (we have enough problems with 'mad cow disease' and crazy politicians). Britain has been virtually free of rabies for over 60 years. **However, there's good news for those who cannot bear to be parted from their cats and dogs, as Britain plans to introduce a new system without quarantine in the year 2000 (see below) on a trial basis.** Under the quarantine laws all mammals other than specific breeds of horses and livestock must spend a period of six months in quarantine in an approved kennel to ensure they are free of rabies and Newcastle disease. Rabies is a serious hazard throughout the world, including many parts of Europe. You can catch this disease if you're bitten, scratched or even licked by an infected dog, cat, fox, monkey, bat or other animal.

Quarantine in Britain applies to all cats and dogs, including guide dogs for the blind. If you're coming to Britain for a limited period only, it may not be worth the trouble and expense of bringing your pet and you may prefer to leave it with friends or relatives during your stay. Before deciding to import an animal, contact the Ministry of Agriculture, Fisheries and Food, Hook Rise South, Tolworth, Surbiton, Surrey KT6 7NF (☎ 0208-330 8174, Internet: www.maff.gov.uk) for the latest regulations, application forms, and a list of approved quarantine kennels and catteries (the ministry also publishes a number of free brochures about rabies). Applications for the importation of dogs, cats and other mammals, should be made at least eight weeks prior to the proposed date of importation. To obtain a licence to import your pet, you must have a confirmed booking at an approved kennel (it's possible to change kennels after arrival), enlist the services of an authorised carrying agent (who will transport your pet from the port to the quarantine kennels), and your pet must arrive at an approved port or airport. Animals must be transported in approved containers, available from air transport companies and pet shops, and must be shipped within six months of the date specified by the licence.

The cost of quarantine for six months is from £75 to £150 a month for a dog, depending on its size (and what it eats) and about £50 a month for a cat. You must also pay for any vaccinations and veterinary costs incurred during your pet's quarantine period. You're permitted, in fact encouraged, to visit your pet in quarantine, but won't be able to take it out for exercise. There are different regulations for some animals, birds for example, serve a shorter quarantine time than other animals, until it's established that there's no danger of psittacosis. Pet rabbits must be inoculated against rabies and cannot be imported from the USA. There's no quarantine for cold-blooded animals such as fish and reptiles. Around 5,000 dogs and 3,000 cats are quarantined each year in Britain.

New Regulations: A new pilot 'Pet Travel Scheme (PETS)' will replace quarantine for qualifying cats and dogs from April 2000. Under the scheme pets must be microchipped (they have a microchip inserted in their neck), vaccinated against rabies, undergo a blood test and be issued with a 'health certificate' ('passport'). The scheme will be restricted to animals imported from rabies-free countries and countries where rabies is under control (initially Western Europe and possibly including North America later), but the current quarantine law will remain in place for pets coming from Eastern Europe, Africa, Asia and South America. The new regulations are expected to cost pet owners around £100 (for a microchip, rabies vaccination and blood test) plus £60 a year for annual booster vaccinations and around £20 for a border check. Shop around and compare fees from a number of veterinary surgeons. To qualify, pets must travel by sea via Dover or Portsmouth, by train via the Channel Tunnel or via Heathrow airport (only certain carriers will be licensed to carry animals). More information is available from the Ministry of Agriculture, Fisheries and Food (MAFF) by phone (☎ 0208-330 6835) or via the Internet (e-mail: pets@ahvg.maff.gov.uk).

An import licence and a veterinary examination is required for some domestic animals, e.g. horses, of which only certain breeds are kept in quarantine. Dangerous animals require a special import licence and you also require a licence from your local council to keep a poisonous snake or other dangerous wild animal, which must be properly caged with an adequate exercise area and must pose no risk to public health and safety. **It's a criminal offence to attempt to smuggle an animal into Britain and it's almost always discovered.** Illegally imported animals are either exported immediately or destroyed and the owners are prosecuted. Owners face (and invariably receive) a heavy fine of up to £1,000 or an unlimited fine and up to a year's imprisonment for deliberate offences. There's no VAT or duty on animals brought into Britain as part of your 'personal belongings', although if you import an animal after your arrival VAT and duty may need to be paid on its value.

There isn't a dog registration or licence scheme in England, Wales or Scotland, which was abandoned some years ago. In Northern Ireland a dog licence must be obtained from your local district council office for a dog aged over six months old. Attempts to introduce a dog registration scheme have been defeated by the government, much to the dismay of veterinary surgeons and the RSPCA, who have mounted a campaign to reintroduce dog registration (which has the support of the vast majority of people).

Before buying a home in a community development such as an apartment block, townhouse development or a development within its own private grounds, you should check whether there are any restrictions regarding pets. Some apartment developments ban dogs and many London developments (and private squares) with private gardens have restrictions on the walking of dogs and some don't allow it at all (when it's allowed, you must usually pay for the privilege and dogs may also need to be kept on a lead).

TELEVISION & RADIO

Television

Watching television (TV), referred to colloquially as the 'box' or 'telly', is Britain's most popular pastime (or a national epidemic, depending on how you view it). This unsocial disease has all but replaced all those boring things like talking, listening to music, exercise, visiting people (particularly people without TVs), or generally doing anything which might exercise the brain or the body (perish the thought!). Most British homes have at least one TV and over 60 per cent have more than one (25 per cent have three or more), and 80 per cent also have a video recorder.

Many families have a TV in each room except

the toilet, particularly in children's rooms where TVs (and computers) serve as tranquillisers for overactive kids, i.e. anytime when they're awake. In households where TV reigns supreme, the box is far more influential with children than parents. However, although TV may have killed off conversation in many homes, in deprived households with only one TV it does wonders for arguments (about which programme to watch). The average Briton is glued to the box for over 15 hours a week or 33 (24-hour) days a year (surprisingly, homes with cable and satellite TV watch little more than those receiving terrestrial TV only). Interactive TV services are the latest offering for couch potatoes and include home shopping and banking, educational programmes, computer games and videos on demand.

While still producing a surfeit of nonsense (e.g. inane quiz shows and soaps, otherwise known as 'tabloid' TV) to cater for TV junkies, British TV (and British produced TV programmes) is generally recognised as the best (or least worst) in the world. British TV companies produce many excellent programmes including documentaries; wildlife and nature programmes; serialised adaptations of novels; TV films; situation comedy; and variety shows, which are sold throughout the world. Other excellent programmes include current affairs, serious music, chat shows and sports coverage. Some three-quarters of Britons get their main information about the world from TV News, although the presentation is becoming more showbiz (newscasters are often stars in their own right). Some critics complain that there's too little live TV, where comedians fluff their lines, jugglers drop their balls and dancers fall about (although there are plenty of live chat shows). Explicit sex is becoming commonplace and has led to the Broadcasting Standards Council trying to ban gratuitous sex scenes.

Standards: The standards for TV reception in Britain aren't the same as in many other countries. TVs and video recorders manufactured for use in the USA (NTSC Standard) and continental Europe won't function in Britain due to different transmission standards. Most European countries use the PAL B/G standard, except for, you guessed it, France, which has its own standard called SECAM. All British channels broadcast on 625 lines ultra-high frequency (UHF) and around 99 per cent of the population live within the transmission range. The British standard is a modified PAL-I system, where the audio signal is shifted to avoid the buzz plaguing the conventional PAL system when, for example, transmitting subtitles or other white areas.

If you bring a TV to Britain from the USA or the continent, you will get either a picture or sound, **but not both.** A TV can be converted to work in Britain, but it's usually not worth the trouble and expense. If you want a TV and video recorder (VCR) that will work in Britain and other European countries (including France) and/or the USA, you must buy a multi-standard model. Some multi-standard TVs also handle the North American NTSC standard and have an NTSC-in jack plug connection allowing you to play back American videos.

Digital TV: All major terrestrial stations are now broadcast in both digital and analogue format and in late 1999 around 90 per cent of viewers could receive digital TV. However, in order to receive digital TV you need a separate aerial and decoder or an integrated TV with a built-in decoder. In addition to providing a superior picture, better (CD) quality sound and wide-screen cinema format (with a digital TV), digital TV also allows for interactive services, digital text and interactive TV (see also **Digital Satellite TV** below).

Stations: In most city and rural areas, five TV stations can be received: BBC1, BBC2, ITV3 (independent television), Channel 4 and Channel 5. In areas where two ITV3 stations overlap, viewers can usually receive both stations. Under the Broadcasting Act 1990, the ITV channel was officially renamed Channel 3, shown as ITV3 in this book, thus allowing all channels to be referred to by a number (although to most people it will always be simply 'ITV'). The BBC channels carry no advertising and are publicly funded through an annual TV licence (see below), the sale of the *Radio Times*, and the trading activities of BBC Enterprises. With the exception of Wales, where many Welsh-language programmes are broadcast, and regional news broadcasts, BBC programmes are the same throughout Britain. All terrestrial TV stations now broadcast for 24 hours a day, as do many satellite and cable stations. Programmes on BBC begin at odd times (e.g. 6.20, 8.05), depending on the length of programmes, as they aren't subject to commercial breaks. ITV programmes usually start on the hour or half hour. The terrestrial TV audience in Britain is fairly evenly divided between BBC and ITV.

TV Licence: An annual TV licence (£97.50 for colour, £32.50 for black and white) is required by all TV owners in Britain. Registered blind people are generously offered a reduction of £1.25 on production of the local authority's certificate for the blind. The fee is linked to the cost of living and is subject to a three-year agreement under the BBC's charter. However, the fee will be increased dramatically from the year 2000 to pay for digital broadcasts. TV licences must be renewed annually and can be purchased from post offices or from TV Licensing, Freepost (BS6689), Bristol BS98 1TL (☎ 0990-226666). A 'Television Licence Application' form must be completed. The licence fee can also be paid by direct debit from a bank or building society account in one payment or in quarterly or monthly payments (which include a small premium). The post office operates a TV licence saving scheme for philatelists, through the purchase of £1 TV licence stamps. If you're leaving Britain, you can obtain a refund on any unexpired three-month period of a TV licence by applying in writing to Customer Services, TV Licensing, Freepost (BS6689), Bristol BS98 1TL.

Cable TV: Cable television in Britain was originally confined to areas of poor reception (e.g. due to natural geographical features or high-rise buildings) or where external aerials weren't permitted. However, there has been an explosion in cable TV in the last decade and it's the fastest growing sector of the TV industry. Over ten million homes can now receive cable TV and there are around three million subscribers (although Britain still has a long way to go to match European countries such as Belgium, the Netherlands and Switzerland, where up to 90 per cent of the populations has access to cable TV).

The new broadband cable systems can carry up to 30 channels including terrestrial broadcasts, satellite TV, channels delivered by videotape and local services. Most cable TV companies provide all the stations offered by satellite TV plus a few others, a total of up to 40 (possibly including local cable TV companies such as Channel One in London). There's an initial connection fee of around £25 for cable TV and a subscription of around £15 a month for the basic package or up to £35 a month for a package including all the premium channels. One of the main advantages is that most cable companies offer inexpensive telephone services, possibly including free local off-peak calls, which can save you enough on your phone bill to pay for your cable TV. Digital TV was introduced in 1999 and is cheaper than satellite digital TV as no extra equipment is necessary. Companies will also offer pay-per-view broadcasts, movies on demand, home shopping and access to the Internet.

Satellite TV: Although many people complain endlessly about the poor quality of TV in their home countries, many find they cannot live without it when abroad. Fortunately the advent of satellite TV in the last decade means that most people can enjoy TV programmes in English and a variety of other languages almost anywhere in the world. Britain is well served by satellite TV, where a number of satellites are positioned carrying over 200 stations broadcasting in a variety of languages.

Astra: Although it wasn't the first in Europe (which was Eutelsat), the European satellite revolution really took off with the launch of the Astra 1A satellite in 1988 (operated by the Luxembourg-based *Société Européenne des Satellites* or SES), positioned 36,000km (22,300mi) above the earth. TV addicts (easily recognised by their antennae and square eyes) are offered a huge choice of English and foreign-language stations which can be received throughout most of Britain with a 60cm (or smaller) dish and receiver. Since 1988 a number of additional Astra satellites have been launched, increasing the number of available channels to 64 (or over 200 with digital TV). An added bonus is the availability of radio stations via satellite, including all the national BBC stations (see **Satellite Radio** on page 83).

Among the many English-language stations available on Astra are Sky One, Movimax, Sky Premier, Sky Cinema, Film Four, Sky News, Sky Sports (three channels), UK Gold, Channel 5, Granada Plus, TNT, Eurosport, CNN, CNBC Europe, UK Style, UK Horizons, the Disney Channel and the Discovery Channel. Other stations broadcast in Dutch, German, Japanese, Swedish and various Indian languages. The signal from many stations is scrambled (the decoder is usually built into the receiver) and viewers must pay a monthly subscription fee to receive programmes. You can buy pirate decoders for some channels. The best served by clear (unscrambled) stations are German-speakers (most German stations on Astra are clear).

BSkyB Television: You must buy a Videocrypt decoder, an integral part of the receiver in the latest models, and pay a monthly subscription to receive all BSkyB or Sky stations except Sky News (which isn't scrambled). Various packages are available costing from around £12 to £30 a month for the premium package offering all movie channels plus Sky Sports. Subscribers are sent a coded 'smart' card (similar to a credit card), which must be inserted in the decoder to switch it on (cards are frequently changed to thwart counterfeiters). Sky subscribers receive a free copy of *SkyTVguide* monthly.

Digital Satellite TV: Digital TV was launched on 1st October 1998 by Sky Television (☎ 0870-424242) in the UK. To watch digital TV you require a Digibox and a (digital) Minidish, costing £200 including installation (the actual cost of the set top box is around £400 without the hefty subsidy paid by BSkyB). Customers must sign up for a 12-month subscription and agree to have the connection via a phone line (to allow for future interactive services). In addition to the usual analogue channels (see above), Sky digital TV offers BBC1 & 2 and Channels 4 and 5 (but not ITV3), plus many new digital channels (a total of 200 with up to 500 possible later). ONdigital (☎ 0808-100 0101) launched a rival digital service on 15th November 1998, which although it's cheaper than Sky digital, provides a total of 30 channels only (15 free and 15 subscription) including BBC1 & 2, ITV3, Channel 4 and Channel 5. Digital TV is also available via cable and terrestrial aerials. Contact your local TV store for further information and installation.

Eutelsat: Eutelsat (owned by a consortium of national telephone operators) was the first company to introduce satellite TV to Europe (in 1983) and now runs a fleet of communications satellites carrying TV stations to over 50 million homes. Until 1995 they had broadcast primarily advertising-based, clear-access cable channels. Following the launch in March 1995 of their Hot Bird satellite, Eutelsat hoped to become a major competitor to Astra, although its channels are mostly non-English. The English-language stations on Eutelsat include Eurosport, Euronews, BBC World and CNBC Europe. Other channels broadcast in Arabic, French, German, Hungarian, Italian, Polish, Portuguese, Spanish and Turkish.

BBC World-wide Television: Although intended for an international audience, it's possible to receive the BBC World-wide TV stations, BBC Prime (general entertainment) and BBC World (24-hour news and information) in Britain via the Intelsat VI and Eutelsat II F1 satellites respectively. BBC Prime is encrypted and requires a D2 Mac decoder and a smartcard (£75 plus VAT per year). BBC World is clear (unencrypted) and is financed by advertising revenue. For more information and a programming guide contact BBC World-wide Television, Woodlands, 80 Wood Lane, London W12 0TT, UK (☎ UK 0208-576 2555). The BBC publishes a monthly magazine, *BBC On Air*, giving comprehensive information about BBC World-wide Television programmes. A programme guide is also listed on the Internet (www.bbc.co.uk/schedules) and both BBC World and BBC Prime have their own websites (www.bbcworld.com and www.bbcprime.com). When accessing them, you need to enter the name of the country so that the schedules appear in local time.

Equipment: A satellite receiver should have a built-in Videocrypt decoder (and others such as Eurocrypt, Syster or SECAM if required) and be capable of receiving satellite stereo radio. A 60cm dish (to receive Astra stations) costs from around £150 plus the cost of installation (which may be included in the price). Larger (from 90cm) motorised dishes cost from £600 to over £1,000. Shop around as prices vary enormously. Systems can also be rented, although renting isn't good value for money. You can also buy a 1.2 or 1.5 metre dish and receive hundreds of stations in a multitude of languages from around the world. If you wish to receive satellite TV on two or more TVs, you can buy a system with two or more receptors. To receive stations from two or more satellites simultaneously, you need a motorised dish or a dish with a double feed (dual LNBs) antenna. **When buying a system, ensure that it can receive programmes from all existing and planned satellites.**

Location: To receive programmes from any satellite, there must be no obstacles between the satellite and your dish, i.e. no trees, buildings or mountains (or anything else) must obstruct the signal, so check before renting or buying a home. Under current planning regulations most householders are permitted to erect one satellite dish aerial without planning permission, providing it's no bigger than 90cm. Dishes can be mounted in a variety of unobtrusive positions. Apartment blocks usually have cable TV or communal aerials. You may need planning permission to install a satellite dish or antenna on a house depending on its size, height, position, the location of the property, and whether or not a dish is already installed. If in doubt contact your local council's planning department. Note that those living in conservation areas and in listed buildings are banned from erecting aerials on buildings (or may be required to mount them so they cannot be seen from public roads). In strong signal areas it's possible to mount a dish indoors, providing there's a direct line to the satellite through a window or skylight.

Programme Guides: Many satellite stations provide teletext information, which include programme schedules. Satellite programmes are also listed in most national daily newspapers, general TV magazines and satellite TV magazines such as *What Satellite, Satellite Times* and *Satellite TV* (the best), available from newsagents or on subscription. The annual *World Radio and TV Handbook* (Billboard) contains over 600 pages of information and the frequencies of all radio and TV stations world-wide.

Radio

Radio reception in Britain is excellent in most parts of the country, including stereo reception, which is clear in all but the most mountainous areas (although FM reception isn't always good in cars). The radio audience in Britain is almost equally split between the British Broadcasting Corporation (BBC) and commercial radio stations (although the BBC has been losing listeners to commercial stations at an alarming rate in recent years). Community and ethnic radio is also popular in many areas and a number of universities operate their own radio stations. In addition to the FM or VHF stereo wave band, medium wave (MW or AM) and long wave (LW) bands are in wide use throughout Britain. Shortwave (SW) band is useful for receiving foreign radio stations. As in other countries, British radio stations scour the country (world?) to find brainless, incoherent, banal dimwits whom they can instantly turn into wallies of the radio waves, known as disc jockeys (some of whom achieve greater fame as even bigger prats on TV).

BBC Radio: BBC operates five network radio stations with easy to remember (if unimaginative) names: BBC Radio 1 (contemporary music, FM 97.6-99.8), BBC Radio 2, dubbed 'the opium of the people', (entertainment, culture and music, FM 88-90.2), BBC Radio 3 (classical music, jazz, drama, discussions, documentaries and poetry, FM 90.2-92.4), BBC Radio 4 (conversation, comedy, drama, documentaries, magazine programmes, news, FM 92.4-94.6, LW 198), BBC Radio 5 Live (news, current affairs and sports, MW 693, 909) and around 40 English BBC local radio stations with some ten million listeners. There's no advertising on BBC radio stations, although it's the main source of income for commercial radio stations (the other is selling T-shirts). BBC radio is financed by the government and the revenue from TV licence fees, as no radio licence is necessary in Britain.

BBC radio programmes are published in national newspapers and Radios 1, 3 and 4 are broadcast both in stereo on FM and in mono on AM. BBC radio programmes are also listed on the BBC TV teletext information service. If you have any difficulty locating the BBC's stations, send a stamped, self-addressed envelope to the BBC, Listener Correspondence, Broadcasting House, Portland Place, London W1A 1AA (☎ 0207-580 4468).

Commercial Radio: Commercial radio is hugely popular in Britain and is Britain's fastest growing entertainment medium. Most cities can now receive at least five commercial stations (over ten in London). However, there are still only some 200 commercial radio stations in the whole of Britain, compared with around 1,000 in France and Italy, and over 9,000 in the USA. The British are avid radio listeners and the majority of people listen to the radio for 20 hours or more each week. Commercial radio is reported to have some 36 million listeners or almost 80 per cent of all adults.

Stations vary from large national stations with vast budgets and millions of listeners to tiny local stations run by volunteers with just a few thousand listeners. They provide a comprehensive service of local news and information, music and other entertainment, education, consumer advice, traffic information and local events, and provide listeners with the chance to air their views, often through phone-in programmes (talkzak). Advertising on commercial radio is limited to nine minutes an hour, but is usually less (although it sometimes appears to be endless, particularly on Capital FM). Britain has three national commercial radio stations: Classic FM (FM 100-101.9) Virgin Radio (popular music, FM 105.8, MW 1197, 1215) and Talk Radio UK (MW 1053, 1089), Britain's first 24-hour, national, speech-only commercial station. Britain's most popular commercial radio station is Capital Radio (Capital FM and Capital Gold plus stations in Birmingham, Kent, Hampshire and Sussex), the world's largest metropolitan radio station with over three million listeners.

Satellite Radio: If you have satellite TV you can also receive radio stations via your satellite link. For example, BBC Radio 1, 2, 3, 4 and 5, BBC World Service, Sky Radio (a popular music station *without DJs*), Virgin 1215 and many foreign (i.e. non-English) stations are broadcast via the Astra satellites. Satellite radio stations are listed in British satellite TV magazines such as *Satellite Times*. If you're interested in receiving radio stations from further afield you should obtain a copy of the *World Radio TV Handbook* (Billboard).

LEARNING ENGLISH

If you don't speak English fluently (or you wish to learn another language) you can enrol on a language course at one of over 5,000 language schools in Britain. Obtaining a working knowledge of English while living in Britain is relatively easy (if learning a language is ever easy!) as you will be constantly immersed in the English language and will have the maximum opportunity to practice. However, if you wish to speak or write English fluently you will probably need to attend a language school or find a private tutor. Over 500,000 students come to Britain each year to learn English, 75 per cent from Western Europe, thus ensuring that English-language schools (over 1,000) are big business. It's usually necessary to have a recognised qualification in English to be accepted at a college of higher or further education in Britain. In many areas there's an ethnic minority language service providing information and counselling in a variety of languages. These organise a wide range of English classes including home tuition, open learning and small classes, at beginner and intermediate levels.

There are English-language schools in all cities and large towns in Britain; however, the majority of schools, particularly those offering intensive courses, are to be found in the south. The largest concentration of schools is in London and the world-famous university towns of Oxford and Cambridge. There are also a large number of schools along the south coast, particularly in Brighton and Bournemouth. Edinburgh is the most popular location in Scotland. The British Tourist Authority (BTA) publish an annual directory, *Learning English,* of English-language schools, including state sector courses and recognised and non-recognised schools (see below). The introduction is written in Arabic, Dutch, English, French, German, Italian and Spanish. A copy can be obtained free from BTA offices abroad or direct from the British Tourist Authority.

You may find it advantageous to choose a school that's a member of Arels-Felco Ltd., the association of recognised English language teaching establishments in Britain. Arels-Felco incorporates ARELS (Association of Recognised English Language Schools) and FELCO (Federation of English Language Course Organisations), and is a non-profit association whose members are recognised as efficient in the teaching of English as a foreign language by the British Council. Members must follow the association's regulations and code of conduct, which include high academic standards and rules governing the welfare of students. Some members of Arels-Felco are registered as non-profit educational trusts (which means VAT isn't payable on fees) and many members cater for the handicapped, including blind, deaf and physically handicapped students. Arels-Felco publish an annual directory of members containing details of all courses, available from Arels-Felco Ltd., 2 Pontypool Place, Valentine Place, London SE1 8QF (☎ 0207-242-3136).

Courses offered by schools that are members of Arels-Felco mainly fall into four categories: general English courses available all year round; courses for executives; junior (9+) holiday courses; and adult (16+) courses. Courses vary in length from one week to six months and cater for all ages from five (in special schools) through to senior citizens. The average class size is around 10 to 12, with 15 usually being the maximum. Most schools are equipped with computers, language laboratories, video studios, libraries and bookshops, and some even have their own restaurants and bars (to help loosen the tongue).

Most language schools offer a variety of classes depending on your current language ability, how many hours you wish to study a week, how much money you want to spend and how quickly you wish to learn. Full-time, part-time and evening courses are offered by many schools, and many also offer residential courses or selected accommodation with local families (highly recommended to accelerate learning). Courses that include accommodation (often half board, consisting of breakfast and an evening meal) usually offer excellent value for money. Bear in mind that if you need to find your own accommodation, particularly in London, it can be difficult and expensive. Language classes generally fall into the following categories:

Category	No. hours a week
compact	10 to 20
intensive	20 to 30
total immersion	30 to 40+

Most schools offer compact or intensive courses and also provide special English courses for businessmen, solicitors, journalists and doctors (among others), and a wide variety of examinations, all of which are recognised internationally. Course fees vary considerably and are usually calculated on a weekly basis. Fees depend on the number of hours tuition per week, the type of course, and the location and reputation of the school. Expect to pay £150 to £250 a week for an intensive course providing 20 to 30 hours of language study per week. A compact course usually costs around £80 to £100 per week and half board accommodation around £80 to £90 a week extra (more in London). It's possible to enrol at a good school for an all-inclusive (tuition plus half-board accommodation) intensive course for as little as £200 per week. In London and other large cities, students in private accommodation may need to spend more time travelling to classes each day.

Total immersion or executive courses are provided by many schools and usually consist of private lessons for a minimum of 30 to 40 hours a week. Fees can run to £1,000 a week or more and not everyone is suited to learning at such a fast rate (or has the financial resources). Whatever language you're learning, don't expect to become fluent in a short period unless you have a particular flair for languages or already have a good command of a language. Unless you desperately need to learn a language quickly, it's best to space your lessons over a long period. Don't commit yourself to a long course of study (particularly an expensive one) before ensuring that it's the correct one for you. Most schools offer a free introductory lesson and free tests to help you find your correct level. Many language schools offer private and small group lessons. **It's important to choose the right course, particularly if you're studying English in order to continue with full-time education in Britain and need to reach a minimum standard or gain a particular qualification.**

Many language schools offer special English classes for au pair girls costing from around £40 to over £150 a term, depending on the number of hours tuition per week. Most courses for au pairs include around four hours study a week. The school year begins in the middle of September and ends in June, and some schools accept au pairs only in the September and January terms (au pairs arriving after Easter may find it difficult to obtain classes). There are usually no classes for au pairs over the summer holiday period (June to mid-September). Among the best value-for-money English courses are those run by state colleges under the control of Local Educational Authorities (LEAs), the Department for Education and Employment or the Scottish Education Department.

Most colleges offer full-time, part-time and vacation English courses for overseas students throughout the year, with fees ranging from around £20 to £80 a week. Many courses are cheaper for EU nationals and may even be free during the daytime for those aged under 18. Colleges usually arrange accommodation for students. A booklet containing a list of colleges and their courses (including courses for English language teachers) is available from the British Association of State English Language Teaching (BASELT), Secretariat, Cheltenham & Gloucester College of Higher Education, Francis Close Hall, Swindon Road, Cheltenham, Glos. GL50 4AZ (☎ 01242-227099).

You may prefer to have private lessons, which are a quicker but generally more expensive way of learning a language. The main advantage of private lessons is that you learn at your own speed and aren't held back by slow learners or dragged along by the class genius. You can advertise for a teacher in local newspapers, on shopping centre or supermarket bulletin boards, university or school notice boards, and through your or your spouse's employer. Your friends or colleagues may also be able to help you find a suitable private teacher. If you're living in Britain and speak reasonable English but need conversational practice, you might consider enrolling in a part-time course at an adult education institute.

Many British universities hold summer and other holiday English language courses for foreigners, e.g. Birmingham, London and Oxford. For a programme contact the Secretary, British Universities Summer Schools, University of Oxford, Department for Continuing Education, 1 Wellington Square, Oxford OX1 2JA (☎ 01865-270378). The British Chamber of Commerce provides an English tuition advisory service in many countries and works closely with English schools, universities and institutions in Britain, covering all aspects of English language teaching. For information contact your local British embassy, consulate or high commission abroad.

CRIME

According to official statistics the number of crimes (apart from violent crimes) being committed have reduced in recent years. However, sceptics believe that people are simply reporting less crime because they consider it a waste of time (the clear-up rate or number of crimes solved is below 20 per cent in most areas). In the last decade there has been an upsurge in car joy-riding (where cars are stolen by kids for 'fun'), muggings, pick-pocketing, car crime, house-breaking and burglary, robbery, fraud, rape and school crime. The number of violent crimes are also increasing, although they are still relatively low compared with many other countries. There are around 500 murders a year in Britain, where you're more likely to choke to death on your food than you are to meet a violent death.

Nevertheless, violent crime has reached shocking proportions in some cities and it's becoming more common among children. The levels of street crime (where men under 30 are most at risk) are far higher than official figures suggest and the actual number of crimes is reckoned to be around four times the number recorded by the police. However, muggings and crimes of violence are still rare in most towns, where you can safely walk almost anywhere day or night. Many crimes are drug-related and are due to the huge increase in drugs flooding into Britain in recent years. The use of hard drugs (particularly cocaine and crack) is a major problem in most British cities, where gangs increasingly use guns to settle their differences. Violent crime and assaults are increasing and the police warn people (particularly young women) against tempting fate by walking alone in dark and deserted areas late at night. The increasing rate of assaults on female students has prompted some universities to issue them with rape (screech) alarms.

For many people in Britain, crime is their number one concern and in some areas people are afraid to leave the relative safety of their homes at any time of day or night. The increase in crime in many areas is attributed by psychologists to poverty, the breakdown of traditional family life, the loss of community and social values in society, and a growing lack of parental responsibility and skills. The failure to deal with juvenile crime is one of the biggest threats facing Britain and many children are out of control by the age of ten or even younger. Riots occasionally occur and are often sparked by a breakdown in relations between police and youths.

Crimes against property are escalating, particularly burglary and housebreaking, car thefts and thefts from vehicles. The number of cars stolen in Britain is the highest (per capita) in Western Europe and burglary is also the highest in Europe. If you work or live in a major city and park your car there, you have a one in four chance of having it stolen or broken into. In London (where around 20 per cent of all crime takes place) professional thieves even steal antique paving stones, railings and antique doors and door casings. Fraud or so-called 'white-collar' crime (which includes credit card fraud, income tax evasion and VAT fraud), costs £billions a year and accounts for larger sums than the total of all other robberies, burglaries and thefts added together.

The authorities' response to the crime wave sweeping Britain has been to 'get tough' with offenders and sentence an increasing number of people to prison terms, particularly women. British courts are increasingly imprisoning people for petty crimes, e.g. minor motoring offences and non-payment of TV licences and council tax. Justice is weighed heavily against women, who are often treated much more harshly than men for the same crimes. The routine imprisonment of women for petty offences has created a crisis in women's prisons, where the number of prisoners has increased by 30 per cent over the last few years. Another anomaly causing concern is the disproportionate percentage of black prisoners, which has led to accusations of racial bias in the courts. Britain sends more people to prison for more offences and sentences more people to life imprisonment than in the whole of the rest of Western Europe.

Although the foregoing catalogue of crime may paint a depressing picture of Britain, it's a relatively safe place to live. In comparison with many other countries, including most other European countries, Britain's crime rate isn't high and the incidence of violent crime is low. If you take care of your property and take precautions against crime, your chances of becoming a victim are small. Note that the rate of crime in Britain varies considerably from area to area and anyone coming to live in Britain should avoid high crime areas if at all possible.

Information: Police forces, central government, local authorities and security companies all publish information and provide advice on crime prevention. Police forces have a local crime prevention officer whose job is to provide free advice to individuals, homeowners and businesses. Most police forces publish comprehensive police *Crime Prevention Manuals*. The Central Office of Information and the Home Office also publish numerous brochures and booklets about crime prevention including *Your Practical Guide to Crime Prevention*, available from police stations, libraries and council offices.

3.

FINANCE

One of the most important aspects of buying a home in Britain and living there (even for relatively brief periods) is finance, which includes everything from transferring and changing money to mortgages and taxes. If you're planning to invest in a property or business in Britain financed with imported funds, it's important to consider both the present and possible future exchange rates. On the other hand, if you live and work in Britain and are paid in sterling, this may affect your financial commitments abroad. **Bear in mind that if your income is received in a currency other than sterling it can be exposed to risks beyond your control when you live in Britain, particularly regarding inflation and exchange rate fluctuations.**

Britain is a credit-financed society and companies queue up to lend you money or give you credit, although they are more circumspect than they were in the '80s when they would lend to anyone. Credit and assorted other plastic cards have largely replaced 'real' money and now account for over 75 per cent of all retail purchases (Britons owe some £16 billion on credit cards). Your financial standing in Britain is usually decided by the number of cards you have, which include credit cards, cash cards, debit cards, cheque guarantee cards, charge cards, store cards, affinity cards and mystery cards. British banks are following America's example and are trying to introduce a cash-less society, and in future to be card-less may equate to being credit-less.

Britain has one of the most unregulated financial service industries in the western world and anyone can set themselves up as an investment expert and charge practically whatever fees and interest they wish. It has been described as the financial rip-off centre of Europe and it's conservatively estimated that finance companies over-charge small investors by over £500 million a year (when Germany was planning to introduce new laws regarding financial services some years ago, its investigators were horrified at what they discovered in Britain). Personal finance is a jungle and there are plenty of predators about just waiting to get their hands on your loot. Always shop around for financial services and never sign a contract unless you know exactly what the costs and implications are. Although bankers, financiers and brokers don't like to make too fine a point of it, they aren't doing business with you because they like you, but simply to get their hands on your pile of chips. It's up to you to make sure that their share is kept to a minimum and that you receive the best possible value for your money. **When dealing with financial 'experts' bear in mind that while making mistakes is easy, fouling up completely requires professional help!**

If you own a home in Britain you can employ an accountant to look after your financial affairs there and declare and pay your local taxes. You can also have your accountant receive your bank statements, ensure that your bank is paying your standing orders (e.g. for utilities) and that you have sufficient funds to pay them. If you let a home through a British management company, they usually perform these tasks as part of their service.

Wealth Warning: If you plan to live in Britain you must ensure that your income is (and will remain) sufficient to live on, bearing in mind currency devaluations and exchange rate fluctuations (if your income isn't paid in sterling), rises in the cost of living (see page 126), and unforeseen expenses such as medical bills or anything else that may reduce your income (such as stock market crashes and recessions!). Foreigners, particularly retirees, often under-estimate the cost of living in Britain and some are forced to return to their home countries after a few years. Although direct taxes (particularly income tax) are relatively low compared with many other

European countries, overall taxes have risen in recent years. The cost of living has been steadily rising in the last decade and Britain is now one of the most expensive countries in Europe in which to live and London one of the most expensive cities in the world.

This section includes information on importing and exporting money; banking; mortgages; taxes (property, income, capital gains, inheritance, gift and VAT); wills; and the cost of living. **Note that the figures and information contained in this chapter are based on current law and Inland Revenue practice, which are subject to change frequently.**

BRITISH CURRENCY

As you're probably aware, the British unit of currency is the pound sterling, which has been very strong (too strong for British exporters) and stable in recent years. Due to the widespread Europhobia generated by elements of the previous Conservative government, Britain declined to join the euro (•) which was launched on 1st January 1999 in Austria, Belgium, Finland, France, Germany, Ireland, Italy, Luxembourg, the Netherlands, Portugal and Spain. Many analysts believe that remaining outside the euro group of countries will do irreparable damage to Britain's economy and London's international financial standing, although the present Labour government has expressed its intention to join in the new millennium (providing the British people approve it in a referendum).

The British pound has a number of colloquial names including quid and smacker. Fiver (£5) and tenner (£10) are also commonly used. The pound is divided into 100 pence and British coins are minted in 1p and 2p (bronze); 5p, 10p, 20p and 50p (cupro-nickel); and one (nickel-brass) and two (bronze outer rim, cupro-nickel centre) pounds. The 20p and 50p coins are seven-sided, while all other coins are round. Smaller, lighter coins have been introduced in recent years, although British coins are still heavier than those in many other countries. Banknotes are printed in denominations of £5, £10, £20 and £50 pounds; the higher the denomination, the larger the note (it's best to avoid £50 notes as many people seem to think they are home-made). Forgery is a problem in most western countries and there are a 'significant number' of forged notes in circulation, so be on your guard if someone insists on paying a large bill in cash.

If you believe that banks have a licence to print money, with respect to Scottish and Northern Irish banks, you would be absolutely correct. Shopkeepers and traders don't legally need to accept notes issued by Scottish and Northern Irish banks (which include a £1 note, replaced by a coin in England and Wales, and a £100 note), even in Scotland and Northern Ireland. Scottish banknotes are naturally accepted without question in Scotland, but they may be rejected in the rest of Britain. Don't take Scottish or Northern Irish banknotes abroad as you will receive a much lower exchange rate than for Bank of England banknotes (that's if anyone will accept them at all). The Channel Islands and the Isle of Man have some local coins and notes, but the monetary system is the same as in the rest of Britain.

IMPORTING & EXPORTING MONEY

Britain has no currency restrictions and you may bring in or take out as much money as you wish, in practically any currency. The major British banks will change most foreign bank notes (but not coins), but usually give a better exchange rate for travellers cheques or eurocheques than for bank notes. In addition to banks, many travel agents, hotels and shops in major cities either change or accept foreign currency, but usually at a less favourable exchange rate than banks. There are currency exchange machines at some international airports where you can change a range of foreign currencies for sterling.

Buying & Selling Currency: When buying or selling foreign currency in Britain you should beware of excessive charges. Apart from differences in exchange rates, which are posted by all banks and bureaux de change, there may be a significant difference in charges. Most high street banks and building societies charge 1 or 2 per cent commission with a minimum charge of £2 or £2.50 (some such as Nationwide have scrapped commission charges). All banks and building societies buy and sell foreign currency, although not all keep foreign currency and you often need to order it two or three days in advance. You can also buy and sell foreign currency at main post offices, although you need to order currency at sub post offices 24 hours in advance. Post offices charge 1 per cent commission on both currency and travellers' cheques, with a minimum fee of £2.50, and accept payment by credit card.

Exchange Rates: It pays to shop around for the best exchange rates (the worst rates are offered by high street banks), particularly if you're changing a lot of money (it's possible to barter over rates in some establishments). Most banks have a spread of up to 8 per cent between their buying and selling rates for foreign currencies. The sterling exchange rate against most European and major international currencies is listed in banks and the quality daily newspapers. **Don't change money at hotels or the ubiquitous independent 'Bureau de Change' in London and other cities unless you have no choice or money to burn, as they levy high charges or offer poor exchange rates.**

Travellers' Cheques: Travellers' cheques are widely accepted in Britain in all major currencies. The commission for cashing travellers' cheques is usually 1 per cent (you need your passport). Lost or stolen travellers' cheques can be replaced in Britain and many countries abroad (the easiest to replace are American Express). Always keep a separate record of cheque numbers. You can buy travellers' cheques commission-free from many building societies (although you may need to be an account holder), stores (e.g. Marks & Spencer) and some travel agents. Most banks charge commission of 1 per cent of the face value. Sterling travellers' cheques are accepted in most countries, although some banks in some European countries (e.g. France) refuse to change all travellers' cheques.

Cash Transfers: If you have money transferred to Britain by banker's draft or a letter of credit, bear in mind that it may take a few days or longer to be cleared. You can also have money sent to you by international money order (MoneyGram) via a post office, a cashier's cheque or telegraphic transfer, e.g. via Western Union (the quickest, safest and most expensive method). You usually need your passport to collect money transferred from abroad or to cash a banker's draft (or other credit note). If you're sending money abroad, it's best to send it in the local currency so that the recipient won't need to pay conversion charges. Note that some countries have foreign exchange controls limiting the amount of money that can be sent abroad.

Insured mail is the only safe way to send cash, as the insured value is refunded if it's lost or stolen.

Postal orders can be sent to Commonwealth countries and a Girobank post office transfer can be made to most countries (usually free when transferring money to a Girobank holder). Eurocheques can be sent within Europe and postcheques (Girobank customers only) to certain countries. You can also send money direct from your bank to another bank via an inter-bank transfer. Most banks have a minimum service charge for international transfers, which generally make it expensive, particularly for small sums. Overseas banks also take a cut, usually a percentage (e.g. 1 or 2 per cent) of the amount transferred.

One thing to bear in mind when travelling anywhere isn't to rely on one source of funds only.

BANKS

The major British banks with branches in most towns throughout Britain (termed 'high street' banks) include the National Westminster, Barclays, Lloyds TSB, HSBC (which took over the Midland Bank) and Abbey National. Other major banks with branches in large towns are the Bank of Scotland, the Royal Bank of Scotland and the Co-operative Bank. There are also telephone banks (including First Direct and Girobank) that don't have branches and are 'open' 24-hours a day. For the wealthy there are many private banks (mainly portfolio management) and foreign banks abound in major cities (there are over 500 foreign banks in the City of London alone). Most banks have Internet websites and many offer online banking, although it's in its infancy with some 500,000 customers only in early 1999. In recent years there has been a flood of new-style 'banks' such as Virgin Direct, supermarkets and stores such as Marks and Spencer, who have shaken up the traditional high street banks with their innovative accounts and services.

British banks provide free banking for personal customers who remain in credit, pay interest on account balances and offer a range of financial services (although they usually *aren't* the best place to buy insurance or pensions). If you do a lot of travelling abroad, you may find the comprehensive range of services offered by a high street bank advantageous. In a small country town or village, there's usually a sub post office, but there isn't usually a bank. Note that many services provided by British banks are also provided by Building Societies (see below).

The relationship between the major banks and their customers has deteriorated in the last decade (particularly during the recession), during which banks dramatically increased their charges to personal and business customers to recoup their losses on bad loans to developing countries. Few people in Britain have a good word to say about their banks which are widely perceived to be profit-hungry, impersonal and definitely not customer-friendly. Complaints against banks have risen dramatically in recent years. British banks have made record profits (running into £billions) in the '90s, which has served only to further irritate customers (who think their banks are ripping them off). Note that often the worst place to buy financial products is from a major high street bank (building societies usually offer better deals).

Not surprisingly banks aren't exactly happy with their poor public image (on a par with that of used car salesmen, estate agents and politicians) and most have been busy trying to improve customer relations by introducing codes of conduct and payments for mistakes or poor service. Many people could save money by changing their banks. You shouldn't allow loyalty to prevent you from switching banks, as when times are hard your bank won't hesitate to withdraw your safety net (during the recession banks were directly responsible for the failure of thousands of small businesses through arbitrarily withdrawing or refusing overdrafts and loans).

Deposit Protection: All banks, including branches and subsidiaries of foreign banks accepting sterling deposits in Britain, must be licensed by the Bank of England and contribute to the Deposit Protection Fund (DPF) which guarantees that 90 per cent of deposits up to £20,000 will be repaid if a bank goes bust. Because of the limit, it's worthwhile spreading your investments around several banks and financial institutions.

Complaints: British banks are very (very) slow to rectify mistakes or to resolve disputes and rarely accept responsibility, even when clearly in the wrong. It has been estimated (based on actual proven cases) that banks routinely overcharge small business customers by hundreds of millions of pounds a year. If your bank makes a mess of your account and causes you to lose money and spend time putting it right, you're quite within your rights to claim financial compensation for your time and trouble in addition to any financial loss. Note, however, that banks typically stall complaints for up to six years and use their financial muscle to wear down customers (some banks fight every case with litigation). If you have a complaint against a British bank and have exhausted the bank's complaints' procedure, you can apply for independent arbitration to the Office of the Banking Ombudsman, 70 Grays Inn Road, London WC1X 8NB (☎ 0207-404 9944).

BUILDING SOCIETIES

Building societies date back to 1775 and were originally established to cater for people saving to buy a home. Savers saved a deposit of 5 or 10 per cent of the cost of a home with the building society, who then lent them the balance. A building society would rarely lend to anyone who wasn't a regular saver, although this changed many years ago. In 1987, the regulations governing institutions offering financial services were changed and as a result banks and building societies now compete head-on for customers. There has been a wave of mergers and take-overs in recent years, and in the past ten years the number of societies has fallen dramatically. Many building societies have converted to banks (called demutualisation) in recent years, earning millions of pounds for account holders. Many people (known as carpetbaggers) have taken advantage of pay-outs by opening accounts at a number of building societies.

Nowadays building societies offer practically all the services provided by banks, including current and savings accounts, cheque guarantee cards, cash cards, personal loans, credit cards, insurance and travel services. In an effort to woo customers away from banks, many building societies produce special brochures and 'transfer packs' (even containing pre-printed 'letters') detailing exactly how to transfer your account. Building societies don't all offer the same services, types of accounts or rates of interest (those offering the best interest rates are often the smaller societies). If you're looking for a long-term investment, the number of branches may not be of importance and members of all building societies can use cash dispensers free of charge at other building society branches via the Link system.

Deposits in British building society accounts are protected by a similar compensation scheme to banks, under which you're guaranteed to receive 90 per cent of your investment (up to a maximum of £20,000) if it goes bust. If you have a complaint against a building society and have exhausted its complaints' procedure, you can apply for independent arbitration to the Office of the Building Societies' Ombudsman, Millbank Tower, Millbank, London SW1P 4XS (☎ 0207-931 0044).

Opening an Account

If you're planning to buy a home in Britain, one of your first acts should be to open a current (or cheque) account with a bank, building society or the Girobank (post office), like over 80 per cent of Britons. Many people have at least two accounts: a current account for their out-of-pocket expenses and day-to-day transactions, and a savings account for long-term savings (or money put aside for a rainy day, which is every other day in Britain). Many people have both bank and building society accounts. Before opening an account compare bank charges, interest rates (e.g. on credit cards) and other services offered by a number of banks. **If you're planning to buy a home with a mortgage, one of the best accounts is an all-in-one account or mortgage current account** (see page 106).

To open an account, you simply go to the bank or building society of your choice and tell them you would like to open an account. You will be asked for proof of identity, e.g. usually a passport or driving licence, plus proof of your UK address (if you have one) in the form of a utility bill. Foreign residents may be required to provide a reference from their employer or a foreign bank. Many banks provide new account holders with a free cash card wallet, cheque book cover and statement file. The facilities you should expect from a current account include a cheque book; a paying-in book; a cheque guarantee card (preferably £100 or £250); interest paid on credit balances; no charges or fees when in credit; a free cash card and lots of local cash machines; a free debit card (preferably aligned with Mastercard or Visa); monthly statements; an automatic authorised overdraft facility; and the availability of credit cards. Most of these are standard.

With a current account you receive a cheque book (usually containing 30 cheques) and a cash card. A cheque guarantee card is usually provided on request and guarantees cheques up to £50, £100 or £250. Note that when using a cheque guarantee card, the card number must be written on the back of the cheque. Most businesses won't accept a cheque without a guarantee card. A cheque book usually also contains paying-in slips (at the back), with which you can make payments into your account. You also receive a separate paying-in book.

Most people pay their bills from their current account, either by standing order or cheque. Bank statements are usually issued monthly (optionally quarterly), interest is paid on deposits (usually quarterly) and an overdraft facility may be provided. Most banks don't levy charges on a current account, providing you stay in credit. However, if you overdraw your account without a prior arrangement with your bank you may be billed for bank charges on all transactions for the accounting period (usually three months).

Cheques: Cheques are usually crossed, which normally takes the form of two parallel lines across the face of the cheque. A crossed cheque theoretically provides additional security, because it can be paid only into a bank account and cannot be cashed at a bank. Banks don't recommend uncrossed cheques, although some will supply them. To obtain cash from a bank, write the cheque in your own name or write 'cash' alongside 'Pay' (but never send a cheque made out to cash through the post). If you make a mistake when writing a cheque, you can change it, but the correction must be initialled.

Take great care when sending cheques through the post, particularly for large amounts, as cheques are sometimes stolen and paid into someone else's account, from which the money is quickly withdrawn. This may be done by someone simply forging an 'endorsement' (signature) on the back of a cheque in the name of the payee, which makes the cheque negotiable. Banks aren't required to check the signatures on the back of cheques and in fact couldn't even if they wanted to. Crooks often steal mail and pay cheques into their own accounts. They simply use the name of the payee but their own account number and banks don't check that the payee and account number tally. This makes a mockery of the safety of cheques! Note that cheques usually take three to five days to clear, although some banks have scrapped the cheque-clearing period on payments and credits cheques of up to £1,000 to accounts before they have cleared.

Cheque Safeguards: There are a number of ways to safeguard your cheques, one of which is to write 'not negotiable' between the lines on a crossed cheque. This means that although the cheque can be signed on the back and handed over to someone else, you have legal rights against the person who cashes the cheque if the endorsement was forged. An additional safeguard is to add the words 'account payee only' to the crossing (in between the two parallel lines). Although this has no legal significance, it means that your bank should only credit the account of the named payee and they would be considered negligent if they credited an 'account payee only' cheque to the wrong account. For extra security, you can add both 'not negotiable' and 'account payee only' to a cheque.

Claims: If a cheque is converted, cashed, negotiated or transferred unlawfully, your bank will probably take refuge behind the law and refuse to accept any responsibility (unless you have £billions on deposit). However, if the amount or other details on a cheque are changed and your bank pays out, it cannot make you liable for the forgery. If you're a victim of fraud and believe your bank or building society was negligent, you should demand compensation. If it isn't offered you should take your case to the ombudsman.

Charges: All banks make a charge for 'bounced' cheques. If you accidentally go into the red for a few days and are charged bank charges for a full month or three months, a complaint to your bank manager in writing, if necessary threatening to transfer your account elsewhere, may get you a reduction (if not, you can always carry out your threat). Most banks and building societies have a long list of service charges for current accounts. Note, however, that providing you stay in credit it's still possible to avoid paying charges by shopping around. If you're thinking of changing banks (or building society), check whether you will lose any important benefits such as a credit card (with a high spending limit) or a preferential loan or overdraft facility.

High-Interest Cheque Accounts: Most banks and building societies offer high-interest cheque accounts for customers who maintain a minimum balance, e.g. £1,000 to £5,000. These accounts offer a range of benefits including a cheap overdraft facility and a £250 cheque guarantee card. Some current accounts pay variable rates of interest depending on the account balance. Interest on high-interest accounts may be paid monthly and there's usually no transaction or monthly fees. However, if you don't need instant access to large sums of cash, you're better off with a savings account than a high-interest cheque account. **It's never advisable to keep a lot of cash in an account with a cash card, as fraudulent withdrawals aren't unknown!** It would appear that many people in Britain have money to throw away, as they keep quite large sums in accounts that pay no interest or minimal interest only, e.g. 0.5 per cent. Naturally banks don't go out of their way to explain to customers the most advantageous accounts for their money, or indeed even explain about account fees or charges (some banks even forbid staff to tell customers about more favourable accounts). Even modest balances in an interest-earning account can earn enough to ward off inflation. If you never overdraw on your current account and aren't being paid interest, you're making a free loan to your bank (something they most certainly *won't* do for you).

Offshore Banking

If you have a sum of money to invest or wish to protect your inheritance from the tax man, it may be worthwhile looking into the accounts and other services (such as pensions and trusts) provided by banks in offshore tax havens such as the Channel Islands (Guernsey and Jersey), Gibraltar and the Isle of Man (around 50 locations world-wide are officially classified as tax havens). The big attraction of offshore banking is that money can be deposited in a wide range of currencies, customers are usually guaranteed complete anonymity, there are no double-taxation agreements, no withholding tax is payable and interest is paid tax-free. Many offshore banks also offer telephone banking (usually seven days a week).

A large number of American, British and other European banks and financial institutions provide offshore banking facilities in one or more locations. Most institutions offer high-interest deposit accounts for long-term savings and investment portfolios, in which funds can be deposited in any major currency. Many people living abroad keep a local account for everyday business and maintain an offshore account for international transactions and investment purposes. However, most financial experts advise investors never to rush into the expatriate life and invest their life savings in an offshore tax haven until they know what their long-term plans are.

Accounts have minimum deposits levels which usually range from £500 to £10,000, with some as high as £100,000. In addition to large minimum balances, accounts may also have stringent terms and conditions, such as restrictions on withdrawals or high early withdrawal penalties. You can deposit funds on call (instant access) or for a fixed period, e.g. from 90 days to one year (usually for larger sums). Interest is usually paid monthly or annually; monthly interest payments are slightly lower than annual payments, although they have the advantage of providing a regular income. There are usually no charges providing a specified minimum balance is maintained. Many accounts offer a cash card (usually aligned with Mastercard or Visa) that can be used to obtain money from cash machines world-wide.

When selecting a financial institution and offshore banking centre, your first priority should be for the safety of your money. In some offshore banking centres bank deposits are guaranteed up to a maximum amount (e.g. £100,000) under a deposit protection scheme should a financial institution go to the wall (the Isle of Man, Guernsey and Jersey all have such schemes). Unless you're planning to bank with a major international bank (which is only likely to fold the day after the end of the world!), you should check the credit rating of a financial institution before depositing any money, particularly if it doesn't provide deposit insurance. All banks have a credit rating (the highest is 'AAA') and a bank with a high rating will be happy to tell you (but get it in writing). You can also check the rating of an international bank or financial organisation with Moody's Investor Service. You should be wary of institutions offering higher than average interest rates, as if it looks too good to be true it probably will be – like the Bank of International Commerce and Credit (BICC) which went bust in 1992.

MORTGAGES

Mortgages (or home loans) in Britain were traditionally provided by building societies, which were created as savings banks for people saving to buy a home. They had a strict lending policy and were reluctant to lend money to anyone who wasn't a regular saver. Nowadays, in addition to building societies, you can obtain a home loan from high street and foreign banks (including offshore banks), insurance companies, mortgage companies (including direct mortgage companies), local authorities and even employers. Competition to lend you money is fierce and homebuyers in Britain have a greater variety of home loan finance available than elsewhere in Europe.

When looking for a mortgage it's important to shop around and compare deals. Most high street banks and building societies offer similar deals and you may get a better deal from a small regional building society, although they may not offer fixed rate mortgages. Major lenders often conceal the best deals, which may only be available through mortgage brokers. Although brokers may not offer you independent advice they can save you money and may be able to offer lower rates, free valuations and more generous cashbacks due to inducements offered by lenders to encourage them to push their products. **It's highly advisable to obtain independent advice before taking out a mortgage in Britain, as mortgage mis-selling is widespread.**

Income: You can usually borrow up to 3.75 times your gross (pre-tax) salary or 2.75 times the joint income of a couple. For example if you earn £25,000 a year and your wife £20,000, you would qualify for a £123,750 mortgage. Note, however that this varies depending on the lender and some will provide only 3.25 times your salary plus the salary of a partner while others lend on the basis of 'affordability', which may allow you to borrow much more than 3.75 times your salary. Up to four people can legally share the ownership of a property, although most lenders allow a maximum of three co-owners. Many people in London and the south-east of England pay between 40 and 50 per cent of their net income in mortgage payments, while in other parts of the country it has fallen to below 30 per cent. Most lenders will give you a 'conditional' decision over the phone and will provide a written 'mortgage promise' that you can show sellers to prove that you're a serious buyer. If you're an employee in steady employment, Britain is one of the easiest countries in the world in which to obtain a mortgage.

Loan-to-Value (LTV): The loan-to-value is the size of the mortgage as a percentage of the price or value of a property. An £80,000 mortgage on a house worth £100,000 is equal to a LTV of 80 per cent. In Britain most borrowers can obtain 90 to 95 per cent mortgages and some lenders offer 100 per cent mortgages (in 1999 some lender were offering up to 125 per cent mortgages!). In many other European countries loans are usually limited to between 50 and 75 per cent of a property's value (the average loan to homebuyers in France, Germany, Holland and Italy is around 60 per cent of the value of a property). Hence the average age of first-time buyers in Britain is around 27, compared, for example, with the mid to late thirties in Germany and Italy. Note that the larger the deposit you can pay (as a percentage of the value), the wider the choice of mortgages and deals available to you.

Mortgage Indemnity Guarantee (MIG): If you borrow more than a certain loan-to-value (LTV), which varies depending on the lender, you must usually take out a mortgage indemnity guarantee (MIG – also called a high lending fee or mortgage risk fee). This is to protect the lender in the event that you're unable to repay the loan and the lender is forced to repossess (see page 107) and sell the property. Many lenders insist on a MIG if you borrow more than 70 or 80 per cent of the value of a property, although many lenders have now dropped MIG on loans of up to 90 per cent of the value of a property. Where applicable the difference between the LTV and the MIG threshold is the amount on which you must pay MIG. For example if you buy a property valued at £100,000 with a 90 per cent mortgage (£90,000) and your lender has a 75 per cent MIG threshold, the amount of the loan attracting MIG will be £90,000 - £75,000 = £15,000. The interest rate charged for MIG varies but if it was 7.5 per cent your premium would be £1,125, which is paid up front or added to the mortgage (although some lenders allow you to pay it over a few years without interest charges). Note that if you add it to the mortgage, a MIG premium of £1,000 would cost you over £3,000 over 25 years, and if you pay a mortgage off early you don't receive a refund of a portion of the MIG.

High-Risk Borrowers: Many lenders won't lend to so-called 'high-risk' borrowers or when they do they levy a higher interest rate. High-risk borrowers generally include the self-employed, contract workers (who are often treated as self-employed), people who have had a lot of jobs in a short period of time, single mothers and divorced women. High-risk borrowers also include those seeking a mortgage for a risky property, e.g. a flat attached to commercial premises such as a shop. They also include those with poor credit ratings who have had mortgage payment arrears (or been repossessed) and people with county court judgements. Around three in ten people are turned down for a mortgage by high street lenders, who usually insist that the self-employed have two or three years' audited accounts to qualify for a standard mortgage or special deals. Some lenders specialise in lending to the self-employed, such as the Bank of Scotland (☎ 0800-810810) and UCB (☎ 0645-501500 – a subsidiary of the Nationwide Building Society, which is a largely untapped market totalling over three million people in Britain.

High-risk borrowers can usually obtain a self-certification (no income qualifier) or special status mortgage of up to 90 per cent of the value, although some lenders will lend up to 75 per cent only. The rates offered to high-risk borrowers are typically 2 to 4 per cent above the standard rates for new customers. Specialist non-status or sub-prime lenders (who lend to high-risk borrowers) include Future Mortgages (☎ 0118-951 4940), the Kensington Mortgage Company (☎ 0207-376 0110), the Money Store (☎ 0800-783 4448) and Paragon Mortgages (☎ 0121-712 2345). Alternatively you can use a mortgage broker to find you a deal, who will charge a fee of around £300. Many people use 'alternative' lenders as a stopgap to rebuild their credit rating or until they can find a better deal, although you need to beware of redemption penalties and avoid the sharks.

Interest Rates: In recent years the cost of a standard variable-rate mortgage has fallen considerably and in late 1999 was below 7 per cent (from a peak of over 15 per cent in 1988), the lowest rate for over 40 years, with most lenders offering even lower short-term rates to new customers. Many experts expect sterling base rates (5 per cent in mid-1999) to come into line with the Euro base rate (which was just 3 per cent in mid-1999) during the next few years. Rates would be even lower if the difference between the rate at which lenders borrow and the rate they charge homeowners hadn't grown over the last few years (profit margins on mortgages in Britain are around double those in many other countries). As the base rate fell to 5 per cent in spring 1999 many lenders refused to pass on cuts to borrowers, ostensibly to protect savers, because when mortgage rates are cut the interest paid to savers must also be reduced. On a £100,000 interest-only mortgage savings would be £485 a year if your interest rate was 0.5 per cent lower, £970 (1 per cent), £1,455 (1.5 per cent), £1,940 (2 per cent), £2,425 (2.5 per cent) and £2,910 (3 per cent).

An important aspect of a mortgage is how interest is calculated, which may be daily, monthly or annually. Daily is the best method for borrowers, as when you make payments (or overpayments) they take effect immediately. With a repayment mortgage, payments include part interest and part capital repayments, and when interest is calculated annually the outstanding debt doesn't decrease daily or even monthly but once a year. This results in you paying interest on money you have already repaid, which has been called downright dishonesty or usury by many analysts! Some lenders claim they cannot calculate interest daily, as it's too expensive to upgrade their computer systems!

The gross monthly payments per £1,000 borrowed for repayment and interest-only mortgages over 20, 25 and 30 years are shown below:

Interest Rate (%)	Repayment Mortgage*			Interest-Only Mortgage#
	20 Years	25 Years	30 Years	
4.00	6.13	5.33	4.82	3.33
4.25	6.27	5.48	4.97	3.54
4.50	6.41	5.62	5.12	3.75
4.75	6.55	5.77	5.27	3.96
5.00	6.69	5.91	5.42	4.17
5.25	6.83	6.06	5.58	4.37
5.50	6.97	6.21	5.73	4.58
5.75	7.12	6.36	5.89	4.79
6.00	7.27	6.52	6.05	5.00
6.25	7.41	6.67	6.22	5.21
6.50	7.58	6.83	6.38	5.42
6.75	7.71	6.99	6.55	5.62
7.00	7.87	7.15	6.72	5.83
7.25	8.02	7.31	6.88	6.04
7.50	8.17	7.48	7.06	6.25
7.75	8.33	7.64	7.23	6.46
8.00	8.49	7.81	7.40	6.67
8.25	8.65	7.97	7.58	6.87
8.50	8.81	8.14	7.75	7.08
8.75	8.97	8.31	7.93	7.29
9.00	9.13	8.48	8.11	7.50
9.25	9.29	8.66	8.29	7.71
9.50	9.46	8.83	8.47	7.92
9.75	9.62	9.00	8.66	8.12
10.00	9.79	9.18	8.84	8.33

* **Repayment Mortgage:** To calculate your mortgage repayments using the above table, simply find the payment that applies to your mortgage rate and term and multiply it by the amount of your mortgage. For example if you borrow £75,000 at 6.75 per cent over 25 years your monthly repayments will be £6.99 x 75 = £524.50.

Interest-Only Mortgage: This column applies only to the interest on your mortgage and the cost of investment element (e.g. endowment, ISA or pension) of your mortgage that's intended to pay off the capital at the end of the loan period must be added.

Discounts: In 1999 there were over 200 mortgage discounts on offer, including fixed rates, discounts and cashback deals. These deals usually run from one to five years, after which the current variable interest rate applies. Although these deals look very attractive there's always a price to pay. In recent years many people have become locked into fixed rate deals that are costing them hundreds or even thousands of pounds a year more than the current variable interest rate. There may also be other restrictions such as early repayment penalties and no capital repayments during the period of a limited fixed, discounted or capped rate of interest. The best deals are offered to new lenders while existing borrowers are ignored, although the days of discount home loans may be numbered if interest rates continue to fall. The things you need to know when considering a discount mortgage include the following:

- the repayment method and time scale;
- the consequences of early repayment and lump sum payments;
- the type of interest rate;
- what the future repayments after any fixed or discounted period may be;
- whether you must take out any insurance through the lender;
- fees such as start-up costs;
- monthly administration charges;
- whether the same terms can be continued if you move house;
- whether you need to pay a percentage lending fee, and if so, how much?

Some deals require you to buy expensive building and contents insurance – typically 30 per cent above identical cover available elsewhere, but it can be double or triple the price – from the lender, who may refuse to give you an insurance quotation until a valuation (which you pay for) has been done. The linking of loans to insurance purchase may be outlawed in future, as it has been with holiday package tours.

Cashback Mortgages: These are traditionally offered with variable rate mortgages and offer up to £20,000 cashback (that you can spend on furniture, decorating and improvements), which is calculated as a percentage of the loan, e.g. from 2 to 8 per cent. Although they sound great – you take out a mortgage and the lender gives you cash! – there's a hidden price including high fees, interest rates and hefty penalties for early redemption. They aren't the best deals around and without a cashback you can obtain a discount off the variable rate for up to five years.

Term: The usual home loan period in Britain is 25 years on repayment mortgages and 40 years for interest-only mortgages linked to an endowment, ISA or pension. Note that reducing the term, say from 25 to 20 years, will save you a lot of money, e.g. £12,000 in interest on a £50,000 repayment mortgage. Most mortgages allow you to pay off lump sums at any time, which can also save you thousands of pounds in interest and reduce the term of your loan. For example a lump sum payment of £5,000 results in a saving of £17,948 on a 20-year mortgage at 7.7 per cent and a payment of £10,000 a saving of £32,551. There are usually minimum lump sum payments, e.g. £500 or £1,000, and lenders may credit lump sum payments immediately, monthly or annually. There are usually penalties with fixed rate loans.

Fixed or Variable Rate: You can generally choose between fixed and variable rate mortgages, where the interest rate goes up and down depending on the base rate. Those who cannot afford an increase in their mortgage repayments are better off with a fixed-rate mortgage, where the interest rate is fixed for a number of years (e.g. one to the whole mortgage term), no matter what happens to the base rate in the meantime. The longer the fixed-rate period, the lower the interest rate offered. If interest rates go down, you may find yourself paying more than the current mortgage rate, but at least you will know exactly what you must pay each month. To judge whether a fixed-rate mortgage is worthwhile, you must estimate in which direction interest rates are heading (a difficult feat even the experts cannot manage). The standard variable rate is usually around 1.5 per cent above the base rate. Building societies typically offer standard variable rate mortgages that are around half a percentage point below high street banks. Some 60 per cent of loans are fixed rate deals and many experts recommend that lenders fix rates to avoid being hit by a rise in the cost of borrowing.

Tracker Mortgages: Tracker mortgages are a variation on variable rate mortgages, where the interest rate is fixed at a set percentage above the base rate. This means that it 'tracks' the base rate and therefore guarantees that your monthly repayments fall (or rise!) in line with the basic rate. Note that some tracker mortgages track the base rate for a number of years only, before reverting to the lender's standard variable rate. Loans may be linked to hefty redemption penalties and you may need to take out life insurance to obtain the best rate (always read the small print). Although relatively new, tracker mortgages are becoming increasingly popular with borrowers, particularly as most lenders have failed to pass on cuts in the base rate in full to borrowers in recent years. Some lenders offer discounts on tracker mortgages for a number of months or years. Rates vary considerably, e.g. from 0.7 to 1.45 per cent above the base rate, so you should shop around for the best rate.

Fees: There are various fees associated with mortgages. All lenders charge an arrangement fee (also called a completion, booking or reservation fee) for establishing a loan, which is either a fixed amount or a percentage of the loan. This is usually from £150 to £400 and is paid when you apply for a loan or when you accept a mortgage. This has been branded a rip-off by mortgage brokers and others in the loan business, particularly as some 20 per cent of purchases fall through and lenders keep the fee. Some lenders charge an up-front application fee and a completion fee when you accept the mortgage. Mortgage brokers may also levy a fee, e.g. 1 per cent of the value of the loan or a fee starting at around £300 to find you a deal. Always check whether fees are refundable if the purchase falls through. There's usually a valuation fee of around £200 and the lender's legal fees, although many lenders now waive these.

MIRAS: Mortgage Interest Relief at Source (MIRAS) is allowed on mortgage interest payments at your highest rate of tax, up to a limit of £30,000. Relief was restricted to 10 per cent on the first £30,000 of a mortgage for the 1999/2000 tax year. For example if your mortgage rate is 7 per cent you pay £2,100 in interest on £30,000, on which tax relief is 10 per cent or £210. **MIRAS will be abolished on April 6th 2000.**

Types of Mortgages: Once you've calculated how much you wish to pay for a home, you must decide what kind of mortgage you want. Although there are many different mortgages on the market, all fall into two main categories: repayment and interest-only. Most interest-only mortgages are linked to an endowment, investment (such as an ISA) or a pension plan.

Repayment Mortgages: These are so called because you repay the original loan and interest over the period of the mortgage, similar to most personal loans. As interest rates rise and fall, your repayments go up or down, but assuming a constant interest rate your payments would remain the same for the period of the loan. One advantage is that the term of the loan can be extended if you have trouble meeting your monthly repayments. A disadvantage of a repayment mortgage is that you don't have a life policy and you must therefore take out a 'mortgage protection' policy to ensure that your loan is paid off if you die. This policy isn't expensive as it pays off the mortgage only if you die before the term of the loan is completed (and the term and amount owed decreases over time). For the majority of people, a repayment mortgage together with adequate life insurance is the best choice.

Interest-Only Mortgages: These are offered by most lenders, where you take out a mortgage loan in the normal way and pay interest as usual. However, instead of agreeing to repay the loan at a fixed date in the future, the loan simply stays in existence until you (not the lender) decide to repay it, which could be anytime from six months to 60 years. Interest-only loans are good for single people with no dependants, heavily mortgaged families, those whose earnings fluctuate and people who expect to inherit money. It isn't necessary to have an insurance policy to repay the loan should you die, but it's advisable if others are dependent on your income. Most lenders will only lend from 50 to 75 per cent of a property's value on an interest-only mortgage *without* a linked investment. For most people with an interest-only mortgage, it's essential to make provision for repaying the capital sum at the end of the original mortgage term, which can be done with an endowment, investment-linked or pension mortgage, which are described below:

Endowment Mortgage: With an endowment mortgage you pay interest over the length of the loan. You also take out an endowment life insurance policy, which will hopefully provide a large enough lump sum to pay off the mortgage at the end of the term, usually 25 years. Your monthly mortgage payments are made up of an interest payment and an insurance (endowment) payment. The policy also carries life insurance, which ensures that if you die the mortgage is paid off in full and any money left over is paid to your estate. The loan and endowment are separate and you can obtain them from different sources. You should obtain independent advice and try to find a lender with a low interest rate and an insurance company with a good track record.

Like all endowment policies, you could be left with a tax-free sum at the end of the term after your loan has been paid off, although there are no guarantees. Endowment mortgages have been performing badly in the last decade and in the late '90s many weren't on target to repay loans, let alone provide a surplus! Many people have had to increase their premiums (for the endowment) because of poor returns and high charges, and some endowments are worth less than the holders have paid in, even after ten years! One advantage of an endowment loan is that the life policy can be transferred when you move house. If moving home results in a bigger loan, you take out a new policy to cover the increase and continue to pay the premiums on earlier policies. Don't allow yourself to be persuaded to surrender an existing policy simply to take out another without good reason. If you surrender your old endowment policy and take out a new policy, you stand to forfeit £thousands as a penalty.

This buying and selling of endowment policies to generate commissions, is called 'churning' in the industry and is encouraged by some lenders. The reason endowment mortgages were so popular is that they were heavily promoted by lenders (who usually don't tell borrowers about the disadvantages, such as high commissions and fees, or alternatives) due to the high commission on the endowment. However, endowment mortgages have plummeted in recent years and now comprise some 30 per cent of the total, compared with 80 per cent in the '80s. Endowment mortgages aren't recommended for first-time buyers with limited financial resources and low salaries, who should consider a repayment mortgage, which is more flexible if you have trouble meeting your repayments. However, they are the best choice for some people.

If you decide on an endowment mortgage, you must then choose the type of policy that suits you. A with-profits policy is the most expensive and therefore isn't so popular nowadays. Bonuses are added regularly, which once paid cannot be taken away, and there's usually also a final termination bonus. Your payments are invested in a wide range of investments and the level of bonuses you receive is determined by the skills (or otherwise) of your fund manager and the performance of the stock market. Don't be taken in by the promise of a huge lump sum in 25 years time, which after inflation has been taken into account may not be worth much. In recent years, with-profits insurance policies have looked less attractive when compared with the alternatives. **It has been estimated that millions of people have been sold 'useless' endowment mortgages in recent years and you should be extremely cautious about taking out one, and should only do so after considering all other options and obtaining independent financial advice.**

Investment-Linked or ISA Mortgages: Investment-linked mortgages are generally linked to an Individual Savings Account (ISA), which replaced Personal Equity Plan (PEP) mortgages in 1999, both of which are tax-free savings schemes. With an ISA mortgage you set up the finance for a home in the usual way, but you repay only the interest (not the capital) on the debt each month. At the same time you take out an ISA where your tax-free monthly contributions should grow over the mortgage term to enable you to repay the capital debt (hopefully with a surplus), in the same way as an endowment mortgage. As a general rule you need to invest £15 a month for each £10,000 of mortgage, e.g. if you have a £100,000 mortgage your make monthly ISA contributions of £150.

The main advantage is that you don't need to pay income tax or capital gains tax on your ISA investment. ISA home loans are more flexible than endowment mortgages as they don't have high start-up fees, they have a fixed life and you can withdraw some of your investment to repay your loan early. You can also usually stop, start and vary contributions without penalty. You do, however, need to take some investment risk and near the end of the term it's important that your investment is switched to low-risk investments to guard against a stock market crash. One drawback is that ISAs are guaranteed to exist for ten years only, although if they are terminated they are likely to be replaced with a similar tax-free savings scheme. Some lenders insist that you also take out a life insurance policy.

Pension-Linked Mortgages: These are broadly similar to endowment mortgages, where monthly interest is paid on the loan. However, with a pension mortgage you pay into a personal pension plan that pays off your mortgage on retirement and also pays you a pension. This is a good choice for the self-employed and for employees who aren't members of a company pension scheme, as the pension premiums attract tax relief at your highest tax rate and you can pay in from 17.5 to 40 per cent of your annual earnings, depending on your age. They are, however, inflexible and you must stipulate a retirement date from the outset. When you retire, 25 per cent of your fund can be taken as a lump sum and used to pay off your mortgage, although there's no guarantee that the pension will produce enough to repay the mortgage.

Flexible or Current Account Mortgage: One of the most profitable innovations for homebuyers in recent years has been the flexible or current account mortgage (also called an 'all-in-one' account), where you operate your mortgage as a current account within certain limits. With a current account mortgage you have your salary paid into your mortgage account, which automatically reduces your mortgage debt and saves you interest until you withdraw money (interest is calculated daily). You also earn the same interest rate on your savings as you pay on your mortgage and you can borrow additional funds at any time at the same interest rate you pay for your mortgage. **Analysts agree that these accounts are difficult to beat and if you make full use of the account you could save tens of thousands of pounds and pay off your borrowing as quickly or slowly as you wish.** A typical £100,000 25-year mortgage could be paid off within 17 years with a flexible mortgage, which are expected to become the standard mortgage in the future. Among the lenders offering this type of loan are Virgin One (☎ 08456-000001, Internet: www.virgen-direct.co.uk), First Active (☎ 0800-550551) and Kleinwort Benson (☎ 0800-317477), although not all allow over payments, payment holidays, a cheque book and borrow back (one that does is the Virgin One Account).

Self-Build Mortgages: If you wish to build your own home (e.g. buying a plot of land, engaging an architect and builder, etc. – you don't need to physically build it yourself), you can obtain a self-build mortgage where the money is released in stages once building has begun until the loan is fully drawn. Note, however, that many lenders won't lend on the cost of the land and you usually need a 20 to 25 per cent deposit. Moneyfacts magazine (☎ 01692-500677) publishes a list of lenders offering self-build mortgages, together with brief terms and conditions. The main lenders include the Bradford & Bingley and Norwich & Peterborough building societies in England and Wales, and TSB Scotland in Scotland. These lenders are prepared to lend on the cost of the land and the construction. The sum you can borrow is calculated on the valuation rather than the cost of a home, therefore you should easily be able to borrow sufficient to build a home. See also **Building Your Own Home** on page 170.

Buy-to-Let Mortgages: In recent years special 'buy-to-let' mortgages have been introduced for those wishing to buy an investment property and have proved very popular. Most lenders will lend a maximum of 75 or 80 per cent of the value of a property (some will lend on up to five properties to a single borrower) and will also lend to first time buyers. Most mortgages are variable rate and some offer a discount for a number of years. Note that if you take out a second mortgage you must inform both lenders that you're paying two mortgages, otherwise you'll be committing mortgage fraud. Surplus rental income can be used to make overpayments on your mortgage and you can have rental payments paid directly into your mortgage 'account' if you have a flexible mortgage (see above).

Re-mortgaging & Redemption Charges: Many people find that it pays to re-mortgage (i.e. take out a new mortgage) if they have a high interest loan, which can save £thousands a year. However, most fixed, capped, discounted and cashback deals come with penalties if you repay your loan early or switch to another deal. Penalty clauses typically keep you tied in for up to seven years and if you redeem the loan early you must repay any benefits or pay up to around nine month' interest. For example six months interest on a £75,000 loan at 7 per cent is £2,625. Mortgage lock-ins and redemption charges have caused a lot of anger in recent years and may be outlawed by the government (if the courts don't do it first). Nevertheless, as the base rate has fallen sharply in recent years, many people find that they can re-mortgage and still save money, providing of course interest rates don't start rising again. Fixed-rate mortgages (where the rate is fixed for the whole term) often have crippling early repayment costs, e.g. £50,000 or more! This is because the lender 'purchased' the money for the loan at a fixed interest rate when the borrower took out the loan. Many people on fixed-rate loans are paying £hundreds or even £thousands a year more for fixed rate mortgages taken out in the last few years before interest rates started falling.

Repossession: If you fall behind with your payments a lender may allow you to re-mortgage your home to reduce your payments. However, if you fall too far behind, for example six months or over one year, or stop paying altogether without notifying your lender, they will eventually take steps to repossess your home. If your home is repossessed it will be sold at auction and if the amount recovered is less than that owed to your lender, you may be sued for the balance by your lender or the MIG company. Note that lenders are required by law to print the following warning in all advertisements and literature: 'Your home is at risk if you don't keep up repayments on a mortgage or loan secured on it.' It means exactly what it says and is why lenders (particularly crooks) are so keen to lend to homeowners. Lenders have been getting tougher with those in arrears in the last decade, during which over 500,000 homes have been repossessed by lenders in Britain.

Advice & Information: Whatever kind of mortgage you want, you should shop around and take the time to investigate all the options available. One way to find the best deal is to contact an independent mortgage broker. Mortgage advice offered by lenders is often misleading and biased and not to be trusted (surveys have found that the mis-selling of mortgages is widespread among high street lenders). The best independent advice is found in surveys carried out by publications such as *Which?* magazine (see **Appendix A**), that accepts no advertisements, and daily newspapers. The best variable, fixed-rate and discount mortgage rates are published in Sunday newspapers such as *The Sunday Times*, *The Sunday Telegraph*, *The Observer* and *The Independent on Sunday*, and in monthly mortgage magazines such as *What Mortgage* and *Mortgage Magazine*. You can also make quick comparisons on the Internet (e.g. www.moneynet.co.uk, www.moneyextra.co.uk, www.ftquicken.com, www.propertycity.co.uk and www.moneyworld.co.uk).

A Mortgage Code for lenders was introduced in recent years and is available from lenders or the Council of Mortgage Lenders, 3 Saville Row, London W1X 1AF (☎ 0207-437 0075). However, it has been criticised as too vague and is already being broken by many lenders.

See also **Mortgage Protection Insurance** on page 65.

Mortgages for Second Homes

Mortgages for second homes are available from most lenders in Britain and a number of offshore banks. In recent years special 'buy-to-let' mortgages (see page 106) have been introduced for those wishing to buy an investment property. However, it's difficult for non-residents to obtain a mortgage for a second home in Britain and usually only up to 75 or 80 per cent of its value can be borrowed. Interest rates for non-residents are also usually higher than for residents. Many people find it difficult to obtain a mortgage outside of Britain for a British home without collateral. If you have spare equity in an existing property (either in Britain or abroad), then it's usually more cost effective to re-mortgage that property than take out a new mortgage for a second home. It involves less paperwork and therefore lower legal fees, and a plan can be tailored to meet your individual requirements. Depending on the equity in your existing property and the cost of a British home, this may enable you to pay cash for a second home.

Foreign Currency Mortgages: It's also possible to obtain a foreign currency mortgage, e.g. in Euros, Swiss francs, US dollars, Deutschmarks or Japanese yen, all currencies with historically low interest rates that have provided huge savings for borrowers in recent years. However, you should be cautious about taking out a foreign currency mortgage, as interest rate gains can be wiped out overnight by currency swings. Most lenders such as high street banks and building societies, advise against taking out foreign currency home loans unless you're paid in a foreign currency (such as Euros). Euro loans are available for expatriates paid in Euros. This offers lower interest rates than sterling, but usually requires a higher deposit (e.g. 30 per cent) and a high booking fee, e.g. £500.

The lending conditions for foreign currency home loans are stricter than for sterling loans and are generally granted only to high-rollers (those earning a minimum of £40,000 or £50,000 a year) and may be for a minimum of £100,000 and a maximum of 60 per cent of a property's value. If you take out a foreign currency loan with an offshore bank, switching between major currencies is usually permitted. When choosing between a sterling loan and a foreign currency loan, be sure to take into account all charges, fees, interest rates and possible currency fluctuations. However you finance the purchase of a second home in Britain, you should obtain professional advice from your bank manager and accountant.

Note that if you have a foreign currency mortgage, you must usually pay commission charges each time you make a transfer to pay your mortgage or remit money to Britain (although some lenders will transfer mortgage payments to Britain each month free of charge or for a nominal amount). If you let a second home, you may be able to offset the interest on your mortgage (pro rata) against rental income.

VALUE ADDED TAX (VAT)

Value Added Tax (VAT) is payable at a standard rate of 17.5 per cent on all goods and services in Britain, with the exception of domestic fuels on which the rate is 8 per cent. The following goods and services are zero rated:

- most food (but not catering, which includes meals in restaurants, cafés, and hot take-away food and drink);
- sales and long leases of new buildings, construction of most new buildings (but not work to existing buildings);
- young children's clothing and footwear;
- books and newspapers;
- mobile homes and house boats;
- dispensing of prescriptions and the supply of many aids for handicapped people;
- the export of goods.

Certain business transactions are exempt from VAT (not the same as zero rated), on which VAT isn't applicable. Exempt supplies include most sales, leases and lettings of land and buildings; insurance; betting, gaming and lotteries; the provision of credit; certain education and training; and the services of doctors, dentists and opticians.

If you're self-employed and your annual turnover (not just profits) is more than £51,000 annually, you must be registered for VAT. A business which makes exempt supplies only cannot register for VAT, but a company making zero-rated supplies can. An individual is registered for VAT, not a business, and registration covers *all* the business activities of the registered person. The prices of some goods, e.g. computers and other business equipment, are advertised or quoted exclusive of VAT (although almost all other advertised prices are inclusive of VAT). The VAT you're charged on goods and services that you use in setting up your business can be reclaimed, subject to certain conditions.

There are stiff penalties for anyone who fails to register for VAT or who makes a false declaration. A serious wrong declaration could result in a 30 per cent penalty (even for accidental errors) plus interest being levied on all underpayments. There are also penalties for making late returns, which must usually be made quarterly (this may be extended to annually for traders with an annual turnover under the £50,000 threshold). If you're in any doubt as to your registration or VAT declarations, you should contact your local VAT office, the address of which is in your local phone book under 'Custom and Excise'. A range of VAT publications and leaflets are published, including *Should I be Registered for VAT* and *The VAT Guide*, copies of which are sent to you when you register. All VAT publications are available on request from VAT offices. Many people believe VAT is actually short for Vague Additions to the Total (it's usually the difference between a reasonable price and too expensive).

It's the declared aim of the EU to eventually have just one universal rate of VAT for the whole union, although this will take some time (i.e. eons) to accomplish.

INCOME TAX

It's hardly surprising that the British don't always see eye to eye with the French. After all it was because of a damned Frenchman (Napoleon) that income tax was introduced in 1799 (the 'good' news is that it was introduced as a temporary measure only and may be rescinded at any time!). Another Frenchman, William the Conqueror, was to blame for the introduction of the budget.

Domicile: Your liability for British taxes depends on where you're domiciled and whether you're a British resident. Your domicile is the country which you regard as your natural and permanent home, so unless you intend to live in Britain permanently you won't normally be considered to be domiciled there. A person can be resident in more than one country, but at any given time can be domiciled in one only. From 1st January 1974 the domicile of a married women hasn't necessarily been the same as her husband's, but is decided using the same criteria as anyone capable of having an independent domicile.

To be regarded as resident in Britain for a given tax year (the tax year in Britain runs from the 5th April to the 6th April of the following year and not a calendar year), you must normally be physically present there for at least part of that year. You will always be regarded as resident in Britain with regard to income tax if you spend six months (183 days) or more there in any one year (whether in one continuous period or during a number of visits). A resident in Britain may be classified as 'resident' or 'ordinarily resident'. Ordinarily resident is broadly equivalent to being habitually resident, i.e. a person who's resident in Britain year after year is ordinarily resident there. A person may be resident but not ordinarily resident in Britain for a given tax year, e.g. he could normally live outside Britain but visit Britain for six months or more in that year. Alternatively he may be ordinarily resident in Britain, but not resident for a given tax year, e.g. he usually lives in Britain but goes abroad for a long holiday and doesn't set foot in Britain during that year. Each tax year is looked at as a whole and a person can be classified only as resident or non-resident for a particular tax year and not, for example, resident for part of the year and non-resident for the remainder.

If you're a new permanent resident in Britain (i.e. someone not ordinarily resident there), you will be considered resident only from the time of your arrival (the same rule applies to anyone leaving Britain for permanent residence abroad, who becomes not ordinarily resident in Britain from the time he left). If you're classified as a resident in Britain, you will be liable to British income tax on all income arising from a source in Britain. If you're a British resident *and* domiciled in Britain, you're liable for taxation in Britain on your world-wide income, including capital gains tax. A booklet entitled *Residents and Non-residents - Liability to tax in the United Kingdom* (IR20) explains the rules outlined above.

Double Taxation Agreements: Britain has double taxation agreements with around 80 countries, which despite the name, are to prevent you paying double taxes and not to ensure that you pay twice. Under double taxation treaties, certain categories of people are exempt from paying British tax. If part of your income is taxed abroad in a country with a double taxation treaty with Britain, you won't need to pay British tax on that income. If you're a British citizen living abroad, you won't usually be liable for British tax providing your absence from Britain covers a complete tax year and you don't:

- remain in Britain for 183 days or more in any tax year;

- have accommodation available in Britain and don't make any visits to Britain no matter how short, unless you're employed full-time abroad;

- visit Britain for more than three months a year in four or more consecutive years.

Besides British taxes, you may also be liable for taxes in your home country. Citizens of most countries are exempt from paying taxes in their home country when they spend a minimum period abroad, e.g. one year. It's usually your responsibility to familiarise yourself with the latest tax procedures in your home country or country of domicile. If you're in doubt about your tax liability in your home country, contact your embassy or consulate. It's possible for some foreigners to live legally in Britain without paying British tax. To qualify you must reside in Britain for less than 183 days in a calendar year or your salary (if applicable) must be paid and taxed by your employer in another country with a 'double taxation' treaty (see above) with Britain. For information about double taxation agreements, refer to the leaflet *Double Taxation Relief* (IR6), available from tax offices.

Tax Rates: Britain has three income tax rates (1999/2000). The first £1,500 of taxable income is taxed at the **lower rate** of 10 per cent. Taxable income from £1,501 to £28,000 is taxed at 23 per cent (this will be reduced to 22 per cent from April

2000), known as the **basic rate** of tax. The **higher rate** tax of 40 per cent is the highest rate of tax on earned income in Britain and is payable on taxable income above £28,000 a year. The rate of income tax payable in Britain is among the lowest in Europe. Your taxable income is your income after all allowances and deductions have been made from your gross income (from all sources).

Like everything in Britain, there's a two-tier tax system, 'first class' for the self-employed and a 'second class' system, called Pay-As-You-Earn (PAYE), for employees. The self-employed pay their tax in arrears (as all employees do in many European countries), whereas an employee's income tax is deducted at source weekly or monthly from his salary by his employer. Although the Inland Revenue (IR) may give individuals a hard time when it comes to paying their tax bills, British companies withhold £billions from the tax authorities each year due to disputed corporation tax bills, plus £billions more that's contested by the self-employed and those owing capital gains tax.

Tax Evasion: Tax evasion is illegal and is a criminal offence in Britain, for which you can be heavily fined or even sent to prison. Nevertheless, there's a flourishing black economy which the Inland Revenue estimate amounts to around £10 billion a year in unpaid tax on undeclared income. The IR has tightened up its ability to collect tax and catch tax dodgers in recent years and carries out investigations into tens of thousands of 'suspicious' tax returns each year (it has 12 months from the date you file a return to launch an enquiry). In most cases where taxpayers owe money, the investigation is conducted out of court with taxpayers making a full disclosure and a monetary settlement.

Tax Avoidance: Tax avoidance, i.e. legally paying as little tax as possible, if necessary by finding and exploiting loopholes in the tax laws, is a different matter altogether (from tax evasion). It's practised by most companies, wealthy individuals and self-employed people, although the opportunities for anyone paying direct PAYE tax are strictly limited. Unfortunately there are few (legal) ways an individual paying PAYE tax can reduce his income tax bill (dying is one of them), although it's possible to appeal against your PAYE coding notice (see page 113) or anything connected with your tax affairs that you believe is incorrect. Whether you're self-employed or an employee, you should ensure that you don't pay any more tax than is necessary.

Accountants: If your tax affairs are complicated or you're unable to understand your own finances (like the majority of people), you should consider employing an accountant to deal with your tax affairs (most high street banks also provide a personal tax service). This probably applies to most self-employed people, but very few who are on PAYE (see page 113). However, don't just pick an accountant with a pin from the phone book, but ask your friends, colleagues or business associates if they can recommend someone. If you're self-employed, you should choose an accountant who deals with people in your line of business and who knows exactly what you can (and cannot) claim.

Substantial tax savings can be made with regard to pensions, independent taxation, and trusts to avoid capital gains and inheritance tax. Some tax avoidance schemes apply only to the very rich as the cost of using them is prohibitive to anyone else. As soon as the Inland Revenue close one loophole tax accountants find another one. Accountant's fees vary from £50 to £150 or more an hour, so ask in advance what the rates are (they're highest in London). Avoid 'high-power' accountants who will cost you the earth. You can reduce your accountant's fees considerably by keeping itemised records of all your business expenses (preferably on computer), rather than handing him a pile of invoices and receipts. Note, however, that a good accountant will usually save you more than he charges in fees.

Tax Changes: Changes in direct or indirect taxation are generally announced in the main Budget Statement in March each year. Changes to income tax come into effect in the following tax year (from 6th April to 5th April), although amendments can be made at any time and some tax changes don't come into effect until a year later. Taxes and allowances quoted in this section largely refer to the 1999-2000 tax year (ending on 5th April 2000).

Information: There are many books published about how to reduce your income tax bill including the Daily Mail *Income Tax Guide* and the Daily Telegraph *Guide to Income Tax*. The Consumer's Association publish an annual *Tax Saving Guide* which isn't sold by newsagents or bookshops but is 'free' to subscribers of *Which?* magazine (see **Appendix A**), plus an annual guide entitled *Which? Way To Save Tax*. A tax guide written especially for the elderly is *Your Tax and Savings* by John Burke, available from Age Concern England. The Inland Revenue publish a huge number of leaflets on every conceivable tax subject, all of which are listed in a leaflet entitled *Catalogue of leaflets and booklets*. Copies of tax leaflets can be ordered by phone from tax offices and tax enquiry centres (TECs), which are usually open from 1000 to 1600. If you have a home or business computer, a number of tax computer programs are available such as *QuickTax* (Intuit) and *TaxCalc* (Which? Books), designed to make it easier to calculate and check your income tax payments.

Finally, never trust the tax man to take only what he should or to allow you the correct allowances and deductions. While the IR won't cheat you deliberately, it isn't uncommon for them to make mistakes. If you pay PAYE tax, make sure that your tax code is correct (see page 113) and never hesitate to dispute a tax bill with which you disagree. It's estimated that Britons pay some £5 billion in unnecessary tax each year (mostly on income) and that savers and investors waste millions of pounds by not taking advantage of tax concessions.

Independent Taxation

Under independent taxation, spouses are allocated their own tax allowances and privacy in their dealings with the Inland Revenue. Each partner has his or her own tax bill and needn't tell the other what they earn or how much tax they pay (not that most people would dream of telling fibs about their income to their spouses). Note, however, that a couple usually need to work together to make the most of independent taxation. Prior to the introduction of independent taxation (April 1990), a wife didn't pay her own tax on savings and investments, even if a couple opted for separate taxation, and her husband was responsible for the tax bill on her investments.

Married couples can reduce their tax bill by switching savings and assets between them. If one partner isn't working it's important to put any savings in the non-working partner's name in an account or investment that pays interest gross, and which allows the interest to be offset against the tax allowance. Despite the savings to be made, many couples are slow to take advantage of tax rules. In addition to a personal allowance, married couples also receive a married couple's allowance, usually claimed by the male partner. The down side of independent taxation is the extra work involved in completing two tax returns and the extra cost if an accountant is employed. The Inland Revenue publish many leaflets about independent taxation and most banks and building societies offer free advice.

Pay As You Earn (PAYE)

Income tax is collected by the Inland Revenue (IR). All employees pay direct income tax or Pay As You Earn (PAYE) income tax, which is deducted from gross salaries at source by employers. PAYE isn't a separate tax, but simply the name given to the system of direct (income) taxation in Britain. Any additional income, whether tax is deducted at source or not, must be declared to the Inland Revenue. This may include part-time employment or income from investments or savings. PAYE tax applies to all income tax which is payable on earnings to which the scheme relates and includes tax at both the basic and higher rates.

Some employers may not deduct PAYE tax from an employee's earnings, particularly in the case of casual or part-time employees, and where the distinction between employee and self-employed is blurred. This is illegal and a hazardous practice for employers, who are responsible for deducting all their employees' income tax at source, unless a person is categorised as self-employed by the tax office. Tax on Unemployment Benefit and other social security benefits, such as Maternity Pay and Statutory Sick Pay, also comes within the PAYE scheme. The PAYE scheme is disadvantageous to many employees, who would be entitled to claim larger and more allowances if they were classified as self-employed, and would also have the benefit of paying their tax in arrears.

PAYE Tax Code

In Britain, the level of tax for those taxed under the PAYE system is denoted by a tax code. A notice of coding 'Form P2 (T)' is sent out in January or February for the tax year starting in April, to both employers and employees (although not everyone receives one each year). When you receive a new code, your notice of coding will show how the calculations have been made. You should check that the deductions, allowances and the total are correct. You don't receive a notice each year, but your current tax code is always given on your pay or wage slip (which you get when you receive your weekly or monthly salary). Your pay slip also shows your gross pay (your salary without any deductions) to date and the amount of tax you have paid to date.

If your circumstances change you should tell the Inland Revenue. They will either send you a new income tax return to complete (see below) or simply change your tax code. You must inform the IR of any changes in your tax status, e.g. marriage, a dependent relative, divorce or separation, which entitles you to an additional allowance, or a change in your income (maybe from a part-time job) or company benefits (e.g. a company car). It's in your interest to do this, as when the Inland Revenue find out later you won't only be liable for any tax owed plus interest, but can also be fined up to 100 per cent of the amount of unpaid tax.

Your tax code is also printed on your P45, a certificate given to you when you leave your employment and which should be given to a new employer when you start a new job. Your P45 shows your PAYE code, your total earnings and how much tax you've paid since the start of the current tax year. If you're unemployed after leaving a job and are eligible to claim Jobseeker's Allowance (i.e. unemployment benefit), you must give your P45 to the benefit office when registering for Unemployment Benefit. When you find a job, the benefit office will give you a P45 for your new employer. If you don't have a P45 when starting a job, e.g. for your first job after school or after arriving in Britain from abroad, you should ask your new employer for a P15 *Notice of coding* form. Complete this form and ask your employer to send it to the IR, who will then give you a tax code (you can send it yourself if you want to keep the information private). Your employer will also complete a P46 form (stating your salary) to notify the Inland Revenue that you're employed by him, which you will be asked to sign. If you don't have a P45 on starting a job, your employer will tax you under a special system called an emergency code. If you pay too much tax, it will be repaid by your employer in your next pay cheque as soon as he receives your PAYE tax code.

Your tax code is made up of a series of numbers (usually three) and a letter, e.g. 645H. The numbers are the total allowances minus the last digit, e.g. allowances of £6457 become code number 645. A code of 0 (zero) applies when you have two or more jobs and your allowances have already been used to calculate the code number for your main employment. Some codes don't have a number or have numbers that don't stand for allowances, e.g. BR or DO. The letter tells the Inland Revenue you tax status as shown below:

Code	Status/Meaning
BR	tax is deducted at the basic rate;
DO	tax is deducted at a higher rate;
H	you're entitled to the personal allowance for those aged under 65 plus the married couple's allowance for those under 65 or the additional personal allowance;
K	deductions from your free-of-tax pay, such as taxable state benefits, exceed your personal allowances;
L	entitlement to the basic personal allowance (for those aged under 65);
NT	no tax is to be deducted;
OT	you receive no allowances after adjustments and tax is deducted at the lower, basic and higher rates depending on your income;
P	entitlement to the personal allowance for those aged 65 to 74;
T	someone who doesn't fall within the above categories (e.g. no allowance due to other employment) or someone whose code should end in H, L, P or V, but doesn't want an employer to know his or her status;
V	someone who's entitled to the personal and married couple's allowance for those aged 65 to 74.

If you have the letter H, L, P or V after your tax number, your employer can alter your tax when allowances are changed by a budget. If you have a T code and allowances are changed by the budget, the IR will need to work out your code again and inform both you and your employer. Codes BR and DO are affected only if the tax rates or bands change. The tax code is used by your employer to calculate the amount of income tax to be deducted from your salary. If it's wrong, tell the Inland Revenue. Never assume that your tax code is correct, but check it yourself or ask an accountant or tax expert to check it for you. If you have any questions about tax, contact any tax office or tax enquiry centre. Around April you should receive a form P60 showing how much tax you have paid in the previous tax year. You should check it and keep it in a safe place as you may be asked to produce it at a later date.

There are a number of forms with which to reclaim tax or ensure you don't pay tax unnecessarily. These include a form P50 which is used to reclaim tax, for example when you return to work after a period of not working, during which you didn't claim Unemployment Benefit. A form P187 is used to reclaim tax if you have no P45 and a form R40(S) is used to reclaim tax if you think you've paid too much (for whatever reason). Students should complete a form P38(S) when they start a holiday job and think their total taxable income for the whole tax year is likely to be *less* than the basic personal allowance. This will ensure you don't pay tax on your holiday earnings or that it's refunded.

Self-Employed

One person in eight in Britain is self-employed, either as a 'sole trader' or in partnership with others. You're generally much better off if you're self-employed, as you can claim more in the way of expenses than employees (paying PAYE tax). Another advantage for the self-employed is the delay between making profits (hopefully) and paying tax on them. To be treated as self-employed, you must convince your tax office that you're genuinely self-employed and in business for yourself. The definition of self-employed is much the same as in most other countries and includes:

- working freelance for a number of clients;
- supplying your own tools or equipment;
- risking your own money in a business;
- having the final say in how the business is run;
- using your home as your office;
- responsibility for meeting losses as well as taking profits;
- the freedom to hire other people on your own terms and paying them out of your own pocket;
- correcting unsatisfactory work in your own time at your own expense;
- paying your own expenses and charging an overall fee for your services.

To check whether you're entitled to be self-employed, contact your local Inland Revenue office (see also leaflet IR56 *Employed or Self-employed*). If they decide that you're self-employed, get your tax office to confirm its decision in writing. Self-employed, as used in Britain, means a 'sole trader' or someone in a partnership, and not someone with a limited company. If you have a Limited Company you must pay Corporation Tax on your profits and will need the services of an accountant to deal with this. If your total turnover is less than £10,000 a year, you aren't required to submit detailed accounts to your tax office, but can give the Inland Revenue 'three-line accounts' showing turnover, expenditure and profits only.

Prior to 6th April 1994, the self-employed weren't required to pay tax on their profits for their first tax year until after the end of that year, as no assessment was made until you had been in business for 12 months. However, from 6th April 1994, new self-employed persons have been taxed on what they earn in the current tax year and not their preceding year's earnings. With the introduction of self–assessment (see page 119), the self-employed (and those who receive income from letting property or who have income from savings or investments that isn't taxed at source) must pay their income tax on account, as advance payments towards their final tax bill. Payments on account are due on 1st January and 1st July each year. The second instalment in July is for the previous tax year ending in April of that year, e.g. the July 2000 payment is the second instalment of income tax for the tax year 1999/2000. Usually each payment is equal to half your tax liability for the previous tax year. Any balance of tax due (for the tax year 1999/2000) must be paid by 31st January 2001.

If you're self-employed, you will also pay class two National Insurance contributions and must also pay class four contributions at 6 per cent on profits between £7,310 and £25,220 a year (1998/99), payable at the same time as your income tax. The following list is a guide to the deductions you can make from your gross income when calculating your taxable profits:

- National Insurance contributions, accident insurance, health insurance and unemployment insurance.

- Premiums for life insurance, endowment and private pensions.

- Business expenses, e.g. car expenses (including travel to and from your place of work), outside or subsidised meals (not free meals), employment-related education and books, and accountant's fees.

- Standard allowances are permitted for many items without proof of expenditure. Personal allowances vary depending on individual circumstances, e.g. single or married, divorced or widowed, and the number of children or dependants.

- Interest charges on loans, overdrafts and leasing contracts.

- Telephone, electricity and office expenses.

- Capital allowances for equipment, e.g. computers, office equipment and car.

- Donations to recognised charities above £600 in a financial year.

You shouldn't hesitate to claim for anything that you believe is a legitimate business deduction. The IR will delete them if they don't agree, but what they will never do is allow you a deduction that you're entitled to and have forgotten to claim. The Inland Revenue publish a number of leaflets for the self-employed including *Starting in Business* (IR28). If you're self-employed, you will probably find it pays to hire an accountant to complete your tax return.

Allowances

Before you're liable for income tax, you're allowed to earn a certain amount of income tax-free. If you earn below your taxable limit, you aren't liable for tax. Everyone has a tax-free personal allowance and a married couple is entitled to an additional married couple's allowance, both of which are increased for those aged 65 and over (even more for the over 75s). Under independent taxation for married couples (see page 112), each partner is wholly responsible for his or her own tax affairs, including both income and capital gains tax. The tax-free allowances for the 1999/2000 tax year are as follows:

Personal Allowance: Every taxpayer has a personal allowance to set against his taxable income. The personal allowance is applicable to all residents in Britain who have an income from any source, e.g. salary, pension, interest on savings or dividends from investments. The personal allowance you receive depends on your age as follows:

Age	Allowance
under 65	£4,335
65 to 74*	£5,720
75 and over*	£5,980

* Pensioners whose income exceeds £16,800 a year have their age allowance reduced by £1 for each £2 of income above this level, until they are reduced to the basic personal allowance.

Married Couple's Allowance: A married couple receive the married couple's allowance in addition to their individual personal allowance outlined above. The married couple's allowance can be split between both spouses or allocated entirely to either spouse. The higher 'age allowance' is paid when either partner qualifies. The married couple's allowance depends on your age as follows:

Age	Allowance
under 65	£1,970
65 to 74*	£5,125
75 and over*	£5,195

* See note above under personal allowance table.

Initially the married couple's allowance is set against the husband's income. Although it's called the married couple's allowance, if the husband doesn't work (e.g. he's a house-husband) and the wife does, then the married couple's allowance can be claimed by her. However, if the husband receives Unemployment Benefit, a pension or any taxable income, it must be set against his allowance first. Anything left over can be transferred to his wife. In the first year of marriage, the husband receives one twelfth of the married couple's allowance for each month he's been married. You must inform your local tax office when you get married in order to claim the allowance. If two people live together as a couple without getting married, they are taxed as two single people and don't receive the married couple's allowance. If a couple is separated or divorced, they're able to claim the allowance for the tax year in which they permanently separate.

An **additional personal allowance** of £1,970 (1999/2000) can be claimed by anyone bringing up children (under the age of 16 or in full-time education) on their own, regardless of whether they are single (unmarried), divorced, separated or widowed. There's a **blind person's relief** of £1,330 for registered blind people and a **widow's bereavement allowance** of £1,970, which is paid to a widow for the year of assessment in which her husband dies and for the following year (providing she doesn't remarry before the start of the next tax year).

Taxation of Property Income

Income tax is payable in Britain on rental income from a British property, even if you live abroad and the money is paid there. All rental income must be declared to the British tax authorities whether you let a property for a few weeks to a friend or 52 weeks a year on a commercial basis. You're eligible for deductions such as repairs and maintenance; security; cleaning and gardening; mortgage interest; management and letting expenses (e.g. inventory and tenancy agreement fees and advertising); council tax; buildings and contents insurance; accountancy charges; service charges; ground rent; and utility charges. If you plan to let your family home for a period while working abroad, it will pay you to have any necessary repairs, modernisation or restoration work done while you're abroad, as the cost can then be offset against your rental income. You should seek professional advice to ensure that you're claiming everything to which you're entitled. You also need to decide how a home in the UK should be owned, as it may be more tax efficient for it to be owned jointly by a couple than in one name only. After personal allowances and expenses have been deducted, often there's little or no tax to pay on rental income.

If a property is let unfurnished the cost of repairing or replacing fixtures and fittings is tax deductible. If a property is let furnished you can claim on the 'renewals basis', where you claim for items that need to be replaced, or use an alternative method called 'wear and tear allowance'. This allows you to claim an annual depreciation equal to 10 per cent of the rent (less council tax and water rates), which is usually more beneficial. Under the wear and tear allowance scheme, when items such as soft furnishings are replaced no additional claim is available against tax, as this has been covered by the 10 per cent allowance. The most beneficial method will depend on your rental income and should be discussed with your accountant.

If you're a UK resident tax on property income is paid on account twice a year on 1st January and 1st July each year, in the same way as for the self-employed (see page 115). If you're a non-resident and don't have a UK letting agent, income tax must be deducted from rental income by your tenant(s) and paid to the Inland Revenue (IR) each quarter on 31st March, 30th June, 30th September and 31st December. If you have a UK letting agent you can apply to have your rental income (which must be over £100 a week) paid gross and pay tax annually in arrears. If an agent provides a full management service, you should apply to the Financial Intermediaries and Claims Office (FICO), Non-Resident Landlord (NRL) section of the IR to have your rental receipts paid gross of tax. Under the NRL scheme, this relieves the agent of the responsibility of deducting basic rate income tax (23 per cent) at source from your rental income. In order to receive approval your tax affairs must be up to date.

The advantages of registration are that you pay your tax annually in arrears after deduction of your expenses and allowances (which helps your cash flow), and aren't required to reclaim money from the Inland Revenue. Note that if you change agents or tenants you must re-register with FICO. More information is provided in a booklet, *Non-resident landlords, their agents and tenants* (IRT140), or you can contact FICO (Non-Residents), St. John's House, Merton Road, Bootle, Merseyside L69 9BB (☎ 0151-472 6208/9, fax 0151-472 6067). The IR also publish *Taxation of Rents: a Guide to Property Income* (IR150).

Landlords (including expatriate or foreign landlords) must complete an annual self-assessment tax return from April after letting commences. If applicable, the return is sent to the address given on the FICO application form, which should be a private address (preferably your UK accountant). If you don't receive a return you must apply for one, as this isn't accepted as an excuse not to file. If you fail to file a return, your application to pay tax in arrears will be revoked by FICO and a penalty could be imposed. Some accountants advise that you file a return even if you make a loss, as it could be offset against future tax.

See also **Capital Gains Tax** on page 122 and **Inheritance Tax** on page 123.

Income Tax Returns

If you're self-employed or a higher-rate taxpayer, you should be sent a tax return annually, although if you pay your income tax through PAYE and your tax affairs are fairly simple, you will rarely receive one. If you think you're paying too much tax, inform your tax office. Similarly, if you aren't paying tax on part of your earnings, it's up to you to inform the tax office. If you don't receive a return (or all the forms required) and need one, it's your responsibility to request it (☎ 0645-000404).

Self-Assessment: A new system called self-assessment was introduced in the 1997/98 tax year (from April 1997) and was the biggest tax reform for 50 years. Under the old system the Inland Revenue issued estimated assessments which could then be challenged by individual taxpayers (an exercise that could become 'confrontational'). Self-assessment embraces some nine million self-employed people, company directors and taxpayers with substantial investment income or complex tax affairs, who must calculate their own tax liability. In theory it's a simpler method of calculating tax, although there are hidden complexities and harsh penalties for late filing, and reservations have been expressed about the IR forcing people to become tax 'experts'. The first few years of self-assessment have been chaotic, with many people wrongly fined and sent incorrect bills.

Schedule: The self-assessment schedule for tax payment for the tax year 1999/2000 is as follows:

Date	Action/Deadline
January/February 2000	PAYE coding notices for tax year 1999/2000 sent.
April 2000	Self-assessment tax returns for the tax year 1999/2000 are sent to taxpayers who are subject to self-assessment.
By 31st May 2000	P60s forms are issued providing details of your taxable pay and tax paid for tax year 1999/2000. P60s apply to all employees and pensioners who receive an income from a previous employer's pension scheme or a private pension plan.

By 6th July 2000	P11D forms issued providing details of your taxable fringe benefits and expenses for tax year 1999/2000. This applies to employees and directors earning £8,500 or more and receiving fringe benefits and/or expenses.
31st July 2000	Second payment on account for 1999/2000 tax year is due (mostly applies to the self-employed).
30th September 2000	Complete and send your return (without calculation) for the tax year 1999/2000 to the IR if you want them to calculate your tax bill.
31st January 2001	Final deadline for sending your tax return and paying any outstanding tax for 1999/2000. If you make payments on account, you must make the first payment for the 2000/2001 tax year. The IR must inform you by this date if it intends to investigate your 1998/99 return.
January/February 2001	PAYE coding notices for tax year 2000/2001 sent.

Completing the Return: Under self-assessment, all taxpayers receive the same standard eight-page return which covers savings, investments, state benefits and pensions, in addition to allowances and reliefs that you wish to claim. You may receive additional forms depending on your sources of income, e.g. those in a partnership. The return is supplied with explanatory notes that are relatively easy to understand and most people can complete it without any trouble. If you need help with your tax form or are unclear about a specific point, you can call the self-assessment helpline (☎ 0645-000444) from 0800 until 2000 from Mondays to Fridays and at weekends. Always keep a copy of your tax form and anything else you send to your tax office. This will be vital if your tax form gets lost in the post or there are any queries later. **Don't forget to sign the return!** All tax records should be retained for five years from the latest date by which the tax return is to be filed.

Filing: Filing is due by 31st January after the end of the tax year, e.g. a tax return for the tax year ending 5th April 2000 must be submitted no later than 31st January 2001. You can also give your figures to the Inland Revenue and have them calculate your tax liability, although if you use this method you must submit your tax return by 30th September of the tax year in question, i.e. four months earlier than if you do the assessment yourself.

Late filing: There are heavy fines for late filing and late payers under the self-assessment scheme. If you miss the deadline for filing your tax return by a single day you must pay an automatic £100 fine (incurred by hundreds of thousands of people each year). Failure to return the tax form by the end of February means a 5 per cent surcharge is levied on the tax owed. If you send in your return after the 31st July (i.e. over six months late) you must pay a further £100 fine, and a delay of 12 months incurs a penalty of up to 100 per cent of the tax payable, plus a discretionary charge of £60 a day until your return is filed. You must also pay interest on unpaid tax bills. You can appeal against a penalty for filing a late return.

Payment on Account: If you're self-employed or receive rental or investment income without having tax deducted at source, you must pay income tax on account. Two payments must be paid on account of tax due, one by 31st January (the same day as filing your return) and the other by 31st July, each amounting to half of your liability for the previous year (excluding tax deducted at source, e.g. on PAYE income). A third balancing payment (or refund if you have over-paid) is made by the following 31st January.

Late payment: Late payment of tax incurs interest charges at a floating rate decided by the Treasury. A delay of 28 days will add a 5 per cent surcharge and a delay of six months a further 5 per cent (total 10 per cent). Interest on surcharges will be due within 30 days of their imposition. In 1999, interest was 7.5 per cent on overdue income tax, although the IR paid just 3 per cent interest if it owed you money.

COUNCIL TAX

The council tax is a property-based tax that replaced the reviled poll tax (or community charge) in 1993, which itself replaced property rates in 1989 in Scotland and in 1990 in England and Wales. The council tax is a local tax levied by local councils on residents to pay for such things as education, police, roads, waste disposal, libraries and community services. Each council fixes its own tax rate, based on the number of residents and how much money they need to finance their services.

The amount payable depends on the value of your home, relative to others in your area, as rated by your local council (not necessarily the market value). Properties in England, Scotland and Wales (there's no council tax in Northern Ireland) are divided into the following bands:

	Property Value		
Band	**England**	**Scotland**	**Wales**
A	up to £40,000	up to £27,000	up to £30,000
B	£40,001-£52,000	£27,001-£35,000	£30,001-£39,000
C	£52,001-£68,000	£35,001-£45,000	£39,001-£51,000
D	£68,001-£88,000	£45,001-£58,000	£51,001-£66,000
E	£88,001-£120,000	£58,001-£80,000	£66,001-£90,000
F	£120,001-£160,000	£80,001-£106,000	£90,001-£120,000
G	£160,001-£320,000	£106,001-£212,000	£120,001-£240,000
H	over £320,000	over £212,000	over £240,000

The tax payable varies considerably depending on the borough or county where you live. In a rural county the council tax may range from between £400 and £500 (band A) to between £900 and £1,250 (band H). You can find out what the council tax is in any town in England and Wales via the Internet (www.upmystreet.com).

The tax includes payments for the county, borough or district council; the local police, fire and civil defence authorities; and possibly a 'special expenses' payment in certain areas. It can usually be paid by direct debit from a bank or building society account, by post with a personal cheque, in person at council offices, by credit card, or at a bank or post office. Payment can be made in a lump sum (for which a reduction may be offered) or in ten instalments a year, from April to January (12 instalments in Scotland). In recent years taxes have increased due to inadequate funding from central government and many councils have been forced to cut services to meet their budgets. Taxes increased by 5 to 10 per cent in many parts of England in 1999.

The full council tax assumes that two adults are living permanently in a dwelling. If only one adult lives in a dwelling (as their main home), the bill is reduced by 25 per cent. If a dwelling isn't a main home, e.g. it's unoccupied or is a second home, the bill is reduced by 50 per cent. Exempt dwellings include those that are unfurnished (exempt for up to six months); undergoing structural alteration or major repair (exempt for up to six months after completion); are left empty for specific reasons (e.g. the occupier is in hospital, a nursing home or prison, or is a student); or are occupied by people under 18 years of age only.

Certain people aren't counted when calculating the number of adults resident in a dwelling, e.g. full-time students and 18 and 19 year-olds who have just left school. If you or someone who lives with you has special needs arising from a disability, you may be entitled to a reduction in your council tax bill. Those receiving Income Support (social security) usually pay no council tax and others on low incomes have their bills reduced. You can appeal against the assessed value of your property and any errors due to exemption, benefits or discounts.

All those who are liable for council tax must register with their local council when they take up residence in a new area and are liable to pay council tax from their first day of residence. A register is maintained by councils containing the names and addresses of all people registered for council tax, which is open to public examination. If you don't want your name and address to appear on the register, e.g. for fear of physical violence, you can apply for anonymous registration. New arrivals in Britain must register with their local council after taking up residence in Britain or after moving house. When moving to a new county or borough, you may be entitled to a refund of a portion of your council tax.

CAPITAL GAINS TAX

Capital Gains Tax (CGT) is applicable whenever you sell or otherwise dispose (e.g. lease, exchange or loss) of an asset, which broadly speaking is anything you own. Anything you sell, from a second home to shares or antiques, which reap profits above £7,100 a year (1999/2000) is liable to CGT payable at your highest rate of income tax, either 10, 23 or 40 per cent (companies pay corporation tax at their normal rate). CGT liability must be included in your income tax return. It's usually payable on private motor vehicles; private homes; household goods and personal effects; SAYE contracts and National Savings certificates and bonds; premium bonds; betting winnings; most life insurance policies; government securities such as 'gilts'; and personal injury compensation.

If an asset disposed of was acquired *before* 31st March 1982, no capital gains tax is usually payable. The value of assets purchased and disposed of after this date are adjusted for the increase in the Retail Prices Index (RPI) between 31st March 1982 and the date of disposal. If the asset was acquired *after* 31st March 1992 then its cost is adjusted for the increase in the RPI between the date of acquisition and its disposal. The adjusted cost is then deducted from the net sales proceeds to arrive at the gain or loss. This calculation is termed the indexation allowance (RPI tables are provided to make calculation easy). To complicate matters further, from 6th April 1998 a new taper relief system was introduced and applies to assets purchased from this date. This works by reducing the tax payable on a gain depending on how long you have owned it. You must own a non-business asset for at least three years and a business asset for at least one year before taper relief reduces your tax bill. The percentage of capital gains payable on a non-business asset reduces to 95 per cent after three years and a maximum of 60 per cent after ten or more years.

If you have two homes, living part of the year in one and part in another, you must choose which is your main residence for capital gains tax purposes. It's best to choose the one on which you think you will make the largest profit as your main home. You should inform the tax office within two years of buying a second home (otherwise the Inland Revenue may decide which property is your main home), although you can change your mind at any time by informing your tax office. Your choice of main residence for capital gains tax purposes shouldn't affect your choice for council tax purposes (see page 121). Note that an unmarried couple can legally own two 'principal' homes, whereby each claims a property as his or her main home.

You can reduce your CGT bill by selling your principal home and making your second home your main home for a period (the Inland Revenue doesn't state how long you must be in residence before you become exempt from CGT). However, if you live in a home for a number of years and then let it for a number of years before selling it, the IR looks at the total gain from the date of purchase to the date of sale. It then divides the gain in proportion to the years the property was used as a primary residence (which are exempt from CGT) and the years it was let (for which CGT is payable). Those who reside abroad are exempt from tax on capital gains arising in the UK, although it's possible to lose all or part of this exemption if any of the owners of a property become resident in the UK for tax purposes.

Under independent taxation, husbands and wives each have an annual capital gains exemption of £7,100 (total £14,200) and it isn't possible for one spouse's losses to be set against the other's gains. Capital gains tax is payable on overseas investments, only when the money is brought back into Britain. The Inland Revenue publish a number of leaflets about capital gains tax. If you're liable for CGT, you should obtain advice from an accountant as you may be able to reduce your tax liability.

INHERITANCE & GIFT TAX

In Britain, inheritance tax (IHT) at 40 per cent is payable on any bequests above £231,000 (1999/2000) when left to anyone other than your spouse or a registered charity (expensive business dying, unless you have lots of debts and no money). The tax-free threshold is usually increased annually and is likely to be much higher when you die (but then so will the value of your estate). The best way to reduce your IHT liability is to simply give some of your money away to family or friends or to a deserving cause (such as struggling authors), so long as it doesn't adversely affect your standard of living. Your liability to inheritance tax can be avoided by judicious financial planning and transferring assets, which is one of the most effective forms of tax planning. One way to avoid IHT is with a trust or an insurance policy, which pays the tax liability (with your children or grandchildren as beneficiaries), although you must live for seven years after setting it up.

You're permitted to give away up to £3,000 a year, which can be carried over for one year. Small gifts up to £250 don't count and you can give £250 to as many people as you wish in one year. Any taxable gifts over £250 made in the previous seven years are included in your estate, although the amount of tax payable is reduced according to a sliding scale. A gift given seven years before death incurs no inheritance tax and relief of from 20 to 80 per cent is given on gifts made between three and seven years before death. Inheritance tax is payable in full on gifts made within three years of death. Tax payable on lifetime gifts (other than those that fall under the seven-year rule) is 20 per cent. You can also make a one-time gift to a non-domiciled spouse of up to £55,000.

Those liable for inheritance tax must submit an account to the IR detailing the assets they have inherited and their value within 12 months of receiving them. There's a fine of £100 for anyone who makes a late declaration and much higher fines for providing fraudulent or incorrect information.

Inheritance tax is a complicated subject and depends on whether you're domiciled in Britain (defined in Inland Revenue leaflet IHT1). Before making any gifts or transfer of property or any bequests in your will (see below), it's vital to obtain legal advice from a solicitor who specialises in inheritance tax. There are a number of useful books including *The Which? Guide to Giving and Inheriting* by Jonquil Lowe (Which? Books).

WILLS

It's an unfortunate fact of life, but you're unable to take your worldly goods with you when you take your final bow (even if you have plans to come back in a later life), so it's better to leave them to someone or something you love, rather than to the Inland Revenue or leave a mess which everyone will fight over (unless that's your intention!). Surprisingly, around two-thirds of Britons die intestate, i.e. without making a will, which means that the inflexible laws of intestacy dictate how the estate is divided. It's estimated that over £750 million in inheritance tax could be avoided if more people planned their taxes and made wills. Most married people in Britain imagine that when they die, everything they own will automatically be inherited by their partner, which isn't true.

A surviving spouse is entitled to as much as half of a house and any other property, plus between £125,000 and £200,000 of the spouse's cash, depending on whether there are any children. If you have no children, then a share of your estate passes to your parents (if they're alive) or other relatives. Under the laws of intestacy, common law spouses have no legal rights. The biggest problem of leaving no will is the delay in winding up your estate (while perhaps searching for a will), which can cause considerable hardship and distress at an already stressful time. Note that when someone dies, an estate's assets cannot be touched until inheritance tax (see above) has been paid and probate (the official proving of a will) has been granted. You usually require probate for estates worth more than £5,000, although you can exclude assets (e.g. a home) owned as 'joint tenants' from this sum.

All adults should make a will regardless of how large or small their assets. If your circumstances change dramatically, for example you get married, you must make a new will as marriage automatically revokes any existing wills under English law. Both husband and wife should make separate wills. Similarly, if you separated or divorced you should consider making a new will, as gifts in a will to an ex-spouse are invalid (but make sure you have only one valid will). A new bequest or a change can be made to an existing will through a document called a 'codicil'. You should check your will every few years to make sure it still fits your wishes and circumstances (your assets may also increase dramatically in value).

If you're a foreign national and don't want your estate to be subject to British law, you may be eligible to state in your will that it's to be interpreted under the law of another country. To avoid being subject to British death duty and inheritance laws, you must establish your country of domicile in another country. Domicile in Britain is defined in Inland Revenue leaflet IHT1 and information is also given in a booklet (IR20) entitled *Residents and Non-residents - Liability to tax in the United Kingdom* (see also page 109). If you don't specify in your will that the law of another country applies to your estate, then British law will apply. If your estate comes under British law, your dependants will be subject to British inheritance laws and tax. Inheritance law is slightly different in Scotland from in the rest of Britain, where part of the estate must be left to any children and where you can hand-write your own will, called a holograph, which doesn't need to be witnessed.

Once you've accepted that you're mortal (the one statistic you can rely on is that 100 per cent of all human beings eventually die), you will find that making a will isn't a complicated or lengthy process. You can draw up your own will (which is better than none), but it's advisable to obtain legal advice from a bank or solicitor who will draw up a simple will for around £50 for a single person, or up to £100 for a couple (fees vary considerably and you should shop around). Some banks will draw up wills only if they are made executors of the estate (see below) and should therefore be avoided. Note than many wills are drawn up incorrectly by solicitors and you may be better off doing it yourself!

It's possible to make two wills, one relating to British and the other to foreign property. Opinion differs on whether you should have separate wills for British and foreign property or a foreign will with a codicil (appendix) dealing with your British property (or vice versa). However, most experts believe it's better to have a British will from the point of view of winding up your British estate (and a will for any country where you own real estate). If you have British and foreign wills you must ensure that they don't contradict one another (or worse still, cancel each other out, e.g. when a will contains a clause revoking all other wills). Note that a foreign will written in a foreign language must be translated into English (a certified translation is required) and proven in Britain in order to be valid there.

For those who would rather do it themselves, a simple will form can be purchased from legal stationers for about 50p, which also provides some guidance on writing your will. Better still buy a copy of the *Make Your Will* action pack produced by the Consumers' Association (see **Appendix A**), which contains three alternative will forms. However, bear in mind that a will must be written in a tax-efficient manner – lawyers have a field day sorting out home-made wills. You *must* have two witnesses (to your signature, not the contents of the will) who cannot be either beneficiaries or your spouse. If you wish you can list all your 'valuables' and who's to get what (the list can be kept separate from the will and changed without altering the will itself).

You'll also need someone to act as the executor (or personal representative) of your estate, which can be particularly costly for modest estates. Your bank, building society, solicitor (the least expensive, but far from cheap), or other professional will usually act as the executor, although this should be avoided if at all possible, as the fees can be astronomical. Banks' fees are based on a percentage of the estate and work out at around £500 or more an hour! **It's best to make your beneficiaries the executors and then they can instruct a solicitor after your death if they need legal assistance.** Keep a copy of your will in a safe place (e.g. a bank) and another copy with your solicitor or the executors of your estate. You should keep information regarding bank accounts and insurance policies with your will(s), but don't forget to tell someone where they are!

There are a number of books on wills including *Wills and Probate* and *What to do when Someone Dies* (Which? Books). Many charities also produce free guides in the hope that you will leave them a bequest. Note that British inheritance law is a complicated subject and it's important to obtain professional legal advice when writing or altering your will(s).

COST OF LIVING

No doubt you would like to know how far your pounds will stretch and how much money (if any) you will have left after paying your bills. Britain has a high cost of living and high rates of duty on everything from petrol to tobacco and alcohol to cars, making it one of the world's most expensive places to live. British consumers pay more for food and most consumer goods than people in most other major countries. While direct taxes are relatively low, indirect taxes are high. In 1998 Britain had the highest cost of living in the world after Japan and Denmark according to figures from Employment Conditions Abroad. London is one of the world's most expensive cities and has a higher cost of living than Amsterdam, Berlin, Luxembourg, Montreal, Munich, New York and Sydney.

Britain's inflation rate is based on the Retail Prices Index (RPI), which gives an indication of how prices have risen (or fallen) over the past year. The prices of around 600 'indicator' items are collected on a single day in the middle of the month (a total of around 130,000 prices are collected for the 600 items in the RPI basket). However, the Institute of Fiscal Studies says that inflation rates have been over-estimated by 1 to 3 per cent because the RPI is woefully out of date. Britain's official inflation rate in early 1999 was around 2.5 per cent.

However, on the plus side Britain's standard of living has soared in recent years and compared with most other European Union countries British workers take home a larger proportion of their pay after tax and social security. The gap between rich and poor in Britain is the largest since records began in 1886 and state pensioners are unable to afford basic 'comforts' such as a healthy diet, a car and an annual holiday. There's a huge gap between the wealthy south of England and the poor north of England, Scotland and Northern Ireland, although the gap was narrowed by the recession in the early '90s. In contrast, the middle classes have never been better off than in recent years and the super rich go on spending sprees buying holiday homes, cruises, yachts, power boats, luxury cars and private aircraft.

It's difficult to calculate an average cost of living, as it depends on each individual's particular circumstances and lifestyle. What is important to most people is how much money they can save (or spend) each month. Your food bill will naturally depend on what you eat and is usually around 50 per cent higher than in the USA, and up to 25 per cent higher than in other Western European countries. Approximately £200 should be sufficient to feed two adults for a month in most areas (excluding alcohol, fillet steak and caviar). Even in the most expensive areas of Britain (i.e. London), the cost of living needn't be astronomical. If you shop wisely, compare prices and services before buying and don't live too extravagantly, you may be pleasantly surprised at how little you can live on. Note that it's also possible to save a considerable sum by shopping for alcohol and other products in France, buying your car in Europe, and shopping overseas by mail and via the Internet (see page 74).

A list of the approximate **MINIMUM** monthly major expenses for an average person or family in a typical provincial town are shown in the table below. **Note that these are necessarily only 'ball park' figures and depend on your lifestyle, extravagance or frugality and where you live in Britain (almost everyone will agree that they are either too low or too high!).** When calculating your cost of living, deduct the appropriate percentage for income tax (see page 109), National Insurance and pensions from your gross salary.

	MONTHLY COSTS (£)		
ITEM	**Single**	**Couple**	**Couple with 2 children**
Housing (1)	300	400	600
Food	100	200	300
Utilities (2)	50	80	100
Leisure (3)	100	100	150
Car/travel (4)	100	125	150
Insurance (5)	25	50	50
Clothing	50	100	150
Council Tax (6)	30	40	60
TOTAL	**£755**	**£1,095**	**£1,560**

(1) Rent or mortgage on a modern apartment or semi-detached house in an 'average' provincial suburb. The amount for a single person is for a bedsit or sharing accommodation (a young person is assumed!). Other costs are for a two (couple) or three-bedroom property (couple with two children). They don't include council or other subsidised housing.

(2) Includes electricity, gas, water and telephone, plus heating bills.

(3) Includes all entertainment, sports and holiday expenses, plus TV licence, newspapers and magazines (which could of course be much higher than the figure given).

(4) Includes running costs for an average family car, plus third party insurance, road tax, petrol and servicing, but not depreciation or credit costs.

(5) Includes all 'voluntary' insurance, excluding car insurance.

(6) This is a guesstimate only, as council tax is based on a property's value.

4.

FINDING YOUR DREAM HOME

After having decided to buy a home in Britain, your first tasks will be to choose the region and what sort of home to buy. If you're unsure where and what to buy, the best decision is usually to rent for a period. The secret of successfully buying a home in Britain (or anywhere else) is research, research and yet more research, preferably before you even set foot there. You may be fortunate and buy the first property you see without doing any homework and live happily ever after. However, a successful purchase is much more likely if you thoroughly investigate the towns and communities in your chosen area; compare the range and prices of homes and their relative values; and study the procedure for buying property. It's a wise or lucky person who gets his choice absolutely right first time, but it's much more likely if you do your homework thoroughly.

Among the many things that attract homebuyers to Britain is the relatively good value for money of property (providing you avoid city centres and the more fashionable areas) and the period architecture and character of British homes, particularly country homes. There's a steady demand for holiday, retirement and investment homes from both Britons and foreigners, although there are few purpose-built, holiday-home developments (as are common in France and Spain). Many Britons own a second home, which has been boosted by soaring property values in recent years (many people have purchased second homes with the spare equity in their principal home). An increasing number of people who work in London and other cities buy a small apartment for accommodation during the week and a large country home (possibly abroad) where they spend their weekends with the family.

Some 70 per cent of Britons own their own homes, one of the highest figures in Europe, and Britain also has the highest level of ownership of second homes in Europe. The average age of first-time buyers is around 27, one of the lowest in the world, compared, for example, with around 35 in Germany and Italy, due largely to easy access to mortgages and the large loans (as a percentage of a property's value) offered by lenders. There are around 2.5 people per household in Britain and 25 per cent of households consist of one person only, a figure that's expected to rise considerably in the next ten years. Four out of five people in Britain live in houses rather than apartments (flats) and most Britons aren't keen on apartment living or townhouses, and want their own detached home with a garden and garage. They prefer more traditional styles and most aren't keen on the more modern high-tech homes favoured by some developers. The British are very mobile and move house more frequently than people in most other countries, with some people moving house every three or four years. The average time spent in a home is around nine years, although people who live in modern homes tend to move more often, e.g. every five years.

The government has estimated that five million new homes will be required by the year 2016, which has led to the countryside being under threat as never before. The huge demand for new homes has led to an increasing amount of land being swallowed up by buildings (the worst affected area is southern England) and it's estimated that one-fifth of England will be built on by the year 2050. There are fears that the infrastructure (particularly roads) could collapse in the south-east due to the one million new homes planned. In 1999 there was an outcry over increased building on 'green field' (virgin land) sites previously banned from development, although the government is trying to encourage more building on 'brown field' sites (any land that has been developed in the past). The British people's dislike for high-rise apartment living has led to more urban sprawl and the march of housing estates across green fields. One of the major problems facing planners is how to regenerate rundown towns and city centres (called 'urban blight') and stop the drift to the countryside. This is a particular problem in some areas of the north of England, where the property market has virtually collapsed due to high unemployment.

Most property in Britain is owned freehold, where the owner acquires complete legal ownership of the property and land and his rights over the property, which can be modified only by the law or specific conditions in the contract of sale. Most houses, whether detached, semi-detached, terraced or townhouses, are sold freehold. However, unlike most other countries, apartments (flats) in England and Wales aren't usually owned outright under a system of co-ownership, and are usually owned 'leasehold', with a lease of, for example, 99 to 999 years (see page 174).

This chapter is designed to help you decide what sort of home to buy and, most importantly, its location. It will also help you avoid problems and contains information about regions; research; British homes; location; renting, house prices; fees; buying new and old; buying land and building your own home; auctions; investments; sheltered housing; mobile homes; leasehold apartments; timeshare (and other part-ownership schemes); estate agents, inspections and surveys, garages and parking; conveyancing; purchase contracts; completion; home improvements and renovation; moving house; moving in; home security; utilities; heating and air-conditioning; property income; and selling a home.

REGIONS

Britain comprises Great Britain (England, Wales and Scotland) and Northern Ireland. For the purposes of this book, England is divided into nine geographical regions, as shown on the map on the following page. (Note that although most surveys divide England into more or less the same regions, the counties included in each region may differ.)

Greater London: Greater London is made up of 32 boroughs (local government administrative areas) covering almost 1,280km² (800mi²) enclosed by the M25 motorway, which circles Greater London. London's main geographical feature is the River Thames, a tidal river that enabled the establishment of an easily defendable port first exploited by the Romans in 43AD. The river flows in wide bends from west to east, dividing the city into northern and southern halves and forming an intrinsic part of London's life. The population of inner London is around eight million, making it Europe's largest city. It's also one of the most cosmopolitan cities in the world and home to people from all corners of the globe, particularly the Commonwealth countries of Africa, Asia and the West Indies. It's a melting pot of the First and Third Worlds, with stark contrasts of wealth and poverty. London is one of the world's great cities and a major tourist attraction, welcoming over twenty million visitors a year.

After a deep recession in the early '90s, London was enjoying an economic boom in 1999. It's one of the liveliest capitals in the world and Britain's centre for government, business, art, entertainment, culture, sport, history, shopping and nightlife. It also houses the largest number of theatres, the most visited museums and some of the best known sights in the world, in addition to having over 1,800 parks and open spaces. London is also Britain's main employment centre, with a huge variety of job opportunities and relatively low unemployment. In common with most

capital cities, the cost of living is high and prices (particularly property) are the highest in Britain, although high salaries compensate to some extent.

For those who are unused to large cities, the sheer size of London can be daunting, although the boroughs (subdivided into districts) are essentially a collection of villages that grew and grew until the city began to assimilate them. Most Londoners don't live in central London, but in the numerous suburbs where life's still largely community based. Wherever you are in the suburbs, you're never far from a traditionally British 'parade' of shops selling the essentials of life and all districts provide amenities such as schools, health and leisure facilities. Much of London's suburbia is characterised by row upon row of brick terraced houses, mainly built in Victorian times to provide housing for the rapidly growing population, or tree-lined avenues of endless semi-detached properties dating from the '20s and '30s.

The price of this sort of typical suburban architecture varies considerably depending on the location, although in general prices in London are much higher than in other parts of Britain. As with all large cities, there's a huge variation in housing quality and price, which exists even within boroughs. The average property price is around £120,000 (£185,000 in central London), although many properties are sold for seven figure sums. Cheaper properties tend to be found in unfashionable 'working class' suburbs mainly situated south of the river in districts such as Clapham and Streatham, or in the East End away from the Docklands, although even here prices have risen dramatically in recent years. Note, however, that the cheaper areas generally have poor housing stock and are subject to the typical inner city problems of neglect, poverty, unemployment and high crime rates.

The 'square mile' enclosing the borough of the 'City of London' (referred to simply as the 'City') is London's financial centre, where the important banks and other financial institutions are situated (the City is virtually uninhabited outside office hours). To the west not far from the City are the best addresses within central London in the districts of Mayfair, Knightsbridge, Kensington and Chelsea, where properties, however small, are always *very* expensive. These areas are characterised by Georgian and Regency developments of formal squares and terraces built in yellow-grey London brick. The affluent suburbs of Hampstead, Highgate, Richmond and Wimbledon are noted for their residential roads lined with huge detached houses with astronomical prices. East of the City is London's Docklands, Europe's biggest urban development area and home to a futuristic cityscape of gleaming high-rise office blocks (dominated by the giant Canary Wharf tower) and waterside housing. After an inauspicious start, it's now becoming fashionable, although much of the office space and housing has still to be occupied and the area still has relatively few amenities.

Communications in London are excellent, particularly public transport, where an extensive network of underground (known as the 'tube') and over-ground trains link all parts of the capital. The bus service is also extensive, although it's much slower than trains during the rush hours. As you would expect, London has outstanding communications with the rest of Britain with frequent trains and bus services to just about anywhere in the country. London is served by five airports (City, Gatwick, Heathrow, Luton and Stanstead), all easily accessible by public transport, which between them provide services to all major domestic and international destinations. London is at the centre of a comprehensive network of motorways including the M1, M2, M3, M4, M11, M20 and M40, and London's ring road, the M25. However, in common with most major cities, it's plagued by chronic traffic problems and most roads are permanently jammed with traffic, making travel by car slow and frustrating. Parking in central London is at best difficult (and expensive) and at worst impossible.

South-East: The south-east region of Britain is comprised of the counties of Bedfordshire, Berkshire, Buckinghamshire, Essex, Hampshire, Hertfordshire, Kent, Oxfordshire, East and West Sussex, and Surrey. The region serves as a dormitory for London's workers and contains the most quintessentially English scenery in Britain. The countryside is dotted with picturesque towns and villages; magnificent castles and stately homes; and a wealth of orchards and market gardens, while the spectacular white cliff southern coastline is lined with typically English seaside resorts. Geographically the area south of London is marked by two chalk ridges, the North and South Downs, running from east to west and creating a rich fertile plain in between known as the Weald, that's heavily exploited for agriculture. In contrast to the rolling hills of the Downs, the north coast of Kent is flat and marshy. The New Forest in Hampshire is the largest area of relatively natural woodland in England and is home to unique flora and fauna, including wild ponies.

The south coast is home to a number of pleasant resorts such as Bognor Regis, Eastbourne, Margate, Ramsgate and Worthing. Brighton, the epitome of the English seaside town, and Hastings are among Britain's largest and most interesting coastal towns. The coastal resorts are popular with retirees and tourists, and are extremely busy on summer weekends. The area also includes several important ports and naval bases such as Dover, the world's busiest passenger harbour, Portsmouth, home to the Royal Navy, and Southampton, famous for shipbuilding and the home port of a number of cruise ships including the Queen Elizabeth II. Away from the coast there are many inland cities of note, particularly Canterbury, an important medieval pilgrimage centre and seat of the Archbishop of Canterbury, head of the Church of England. Other important towns include Winchester with its spectacular 10th century cathedral, Royal Tunbridge Wells and Guildford. Smaller coastal towns worthy of mention include Lewes, Rye and Sandwich, with its perfectly preserved medieval centre. The royal residence of Windsor Castle and Eton, home to Britain's most famous public school, two enduring symbols of the British class system and premier tourist attractions, are also found in this region. The Isle of Wight (234km²/147mi²), situated to the south of Portsmouth, is one of Britain's sunniest spots and a popular holiday destination.

North of London, the counties of Bedfordshire, Essex and Hertfordshire have a number of interesting historic towns including Bedford, Colchester (Britain's oldest recorded town and the capital of Roman Britain), Hertford (nearby Hatfield House is one of Britain's most important stately homes) and St. Albans (a Roman town with a superb 11th century abbey church). There are also a number of notable new towns in the area designed and developed since the second world war, including Stevenage, Welwyn Garden City and Milton Keynes, noted for its landscaping and modern town planning. East of London are the seaside resorts of Clacton-on-Sea and Southend-on-Sea, one of Britain's most lively and popular resorts. To the north-west of London is Oxford, one of the world's most famous university (12th century) towns, and a Mecca for tourists who flock to admire the ancient colleges with their golden (dreaming) spires and riverside views.

Architecture in the south-east varies from thatched stone cottages in the western counties to weatherboard, pantile houses in Kent, which is also famous for its characteristic oast houses with their towers and tall slanted chimneys (the towers contained kilns where hops were roasted before being sent to breweries). Many of the seaside towns are lined with elegant Regency-style houses. The south-east is the most affluent region in Britain (outside London) and consequently property prices are high in most parts, with the average around £105,000. Communications are excellent throughout the region, particularly trains, with an extensive network of lines radiating out from London to all areas. There are also good bus services throughout the region, which is served by many motorways including the M1, M2, M3, M4, M11, M20, M23, M25 and A1/M, although roads are busy and prone to jams during rush hours. The region is served by London's two major international airports, Gatwick and Heathrow, plus Luton and Stanstead airports to the north of London and a number of regional airports. The southern ports (e.g. Dover and Portsmouth) and the Channel Tunnel provide the shortest (35km/22mi from Dover) and main sea route to the European mainland.

South-West: The south-west region of Britain contains the counties of Avon, Cornwall, Devon, Dorset, Gloucestershire, Somerset and Wiltshire. The tapering south-west peninsula culminates in the rugged cliffs of western Cornwall, where the southern most point of Britain, the Lizard Peninsula and Lands End, form the characteristic 'big toe'. The western corner of the region is known as the West Country and offers unique scenery, attractive towns and villages, and a wide range of tourist attractions. The south-west is essentially rural and agriculture is the main industry, although tourism is almost as important. In the east, the counties of Gloucestershire, Wiltshire and Dorset contain many beautiful, unspoilt villages, particularly in the Cotswolds where the honey-yellow, Cotswold stone houses enclosed by dry-stone walls have a unique charm. The curious ancient hill 'carvings' in the chalk downs, particularly the Giant at Cerne Abbas and the prehistoric monument at Stonehenge, are world famous. Devon is largely comprised of two national parks: Dartmoor, with the wildest and bleakest scenery in the country, and Exmoor, with the highest cliffs in England, both of which are havens for walkers and nature lovers. The South West Coast Path (613mi/981km) provides spectacular coastal walking along its whole length.

The most important cities in the region include Bath, an architectural gem with perfectly preserved Roman baths, Bournemouth (a major retirement area), Bristol (the south-west's largest city with an important university and major port), Exeter (known for its university), Gloucester (with its fine cathedral), Plymouth (an historic maritime centre, from where Sir Francis Drake launched his attack against the Spanish Armada), Salisbury (home of one of England's most beautiful cathedrals) and Swindon, an important business centre and Britain's 'silicone valley'. The seaside towns of Brixham, Paignton and Torquay form what's known as the 'English Riviera', complete with palm trees and a mild climate. Away from the major towns, life is village based and generally slow, except for during the summer months when the region is packed with tourists,

Cornwall with its rugged coastline and quaint harbours, provides a haven for smugglers past and present, and is culturally different from the rest of the south-west and has more in common with the Celts of Wales, Ireland and Brittany (France). Efforts are being made to revive the (all but extinct) Cornish language, which was last spoken by large numbers in the 18th century. Cornwall used to be noted for its tin and copper mines, whose abandoned ruins now dot the landscape. Nowadays tourism forms the basis for most employment, although outside the summer season jobs are scarce and it's one of the poorest counties in Britain. The Isles of Scilly, a collection of over 100 rocky islands of which only five are inhabited, lie some 45km/28mi south-west of Lands End. The islands are bathed by the Gulf Stream and enjoy an exceptionally mild climate and are the only place in Britain where subtropical gardens can be seen. Communication with the islands by air and sea is good during the summer, although somewhat sporadic at other times.

Communications and transport in the south-west are generally good, although the rural nature of the area makes travel by private car preferable, providing you avoid the coastal roads and major towns in summer. In the eastern part of the region communications are generally better with a number of fast roads, such as the M4 and M5 motorways, which serve Bristol and Exeter respectively and connect with the rest of the country. There's also a comprehensive train service with frequent connections to London and other major cities. Bristol has an international airport and also provides regular domestic flights to other parts of the country. In Devon and Cornwall public transport isn't particularly good and a car is usually essential. There's just one railway line serving the region, which terminates at Penzance (five hours from London) and bus services outside the towns are sporadic. Exeter has a small regional airport serving a number of international destinations during summer and domestic airports throughout the year. House prices in the area are just above the national average at around £80,000, although property in the more remote areas is cheaper and prices in popular spots such as Bath and Torbay are high.

West Midlands: The West Midlands region contains the counties of Hereford and Worcestershire, Shropshire, Staffordshire, Warwickshire and the West Midlands (county). This patchwork of counties contains a stark contrast between natural beauty and sprawling industrial cities such as Coventry and Birmingham. To the west, the countryside consists of gentle hills, interspersed with sleepy market towns and villages. Shropshire on the Welsh border is peaceful and uncrowded, and boasts two of the most attractive towns in Britain, Shrewsbury and Ludlow. It's also where the industrial revolution started (at Ironbridge) over 300 years ago when Abraham Darby produced the world's first iron. Other popular attractions in the region include Blenheim Palace, Warwick Castle, Stratford-upon-Avon (Shakespeare's birthplace), Worcester (famous for porcelain and its cathedral) and Britain's premier theme park, Alton Towers.

In stark contrast to the many peaceful rural settings and idyllic towns are the heavily industrialised areas at the region's centre. Coventry was once a major car and aircraft manufacturing centre, although only a handful of factories remain. Birmingham is Britain's second-largest city and was one of the pioneers of the industrial revolution, known during the 19th century as the 'workshop of the world'. However, despite the collapse of many industrial activities it remains an important manufacturing centre. Stoke-on-Trent was once the china-making capital of the world and forms part of the 'six towns' that make up the Potteries area where such famous names as Royal Doulton, Spode and Wedgwood still have their factories.

Communications in this part of Britain are excellent, particularly by road and rail, and the region is intersected by a network of motorways and major rail routes. Bus services between major destinations are also fast and frequent and cities have comprehensive local bus services. Birmingham airport is growing fast and serves an increasing number of international destinations plus all the main domestic airports. Property prices in the area are below average with houses costing around £70,000, although property in certain cities and towns is expensive.

East Midlands: The area of the East Midlands is comprised of the counties of Derbyshire, Leicestershire, Lincolnshire, Northamptonshire and Nottinghamshire, and, like the West Midlands, is a mixture of spectacular natural beauty and important industrial centres. Britain's first national park, the Peak District is found in Derbyshire and provides some of England's most striking scenery with its darker, harsher north and more pastoral south. The region is well known for its splendid walking (Britain's most celebrated long-distance footpath, the Pennine Way, starts in the area), caving and climbing opportunities. Britain's most famous forest, Sherwood (and its links to Robin Hood), is also situated here, although it's just a shadow of its former size and glory. The flat, fertile fenlands of Lincolnshire, where bulb growing is a major industry, provide a stark contrast to the Peak District. Derby was an important railway centre and maintains some industrial activity together with the cities of Leicester and Nottingham, once known for its hosiery and lace industries. Lincoln boasts one of the country's most spectacular cathedrals and Skegness (affectionately know as 'Skeggy') in Lincolnshire was Britain's first established seaside resort.

Communications in the area are good and the region is amply served with an excellent network of road (both the M1 and A1/M serve the area) and rail routes. However, communications in rural areas can be poor and it's advisable to have your own transport. The architecture in the region varies widely from a distinct Dutch influence in the east, where gables and windmills abound, particularly in the area of Lincolnshire known as 'Little Holland', to characteristic stone cottages with slate roofs in Derbyshire. Property in the East Midlands is reasonably priced, with the average house costing in the region of £60,000.

East Anglia: East Anglia contains the counties of Cambridgeshire, Norfolk and Suffolk, and is the most easterly region of Britain forming the characteristic round 'bulge'. The region is largely overlooked by tourists, with the notable exception of Cambridge (home to one of Britain's oldest universities), and is something of a backwater. Geographically it's similar to the low countries and in its northern area has a distinctive Dutch feel, which is reflected in its architecture of windmills and Dutch gables. The region has no uplands and the rural landscape consists mostly of flat or gently undulating agricultural land crowned by seemingly endless skies and a unique intensity of light captured by England's most famous landscape artists, Constable and Gainsborough.

The scenery in East Anglia is generally bleak, although attractive in parts. Much of the previous marshland has been drained to form vast expanses of flat fertile black soil used for agriculture. The farmlands are dotted with 'timewarp' medieval villages with timber framed and plaster fronted houses, dominated by huge churches that are the legacy of the rich wool trade in the 18th and 19th centuries. To the north, the Norfolk Broads comprise over 30 broads (large areas of fresh water formed where rivers widen), which are a Mecca for boating enthusiasts and birdwatchers. The long East Anglia coastline has a wealth of traditional British seaside resorts, ranging from the sedate Lowestoft (the most easterly point in Britain) and Wells-next-the-Sea, to the decidedly noisier and more popular Great Yarmouth. The region has the lowest rainfall in the country, but can be cold in winter due to strong north-easterly winds. Cambridge is the historic and cultural capital of the area with its thirty university colleges, sixteen of which have medieval origins (the university was founded in the 13th century) and the magnificent Kings College Chapel. Other interesting cathedral cities include Ely and Norwich.

Communications in East Anglia (where there are no motorways) are poor, particularly if you need to rely on public transport. Roads tends to be slow and meandering, reflecting the slower pace of life in this rural area, and buses are infrequent or non-existent in some places and where they exist routes can be tortuous. The ports of Felixstowe and Harwich operate ferries to northern Europe and Scandinavia, and there's a busy regional airport at Norwich with flights to a number of continental destinations. Average property prices are slightly below the national average at around £70,000, although East Anglia isn't one of Britain's cheapest regions.

Yorkshire & Humberside: The historic white rose region of Britain known as Yorkshire (the Humber River or Humberside marks the region's southern border) is divided into the counties of North, South and West Yorkshire. Yorkshire's main geographical feature are the Pennines, which dominate the region (dividing it into east and west sections) and are the source of countless rivers that provide water for the region's industry. To the north lie the dramatic North Yorkshire Moors, a vast expanse of heather covered moorland largely untouched by man and inhabited mostly by sheep. In the south, the green meadows of the Yorkshire Dales, punctuated by austere stone villages and rivers, comprise one of Britain's most beautiful areas. The Yorkshire coast is a collection of spectacular bays and bustling harbours such as Whitby and popular resorts that include Bridlington and the spa town of Scarborough. The historic city of York is one of Britain's great cities and has been the capital of the north for over 2,000 years; it boasts some of the most impressive surviving medieval fortifications in Europe, dominated by the Gothic Minster (cathedral).

In the south of the region lie the cities of Bradford, Leeds and Sheffield and Britain's industrial heartland. Bradford is the centre of Britain's textile industry, Leeds dominated the wool industry until the middle of the 20th century, while Sheffield has always been synonymous with coal mining and the steel industry, which led to the vast urban development of the area. In recent years there has been a sharp decline in these industries and unemployment has become a chronic problem in some areas; however, all Yorkshire's major cities have important universities and are lively and dynamic places in which to live. Like many other industrial cities, Leeds has been regenerated in the last decade and is Britain's second most important financial centre after London. The triangle bounded by York, Leeds and Harrogate has been dubbed the 'golden triangle' and is the region's most desirable residential area.

Communications are good in most areas of Yorkshire, especially in the south where there's a number of motorways (notably the M1 and M62) and good rail connections (York is one of Britain's main termini). However, in rural areas such as the East Riding and the North Yorkshire Moors, a car is necessary as buses are few and far between. The region is served by ferries to the low countries from the port of Kingston-upon-Hull and there are a number of regional airports (including Leeds-Bradford) serving international destinations (Manchester international airport is also close by). Yorkshire's climate is generally much colder than further south, particularly on the east coast, and it often experiences snowfalls in winter. House prices are generally lower than in the rest of the country, with an average home costing around £55,000.

North-West: The north-west region of Britain contains the counties of Cheshire, Lancashire, Greater Manchester and Merseyside. The north-west was the birthplace of the industrial revolution, introduced the world's first passenger trains, spawned the Beatles and the Merseybeat, and is home to some of the world's most famous football clubs (including Liverpool and Manchester United). Liverpool, with its dramatic setting on the Mersey estuary, was once Britain's second port, specialising in the transportation of slaves and then immigrants to the New World. Consequently it's home to a cosmopolitan population (Scousers) known for their spirit and wit. Despite its glorious past, Liverpool's economic collapse has been dramatic in recent decades and the city's appearance is a stark contrast of grandeur and decay.

Manchester also has a vibrant history as the centre of Britain's weaving industry and has similarly seen economic decline in some areas, although it remains one of the country's most important commercial and financial centres, and its second most dynamic city after London. Both Liverpool and Manchester have innovative arts and cultural scenes and a bustling nightlife. The north-west coast close to the cities isn't particularly attractive although one of Europe's liveliest seaside resorts and Britain's top attraction, Blackpool, is found here. Its world famous pleasure beach and illuminations attract over eight million visitors a year. Further north, Morecombe is an elegant resort and a popular retirement area.

Communications in all areas of the north-west are excellent, with Manchester's international airport the largest outside London, serving over 11 million passengers a year, while Liverpool airport operates services mainly to Ireland and other regions of Britain. The region is served by a number of motorways (including the M6 and M62) and fast train services connect it with the rest of the country. The climate on the west side of the Pennines is generally mild, although it can be extremely wet at any time of the year (Manchester is noted for its rain). The cost of property is well below the national average, with the average price of a home around £60,000. However, some areas are much sought after, particularly the northern part of Cheshire where the local jet set lives and luxury homes cost millions of pounds. The centre of Manchester has been completely regenerated in recent years, where many old buildings have been converted into luxury apartments.

North: The northern region of Britain is comprised of the counties of Cumbria, Cleveland, Durham, Northumberland, and Tyne and Wear. It's dominated by the northern Pennines, with their rugged desolate moorland setting, and to a lesser extent the more gentle Cheviot Hills. Northumberland is Britain's wildest county with a vast array of castles and battlefields testifying to the ancient struggles with the Scots. To the north lies the 117km/73mi Hadrian's Wall, built by the Romans to keep the Scots at bay and still largely intact. The dramatic windswept eastern coastline is dotted with castles set on rocky outcrops included Lindisfarne on Holy Island, the cradle of Christianity in England. The region is largely unspoilt with extensive beaches, quiet resorts and golf courses, and is a paradise for walkers and birdwatchers.

Durham is the most dramatic of all English cathedral cities with its Norman cathedral and castle and a prestigious university. It was an important mining centre and is surrounded by former coal mining villages (mining has declined dramatically in the last few decades) and together with Darlington was at the centre of the development of the railways during the Industrial Revolution. Tyne and Wear, the conurbation centred on Newcastle-upon-Tyne, is one of Britain's most important ports with steel, shipbuilding and engineering industries. These have been in sharp decline in recent decades and Newcastle has struggled to survive, although the city (with its characteristic six bridges over the Tyne) has a lively atmosphere and is home to one of Europe's largest shopping complexes, the Metro Centre at Gateshead.

In the north-west lies Cumbria and the Lake District, Britain's most beautiful corner with its breathtaking lakes and mountain scenery, and literary connections with Wordsworth and Beatrix Potter. The lakes, fells and dales are a haven for walkers, climbers and day-trippers, which means the area is often very crowded, particularly in the summer months (it receives over ten million visitors a year). The main towns of Keswick and Windermere are popular for holiday and retirement homes.

Communications in the region aren't particularly good apart from the city of Newcastle, which is served by trains from London and has a small international airport and a good road network (but no motorways apart from a stretch of the A1). There's a train service running north from Durham or east to Carlisle, but other transport options are sparse, particularly in Northumberland. The climate in this part of Britain can be particularly harsh in winter. Property prices reflect the remoteness and difficult economic conditions of the area and are the lowest in the country, with an average home costing around £55,000.

Scotland: Scotland (pop. 5.2 million) is comprised of 12 regions that include the Borders, Central, Dumfries and Galloway, Fife, Grampian, Highland, Lothian, Orkney Islands, Shetland Islands, Strathclyde, Tayside and the Western Isles. It has been united with England for the past three centuries, although a Scottish Government was established in 1999 with wide-ranging autonomy. Scotland is the least densely populated part of Britain (67 inhabitants per km²/25.8 per mi²) and three-quarters of its population live in the central lowlands. Its main cities are Edinburgh (the capital and seat of government), Glasgow, Aberdeen and Dundee. Scotland contains vast areas of wild, unspoilt landscape largely comprised of mountains (including Britain's highest peak, Ben Nevis, 4,406ft/1,343m), hills and glacier lakes known as 'lochs'. The Scots have a strong sense of national identity based on deep cultural and historical roots, and their own language, Gaelic, spoken by a small minority of the population (mainly on its northern islands). Off its long coastline lie hundreds of wild and remote islands, most of which are uninhabited.

Edinburgh is a World Heritage Site with some 16,000 listed buildings among its sixteenth century tenements in the Old Town and the Georgian masterpieces in the New Town, all of which are dominated by the volcanic crag of Castle Rock and Edinburgh Castle. The city boasts a lively arts and cultural scene and its August International Festival is one of the world's largest and most important art festivals, while its New Year (Hogmanay) celebrations are famous world-wide. Many of Scotland's service industries are based here. On the west coast, Glasgow is a complete contrast to the more sedate Edinburgh and is one of Britain's largest and liveliest cities with interesting Victorian architecture. The city is essentially working class and when its traditional industries collapsed, its inhabitants suffered decades of problems including high unemployment, poor health, substandard housing and crime. However, in recent years Glasgow has reinvented itself and although the old problems still remain to a lesser extent, it's now Britain's third most popular tourist destination. It has excellent arts and nightlife scenes second only to London.

Southern Scotland is a collection of gently rolling fields in the east and high hills in the west, where Dumfries and Galloway is one of the most isolated areas and boasts majestic scenery similar to the Lake District (but without the tourists). Central Scotland is divided into two by the Highland Line geographical fault that divides the southern hills and plains from the wild northern peaks. This area is home to Aberdeen, a lively attractive city with a long history of sea trade and now the North Sea oil industry's onshore base, St Andrews (the home of golf), Dundee and Stirling (with its spectacular castle). The Highlands in the far north are characterised by wide-open spaces and huge lochs and mountains, and are one of Europe's few remaining wilderness areas. The Great Glen, a series of deep narrow lochs linked by the Caledonian Canal, divides the southern and northern Highlands. Inverness is the Highland's capital and Aviemore, in the Cairngorms to the south, is Britain's most popular ski resort.

Scotland's islands lie mainly off the west and north coasts. Some are relatively near the mainland such as the Isle of Skye, which is accessible via a bridge, while the Shetlands are some 112km/70mi offshore and are almost as much a part of Scandinavia as they are of Scotland. All the islands have frequent ferry services and some have airports, although both are subject to the ever-changing weather conditions. The islands are particularly popular with walkers, climbers and birdwatchers, especially during the summer months. The traditional island architecture of crofts (single storey, peat-burning dwellings) still abounds and many of the islands are fervently nationalist and home to most of Scotland's Gaelic speakers.

Communication in Scotland is excellent between the cities in the south, all of which are linked by motorways and railway lines, and Glasgow has an international airport (Edinburgh airport handles mainly domestic flights). However, once you leave the south communications are poor and outside the major cities it's essential to have private transport. There are regular ferry services to all the major islands (and to Ireland), although travel between the islands and the mainland is by no means cheap, and in the case of the Shetlands, very expensive. The region has the wettest and coldest climate in Britain, although it can be surprisingly mild at times during the winter in the south. Scotland is one of Britain's cheaper property regions, where the average home costs around £60,000, although in the major cities prices are much higher, particularly in Edinburgh where a housing shortage has caused prices to spiral.

Wales (Cymru): Wales (pop. three million) is a principality made up of the counties of Clywd, Dyfed, Glamorgan, Gwent, Gwynedd and Powys. Constitutionally it's close to England and the two countries have been unified since 1535, although (as in Scotland) a democratically elected Assembly for Wales was established in 1999. However, the Welsh have a fervent sense of national identity and are proudly independent in outlook and culture, particularly in music and literature. The Welsh language is spoken in all parts of the country and for many, particularly in Mid and North Wales, it's their first language. Two-thirds of the population live in the southern valleys and lower-lying coastal areas concentrated around the capital city of Cardiff and Swansea. For all its proximity to England, Wales is a country apart and much of the landscape is hilly or mountainous, dominated by the Snowdonia National Park in the north, a classic, post-glacial setting with the second highest peak in Britain (Mount Snowdon, 3,560ft/1,085m).

South Wales is densely populated and is one of the most heavily industrialised regions of Britain. The valleys were heavily exploited for iron and coal, although in recent decades the mining industry has been decimated and now only some 90 small private mines are in operation. As a consequence, unemployment and migration are high in Wales and alternative employment has been sought, mainly in tourism and service industries, which now employ two-thirds of the population. The region has been particularly successful in attracting foreign investment and many international companies have factories in South Wales, where Cardiff is a prosperous university city with a lively arts scene. The south coast is an area of outstanding natural beauty, particularly the Gower Peninsula.

Mid Wales is essentially rural with few inhabitants (except for one-quarter of the European Union's sheep population) and with its lakes and mountains, provides exceptional, unspoilt walking country. The Brecon Beacons National Park covers a large area of high grassy ridges interspersed with wooded valleys, all of which is virtually untouched by man. Aberystwyth on the coast is an attractive university town and the area's main centre. North Wales is dominated by Snowdonia and is noted for its abundance of rivers, lakes, waterfalls, forests and glacial valleys. The area is also famous for its slate mines (now disused) and gold mining. Perfectly preserved medieval castles including Beaumaris, Caernarfon and Conway line the coast, which also has a number of popular seaside resorts such as Llandudno and Prestatyn. In the north-west, Anglesey is Britain's largest island (although joined to the mainland by a causeway) and a popular holiday destination.

Communications in the south of Wales are excellent, where the M4 motorway connects Swansea and Cardiff with London and there are a number of other fast roads in the area. Trains services are regular along the south coast and into England and Cardiff has an international airport. Communications in other parts of Wales are difficult and time-consuming, particularly if you wish to travel from south to north, where the hilly terrain makes private transport a necessity. Trains run from Shrewsbury to Aberystwyth and along the north coast, where the A55 is a good fast road. Regular ferries to Ireland operate from Fishguard and Swansea in the south and Holyhead in the north. Wales has a mild climate although it can be windy and its rainfall is much higher than average (its reservoirs provides many regions of England with water). Property in Wales is generally much cheaper than the rest of Britain, with the average house costing around £60,000, although prices vary wildly with homes in Cardiff quite expensive and those in remote rural areas relatively cheap.

Northern Ireland (Ulster): Northern Ireland (pop. 1.6 million) lies 21km/13mi off the Scottish coast and has a 488km/303mi border with the Irish Republic. The province is made up of the six counties of Antrim, Armagh, Down, Fermanagh, Londonderry and Tyrone, although around half the population lives in the eastern coastal region, where the capital, Belfast, and most of the region's industry is situated. Northern Ireland is one of the least familiar parts of Britain and for many years has been the scene of a bloody conflict between Protestant and Catholic groups who have done great damage to the region's economy (although the recent peace accord has brought some calm to the area). Whatever their religion, the Northern Irish are among the friendliest and most hospitable people in Britain, and all share ancient music and dance traditions. A strong sense of identity prevails, although allegiances may be to Britain or the Irish Republic.

Northern Ireland is noted for its lakes, rolling hills, quiet villages and white Atlantic beaches. The northern coast is strung with castle ruins, small seaside resorts and excellent beaches and fishing ports, while in the south the Mourne Mountains are famous for their spectacular changing scenery. The region's major attraction is the Giant's Causeway in the north, a series of unique volcanic rock formations forming columns, some as high as 40 feet (12m). The region contains Britain's largest lake, Lough Neagh, covering an area of 245km² (153mi²) which is the source of a lucrative eel industry. Sheep farming is a major industry, along with whiskey distilleries. Fishing and golf are popular pursuits in the region and there are ample opportunities to practice both. Armagh is Ireland's religious capital and was the home of St. Patrick, the patron saint of Ireland.

Belfast is home to almost half a million people and boasts a fine setting at the mouth of the river Lagan. The city has much in common with Liverpool and Manchester, and was one of Britain's pioneers during the industrial revolution when the development of industries such as linen, printing and shipbuilding doubled the size of the city every ten years. Nowadays much of its industry is in decline and it has the highest unemployment in Britain. However, Belfast still has the world's largest dry dock and the tobacco and aeronautical industries remain healthy. The city has been extensively renovated in recent years, with many new leisure and shopping centres, and there's a lively arts scene.

Communications around Belfast are excellent and the city has a busy international airport and frequent ferry services to mainland Britain. Away from the capital, however, communications tend to be slow, particularly in the more remote areas. Northern Ireland has a mild climate, albeit wet and windy. House prices in the region are lower than in mainland Britain, with the average home costing around £55,000.

RESEARCH

There's a huge choice of property for sale in Britain in most areas, although in some areas (such as London and the south-east) there are a lot more buyers than sellers. As when buying property anywhere, it's never advisable to be in too much of a hurry. Have a good look around in the region(s) you have chosen and obtain an accurate picture of the kinds of property available, the relative prices and what you can expect to get for your money. However, before doing this you should make a comprehensive list of what you want (and don't want) from a home so that you can narrow the field and save time on wild goose chases.

Note that it's sometimes difficult to compare homes in different regions as they often vary considerably and few houses are exactly comparable. Properties range from period terraced, semi-detached and detached houses, to modern townhouses and apartments with all modern conveniences; from dilapidated country mansions and castles requiring complete renovation to luxury modern executive homes and vast penthouses in converted buildings. You can also buy a plot of land and have an individually designed house built to your own specifications. If, however, after discussing it with your partner one of you insists on a new luxury apartment in London and the other an 18th century castle in Scotland, the best solution may be to get a divorce!

Although property in Britain is relatively expensive compared with many other European countries, the fees associated with the purchase of property are among the lowest in Europe and add around 3 to 5 per cent of the cost. To reduce the chances of making an expensive error when buying in an unfamiliar region, it's often prudent to rent a home for a period (see **Renting** on page 155), taking in the worst part of the year (weather-wise). This allows you to become familiar with the region and weather, and gives you plenty of time to look for a home at your leisure. Wait until you find something you fall head over heels in love with and then think about it for another week or two before rushing headlong to the altar! It's sometimes better to miss the 'opportunity of a lifetime' than end up with an expensive pile of bricks around your neck. However, don't dally too long as good properties at the right price don't remain on the market for long.

One of the mistakes people make when buying a rural property in Britain is to buy a house that's much larger than they need with a large plot of land, simply because it offers such good value. Don't, on the other hand, buy a property that's too small. Bear in mind that extra space can easily be swallowed up, and when you have a home in Britain you will probably discover that you have more relatives and friends than you ever thought possible! If you're looking for a holiday home you may wish to investigate mobile (park) homes or a scheme that restricts your occupancy of a property to a number of weeks each year. These include shared ownership, leaseback, time-sharing and a holiday property bond. Don't, however, rush into any of these schemes without fully researching the market and before you're absolutely clear about what you want and what you can realistically expect to receive for your money.

The more research you do before buying a property the better, which should (if possible) include advice from people who already own a house there, from whom you can usually obtain invaluable information (often based on their own mistakes). A huge number of magazines and newspapers (see **Appendix A**) are published for homebuyers in Britain and property exhibitions are also staged throughout the year. Property is advertised for sale in all major newspapers (many of which contain property supplements on certain days) and local free newspapers. Information about properties for sale is also available on the Internet, where many estate agents have websites (see page 179). Numerous books are published for homebuyers in Britain (see **Appendix B**) and building societies and banks publish free booklets, most of which contain excellent (usually unbiased) advice.

AVOIDING PROBLEMS

The problems associated with buying property in Britain have been highlighted in the last decade or so, during which the property market has gone from boom to bust and back again in many regions. From a legal point of view, Britain is one of the safest countries in the world in which to buy a home and buyers have a high degree of protection under British law. However, you should take the usual precautions regarding contracts, deposits and obtaining proper title. Many people have had their fingers burnt by rushing into property deals without proper care and consideration, and it's all too easy to fall in love with a home and sign a contract without giving it sufficient thought. If you're uncertain, don't allow yourself to be rushed into making a hasty decision, e.g. by fears of an imminent price rise or because someone else is interested in a property. It's vital to do your homework thoroughly and avoid the 'dream sellers' who will happily prey on your ignorance and tell you anything in order to sell you a property.

The vast majority of people buying a home in Britain don't obtain independent legal advice and most of those who experience problems take no precautions whatsoever. Of those that do take legal advice, many do so only after having run into problems. The most important point to bear in mind when buying property in Britain is to obtain expert legal advice from someone who's familiar with British law. As when buying property in any country, you should never pay any money or sign anything without first taking legal advice. You'll find the relatively small cost (in comparison with the cost of a home) to be excellent value for money, if only for the peace of mind it affords. Trying to cut corners to save a few pounds on legal costs is foolhardy in the extreme when a large sum of money is at stake. You may be able to obtain a list of solicitors who speak your national language and are experienced in handling British property sales, either in Britain (e.g. from the Law Society) or in your home country.

It may also be possible to find professionals in Britain (e.g. architects and surveyors) who speak your native language, although you shouldn't assume that because you're dealing with a fellow countryman that he'll offer you a better deal or do a better job than a Briton (the contrary may be true). It's wise to check the credentials of all professionals you employ, whether British or foreign. Note that it's *never* advisable to rely solely on advice proffered by those with a financial interest in selling you a property, such as a developer or estate agent (see page 178), although their advice may be excellent and totally unbiased.

Among the most common problems experienced by buyers in Britain are buying in the wrong area (rent first!); buying a home that's unsaleable; gazumping (see below); buying too large a property and underestimating renovation costs; not having a survey done on an old property; not taking legal advice; not including the necessary conditional clauses in a contract; over-charging by vendors and agents; taking on too large a mortgage; and property management companies going bust or doing a moonlight flit with owners' rental receipts.

However, many of the problems associated with buying property in some other European countries are rare in Britain, such as buying a property without a legal title; properties built or extended illegally without planning permission; properties sold that are subject to embargoes; properties sold by a bankrupt builder or company; undischarged mortgages from the previous owner; builders absconding with the buyer's money before completing a property; claims by relatives after a property has been purchased; properties sold to more than one buyer; and people selling properties that they don't own.

Gazumping: When buying a resale home (you cannot be gazumped when buying a new home) in England, Wales or Northern Ireland, prospective buyers make an offer which is subject to survey and contract. Either side can amend or withdraw from a sale at any time before the exchange of contracts (when a sale is legally binding), which is an average of 12 weeks after the acceptance of an offer. In a sellers' market, gazumping (where a seller agrees to an offer from one prospective buyer and then sells to another for a higher amount) is rampant and *isn't illegal.* Sellers and estate agents don't take a house off the market when an offer has been accepted because the buyer may change his mind or take to long to complete the deal. Some agents may, however, agree not to show a property to other prospective buyers, but others actively seek higher bids up until the exchange of contracts. An agent is legally obliged to tell a vendor of all offers received on a property.

Don't take it personally if the vendor receives a better offer after accepting yours and asks you to match or better it – if you really want the property it may be better to swallow your pride. Around 30 per cent of offers that are accepted fail to reach completion for one reason or another – most house sales are part of a chain of sellers and buyers (around seven or eight isn't uncommon) and only one link needs to fail to jeopardise a whole series of sales. If you're a foreigner and a first-time buyer you will be delivered from the dreaded chain and will also be eligible for special mortgage terms (see page 98) offered to first-time buyers.

The conveyancing process in Britain is among the slowest in the world, with the average time required to complete a sale twice as long as in many other countries. There are proposals to speed up the home buying process (to around four weeks), by requiring vendors to produce a 'seller's pack' (at a cost of between £350 and £500), which includes commissioning a survey, collecting the title deeds and conducting local council searches before putting a home on the market. It's hoped that this will reduce the risk of gazumping, although many people believe that following the example of Scotland (see below) or other countries is the only way to stamp it out altogether.

Without a financial penalty (such as a deposit as in other countries) it's very unlikely that gazumping will be eradicated, particularly when some buyers are willing to pay double the asking price and may even pay in cash! You can hardly blame a vendor for accepting a higher offer, particularly when he doesn't know whether the lower offer will even go through. In a sellers' market your chances of being gazumped are very high (in 1999 it was blamed for wrecking one in seven deals) and it's so prevalent that you can now take out insurance against being gazumped after having paid for a survey and legal fees.

You can reduce the chances of being gazumped by exchanging contracts as soon as possible and trying to encourage a seller to sign a lock-out agreement where you have the exclusive purchasing right for a number of weeks (although most sellers won't agree to this and when they do you may need to pay for the privilege). To avoid gazumping, the American system, which allows contracts to be exchanged the same day a sale is agreed has been introduced by some solicitors. Most people agree that the present system is immoral, with both buyers and sellers reneging on deals with impunity, often just days before they are due to exchange contracts (and after a prospective buyer has paid hundreds and possibly thousands of pounds in legal fees and a survey).

There's no gazumping in Scotland as neither side can pull out of a deal once an offer has been made and accepted. When you wish to purchase a property in Scotland your solicitor contacts the seller's solicitor and notes your interest. Once the seller's solicitor has had sufficient interest, he'll usually fix a closing date, by which time all offers must be submitted in writing. Once your offer in writing is accepted, it's legally binding and you cannot pull out, therefore it's vital that you have a survey done (and have the necessary finance) before making an offer. The problem with this system is that each prospective buyer must have his own survey done (as in England and Wales), which has prompted a proposed change in the law where the seller is responsible for having a survey done prior to selling a property. This is an excellent idea, although the surveyor would have to be legally responsible for any errors to both the vendor *and* buyer (at present he's responsible only to the person who commissioned the survey).

Gazundering: This is the term used when a prospective buyer threatens to pull out at the last minute unless the seller reduces the price. Often the vendor has already arranged to buy a new home and is forced to go through with the deal. Although rare, gazundering is more common in a flat housing market where prices are static or falling and buyers are thin on the ground. To get their own back on 'gazunderers', some vendors strip houses bare, removing carpets and anything that wasn't specifically included in a sale – one vendor even went so far as to dig up the tennis court!

Negative Equity: During the recession in the early '90s Britain experienced an unprecedented collapse in property values, resulting in almost two million households with negative equity (where the amount owed on the mortgage exceeds the value of a property). Negative equity was widespread in the south-east (where over 25 per cent of owners were affected in some areas), although there was virtually none in Scotland and Northern Ireland. However, due to the surge in house prices in 1999 most negative equity is expected to have been eradicated by the year 2000 (unless interest rates start climbing again).

Repossessions: Due mainly to increasing interest rates, over two million people fell behind with their home loan payments in the early '90s and around 50,000 people a year had their homes repossessed by their lenders. Many repossessions weren't contested by owners who preferred to simply hand over the keys to their lender (see page 107). This is illegal and indemnity insurers (the insurance company who provides the lender with mortgage guarantee insurance when a home loan exceeds a certain percentage of the purchase price) often pursue errant borrowers if they default, for whatever reason. There were some 35,000 repossessions in 1998 and around 16,000 in the first half of 1999. Repossessions are expected to soar in the next few years as people who over-mortgaged themselves to get a foot on the property ladder fail to keep up their repayments.

Miscellaneous: It's important to deal only with a qualified and licensed estate agent, and to engage a solicitor before signing anything or paying any money. A surveyor may also be necessary, particularly if you're buying an old property or a property with a large plot of land. Your solicitor or conveyancer (see page 184) will carry out the necessary searches regarding such matters as ownership, debts and rights of way. Enquiries must be made to ensure that the vendor has a registered title and that there are no debts against a property. Your solicitor must make sure that the person selling a property is the sole owner or has the right to sell. It isn't unknown for a husband or wife to sell a home without telling his or her spouse, forge the spouse's signature and disappear with the proceeds, in which case the buyer may end up owning half a house only. It's also important to check that a property has the relevant building licences, conforms to local planning conditions and that any changes (alterations, additions or renovations) have been approved by the local council. Finally, if there's any chance that you will need to sell (and recoup your investment) in the short term, it's important to buy a home that will be saleable. A property with broad appeal in a popular area will usually fit the bill, although it will need to be very special to sell quickly in some areas.

BRITISH HOMES

British homes are usually built to high structural standards and whether you buy a new or an old home, it will usually be extremely sturdy. There are stringent planning regulations in most areas regarding the style and design of new homes and the restoration of old (listed) buildings. Britain offers a vast choice of properties (few countries have such a variety of housing), including some of the most luxurious and expensive homes in the world. Most British families live in houses rather than apartments. At the bottom end of the market they are likely to be terraced or semi-detached houses, whereas more expensive homes are detached and are built on a half or one acre (2,000 to 4,000m²) plot. In recent years Britons have taken to apartment living in the major cities (often more out of necessity than choice), many of which are tasteful conversions of old buildings that have been converted into luxurious loft apartments. Many single people live in huge apartments or large houses and generally people live in as much space as they can afford.

The British generally prefer older homes with 'charm and character' to modern homes, although you often find pseudo period features such as beams and open fireplaces in new homes. Some new luxury homes are built to modern standards using reclaimed materials, thus offering the best of both worlds. Although new properties may be lacking in character, they are usually well endowed with modern conveniences and services, which certainly cannot be taken for granted in older properties. Standard fixtures and fittings in modern houses are more comprehensive and generally of better quality than those found in old houses. Central heating, double or triple-glazing and good insulation are standard in new houses and are essential in Britain's climate. Central heating may be gas (the most common) or oil-fired or a home may have electric night-storage heaters. Air-conditioning is rare in Britain, although many luxury apartments and houses have what's called comfort cooling, air cooling or a climate controlled refrigerated air system. Swimming pools are rare in Britain, although indoor pools are becoming more popular in large luxury homes.

In the last decade or so, apartment and townhouse conversions have been common throughout the country and include former stately homes, hospitals, schools, churches, mills, warehouses, offices and factories. Barn conversions are also popular (and very expensive), but rare due to the lack of barns (you can also have a 'barn' home built from new). Loft conversions are popular due to their very high (cathedral) ceilings and general spaciousness.

Old homes: Old homes usually refers to pre-1940 and homes built prior to 1900 are often referred to as period homes, e.g. Georgian or Victorian. Older, larger homes often contain a number of interesting period features including high ceilings, fireplaces, sash windows, panelled doors, elaborate staircases, attics, cellars, alcoves and annexes. Fireplaces are usually a principal feature in most old houses, even when central heating is installed. Floors in old homes are often made of wood, which may be polished, although they are more likely to be carpeted. Walls are either painted or papered (in older homes the walls are more likely to be papered). Most older, smaller homes (e.g. semi-detached and terraced houses) were often built without modern conveniences such as central heating, double glazing, fitted kitchens and proper bathrooms, although most have now been modernised and contain similar mod cons to new homes. However, in some old homes that haven't been modernised there may be no bath or shower room or even an inside toilet! If a home has gas central heating, it will usually also have a gas water heater (otherwise it will have an electric immersion heater).

Modern Homes: Modern homes are built in a vast range of styles and sizes, from small studio and one-bedroom apartments and townhouses, to huge luxury 'executive' detached homes on large plots and luxury penthouse apartments. Most new homes in England and Wales (around 60 per cent in Scotland) are built with brick and block cavity walls, and only some 10 per cent are timber frame construction (40 per cent in Scotland). New houses are usually (but not always) built to higher standards than older houses and include thermal insulation, double glazing, central heating and extensive ventilation. They also usually contain a high level of luxury features such as tiled kitchens, deluxe bathroom suites, fitted wardrobes, fitted kitchens with cookers and refrigerators (possibly also dishwashers and microwave ovens), smoke and security alarms, and optional co-ordinated interior colour schemes. Refrigerators and stoves are usually quite small in British homes. Modern homes usually have a separate utility room off the kitchen where the washing machine and dryer are stored. A modern home has at least one full bathroom (in luxury homes all bedrooms may have en suite bathrooms) and a separate toilet or shower room. Homes rarely have shower rooms and no bath.

The most common types of homes in Britain include the following:

Bedsit: A studio flat with one room for living and sleeping.

Bungalow: A single-storey detached or semi-detached house. Popular with the elderly as they have no stairs.

Cottage: Traditionally a pretty, quaint house in the country, perhaps with a thatched roof (although the name is often stretched nowadays to encompass almost anything except a flat). May be detached or terraced.

Detached house: A house that stands alone, usually with its own garden (possibly front and rear) and garage.

Flat: An apartment or condominium, usually on one floor. A block of flats is an apartment building, high-rise tower block or possibly a large house that has been converted into flats.

Houseboat: These are popular in cities (with waterways!) and modern houseboats are luxurious and spacious. One of the drawbacks is finding a suitable mooring, which costs over £2,000 a year in London.

Maisonette: Part of a house or apartment block forming separate living accommodation, usually on two floors with its own outside entrance.

Mews house: A house that's converted from old stables or servants' lodgings (usually 17th to 19th century) and is the town equivalent of a genuine cottage. These are common in London and very expensive.

Mobile (park) home: A pre-fabricated timber-framed home that can be moved to a new site, although most are permanently located on a 'home park'.

Period property: A property built before 1900 and named after the period in which it was built, e.g. Elizabethan, Georgian or Victorian.

Semi-detached house: A detached building containing two separate homes joined in the middle by a common wall.

Stately home: A grand country mansion or estate, usually a few centuries old, many of which are owned by Britain's oldest titled families and open to the public.

Terraced house: Houses built in a row of three or more usually two to five storeys high.

Townhouse: Similar to a terraced house but more modern and larger, often with an integral garage.

RELOCATION AGENTS

If you know what sort of property you want, how much you wish to pay and where you want to buy, but don't have the time to spend looking, e.g. you live abroad, you can engage a relocation agent or property search company to find a home for you. This can save you considerable time, trouble and money, particularly if you have special or unusual requirements. Many relocation consultants act as buying agents, particularly for overseas buyers, and claim they can negotiate a better deal than private buyers (which could save you the cost of their fees). Some specialise in finding exceptional residences costing upwards of £250,000. Agents can usually help and advise with all aspects of house purchase and may conduct negotiations on your behalf, organise finance (including bridging loans), arrange surveys and insurance, organise your removal to Britain and even arrange quarantine for your pets (see page

75). Most agents can also provide a comprehensive information package for a chosen area including information about employment prospects, health services (e.g. local hospitals), local schools (state and private), shopping facilities, public transport, amenities and services, sports and social facilities, and communications.

Agents charge a fee of 1.25 to 1.5 per cent of the purchase price (or up to 2 per cent in London) and an up-front retainer of between £300 and £1,000. The retainer is deducted from the fee when a property is purchased, but if no deal is done it's usually non-returnable. To find an agent contact the Association of Relocation Agents (ARA), PO Box 189, Diss, Norfolk IP22 1PE (☎ 01359-251800, Internet: www. relocationagents.com) or look in the Yellow Pages under 'Relocation Agents'.

If you just wish to look at properties for sale in a particular area, you can make appointments to view properties through estate agents (see page 178) in that area and arrange a viewing visit. However, you must make *absolutely certain* that agents know exactly what you're looking for and obtain property lists in advance.

CHOOSING THE LOCATION

The most important consideration when buying a home is usually its location – or as the old adage goes, the *three* most important points are location, location and location! A property in a reasonable condition in a popular area is likely to be a better investment than an exceptional property in a less attractive location. There's no point in buying a dream property in a terrible location. Britain provides almost anything that anyone could want, but you must choose the right property in the right spot. The wrong decision regarding location is one of the main causes of disenchantment among those who purchase property in Britain.

Where you buy a property will depend on a range of factors including your personal preferences, your financial resources and, not least, whether you plan to work in Britain. It's advisable to make a list of what you absolutely MUST have and what your definitely WON'T consider, which will help narrow the market considerably. If you already have a job in Britain, the location of your home will probably be determined by the proximity to your place of employment. However, if you intend to look for employment or start a business, you must live in an area that allows you the maximum scope. Unless you have reason to believe otherwise, you would be foolish to rely on finding employment in a particular area. If, on the other hand, you're looking for a holiday or retirement home, you can live virtually anywhere. When seeking a permanent home, don't be too influenced by where you have spent an enjoyable holiday or two. A town or area that was acceptable for a few weeks holiday may be far from suitable, for example, for a retirement home, particularly regarding the proximity to shops, medical facilities and other amenities.

If you have little idea about where you wish to live, read as much as you can about the different regions of Britain (see page 131) and spend some time looking around your areas of interest. Note that the climate, lifestyle and cost of living can vary considerably from region to region. Before looking at properties it's important to have a good idea of the type of property you're looking for and the price you wish to pay, and to draw up a shortlist of the areas or towns of interest. If you don't do this, you're likely to be overwhelmed by the number of properties to be viewed. Estate agents usually expect serious buyers to know where they want to buy within a 30 to 40km (19 to 25mi) radius and some even expect clients to narrow it down to specific towns and villages.

The 'best' area in which to live depends on a range of considerations, including the proximity to your place of work, schools, pub, country or town, shops, public transport, pub, sports facilities, beach, pub, etc. There are beautiful areas to choose from throughout Britain, most within easy travelling distance of a town or city (and a

pub). Don't, however, believe the times and distances stated in adverts and by estate agents. When looking for a home, bear in mind travelling times and costs to your place of work, shops and local amenities (such as restaurants and pubs!). If you buy a remote country property, the distance to local amenities and services could become a problem, particularly if you plan to retire to Britain. If you live in a remote rural area you will need to be much more self-sufficient than if you live in a town and will need to use the car for everything, which will add significantly to the cost of living (and the traffic congestion will drive you mad).

If possible you should visit an area a number of times over a period of a few weeks, both on weekdays and at weekends, in order to get a feel for the neighbourhood (walk, don't just drive around!). A property seen on a balmy summer's day after a delicious pub lunch and a few glasses of your favourite tipple may not be nearly so attractive on a subsequent visit lacking sunshine and the warm inner glow. If possible, you should also visit an area at different times of the year, e.g. in both summer and winter, as somewhere that's wonderful in summer can be forbidding and inhospitable in winter. In any case, you should view a property a number of times before making up your mind to buy it. If you're unfamiliar with an area, most experts recommend that you rent for a period before deciding to buy (see **Renting** on page **¡Error!Marcador no definido.**). This is particularly important if you're planning to buy a permanent or retirement home in an unfamiliar area. Many people change their minds after a period and it isn't unusual for families to move once or twice before settling down permanently.

If you will be working in Britain, obtain a map of the area and decide the maximum distance you wish to travel to work, e.g. by drawing a circle with your workplace in the middle, taking into account traffic congestion and public transport. Obtain large-scale maps of the area where you're looking, which may even show individual buildings, thus allowing you to mark the places that you've seen. You could do this using a grading system to denote your impressions. If you use an estate agent, he will usually drive you around and you can then return later to those that you like most at your leisure (providing that you've marked them on your map!).

There are many points to consider regarding the location of a home, which can roughly be divided into the local vicinity, i.e. the immediate surroundings and neighbourhood, and the general area or region. General information can be found in guidebooks and on the Internet (e.g. www.homedirectory.com, www.goodhomes. beeb.com and www.upmystreet.com, which have links to other useful sites). Take into account the present and future needs of all members of your family, including the following:

- Check for signs of urban blight. Many once desirable suburbs surrounding Britain's major cities are in a crisis of neglect with increasing crime and a breakdown of the community. Indications are unkempt homes, gardens and streets; dumped cars and rubbish in streets; broken streetlights and signs; boarded-up shops and a profusion of second-hand shops; few local services; high crime rates; and stagnating property prices.

- If the climate (see page 52) is an important factor in buying a home in Britain, you should bear in mind both the winter and summer climate, the position of the sun, the average daily sunshine, plus the local rainfall and wind conditions. The orientation or aspect of a building is vital; if you want morning or afternoon sun (or both) you must ensure that balconies, terraces and gardens are facing the right direction.

- Check whether an area is particularly prone to natural disasters such as floods, storms or forest fires. If a property is located near a coast or waterway, it may be expensive to insure against floods, which are a constant threat in some areas. Despite Britain's high rainfall, some areas are affected by drought and there may be water restrictions during the summer.

- Noise can be a problem in some cities, holiday resorts and developments. Although you cannot choose your neighbours, you can at least ensure that a property isn't located next to a busy road, railway line, airport, industrial plant, commercial area, discotheque, night club, bar or restaurant (where revelries may continue into the early hours). Look out for objectionable properties that may be too close to the one you're considering and check whether nearby vacant land has been 'zoned' for commercial activities or tower blocks. Be wary of homes near airports, even small private airports. A planned expansion of flight-paths for jet aircraft is expected to affect over one million homes in the new millennium (unless somebody invents a silent jet engine), with as many as 13,000km² (5,000mi²) affected. The south-east of England will be particularly badly affected.

- Check for any surrounding trees on a neighbour's property or possible extensions and walls that could block your light (you have no right to light enshrined in law). If a house overlooks a village green (or green field land), don't assume that it will always be there as some have been sold off by councils to developers – nothing is safe from the hordes of rampaging developers sweeping across Britain!

- Bear in mind that if you live in a popular tourist area you will be inundated with tourists in summer. They won't just jam the roads and pack the public transport, but may also occupy your favourite table at your local pub or restaurant (heaven forbid!). Although a property on the beach or in a marina development may sound attractive and be ideal for short holidays, it isn't always the best choice for permanent residents. Many beaches are hopelessly crowded in the high season, streets may be smelly from restaurants and fast food joints, parking impossible, services stretched to breaking point, and the incessant noise may drive you crazy. If you're buying a permanent home it's important to check your prospective neighbours, particularly when buying an apartment. For example, are they noisy, sociable or absent for long periods? Do you think you will get on with them?

- Do you wish to be in a town or do you prefer the country? Inland or on the coast? How about living on an island? Bear in mind that if you buy a property in a remote area, you will probably have to tolerate poor public transport (or none at all), long travelling distances to a town of any size, solitude and remoteness. You won't be able to pop along to the local bread shop, drop into the local pub for a drink with the locals or have a choice of restaurants on your doorstep. In a town or large village, the market will be just around the corner, the doctor and chemist close at hand, and if you need help or run into any problems, your neighbours will be close by.

In the country you will be closer to nature, will have more freedom (e.g. to make as much noise as you wish) and possibly complete privacy, e.g. to sunbathe or swim *au naturel*. Living in a remote area in the country will suit nature lovers looking for solitude who don't want to involve themselves in the 'hustle and bustle' of town life. If you're after peace and quiet, make sure that there isn't a busy road or railway line nearby or a local church within 'DONGING!' distance. Note, however, that many people who buy a remote country home find that the peace of the countryside palls after a time and they yearn for the more exciting city nightlife. If you have never lived in the country, it's advisable to rent first before buying. Note also that while it's cheaper to buy in a remote or unpopular location, it's usually more difficult to find a buyer when you want to sell.

- If you're planning to buy a large country property with an extensive garden or plot of land, bear in mind the high cost and amount of work involved in its upkeep. If it's to be a second home, who will look after the house and garden when you're away? Do you want to spend your holidays mowing the lawn and cutting back the undergrowth? Do you want a home with a lot of outbuildings? What are you going to do with them? Can you afford to convert them into extra rooms or guest or self-catering accommodation?

- If you will be working in Britain, how secure is your job or business and are you likely to move to another area in the near future? Can you find other work in the same area, if necessary? If there's a possibility that you may need to move in a few years' time, you should rent or at least buy a property that will be relatively easy to sell and recoup the cost.

- What about your partner's and children's jobs or your children's present and future schooling? What is the quality of local schools? Even if your family has no need or plans to use local schools, the value of a home is often influenced by their quality and location. Many people pay dearly to live within the catchment area of a good state school, which is a big selling point that can add tens of thousands of pounds to the value of a property. Homes near foreign and international schools command high prices from foreign buyers.

- If you're planning to buy an apartment or townhouse, or a detached home on a private estate, you should check whether children and pets are permitted. Some estates prohibit children aged from 4 to 18 from living there (an experiment in 'family-free' living) and pets may also be banned. There may also be other restrictions (see **Leasehold Apartments** on page 174).

- What local health and social services are provided? How far is the nearest hospital with an emergency department?

- What shopping facilities are provided in the local neighbourhood? How far is it to the nearest sizeable town with good shopping facilities, e.g. a supermarket? How would you get there if your car was out of commission? Note that many villages have few shops or facilities and may not be a good choice for a retirement home.

- What is the range and quality of local leisure, sports, community and cultural facilities? What is the proximity to sports facilities such as a beach, golf course or waterway?

- Is the proximity to public transport, e.g. an international airport, sea port or railway station, or access to a motorway important? Don't believe what you're told about the distance or travelling times to the nearest motorway, airport, railway station, port, beach or town, but check for yourself. A fast rail link to London and other major cities can increase the value of a property considerably, while a home near a busy main road or motorway (within the sound of traffic noise, even if it cannot be seen) will be greatly devalued.

- If you're planning to buy in a town or city, is there adequate private or free on-street parking for your family and visitors? Is it safe to park in the street? In some areas it's important to have secure off-street parking if you value your car. Parking is a problem in most towns and cities, where private garages or parking spaces are rare and very expensive. Bear in mind that an apartment or townhouse may be some distance from the nearest road or car park. How do you feel about carrying heavy shopping hundreds of metres to your home and possibly up several flights of stairs? Traffic congestion is also a problem in most towns.

- What is the local crime rate? In some areas, the incidence of housebreaking and burglary is extremely high. Due to the higher than average crime rate, home insurance is higher in major cities and some resort areas. Check the crime rate in the local area, e.g. burglaries, housebreaking, stolen cars and crimes of violence. Is crime increasing or decreasing? Bear in mind that professional crooks like isolated houses, particularly those full of expensive fixtures and fittings, furniture and other belongings, that they can strip bare at their leisure. You're much less likely to be a victim of theft if you live in a village, where crime is usually low (strangers stand out like sore thumbs in villages, where their every move is monitored by the local populace).

- Do houses sell well in the area, e.g. in less than three months? Generally you should avoid neighbourhoods where desirable houses routinely remain on the market for three months or longer (unless the property market is in a severe slump and nothing is selling).

- A final consideration when choosing the location of a property is the likelihood of it being affected by radon. It's estimated that over 100,000 homes throughout Britain are affected, particularly in the south-west of England. Radon is a naturally occurring radioactive gas formed underground by the radioactive decay of uranium, which is present in small quantities in rocks and soil. For the majority of people the radiation dose received from radon isn't high enough to be a cause for concern and after surfacing in the open air it's quickly diluted to harmless concentrations. However, when it enters an enclosed space, such as a house, it can sometimes build up to potentially dangerous concentrations. The acceptable limit for radon concentration (known as the 'reference level') is 200 becquerels per cubic metre of air ($200Bq/m^3$). It has been shown that prolonged exposure to concentrations of radon above this level increases the chance of contracting lung cancer, and in a minority of homes and other buildings in Britain with high radon levels there's a significant health risk for occupants. **You can have a test carried out to check the level of radon in a building or on a plot of land.**

RENTING

If you're uncertain about exactly what sort of home you want and where you wish to live, it's advisable to rent a property for a period in order to reduce the chances of making a costly error. Renting long-term before buying is particularly prudent for anyone planning to live in Britain permanently. If possible, you should rent a similar property to that which you're planning to buy, during the time of year when you intend to occupy it. Some schemes allow you to rent first with an option to buy later. Renting allows you to become familiar with the weather, the amenities and the local people; to meet other foreigners who have made their homes in Britain and share their experiences; and not least, to discover the cost of living for yourself. Providing you still find Britain alluring, renting 'buys' you time to find your dream home at your leisure. You may even wish to consider renting a home in Britain long-term (or 'permanently'), as it saves tying up your capital and can be surprisingly inexpensive in many regions. Some people let their family homes abroad and rent one in Britain for a period (you may even make a profit!).

Long-Term Rentals: Britain has a strong rental market and it's possible to rent every kind of property, from a tiny bedsit (studio apartment) to a huge country mansion. Most rental properties in Britain are let furnished, particularly for lets longer than one year, and long-term unfurnished properties are difficult to find. The reason is historical, as until January 1989 landlords had greater protection under the law if properties were let furnished, although this is no longer the case. From 1997 all new tenancies have automatically been short-hold tenancies unless rents are over £25,000 a year or other arrangements (such as company lets) are agreed in writing. There's no initial minimum let of six months (as before) and a shorter term can be agreed between the landlord and tenant. You shouldn't pay a letting agent an up-front fee to find you a property, which is illegal (although some agents demand fees).

Rental costs vary considerably depending on the size (number of bedrooms) and quality of a property, its age and the facilities provided. However, the most significant factor affecting rents is the region of Britain, the city and the particular neighbourhood. Most rents are negotiable, although this depends on the local rental market. Long-term monthly rents are roughly as follows:

No. of Bedrooms	Monthly Rent
bedsit/studio	£200 to £450
1	£350 to £600
2	£400 to £800
3	£500 to £1,200
4	£600 to £2,000 +++

The rents shown above are for good quality modern or renovated properties and don't include properties located in the central area of large towns, in major cities or in exclusive residential areas, for which the sky's the limit. In London, rents are at least 50 per cent higher than the minimum shown above, while in some remote country areas they may be lower.

Short-Term Rentals: Britain has a wide choice of short-term, self-catering accommodation, particularly in resort areas and major cities. You can choose from literally thousands of cottages, apartments, townhouses, detached houses, bungalows, mobile homes, and even castles and mansions. Most property is available for short holiday lets only, e.g. for a few weeks or months, particularly during the peak summer season. Note that when the rental period includes the peak letting months of July and August, the rent may be prohibitive. Standards vary considerably, from dilapidated, ill-equipped cottages to luxury houses with every modern convenience. A typical holiday rental is a small cottage or self-contained apartment with one or two bedrooms (sleeping four to six and usually including a sofa bed in the living-room), a living/dining room, kitchen and bathroom. Always check whether a property is fully equipped (which should mean whatever you want it to mean!) and whether it has central heating if you're planning to rent in winter.

For short-term lets the cost is usually calculated on a weekly basis (Saturday to Saturday). For holiday rentals, the year is generally split into three rental periods: low (October to April), mid (May and September) and peak (July and August). A rural property sleeping two costs from around £300 a week in the low season and from £400 a week in the peak season, while a property sleeping four costs from some £400 a week in the low season to around £500 in the high season (you may be able to negotiate a reduction for long stays). At the top end of the scale you can easily pay £1,000 to £2,000 a week for a luxury apartment or house in London. Serviced apartments in London and other cities can usually be rented by the day, week or month. Major rental agents include Foxtons (☎ 0207-704 5040 – who publish a World-wide Apartments catalogue), Landmark Trust (☎ 01628-825925), Rural Retreats (☎ 01386-701277), Vivat Trust (☎ 0207-930 8030, Internet: www.vivat.org.uk), English Country Cottages (☎ 01328-864041, Internet: www.english-country-cottages.co.uk) and National Trust Holiday Cottages (☎ 01225-791199). Self-catering accommodation is advertised in magazines and national newspapers such as *The Sunday Times*, *The Observer* and *Dalton's Weekly*.

If you're looking for a rental property for say three to six months, it's best not to rent unseen, but to rent a holiday apartment for a week or two to allow yourself time to look around for a long-term rental. Properties for rent are advertised in British newspapers and magazines, including expatriate publications, and can also be found through property publications in many countries (see **Appendix A** for a list). Some estate agents offer short-term rentals and they can also be found through local tourist offices in Britain and the British Tourist Authority (which has offices in many countries), travel agents, the Internet and many overseas newspapers.

Hotels, etc.: Hotel rates in Britain vary depending on the time of year, the exact location and the individual establishment, although you may be able to haggle over rates outside the high season and for long stays. In most rural towns, a single room costs from around £20 and double rooms from £30 per night. You should expect to pay at least double or treble these rates in a major city, where cheap hotels are often used as permanent accommodation. Hotels aren't a cost-effective solution for home hunters, although there's often little choice if you need accommodation for a short period only. Bed and breakfast accommodation is also widely available in Britain, although it isn't particularly cheap (for budget accommodation you need to choose a hostel). There are also apartment hotels in London and other major cities.

Home Exchange: An alternative to renting is to exchange your home abroad with one in Britain for a period. This way you can experience home living in Britain for a relatively small cost and may save yourself the expense of a long-term rental. Although there's an element of risk involved in exchanging your home with another family (depending on whether your swap is made in heaven or hell!), most agencies thoroughly vet clients and have a track record of successful swaps. There are home exchange agencies in most countries, many of which are members of the International Home Exchange Association (IHEA).

There are many home exchange companies in the USA including HomeLink International (16,500 members in around 50 countries), Box 650, Key West, FL 33041, USA (☎ 305-294 7766 or 800-638 3841). Two long-established home exchange companies in Britain are HomeLink International, Linfield House, Gorse Hill Road, Virginia Water, Surrey GU25 4AS (☎ 01344-842642, Internet: www.homelink.org), who publish a directory of homes and holiday homes for exchange, and Home Base Holidays, 7 Park Avenue, London N13 5PG (☎ 0208-886 8752, Internet: www.homebase-hols.com). Other agencies include Green Theme International (☎ 01208-873123, Internet: www.green-theme.zb.net), Intervac Home Exchange (☎ 01225-892208, Internet: www.intervac.com) and the Worldwide Home Exchange Club (☎ 01892-619300, Internet: www.wwhec.com).

HOUSE PRICES

Buying a home in Britain has traditionally been an excellent investment, although this was severely tested in the early '90s when property investment was anything but as safe as houses! Unlike people in many other countries, the British see buying a home as an investment and many trade up every five years or so to increase the value of their main asset. Prices generally rise by between 5 and 10 per cent a year, although in recent years it has been possible to double your money within a few years in London and the south-east, while in the north of England prices have been falling.

Britain generally has a fairly buoyant property market in most regions, although in recent decades it has been prone to boom and bust cycles (in common with the British economy). In 1956 the price of the average house in Britain was £2,000 and it had still only doubled by 1966. The boom came in the early '70s, when prices jumped by around 90 per cent in three years to over £11,000 in 1973. The next big increases came at the end of the '70s, when prices rose steadily until skyrocketing in the late '80s. However, the boom years of the late '80s (when property values were doubling every few years in some areas) ended in a disastrous collapse during the recession of the early '90s, when many people lost their homes when mortgage interest rates soared to over 15 per cent. It took almost ten years for house prices to return to what they were at the end of the '80s; in 1998 the average property price was around £65,000, which was about the same as in 1989, although by autumn 1999 it had climbed to around £75,000.

In 1999, Britain was in the midst of one of the biggest property booms of all time, inspired by a shortage of property and low mortgage rates (in 1999 you could buy a home for twice the price in 1990 and still have lower mortgage payments). However, it was a highly selective boom that varied considerably depending on the region. Where house prices are concerned Britain can be divided into two nations. In London and the south-east prices were rising at around 20 per cent a year in some areas and towns, while in the depressed areas of the north of England property values were falling. For example, in mid-1999 the average price in Chiswick (an inner suburb of London) was £300,000 compared with Stoke £30,000 (west midlands) and just £12,000 in Newcastle (north-west).

House prices in London are now astronomical, with a small old-fashioned, one-bedroom apartment costing around £100,000 and a two-bedroom apartment in a new development costing £300,000 or more. (The cost of office space in central London has also rocketed and in mid-1999 was the second most expensive in the world after Tokyo, at around £50 per ft²/£550 per m².) For the price of a new apartment in London, where £1 million homes are commonplace, you can buy a modern three or four-bedroom detached house almost anywhere else in the country. However, it's expected that the sheer quantity of homes being built in some areas of London will eventually put a brake on prices.

In many areas each vendor has the pick of up to five buyers, which rises to 11 buyers for each property in the south-east (in contrast, it's just two in the north-west). Some vendors invite sealed bids and the winning bids are up to double the guide price. Buyers have had to move quickly in recent years, as good properties at realistic prices have been snapped up by cash buyers as soon as they come onto the market. Not surprisingly, first-time buyers are finding it hard to get their foot on the property ladder. One way is to buy with a friend or an unmarried partner, although you must ensure that you have a watertight contract, otherwise if a home is in the name of one person he or she will get the lot and you will have no legal rights! You may also be able to buy part of a home and rent the rest from a council or housing association (over 100,000 people own their homes this way).

If you're anxious to climb onto the bandwagon, bear in mind that while many analysts expected the boom to last a number of years, others feared a crash was imminent. However, you need to take what the 'experts' say with a pinch of salt as virtually nobody saw the boom coming (in late 1998 many agents were forecasting stagnation and advising their clients to wait before buying!) and even fewer will see the bust coming until it strikes (if indeed, it does)! Not surprisingly, Britain leads the world in boasting about house prices and, more importantly, property appreciation. Despite the high prices, overall British house prices are still below those in Germany, Ireland, the Netherlands and Norway in Europe.

In mid-1999 the approximate average cost of a house in Britain's regions (see the map on page 132) were:

Region	Average Price
Greater London (Central)	£120,000 (£185,000)
South-East	£105,000
South-West	£80,000
West Midlands	£70,000
East Midlands	£60,000
East Anglia	£70,000
Yorkshire & Humberside	£55,000
North-West	£60,000
North	£55,000
Scotland	£60,000
Wales	£60,000
Northern Ireland	£60,000

As with most things, higher-priced houses, e.g. over £250,000 (which outside London are usually termed executive or prestige homes by estate agents), generally provide much better value for money than cheaper houses, with a proportionately larger built area and plot of land, better build quality, and superior fixtures and fittings. Most semi-detached and detached houses have single or double garages included in the price. When property is advertised in Britain, the number of bedrooms and bathrooms is always given and possibly other rooms such as a dining room, lounge (living/sitting room), study, breakfast room, drawing room, library, playroom, utility, pantry, cloakroom, cellar and conservatory. More expensive properties often simply list the number of reception rooms (e.g. lounge, dining room, study, drawing room, etc.). The total living area in square feet or square metres is almost never stated in ads.

. To get an idea of property prices in different regions of Britain, check the prices of properties advertised in daily and weekly newspapers, newspapers published by estate agents and the price guides in property magazines (see **Appendix A** for a list). Property prices in almost every town in England and Wales can be found on the Internet, e.g. www.upmystreet.com, which claims to be 98 per cent accurate. Before deciding on the price, make sure you know exactly what's included in the sale and have fixtures and fittings and anything you're buying listed in the contract.

Buying at Auction

Buying at auction is becoming increasingly popular in Britain and the number and variety of properties (from terraced houses to country mansions) sold at auction is increasing each year, as is the number of potential bidders, which may be as many as 400 or 500. Auctions really came into their own in the early '90s when lenders used them to dispose of thousands of repossessed properties, although these now comprise only a small percentage of properties sold at auction. Note that when buying at auction you need to move fast as they're usually advertised only three to six weeks in advance and payment must be made in full within around four weeks of a successful bid. In addition to being a quick way to buy a home, you can also save money and there's no possibility of being gazumped! The disadvantages include survey and legal costs, which will be wasted if you're out-bid. Bear in mind when buying a property for modernisation or renovation that the costs can be astronomical.

It's advisable to attend a few auctions before bidding to familiarise yourself with the procedure. Before bidding at an auction, you must have the purchase contract (and title) of the property approved by your solicitor; obtain a valuation or survey, which may be provided by the auctioneer; and obtain a mortgage guarantee certificate from a lender in advance if required (in which case the lender will have a valuation done). When you have had a bid accepted at auction the house is legally yours and you must pay a deposit of around 10 per cent (in cash or by banker's draft – no personal cheques) and usually have 14 to 28 days to pay the balance. Bear in mind that when bidding at auction you bid unconditionally and if you're successful your deposit is at risk if you cannot complete the purchase for any reason (you cannot back out as with a private purchase). You should arrange buildings insurance (see page 60) as soon as possible after buying a property.

Note also that guide prices given by agents prior to an auction tend to be deliberately conservative in order to attract prospective buyers and the actual selling price is often so much higher than the guide price. The guide price isn't the same as the reserve price, which is the lowest price the seller is willing to sell for. If no-one bids above the reserve price, a property will remain unsold. However, if you're among the last bidders for a property that's withdrawn, you should tell the auctioneer afterwards if you're willing to improve your bid, as the seller may accept your offer. An auctioneer may also bid up a property to the reserve price himself, which isn't illegal and is a common practice when bidding is slow. You should take care not to go above the amount you have decided a property is worth or what you're willing to pay (if you go above a mortgage valuation you must fund the extra yourself), as it's easy to get carried away when bidding!

It isn't necessary to attend an auction in person and you can engage a solicitor to bid for you (when you must provide written instructions) or bid by phone, but you must arrange finance beforehand with the auctioneer. It may also be possible to buy a property before an auction – when prior offers are invited the publicity may contain the words 'unless previously sold' – in which case a purchase contract must be signed before the auction for a property to be withdrawn. If you plan to bid for a property, you should register your interest before the auction so that you can be informed if it's sold beforehand. The auctioneer's fee is usually the same as when buying from an estate agent (e.g. 2.5 per cent), but may vary depending on the value of the property and in some cases may be subject to negotiation.

Information: Information about auctions is available from the Incorporated Society of Valuers and Auctioneers (☎ 0207-235 2282, Internet: www.isva.co.uk) and Auctioninfo Ltd., PO Box 62, Daventry NN11 3ZY (☎ 01327-361732, Internet: www.auctioninfo.co.uk), which provides news and information about auctions throughout the country. The Auctioninfo website provides links to auctioneers' websites (e.g. www.theauctionchannel.com operated by Allsop & Co.), which provide online catalogues and details of individual homes for sale. Auctioneers publish catalogues that are mailed to prospective buyers. It costs around £400 to have a property included in a catalogue. The London Auction List (☎ 08700-777733) provides a list of properties for sale in London for £29 for three months and Faxwise (☎ 0207-720 5000) provides a results and catalogue service to auction buyers and sellers, plus a service called AuctionWatch. For £110 for three months or £350 for a year they will search catalogues produced by some 80 auction houses around the country for the particular type of property you're looking for.

Buying for Investment

In recent years British property has been an excellent investment, particularly in London and the south-east of the country. In 1999 the property market in London and the south-east was out-performing the stock market and all forms of savings, and provides both capital growth and income (if you let a property). Anyone who invested in London property in the last few years would have made a killing. Houses in some areas of London have almost doubled in the last few years and even in the worst areas look likely to double in five years. Prices in London have been fuelled by investors and in recent years many foreign buyers have purchased new homes off-plan without even seeing them. Some two-third of new homes in London are purchased for investment.

There are various kinds of property investment. Your own home is an investment of sorts in that it provides you with rent-free accommodation (although for most people who plan to live in a property, it's best to buy a home, not an investment!). It may also yield a return in terms of increased value (a capital gain), although that gain may be difficult to realise unless you trade down or move to another area or country where property is less expensive. Of course, if you buy property other than for your own regular use (i.e. a property that isn't your principal home), you'll be in a position to benefit from a more tangible return on your investment. There are essentially four main categories of investment property:

- A holiday home, which can provide a return in a number of ways. It can give you and your family and friends rent-free accommodation while (you hope) maintaining its value, or you may be able to let it to generate supplementary income. It may also produce a capital gain if property values rise faster than inflation (as they have in Britain in many areas in recent years).

- A home for your children, which may also realise a capital gain. In recent years many parents have purchased homes for their children while at university, which they then share with fellow students (who pay rent). Not only does this save on rentals, but it's also an excellent investment as rental property in university towns is always in high demand.

- A business property, which could be anything from bed and breakfast accommodation to a shop or office.

- A property purchased for pure investment, which could be a capital investment, to provide a regular income or both. In recent years many people have invested in property to provide an income in their retirement.

A property investment should be considered over the medium to long term (see **House Prices** on page 157), say a minimum of five years and preferably 10 to 15 years. **Bear in mind that property isn't always 'as safe as houses' and property investments can be risky over the short to medium term.** You also need to take into account income tax if a property is let (see **Taxation of Property Income** on page 118) and capital gains tax (see page 122) when you sell a second home, although if you're a non-resident it will be exempt.

Good investments include period properties built before 1919; four and five-bedroom houses; reasonably priced flats and maisonettes in the central area of cities; large loft apartments and penthouses; homes with garages (particularly in cities) or even better, double garages; riverside and harbour properties; homes near good state schools and near international schools; and property in university towns. According to some experts, prices in historic towns are set to boom in the next decade, with Bath, Cambridge, Cheltenham, Chester, Exeter, Hay-on-Wye, Norwich, Stratford-on-Avon, Windermere and York just a few places where prices have been tipped to rise sharply. A desirable address (postcode) can upgrade a property from an ordinary house to a desirable residence and one street away can make all the difference in value. Note, however, that the prices of property within a mile or two of a fashionable area may be much better value for money, simply due to a different postcode, and will often have better potential for price increases. If you're planning to buy in London, it may be more profitable to look for an up-and-coming area for maximum profit, rather than an area that's well established with fashionable restaurants, pubs and wine bars.

Properties to avoid generally include one-bedroom apartments, property in rundown areas or areas with high unemployment, unusual or non-traditional houses without universal appeal, poorly designed homes, apartments attached to commercial premises (e.g. above shops), houses near to any source of noise such as a busy motorway, holiday lodges (which also have high service charges), and nondescript 'ultra-modern' homes built in the '60s, '70s and '80s (which are difficult to sell in some areas).

Buying to Rent: When buying to rent, you must ensure that the rental will cover the mortgage (if applicable), outgoings and void periods. Bear in mind that in some areas rents are falling and there are doubts over whether the rental market can absorb the ever-growing number of buy-to-let properties. Gross rental yields (the annual rent as a percentage of a property's value) are from around 5 to 10 per cent a year (although gross yields of 15 per cent or more are possible in London) and net yields two to three per cent lower. Yields vary considerably depending on the region or city and the type of property, and are generally highest on apartments in London, although they can be just as high in cities such as Manchester, where property costs much less. Special buy-to-let mortgages (see page 106) were introduced in recent years for those planning to buy an investment property, under a scheme introduced by the Association of Residential Letting Agents (☎ 01923-896555). It has proved so popular that some estate agents have opened 'buy-to-let' departments.

Before deciding to invest in a property, you should ask yourself the following questions:

- Can I afford to tie up capital in the medium to long term, i.e. at least five years?
- How likely is the value of the property to rise during this period?
- Can I rely on a regular income from my investment? If so, how easy will it be to generate that income, e.g. to find tenants for a property? Will I be able to pay the mortgage if the property is empty, and if so, for how long?
- Am I aware of all the risks involved and how comfortable am I with taking those risks?
- Do I have enough information to make a rational decision?

See also **Mortgages for Second Homes** on page 107, **Property Income** on page 204 and **Taxation of Property Income** on page 118.

Sheltered Housing

For those who are retired or nearing retirement age, purpose-designed retirement homes (referred to as sheltered housing in Britain) can be purchased in most regions. Most sheltered housing is restricted to those aged over 55 or 60 and shouldn't be confused with residential or nursing home, as owners generally need to be mobile and able to look after themselves. However, help may be provided ranging from shopping and cleaning to full domestic services. Owners live in their own apartments, townhouses or cottages, which may be purpose-built or a conversion of a large country home. Sheltered housing is either located in a town with easy access to public transport or in an outstanding rural location with beautiful gardens. Individual homes may contain 'luxury' features such as a conservatory, and storerooms, garages or underground parking are usually provided.

Sheltered housing offers special features, facilities and convenience for the elderly and retired, including communal libraries and guest suites that can be booked for visitors. One of the most important features is that help is at hand 24-hours a day, either from a live-in warden or caretaker or via an alarm system linked to a control centre. Some of the larger developments are modelled on those in the USA with private amenities such as a theatre, restaurant, bar, launderette, shop, putting and golf course, swimming pool, tennis and bowling green. All developments levy annual service charges, which are usually between £1,000 and £3,000 a year for a two-bedroom property, depending on the services and amenities provided. When you leave you can sell your property on the open market or take advantage of a guaranteed buy-back scheme, where the market value is determined by the price of the most recent comparable sale.

Sheltered housing is a booming niche market and there are many retirement developments in Britain comprising over 100,000 private dwellings. It isn't, however, a cheap option, with a two-bedroom home costing from £75,000, depending on the location and quality, and prices in some areas well over £150,000. Despite the relatively high prices, homes sell quickly and you usually need to buy off plan in the most popular developments. There are a number of specialist development companies including the English Courtyard Association (☎ 0800-220858), Beechcroft (☎ 01491-834975) and Pegasus (☎ 0870-120 8844).

Mobile or Park Homes

Mobile homes (owners prefer to call them park homes) have increased in popularity in recent years and there are now around 1,200 sites in Britain with over 200,000 permanent residents. Park homes designed for residential use come in a wide range of styles, shapes and sizes, and are built to a high standard with luxury homes almost indistinguishable from permanent homes. Homes have timber frames with weatherproof exteriors and double-glazed windows, and many have a higher insulation rating than a conventional brick and mortar home. Homes are plumbed with all mod cons and are cemented to the ground, although they aren't as structurally sound as brick-built homes and are more vulnerable to fires and high winds. Note that despite the 'mobile' tag, modern park homes aren't very mobile, particularly as many have added rooms and carports permanently attached to the ground.

Homes cost from £20,000 to £100,000 depending on the size and luxury, with most in the £30,000 to £60,000 price range, or around half to two-thirds of the price of a similar size brick-built home. Resale homes are often sold furnished. When comparing prices, check the standard features and exactly what the price includes. Park homes offer good safety and security and are popular with retirees (many parks are exclusively for the retired). Many parks ban children as permanent residents and may also prohibit dogs and activities such as cycling. Parks are often like self-sufficient villages with their own village shop, pub, restaurant, meeting hall and amenities (such as a bowling green).

Before choosing a mobile home park, you should talk with other owners and ask them about a park's ground rent (annual fees), facilities and management. Read a contract carefully, so that you know exactly what's included and excluded from the rent. Ground rents are typically £75 to £125 per month (£1,200 to £1,500 a year), depending on the park and its amenities. It's important to take the same precautions when buying a park home as when buying a traditional home and to have a sales contract checked by your solicitor. You should also ensure that a park is a member of the BHHPA (see below) or a similar organisation. The Mobile Homes Act 1983 provided park home owners with security of tenure and gave them the right to sell their homes or leave them to close members of their family. Note, however, that each time a home changes hands the landlord (park owner) usually receives 10 per cent of the purchase price.

For information about life in a park home you can contact the British Park Home Residents Association, 3 Lewis Way, Lamins Lane, Killarney Park, Bestwood, Notts. NG6 8UJ or the National Association of Park Home Residents, Flat 1, 6 Rhiw Bank Avenue, Colwyn Bay, North Wales LL29 7PH. For information about parks, obtain a directory from the British Holiday and Homes Parks Association (BHHPA), Chichester House, 6 Pullman Court, Great Western Road, Gloucester GL1 3ND (☎ 01452-526911, Internet: www.parkhome.co.uk).

FEES

The total fees (also called closing or completion costs) payable when buying a house in Britain are among the lowest in the world and total between 3 and 5 per cent for a property costing up to £250,000. Fees are never included in the price quoted for a property. Almost all fees are calculated as a percentage of the cost of a property, therefore the more expensive the property, the higher the fees. Even removal costs will be higher if you have a large house (unless you have a lot of empty rooms). If you're buying and selling, you must consider the cost of both transactions. In 1999 the average cost of buying a £100,000 property was around £3,500 (excluding mortgage indemnity guarantee insurance – see page 99) and the cost of selling a similar property was some £2,500, making a total cost of around £6,000. Note that many fees are associated with a mortgage and if you're a cash buyer your fees will be lower. The fees for buying or selling a home in Britain aren't tax deductible.

Fees vary considerably depending on the price, whether you have a mortgage, whether you're buying via an agent or privately, and whether you have employed a solicitor or other professionals such as a surveyor. There's no such thing as the declared value in Britain and fees are always paid on the actual price paid. Theoretically it would be possible to under-declare the price (so that a buyer can save on stamp duty and a vendor on capital gains tax) and for a vendor to receive part of the price 'under-the-table', although this practice is virtually unknown in Britain.

If you're buying a property without selling one, you'll be faced with the following fees:

- **Stamp duty:** If you're buying a property costing over £60,000 you must pay a property tax, called stamp duty. Stamp duty isn't payable on 'fixtures and fittings' such as carpets, curtains, light fittings or kitchen appliances which may be included in the purchase price, therefore you should have your solicitor price them separately. Stamp duty is paid by your solicitor to the Inland Revenue.

Property Price	Stamp Duty
below £60,000	0
£60,000 to £250,000	1%
£250,001 to £500,000	2.5%
over £500,001	3.5%

- **Solicitor's or Licensed Conveyancer's Fees:** There's no fixed charge, but you should allow for 0.5 to 1 per cent of the purchase price (plus VAT). Some conveyancers will quote a fixed fee in advance. This should include searches (see page 184), although these may be charged separately.

- **Valuation:** You must pay for the valuation of a property before a lender will offer you a loan (even if you decide not to go ahead with the purchase). Check the cost in advance, which varies depending on the lender and the value of the property. The valuation for a £100,000 property costs from £150 to £200 (plus VAT), although many lenders now waive this fee.

- **Survey:** You should consider having a 'homebuyer report' or a 'full structural survey' carried out, particularly on an old property. The homebuyer report is a fairly brief assessment of the general condition of the property, together with a valuation, and costs around £300 (plus VAT) for a £100,000 property. A full structural survey is much more detailed and usually costs from £400 to £600 for a £100,000 property, depending on the surveyor, the property and what's included in the report. When combined with the lender's valuation, a homebuyer report or structural survey should be cheaper.

- **Land Registry Fees:** These are payable each time a property is sold and are to record the change of owner in the property register. The fee varies depending on whether the land is already registered or not (most property in England and Wales is registered). There's a sliding scale of charges depending on the value of the property, as shown in the table below:

Value of Property	Land Registry Fee
below £40,000	£40
£40,001 to £60,000	£70
£60,001 to £80,000	£100
£80,001 to £100,000	£150
£100,001 to £200,000	£200
£200,001 to £500,000	£300
£500,001 to £1,000,000	£500
£1,000,001 to £5,000,000	£800
over £5,000,000	£1,200

- **Mortgage Indemnity Guarantee (MIG):** If you borrow more than a certain loan-to-value (LTV), which varies depending on the lender, you must usually take out a mortgage indemnity guarantee (MIG – also called a high lending fee or mortgage risk fee). This is to protect the lender in the event that you're unable to repay the loan and the lender is forced to repossess (see page 107) and sell the property. Many lenders insist on a MIG if you borrow more than 70 or 80 per cent of the value of a property, although some have dropped MIG on loans of up to 90 per cent of the value of a property (see page 98).

- **Arrangement or Acceptance Fee:** This is usually from £150 to £400 and is paid when you apply for a loan or when you accept a mortgage.

- **Lender's Legal Fees:** Your lender's legal fees are usually around £300 (plus VAT) on a £100,000 property, although some lenders waive this fee.

- **Buildings Insurance:** It's a condition of your lender that a property is fully insured against structural damage, etc. (see page 60).

- **Removal Costs:** Although not a fee as such, the cost of moving house must be taken into account and should include insurance against breakages or loss (see page 190). You should expect to pay around £500 for a typical three to four-bedroom house.

Running Costs: In addition to the fees associated with buying a property, you must also take into account the running costs. These include council tax (see page 121); buildings insurance (see page 60); contents insurance (see page 62); standing charges for utilities (electricity, gas, telephone, water); ground rent or service charges for a leasehold apartment (see page 174); upkeep of private grounds; mortgage protection insurance (see page 65); garden and pool maintenance; and an agent's management fees if you let a property. Annual running costs usually average around 2 to 3 per cent of the cost of a property. All those who are liable for council tax must register with their local council when they take up residence in a new area and are liable to pay council tax from their first day of residence.

BUYING A NEW HOME

Although new homes may lack the charm and character of older buildings, they offer attractive financial and other advantages, including better resale values (in recent years new homes have commanded a price premium of up to 15 per cent over comparable second-hand properties). New homes are generally maintenance-free and there are no costs or problems associated with renovation or modernisation. It's often cheaper to buy a new home than modernise or renovate an old property, as the price is fixed, unlike the cost of renovation which can soar way beyond estimates (as many people have discovered to their cost!). If required, a new property can usually be let immediately and modern homes have good resale potential and are considered a good investment by most buyers. **You also cannot be gazumped!** On the negative side, new homes are usually smaller than old properties with lower ceilings and less sense of space, and they rarely come with a large plot of land.

The standard of new buildings in Britain is strictly regulated and they must conform to stringent building regulations and energy efficiency standards. Developers generally employ high standards of materials and workmanship and homes have higher specifications than old houses, including double or triple-glazing, cavity and under-floor insulation, and central heating. Most new buildings use low maintenance materials and have good insulation and ventilation, providing lower heating bills and keeping homes cooler in summer. Luxury 'intelligent' homes have discreet systems that allow you to control the temperature, lighting, security, music and TVs via wall-mounted or remote controls. Some developers even offer specially designed live-work homes for people who work from home (these are becoming popular in London).

Most new homes are made of brick (some 10 per cent in England and Wales are of timber frame construction) and some employ steel-framed panels, a new approach in Britain but used widely in Australia and the USA. Frames are pre-fabricated with foam insulation board ready for bolting together, which increases fuel efficiency and sound insulation. Although still rare, stone (usually from a local source) is again in vogue as a building material for new homes. Homes with thatched roofs have always been popular and nowadays many builders offer 'thatched' homes of almost any size.

A huge variety of new properties are available in Britain including apartment and townhouse developments – some of which are conversions of old buildings, although for all intents and purposes these qualify as new homes – standard family homes built on new estates, and a wide range of individually designed detached houses (including vast mansions). Waterside homes are popular and many new harbour developments have been built in recent years (waterfront homes are also marketed by estate agents at the London Boat Show held at Earls Court Exhibition Centre in January). Although rare, golf properties are in demand and may include a year's free membership of a golf club. Mock period homes (also called 'nouveau-riche' style) are common and include a vast range of styles. In some areas new homes must be styled to blend in with existing homes and many builders offer a number of 'mock' period styles. Some developers build mock period homes using recycled materials (e.g. bricks, tiles, oak timber beams, fireplaces, doors, etc.) from old properties, thus offering the best of both worlds for those who cannot decide between an old period home and a maintenance-free new home. Some developers event create new houses in the style of barn conversions to keep up with demand.

Many new properties are part of purpose-built developments, which may offer a range of sports facilities such as a golf course, swimming pool, tennis and squash courts, and a gymnasium or fitness club. Developments also include a bar and restaurant. Some properties built on a private estate have a resident's association or management committee to manage the upkeep of roads, landscaping, trees, plants, lamps, etc., for which owners pay an annual fee. There are usually also a number of restrictive covenants that owners must adhere to (see page 177). Unlike in some other countries, most developments in Britain are designed as permanent and not second or holiday homes. The cost of land is usually included when buying a detached house on its own plot, unless you agree a separate contract for the land and the house. Most new homes are sold direct by property developers or builders, although they may also be marketed by agents. New developments have a sales office and usually have a show house or apartment. Homes built within private estates or grounds often have excellent security including electronic gates, security lights and alarms linked to a central monitoring station.

Most new properties are covered by the National House Builders Council's (NHBC) Buildmark 10-year warranty or the Zurich Municipal building guarantee, and many lenders refuse to lend against a new house without a warranty. The NHBC warranty covers the owner for claims up to £10,000 against the builder's failure to complete the house, for the loss of a deposit or any expenses incurred in completing building work. During the first two years the builder is supposed to make good any defects arising from his failure to meet NHBC requirements, but take care, as some builders will do almost anything to avoid meeting their obligations. During the next eight years you're insured against major structural damage caused by defects in the structure, subsidence or heave only. If you suspect any building defects within the first two years, you should inform the NHBC in writing and have a survey done to check that your property is sound. The Zurich Municipal building guarantee provides a similar 10-year warranty, including protection against a builder going bust before a property is completed.

Buying new isn't, however, all roses and many new houses have a long list of faults. Your best insurance when buying a new house is the reputation of the builder. It pays to buy from a long-established builder with a reputation for quality, although the price may be marginally higher than buying from a builder who uses 'cowboy' contractors and refuses to honour his warranty. Before buying a new home you should check what other developments the builder or developer has completed recently and ask the owners what problems they have experienced. It isn't unusual for new homes to have hundreds of faults, most minor but some major. The NHBC warranty (which is half funded by developers) is next to useless when it comes to getting 'minor' faults rectified and the NHBC has been accused of being slow to act and insufficiently tough on builders (the building trade enjoys the luxury of self-regulation).

When buying a new property in a development, you're usually obliged to buy it off-plan, i.e. before it's built. In fact, if a development is built and largely unsold, particularly a quality development in a popular area, it usually means that there's something wrong with it (unless the market is in a slump)! The contract contains the timetable for the property's completion; payment dates; the completion date and penalties for non-completion; guarantees for building work; and a copy of the plans and drawings. Payments are spread over the period of construction, with payments in stages as the building work progresses.

If you're buying a property off-plan, you may be able to choose your bathroom suite(s), kitchen cupboards, wallpaper and paint, wall and floor tiles, and carpets, which may be included in the price. You may also be able to alter the interior room layout, although this will usually increase the price. Note that it's advisable to make any changes or additions to a property during the design stage, which usually cost much more later. New homes in Britain often contain a high level of 'luxury' features, depending on the particular development and the price. Executive homes with four or five bedrooms usually have three or four en suite bathrooms with separate showers; built-in wardrobes in all bedrooms; four reception rooms; a double integral garage; solid oak doors; designer kitchens with top quality appliances; ceramic floors in kitchens, bathrooms and cloakrooms; a security system; conservatory; kitchen breakfast room; utility room and possibly a cellar.

Developers may be willing to negotiate over the price or include extras free of charge, particularly if a development isn't selling well. Some developers will even pay your deposit, legal and survey fees (funded by a discount from the developer and cashback from the lender). Many developers offer a part exchange deal on your existing home, although you should be wary of such schemes. Most developers knock 10 per cent off the value of your home to cover their expenses and the valuation is also likely to be on the low side. Some even agree a price for your home and then reduce the offer a week before you're due to move (a form of gazundering – see page 146). You must be trading up and your home mustn't usually be worth more than 75 per cent of the new home you're buying.

Resale Homes: Buying new doesn't always mean buying a brand new home where you're the first occupant. There are many advantages in buying a modern resale home, which may include better value for money; an established development with a range of local services and facilities in place; more individual design and style (than an old home); the eradication of 'teething troubles'; furniture and other extras included in the price; a mature garden and trees; and a larger plot of land. With a resale property you can see exactly what you will get for your money (unlike when buying off-plan), most problems will have been resolved, and the previous owners may have made improvements such as an extension that may not be fully reflected in the asking price. The disadvantages of buying a resale home depend on its age and how well it has been maintained. They may include a poor state of repair and the need for refurbishment; few benefits of a brand new home unless it has been modernised; the need for redecorating and new carpets; poorer build quality and inferior design; no warranty; termite or other infestations; and the possibility of incurring high assessments for repairs in leasehold properties.

Information: Home and property magazines (see **Appendix A**) contain a wealth of information, including a list of new developments throughout Britain, and numerous advertisements from builders and developers. Daily newspapers are a good source of information, particularly the quality Saturday and Sunday newspapers such as *The Times* and *The Sunday Times* and *The Telegraph* and *The Sunday Telegraph*. Many home and property exhibitions are held throughout Britain including the 'Daily Mail Ideal Home Show' staged in March at the Earls Court Exhibition Centre (London), the biggest and best of all, the 'House & Garden Fair' (held in June at the Olympia Exhibition Centre, London) and various shows staged by Homebuyer Events Limited (☎ 0208-877 3636, Internet: http://eu-net.com/homebuyer) and Property & Investment Shows (☎ 0208-876 1979, Internet: www.propertyshows. com). You can also find information about new home developments on the Internet (e.g. www.yournewhome.co.uk/newsearch/index.htm).

Buying Land

You must take the same care when buying land as you would when buying a home. The most important point when buying land is to ensure that it has been approved for building and that the plot is large enough and suitable for the house you plan to build. When a plot of land has planning permission, the maximum size of building (in square feet) that can be built is usually stated. If you buy land from an agent, it will usually already have planning permission, but if it doesn't it should be made a condition of purchase. Some plots are unsuitable for building as they are too steep or require prohibitively expensive foundations. Also check that there aren't any restrictions such as high-tension electricity lines, water pipes or rights of way that may restrict building. Note also that the cost of providing services to a property in a remote rural area may be prohibitively expensive and it must have a reliable water supply. Always obtain confirmation in writing from the local town hall that land can be built on and has been approved for road access. It's also worth checking whether a plot is in an area where there are high levels of radon gas (see page 154) or problems with subsidence.

Most builders offer package deals that include the land and the cost of building your home. However, it isn't always advisable to buy the building plot from the builder who's going to build your home, and you should shop around and compare separate land and building costs. If you do decide to buy a package deal from a builder, you *must* insist on separate contracts for the land and the building, and obtain the title deed for the land before signing a building contract. Obtain a receipt showing that the plot is correctly presented in the land register and check for yourself that the correct planning permission has been obtained (don't simply leave it to the builder). If planning permission is flawed you may need to pay extra to alter the building or it may even have to be demolished!

The Cost: The cost of land in Britain varies considerably depending on the area, e.g. from around £25,000 to £100,000 or more for a half-acre plot. Prices have escalated sharply in recent years in many areas, fuelled by the demand for new homes. Land can represent up to half the cost of building a home, although it's still possible in many areas to buy a plot of land and build a bigger and better home for far less than the cost of a property built by a developer or a resale property. Prime sites are at a premium in many areas and many larger homes on a sizeable plot of land are bought by developers who knock them down and build a development of apartments, townhouses or individual detached homes. Many self-builders find a plot of land with a derelict building on it, which they may be able to divide into smaller plots to recoup some of the cost.

Information: The National Land Finding Agency (☎ 01371-876875) has thousands of sites on its books – you can access its database for three months for around £30. Plotfinder (☎ 01527-834435), a service of *Homebuilding & Renovating* magazine (☎ 01527-834499, Internet: www.ihomes.co.uk), and *Build It* magazine (☎ 0208-549 2166 or 01732-452020) are also good sources of plots for sale. Homelands of England (☎ 01572-822111) sell building plots ready for building with planning permission, telephone lines, electricity, water, mains gas and drainage (called serviced land and common in the USA).

Building Your Own Home

Self-building is increasingly popular in Britain, where over 30,000 people build their own homes each year. If you want to be far from the madding crowd, you can buy a plot of land and have an individual, architect-designed house built to your own design and specifications or to a standard design provided by a builder. You can even build it yourself, as many people do, although you will need professional help with some (many) jobs and it will need to be approved by building inspectors. Note that building permission can be difficult to obtain in some regions (depending on what you want to build) and building a home in Britain, or anywhere else for that matter, isn't recommended for the timid. It's advisable to engage companies and manage the project yourself if you're up to it, otherwise you will need to hire an architect or master builder to do it for you. Some self-build schemes involve a group of families building their homes together under the guidance of a self-build project management company, such as Wadsworth Landmark (☎ 0117-940 9800).

Planning Permission: If a plot of land doesn't have planning permission, you need to decide whether to apply for outline planning permission, which is a sort of agreement in principle – a way of 'testing the water' if you're unsure whether permission will be granted. The costs involved are less, but you cannot start building until full approval has been granted. Once outline planning permission has been given, you can submit detailed plans for approval. Alternatively, you can make a full application for planning permission from the start. This will save you time but, if it's refused, you'll have wasted money on producing plans and drawings. As they say, "you pays your money and you takes your choice", although by taking expert advice you can minimise any risks involved. If you employ an architect, he will apply for planning permission on your behalf. Note that it can take weeks or even months for planning permission to be approved. Application forms are available from the local council's planning department. The Department of the Environment publishes a booklet, *Planning Permission: A Guide for Householders*, available from planning offices, and the Royal Town Planning Institute publish a leaflet entitled *Where to Find Planning Advice*.

The Cost: When building your own home, land and building costs are usually separate (see above for information about buying land). Building your own home allows you to not only design your own home, but to ensure that the quality of materials and workmanship are first class. Building costs range from around £50 to £55 per ft² (£550 to £600 per m²) for a standard brick house, and £60 to £65 per ft² (£650 to £700 per m²) for a half-timbered home. Many companies sell pre-fabricated or kit homes for self-builders, which can be built in 12 weeks or less. The cheapest homes are kit timber-frame houses, where you buy the frame and supply the bricks and other materials separately. American-style timber homes are becoming popular and are offered by a number of companies including Leisuredeck (01442-242700), Timberpeg Post and Beam Homes (☎ 01727-841957) and Lindal Cedar Homes (☎ 01949-842551). One of the advantages of timber homes is that they have exceptionally low heating costs. Japanese style homes are striking and can be built for around half the cost of a traditional architect-designed house, although you may have difficulty obtaining planning permission (which applies to anything out of the ordinary). However, you have a good chance if it's in a secluded position and isn't over-looked by other properties.

The cost of a 1,500ft² home (140m²) is from around £50,000 to convert an existing building, £75,000 for a brick or timber frame home and £100,000 for an architect-designed house. VAT on materials and labour for the construction can be reclaimed within three months of completion. Note that the largest mortgage for self-builders is usually 75 to 80 per cent of the cost of the land and building combined (see **Self-Build Mortgages** on page 106). On completion, self-build homes are typically valued at around 30 to 40 per cent more than the total building cost (land, labour and materials).

Architect-Designed Homes: You should expect to pay at least 10 per cent more for an individually-designed house than for a standard builder's offering. An individual architect-designed house may also command a much higher selling price, as there are always buyers around who will pay a premium for individuality. You must ensure that the architect will be available to supervise a project and you should also check periodically yourself that nothing is going drastically wrong. When looking for an architect and builder, it's advisable to obtain recommendations from local people you can trust, e.g. a real estate agent or builder, or alternatively you can contact the Association of Self-Build Architects (☎ 0800-387310).

An architect should be able to recommend a number of reliable builders or contractors, but you should also do your own research, as the most important consideration when building a home is the reputation of the builder. However, you should be wary of an architect with his 'own' builder (or a builder with his own architect), as it's the architect's job to ensure that the builder does his work according to the plans and specifications (so you don't want their relationship to be too cosy). Inspect other homes a builder has built and check with the owners what problems they have had and whether they're satisfied. Planning permission and building plans must be obtained in advance and if you build without planning permission, in the wrong place or deviate from the plans, you could be legally forced to demolish the property (it happens). The authorities in Britain *never* turn a blind eye to planning infringements, as is common in some other European countries. If you employ a builder you should ensure that his work is covered by the NHBC Buildmark 10-year warranty or the Zurich Municipal building guarantee scheme (see page 167).

Contracts: You should obtain written quotations from a number of builders before signing a contract. The contract must include a detailed building description and a list of the materials to be used (with references to the architect's plans); the exact location of the building on the plot; the building and payment schedule, which should be made in stages according to building progress; a penalty clause for late completion; the retention of a percentage (e.g. 5 to 10 per cent) of the building costs as a guarantee against defects; and how disputes will be settled. Ensure that the contract includes all costs including the architect's fees (unless contracted separately); landscaping (if applicable); all permits and licences; and the connection of utilities (water, electricity, gas, etc.) to the house, not just to the building site.

Before accepting a quotation, it's advisable to have it checked by an independent building consultant or engineer to confirm that it's a fair deal. You should check whether the quotation is an estimate or a fixed price, as sometimes the cost can escalate wildly due to contract clauses and changes made during building work. It's important to have a contract checked by your solicitor, as building contracts are often heavily biased in the builder's favour and give clients few rights.

Information: Information about building a home is available from a number of sources including *Homebuilding and Renovating* magazine (☎ 01527-834499, Internet: www.ihomes.co.uk), *Build It* magazine (☎ 01732-452020), the Self-Build Association (☎ 01908-587596, Internet: www.thisis. co.uk/assoc_selfbuild) and the Federation of Master Builders (☎ 0207-242 7583, Internet: www.fmb.org.uk). There's also a National Self-Build Homes Show (☎ 0207-865 9042/0208-466 4066) held at Alexandra Palace (London) in September.

BUYING AN OLD HOME

In Britain, the term 'old home' usually refers to a building that's pre-1940, while homes built prior to 1900 are generally referred to as period homes, for example Tudor, Elizabethan, Georgian, Victorian or Edwardian. If you want a property with abundant charm and character; a building for renovation or conversion; outbuildings or a large plot of land; then you must usually buy an old property. Britain has a wealth of beautiful historic buildings, particularly 17th to 19th townhouses and country mansions. When buying an old building you aren't just buying a home but a place of history, a piece of cultural heritage, and a unique building that represents the architects' and artisans' skills of a bygone age. Old homes in Britain cover the whole spectrum from village houses to castles, farmhouses to mansions.

Homes with thatched roofs are attractive and very popular, although they are prone to fires (fire protection and an alarm system are essential). Before buying a home with a thatched roof you should check that it's in good condition, as the skills are disappearing and roofs are expensive to replace (they last anything from 20 to 90 years). Conversions of old buildings are popular in Britain and highly individual homes have been created from old schools, churches, railway stations, coach houses, windmills, towers, mills and barns – you name it and it has been converted to a comfortable home somewhere in Britain. An economical way to live in an historic building (often within private grounds) is to buy an apartment or townhouse in a building that has been converted, which include many former stately homes, hospitals, warehouses and factories.

Inexpensive old houses are available in some areas, but most have been snapped up and modernised years ago, and those that are left are generally no longer the bargains they once were. In rural areas it's still possible to buy old properties requiring total renovation or even total restoration, although they are rarer nowadays and are by no means cheap. The British have a passion for rescuing old tumbledown houses and restoring them to their former glory, and 'ruins' sold at auction often far exceed their reserve price. Note, however, that it's very expensive to restore an old property and can cost more than building a new house, particularly if you do it properly using reclaimed materials. Many people are lulled into a false sense of security and believe they are getting a wonderful bargain, without fully investigating the renovation costs, which are invariably higher than you imagined or planned! Some properties even lack basic services such as electricity, a reliable water supply and sanitation. If you're planning to buy a property that needs renovation, obtain an *accurate* estimate of the costs *before* buying it! While you usually get more for your money when buying an old home, the downside is that they require much more maintenance and upkeep than new homes, and heating costs can be high unless a property has good insulation.

Old properties can, however, provide better value than new homes, although you must check their quality and condition carefully. As with most things in life, you generally get what you pay for, so you shouldn't expect a fully restored property for £50,000 or even £100,000. At the other end of the scale, for those who can afford them there's a wealth of beautiful mansions, castles and stately homes with extensive grounds (some country homes even come with their own golf courses!). Substantial period homes certainly don't come cheap and country homes costing upwards of £500,000 are in high demand, particularly from foreign buyers. If you aspire to live the life of the landed gentry in your own stately home, bear in mind that the cost of their upkeep is usually *astronomical*. As a consequence many mansions have been converted into luxury apartments and townhouses in recent years.

Private gardens: Many London squares and developments have private communal gardens for the exclusive use of residents', which can add considerably to the cost of a property. London's shared gardens date back to the 19th century when the landed gentry came up to town for the season. They often have strict rules and regulations such as no animals (although you may be able to exercise your dog), ball games, barbecues, large parties and unsupervised children – their peace and tranquillity adds to their charm. Residents pay an annual fee and receive a key.

If you're looking for something unusual try Pavilions of Splendour, 22 Mount View Road, London N4 4HX (☎ 0208-348 1234, Internet: www.heritage.co.uk/ apavilions/poshtml2.html) or Save Britain's Heritage (☎ 0207-253 3500, Internet: www.savebritainsheritage.org), which is a charity set up to save endangered buildings. See also **Home Improvements & Renovation** on page 187.

LEASEHOLD APARTMENTS

Most property in Britain is owned freehold, where the owner acquires complete legal ownership of the property and land and his rights over the property, which can be modified only by the law or specific conditions in the contract of sale. Most houses, whether detached, semi-detached, terraced or townhouses, are sold freehold. However, this doesn't apply to apartments (flats), which are usually sold leasehold where 'ownership' is limited to the life of the lease, for example, 80 to 100 years for an old building and up to 999 years for a new building. (Unlike in most other countries, where apartments or condominiums are owned outright under a system of co-ownership.)

Most apartments in England and Wales are sold leasehold, although it's rare in Scotland. A property can change hands several times during the life of a lease and when the lease expires the property reverts to the original owner (the freeholder). When buying a leasehold apartment, the most important consideration is the length of the lease, particularly if it has less than around 50 years to run, in which case you will have difficulty obtaining a mortgage. Most experts consider 75 years to be the minimum lease you should consider. Leases often contain special terms and conditions, which should also be taken into account.

It's sometime possible for lessees to buy the freehold of their apartments and they may have a statutory right of first refusal if the landlord plans to sell. A lease may also be renewable, which must usually be contained in the leasehold agreement. In 1993 the Leasehold Reform, Housing and Urban Development Act gave certain lessees the right to acquire the freehold or a lease for a further 50 years. This right is available to tenants who have lived in a property for the preceding three years or three of the previous ten years, when the original lease was for 21 years or longer and the ground rent is above a certain threshold. For information contact the Leasehold Enfranchisement Advisory Service (☎ 0207-493 3116), which provides free advice and maintains lists of valuers and solicitors who specialise in leasehold properties. If you sell a lease that was drawn up prior to 1996, you must ensure that your solicitor includes am indemnity in the contract that allows you to pass liability for any debts on to the new leaseholder, otherwise you could be held liable – this anomaly was abolished in the Landlord and Tenants (Covenants) Act of 1995.

Apartments are common in London and other cities, but rare elsewhere, particularly in small towns, where they are unpopular and tend to be budget accommodation. In recent years many old properties including stately homes, hospitals, warehouses, offices and factories have been converted into luxury apartments, which have proved extremely popular in London and other cities where houses are rare and prohibitively expensive. However, although there's often little choice if you want to live in a city, many young professionals prefer to live in apartments rather than houses. So called 'mega-apartments', i.e. huge open plan apartments, and loft apartments with double or triple height 'cathedral' ceilings are popular in London and other cities, as are penthouses, some of which sell for £5 million (£1,000 per square foot) or more in London. They are often an emotive purchase, where you pay dearly for the panoramic views.

New apartments (particularly in London) are invariably lavishly appointed, which is essential nowadays if they are to sell well. The best apartments are beautifully designed and fitted, with developers vying with each other to design the most alluring interiors. These include designer kitchens complete with top quality appliances, en suite bathrooms with separate showers; fitted carpets; built-in wardrobes; ceramic floors in kitchens and bathrooms; and telephone and TV points (including cable) in all rooms. Luxury apartments often have a discreet system that allows you to control the temperature, lighting, security, music and TVs. Many luxury apartments and houses also have air-conditioning or what's called comfort cooling, air cooling or a climate controlled refrigerated air system.

Modern developments often have a leisure complex with swimming pool and gymnasium, sauna, Jacuzzi, tennis courts, plus secure parking and landscaped gardens. Sports facilities are often the clincher in an inner-city development. Some developments also have an in-house medical centre, business centre, private meeting rooms for residents' exclusive use, a restaurant and a bar. Security is a key feature of most developments, which may have a 24-hour caretaker/concierge, CCTV surveillance and a security entry system with entry phones (some even have a video entry system that takes a picture of callers who press your door button when you aren't at home!).

Advantages: The advantages of owning an apartment include increased security; lower property taxes than detached homes; a range of sports and leisure facilities; community living with lots of social contacts and the companionship of close neighbours; no garden, lawn or pool maintenance; fewer responsibilities than with a house; ease and low-cost of maintenance; and they are often situated in locations where owning a detached home would be prohibitively expensive, e.g. a city centre.

Disadvantages: The disadvantages of apartments may include excessively high service charges (owners may have no control over increases); restrictive covenants and regulations; a confining living and social environment and possible lack of privacy; noisy neighbours; limited living and storage space; and expensive covered or secure parking (or no secure parking).

Before buying an apartment it's advisable to ask current owners about the development. For example, do they like living there, what are the charges and restrictions, how noisy are other residents, are the recreational facilities easy to access, would they buy there again (why or why not), and, most importantly, is the development well managed? You may also wish to check on your prospective neighbours. An apartment that has other apartments above and below it is generally more noisy than a ground or top floor apartment. If you're planning to buy an apartment above the ground floor, you may wish to ensure that the building has a lift. The ground or garden level apartments (along with the penthouse) are more prone to thefts and an insurance company may insist on extra security before they will insure a property. Note that upper floor apartments are both colder in winter and warmer in summer, and incur extra charges for the use of lifts. Apartments under the roof may also have temperature control problems (hot in summer, cold in winter), although they enjoy better views.

Cost: Prices of apartments vary considerably from as little as £20,000 for a studio or one-bedroom apartment in a small town to £100,000 for a small old-fashioned, one-bedroom apartment and £300,000 or more for a new two-bedroom apartment in central London. Prices in London, where many apartments are purchased by investors, have risen considerably in recent years and in 1999 were £600 to £700 per ft² (£6,500 to £7,500 per m²) in prime areas. The price often includes a year's free membership of the health club. Bear in mind that amenities such as a health club or gymnasium don't come cheap and there are often high service charges, e.g. £4,000 a year, which may include hot water and heating. However, cheaper apartments are available in London's Docklands and south of the River Thames, where loft conversions can be purchased for around £250 per ft² (£2,700 per m²). Apartments in cities are a good investment and have excellent letting potential, always assuming that the rental market doesn't become saturated. Penthouses sell like hot cakes, although few people can afford the astronomical prices (often in the £millions). The best-selling apartments are spacious with at least two bedrooms and good views. Note that in popular developments you must usually buy off plan long before a development is completed.

In an older development, you should check whether access to private grounds and a parking space are included in the lease. Garages and parking spaces may need to be purchased separately. If you're buying a resale property, check the price paid for similar properties in the same area or development in recent months, but bear in mind that the price you pay may have more to do with the seller's circumstances than the price fetched by other properties. Find out how many properties are for sale in a development; if there are many on offer you should investigate why, as there could be management or structural problems. If you're still keen to buy you can use any negative aspects to drive a hard bargain. Note that apartments aren't universally popular, particularly one-bedroom apartments, and can be difficult to sell.

Service Charges: Apartment owners pay service charges for the upkeep of communal areas and for communal services. Charges are calculated according to each owner's share of the development and not whether they are temporary or permanent residents. A proportion of the common elements is usually assigned to each apartment owner depending on the number and size of apartments in a development. Ground floor owners don't usually pay for lifts and the amount that other owners pay depends on the floor (those on the top floors generally pay the most because they use the lifts most). Service charges include such things as road and pathway cleaning; garden maintenance; cleaning, decoration and maintenance of buildings; caretaker; communal lighting in buildings and grounds; water supply (e.g. swimming pool, gardens); insurance; administration; and fees for communal facilities such as a health club or gymnasium. Service charges may also include heating and hot water. Buildings insurance is provided by the freeholder, but you're usually required to have third party insurance for damage you may cause to other apartments (e.g. through flood or fire).

Always check the level of service charges and any special charges before buying a community property. Fees are usually billed monthly or bi-annually and adjusted at the end of the year (which can be a nasty shock) when the actual expenditure is known and the annual accounts have finalised. If you're buying an apartment from a previous owner, ask to see a copy of the service charges for previous years, as owners may be 'economical with the truth' when stating service charges, particularly if they are high. Fees vary considerably and can be relatively high (e.g. £4,000 a year) for luxury developments with a high level of amenities such as a health club and swimming pool. They may also increase annually. An apartment block in a city with a resident caretaker will have higher community fees than one without, although it's preferable to buy in a block with a caretaker. If a management company is employed to manage and maintain an apartment block, the service fees are likely to be higher, but the building is also likely to be maintained better. High fees aren't necessarily a negative point (assuming you can afford them), providing you receive value for money and the development is well managed and maintained. The value of a leasehold apartment depends to a large extent on how well it's maintained and managed.

Disputes over service charges can be acrimonious, although they are usually confined to old buildings. Service charge disputes between apartment owners and landlords should be heard by a Leasehold Valuation Tribunal (LVT), with a panel comprising a solicitor, valuer and a third experienced person, and not by county courts. In the past landlords have used threats of expensive court action to intimidate flat owners into paying higher fees. Many landlords have increased their service charges significantly in recent years, which often bear little or no relationship to actual costs, and many people have been hit by high charges for major repairs (see below). It's essential when buying a leasehold property to take legal advice and have the lease checked by a solicitor.

Maintenance & Repairs: If necessary, owners can be assessed an additional service charge to make up for any shortfall of funds for maintenance or repairs. You should check the condition of the common areas (including all amenities) in an old development and whether any major maintenance or capital expense is planned for which you could be assessed. Beware of bargain apartments in buildings requiring a lot of maintenance work or refurbishment. Most developments have a sink or reserve fund to pay for major expenses, which is funded from general service charges.

Ground Rent: Ground rent is a nominal rent for the land on which an apartment block is built and is usually around £100 a year. The lease should indicate whether the ground rent is fixed or whether it can be reviewed after a certain period.

Covenants & Restrictions: Covenants are legally binding obligations of the freeholder and leaseholder to do or refrain from doing certain things, while restrictions are regulations governing how leaseholders are required to behave. Restrictions usually include such things as noise levels; the keeping of pets; renting; exterior decoration and plants (e.g. the placement of shrubs); garbage disposal; the use of gymnasiums and other recreational facilities; parking; business or professional use; and the hanging of laundry. Check the regulations and discuss any restrictions you're unsure about with residents. Permanent residents should avoid buying in a development with a high percentage of rental units, i.e. units that aren't owner-occupied, although you may have little choice in London.

ESTATE AGENTS & SOLICITOR AGENTS

Most property in Britain is bought and sold through estate agents (they aren't called real estate agents, realtors or brokers in Britain) who sell property on commission for owners, although an increasing number of people are selling their own homes (see page 209). In Scotland, most property sales are handled by solicitor agents, whose property centres provide a one-stop shop for buying, selling and conveyancing. Consequently the whole process of property buying is generally much quicker and cheaper in Scotland. A solicitor agent also isn't tied to any financial institution and is obliged to provide a genuine independent financial advice.

Property sold by estate agents and solicitor agents is said to be sold by private treaty, a method of selling a property by agreement between the vendor and the purchaser, either directly or through an estate agent. Although there are nationwide chains of estate agents in Britain, e.g. covering England and Wales, most agents are local and don't have a nationwide listing of properties in other regions. There's no multi-listing system in Britain, as for example in North America, and agents jealously guard their list of properties from competitors. If you wish to find an agent in a particular town or area, look under estate agents in the local Yellow Pages (available at main libraries in many countries), check the Internet (see below) or hire a relocation agent (see page 149) to find you a home. Many estate agents are also letting and management agents.

Note that estate agents in England and Wales aren't required to have any professional training or qualifications and don't need to be members of any professional organisations (although most are). Estate agents have a terrible public image (it's the occupation that dare not speak its name!) and given a choice many people would rather buy a house from a used car dealer than from an estate agent. There's very little control over estate agents, some of who deliberately force up prices, misrepresent properties or have an undisclosed personal financial interest in a property. The big losers are often those selling a home, as to push a deal through an agent may discourage higher offers (particularly if the lower offer is funded by a mortgage through the agent) or keep the price low by telling buyers how much to offer. Both are illegal as estate agents are required by law to obtain the best deal they can for the vendor.

Other shady deals (all of which are illegal) include accepting money from a buyer to 'ring-fencing' a property sale (reject higher bids) at the same time as taking legitimate fees from sellers; tipping off property developers to undervalued properties owned by naïve sellers in return for a slice of the profit; holding back under-priced, repossessed houses for developers and other favoured buyers in return for a 'cut'; intimidating buyers into bidding over the market price with fictitious 'other' bids; coercing sellers into signing restrictive 'sole agency' agreements (this practice is widespread); and insisting on buyers buying insurance or obtaining a mortgage through the agent's own financial services division. It pays to use more than one agent when selling to avoid dirty tricks. An agent isn't permitted to over-elaborate on property descriptions under the Property Misdescriptions Act 1991, prior to which a garden shed could resemble a palace in 'agent-speak'.

Many estate agents are owned by banks and other financial institutions, and offer only the financial products of their owners, which means that you don't receive independent financial advice and are unlikely to obtain the best mortgage or insurance deal from them. You may receive a better service from the owner-proprietor of a long-established family business than from one of the large chains. Some large estate agents (e.g. Hambro Countrywide) offer an in-house conveyancing service, although you may be better off with an independent solicitor or conveyancer, as an agent's services could easily lead to conflicts of interest. In response to this incursion onto their turf, some solicitors in England and Wales have now started selling properties, as is normal practice in Scotland.

If possible, you should decide where you want to live, what sort of property you want and your budget *before* visiting Britain. Obtain details of as many properties as possible in your chosen area and make a shortlist of those you wish to view. Usually the details provided by agents are sparse and few provide detailed descriptions of properties. In certain areas popular with foreign buyers (such as London), local agents may work with overseas agents in certain countries. Agents who advertise in foreign journals or who work closely with overseas agents may provide colour photographs and a full description, particularly for expensive properties. The best agents provide an abundance of information. Agents vary enormously in their efficiency, enthusiasm and professionalism, and if an agent shows little interest in finding out exactly what you want you should look elsewhere. If you're an overseas buyer, you should confirm (and reconfirm) that a particular property is still for sale and the price before travelling to Britain to view it.

Note that an agent may ask you to sign a document before showing you any properties, which is simply to protect his commission should you obtain details from another source or try to do a deal with the owner behind his back. In Britain you're usually shown properties personally by agents and won't be given the keys (particularly to furnished properties) or be expected to deal with tenants or vendors directly. You should make an appointment to see properties, as agents don't like people just turning up. If you make an appointment you should keep it or call and cancel it. If you happen to be on holiday it's okay to drop in unannounced to have a look at what's on offer, but don't expect an agent to show you properties without an appointment. If you view properties during a holiday, it's advisable to do so at the beginning so that you can return later to inspect any you particularly like a second or third time. Agents may offer open viewing of some properties on certain days without an appointment. Note that few agents work at weekends or in the evenings.

You should try to view as many properties as possible during the time available, but allow sufficient time to view each property thoroughly, to travel and get lost between houses, and for breaks for sustenance. Although it's important to see sufficient properties to form an accurate opinion of price and quality, don't see too many in one day (between six and eight is usually a manageable number) as it's easy to become confused about the merits of each property. If you're shown properties that don't meet your specifications, tell the agent immediately. You can also help the agent narrow the field by telling him exactly what's wrong with the properties you reject. It's advisable to make notes of both the good *and* bad features and take lots of photographs of the properties you like, so that you're able to compare them later at your leisure (but keep a record of which photos are of which house!). It's also wise to mark each property on a map so that should you wish to return, you can find them without getting lost (too often). The more a property appeals to you, the more you should look for faults and negative points; if you still like it after stressing all the negative points it must have special appeal!

Internet: You can search for an estate agent or property on the Internet, which has come a long way in recent years and is expected to dominate the market in the next decade (in the USA some 70 per cent of homes are advertised on the Internet). It's particularly useful when you're looking for a property from abroad, when the Internet can be a good place to start and allows you to peruse property lists at your leisure. Some agents offer virtual viewing whereby you can take a guided tour around a property via your computer. Among the many good websites available are (in no particular order) www.propertylive.co.uk, www.houseweb.co.uk www.findaproperty. com, www.propertyargus.co.uk (Wales), www.homedirectory.com, www.property-seeker.co.uk, www.realestate.com, www.hot-property.com/scripts/lootsite.dll, www. propertyandland.uksw.com, www/home2view.co.uk http://beeb/ukplus.co.uk/, www. propertyfinder.co.uk, www.propertycity.co.uk, www.homes-on-line.com, www. propreg.com and www.faronsutaria.co.uk (which is a multi-lingual site). Most of the above sites aren't dedicated to single agents and many allow you to search for homes and agents throughout Britain, e.g. by location and price. Many estate agents produce free newspapers and magazines containing details of both old and new houses, and colour prospectuses for new property developments.

Always choose an estate agent that's a member of a professional organisation, such as the National Association of Estate Agents (NAEA, ☎ 01926-496800, Internet: www.naea.co.uk). You should also check whether an agent is a member of the Ombudsman Scheme for Estate Agents (☎ 01722-333306), whose members must abide by a code of practice and to whom you can complain if you have a problem. See also **Selling a Home** on page 209.

INSPECTIONS & SURVEYS

When you have found a property that you like, you should make a close inspection of its condition. Obviously this will depend on whether it's an old home in need of renovation or a modern home. Some simple checks you can do include testing the electrical system, plumbing, mains water, hot water boiler and central heating. Don't take someone else's word that these are functional, but check them yourself. Although building standards in Britain are generally high, you should never assume that a building is sound, as even relatively new buildings can have serious faults (although rare). Before commissioning a survey there are a number of obvious signs of damage or decay that you can spot without being an expert.

An old property may show visible signs of damage and decay, such as bulging or cracked walls, rising damp, missing roof slates and rotten woodwork. Take a close look at both internal and external walls, e.g. for cracks or signs of damp (tidemarks or discoloured plaster, particularly on the ground floor or in the basement). Cracks might indicate signs of subsidence, which should be avoided at all costs (also check that the exterior walls are vertical). A few small cracks in walls don't necessarily indicate subsidence as many small cracks happen naturally as houses age. Bear in mind that houses built before 1960 are more likely to be more prone to subsidence, because the foundations tended to be shallower. Damp is one of the most difficult and expensive problems to eradicate (if any damp proofing or other repair work has been carried out, check whether it's guaranteed). Some areas are prone to flooding, storms and subsidence, and it's advisable to check an old property after a heavy rainfall, when any leaks should come to light. Check the roof (with binoculars if necessary) for signs of dislodged slates and leaks in the roof space.

Check that the mortar isn't soft or weathered, that cracks aren't present in the brickwork and that the air-bricks are present and aren't blocked. Examine wooden window frames for signs of rot. If new windows (e.g. double glazing), central heating, re-wiring or re-plumbing are required it will be expensive and should be reflected in (or deducted from) the asking price. Check the quality of any building work or 'improvements' that have been carried out and whether work is guaranteed (when it should be backed by an industry-recognised warranty). Examine the state of the interior and exterior decoration. If it's poor it may indicate that more important repairs have been neglected or fixed temporarily. Check the state of the garden and whether it will need professional work (landscaping is expensive).

British Lenders insist on a valuation before approving a loan, although this usually consists of a perfunctory check to confirm that a property is worth the purchase price. Around half of all buyers in Britain don't have a survey carried out when buying a property, which is risky considering that around one in five properties are found by surveyors to have major faults, such as damp or dry rot. Serious defects are often found in properties less than ten years old and it's important that you discover them before you buy. A property vendor in Britain doesn't need to inform prospective buyers of any defects that might exist in a property, although there are plans to introduce a seller's survey as part a new package designed to speed up the home buying process and reduce gazumping.

Property inspections should be carried out by a qualified surveyor only, who should be a member of the Royal Institute of Chartered Surveyors (RICS) or the Incorporated Society of Valuers & Auctioneers (ISVA). Members of both the RICS and the ISVA must have professional indemnity insurance, which means you can happily sue them if they do a bad job. Put your instructions in writing and include anything you particularly want inspected, plus details of any major work you're planning to have done after moving in. Check what you'll receive for your money and obtain a written estimate that includes VAT and all expenses. It's important to find a good surveyor you can trust to do a good job, as a bad survey can be just as expensive as none at all (as many buyers have found out to their cost).

You may be able to find a foreign surveyor practising in Britain, who will write a report in your own language. However, bear in mind that a British surveyor will have an intimate knowledge of local properties and building methods. If you employ a foreign surveyor, you must ensure that he's experienced in the idiosyncrasies of British properties and that he has professional indemnity insurance covering Britain. A home inspection can be limited to a few items or even a single system only, such as the wiring or plumbing in an old house. If you want an inspection on an unusual property, such as a thatched cottage or period home, then you should choose a surveyor with experience of these.

There are three levels of property inspections in Britain: a valuation, a homebuyer report and a full structural survey.

Valuation: If you're obtaining a loan to purchase a property, your lender must be satisfied that the property provides sufficient security for the loan, and he'll therefore carry out an independent valuation which you must usually pay for (whether or not you go through with the purchase). Check the cost in advance, which varies depending on the lender and the value of the property. A valuation for a £100,000 property costs from £150 to £200, although many lenders now waive this fee. Although it's carried out by a qualified surveyor, it's merely a cautious assessment of the value of the property and not a survey. It's a gamble to rely on a valuation report as it's no guarantee that a property is structurally sound. You may be able to combine a homebuyer report or full structural survey with your lender's valuation, which should save you money, although you may prefer to use a surveyor who has been personally recommended to you or who you have used before. Note that if your lender's valuation is less than the asking price, you may have to pull out of the deal if you cannot get the seller to reduce the price or raise more cash.

Homebuyer Report: A homebuyer report (or homebuyer survey and valuation report/HSVR) is a concise report on the condition of a property, together with a valuation, and costs around £250 for a £100,000 property and £350 for a £200,000 property (the cost also depends on the age of the property). In addition to a mortgage valuation, it includes the current open market value and an opinion of how saleable the property may be in future. Any major defects in the property will be listed, along with recommendations about any further investigations required. The property will be inspected only where it's reasonably accessible and no test is made of the plumbing, heating, electrical or drainage systems (etc.). A homebuyer report isn't much cheaper than a full structural survey and therefore, unless you have a good reason not to, you should consider having a full structural survey carried out. A homebuyer report isn't usually considered sufficient for large houses over say 2,000 ft² (around 200m²), old properties (pre-1940), and converted or purpose-built apartments.

Full Structural Survey: A full structural survey is normally tailored to individual requirements and is particularly suited to larger, older, more complex properties, which may be outside the scope of a homebuyer report. A full structural report usually costs between £300 and £600 depending on the value, size and age of a property and its condition. You should shop around and obtain a few quotes – you may be able to negotiate a lower price. Some people delay having a full structural survey done until both parties are ready to exchange contracts, as it's expensive having a report done for each house you're interested in. Only one in four property buyers in Britain has a full structural survey carried out. The surveyor will examine everything that's reasonably visible, in addition to reporting on the construction and condition of a property. A structural survey includes the structural condition of all buildings, particularly the foundations, roofs, walls and woodwork; plumbing, electricity and heating systems; and anything else you want inspected such as a swimming pool and its equipment, e.g. filter system or heating.

Discuss with a surveyor exactly what will be included in a survey, and most importantly, what will be excluded. You may need to pay extra to include certain checks and tests, as the conditions of this type of report are a matter of negotiation between you and your surveyor. Typical extras may include an environmental survey and an energy efficiency rating. The surveyor will also advise on any repair costs and the suitability of proposed improvements or extensions you plan to make. Although the scope of the inspection is greater than a valuation or homebuyer report, there will still be some inaccessible parts of the structure and limitations. If you want a detailed survey, make sure that the seller will allow your surveyor free access to the property, e.g. to the roof space (loft), and allow him to pull up carpets to examine floorboards. You will receive a written report on the structural condition of a property, including anything that could become a problem in the future. Some surveyors will allow you to accompany them and they may produce a video of their findings in addition to a written report.

Sometimes the valuation or surveyor's report shows that a property is in poor condition or that there are structural faults or other problems such as dry rot, woodworm or rising damp. If the poor condition isn't already reflected in the purchase price, you should negotiate a reduction to cover the cost of repairs or renovation. If a property needs work doing on it, you shouldn't accept what you're told regarding the costs of repairs, but should obtain a quotation in writing from a local builder. Note also that a lender may not provide a mortgage on a property in poor condition and may insist that certain work is carried out before a mortgage is approved.

When buying a rural property in Britain, you may be able to negotiate the amount of land you want included in the purchase. If you're buying a property with a large plot of land you should have the land surveyed by a land surveyor. If a property is part of a larger plot of land owned by the vendor or the boundaries must be redrawn, you will need to hire a surveyor to measure the land and draw up a new plan. You should also check the land registry to find out what the land can be used for and any existing rights of way.

It's important to find out what the land a house is built on was previously used for, as some homes have been built on unsafe sites such as rubbish tips or chemical factories. You should also check what's in the ground (e.g. radon – see page 154) and what's under it (e.g. an old mineshaft). Many houses in Britain are built on clay, which is prone to shrinking in prolonged hot weather, resulting in houses literally cracking up (usually due to inadequate foundations). If this isn't visible to the eye as cracked walls, ceilings or floors, a structural survey should reveal whether there's a problem. You may also wish to have a property checked for termites and other pests, which are common in some areas.

Bear in mind that many surveyors miss problems or even include non-existent problems and some recommend unnecessary specialists. Many surveys are hedged with get-out clauses that try to limit the surveyor's liability. If your new home turns out to have damp, dry rot or to be infested with death-watch beetles, which your surveyor has failed to discover, you can usually successfully sue him for damages (although it's advisable to give your surveyor written instructions in respect to these and other possible problem areas). Members of the RICS and ISVA must have an in-house complaints' procedure and also have compulsory arbitration schemes in the event of a dispute. There's a fee of £235 for arbitration for claims of up to £50,000, which should save most people having to go to court to receive compensation. Any complaints should be made in the first instance to your surveyor or his professional body (see **Appendix A**).

GARAGES & PARKING

A garage or private parking space isn't usually included in the price when you buy an apartment or townhouse in Britain, although private parking may be available at an additional cost, possibly in an underground garage. Modern semi-detached and detached homes always have a garage or car port. Smaller homes usually have a single garage, while larger 'executive' homes often have integral double garages or garaging for up to four cars. Parking isn't usually a problem when buying an old home in a rural area, although there may not be a purpose-built garage.

When buying an apartment or townhouse in a modern development, a lock-up garage or parking space may be available as an extra. Note that the extra cost of a garage or parking space isn't always recouped when selling, although it makes a property more attractive and may clinch a sale. In suburban and rural areas, a garage is essential and a double garage is even better. The cost of parking is an important consideration when buying in a town or city in Britain, particularly if you have a number of cars. It may be possible to rent a garage or parking space, although this can be prohibitively expensive in cities. Bear in mind that in a large development, the nearest parking area may be some distance from your home. This may be an important factor, particularly if you aren't up to carrying heavy shopping hundreds of metres to your home and possibly up several flights of stairs.

Without a private garage or parking space, parking can be a nightmare, particularly in cities or during the summer in busy holiday resorts. Free on-street parking can be difficult or impossible to find in cities and large towns, and in any case may be inadvisable for anything but a wreck. A lock-up garage is important in areas with a high incidence of car theft and theft from cars (e.g. most cities), and is also useful to protect your car from climatic extremes such as ice, snow and extreme heat.

CONVEYANCING

Conveyancing (or more correctly 'conveyance') is the legal term for the process by which ownership of property is transferred from one person to another. A conveyance is a deed (legal document) that conveys a house from the vendor (seller) to the buyer, thereby transferring ownership. Most people employ a solicitor or licensed conveyancer to do the conveyancing, although you can do it yourself. There are two main stages when your conveyancer will become involved. The first stage takes you up to the exchange of contracts (see page 185) and the second leads to the completion of the sale (see page 186), when you become the new owner. In Scotland the procedure differs from the rest of Britain, as conveyancing is carried out only after an offer has been accepted, which is legally binding on both parties (see **Purchase Contracts** on page 185).

Property conveyancing in Britain is usually done by a solicitor (lawyer), a solicitor's agent (Scotland only) or a licensed conveyancer, and can theoretically be completed in a afternoon but usually takes two to three months. The process in Britain is among the slowest in the world, with the average time required to complete a sale twice as long as in many other countries. There are proposals to speed up the home buying process to around four weeks, by requiring vendors to produce a 'seller's pack' (see page).

Conveyancing includes ensuring that a proper title is obtained; arranging the necessary registration of the title; checking whether the land has been registered and the existence of any restrictive covenants; enquiring about any planned developments that might affect the value of the property (like a new railway line or motorway through your garden); and drawing up a contract of sale. If the property is a leasehold apartment, the lease and all its clauses must also be checked. Anyone has the right to inspect the Land Registry's records and check who owns land or property registered in England and Wales, whether or not there's a mortgage attached to it and any restrictions of use or unusual rights of way (in Scotland it's also possible to inspect the Registry's copies of registered mortgages). A free leaflet entitled *The Open Register – A Guide To Information Held By The Land Registry* is available from HM Land Registry, Lincoln's Inn Fields, London WC2A 3PH and regional offices.

Prior to 1988, the cost of conveyancing was kept artificially high in England and Wales by the monopoly maintained by solicitors. Since 1988 buyers have also been able to employ a licensed conveyancer, which has brought costs down to the current average of 0.5 to 1 per cent of the purchase price (still a nice little earner for a bit of paper work that's often relegated to a solicitor's clerk). Some conveyancers will quote a fixed fee in advance. Disbursements, which include fees such as stamp duty, land registry fees and search fees, are payable to the conveyancer separately on completion (see page 186). Some large estate agents in England (e.g. Hambro Countrywide) offer an in-house conveyancing service, although you may be better off with an independent solicitor or conveyancer, as an agent's services could easily lead to conflicts of interest.

Your conveyancer will need to know the name of the estate agent (if applicable), the property details, a list of any special points such as items that are included in the sale (carpets, appliances, furniture, etc.), and anything agreed regarding the condition of a house. He will also need details of your sources of finance (bank, building society, etc.). If applicable, give him a contact name and telephone number for your prospective lender and tell him the time scale in which you would like to take possession. If you're selling, your solicitor will need details of where the deeds are, your mortgage account number (if applicable), the name of your lender, and the branch office and telephone number. He will require copies of planning consents for any work you've had done on the house and details of any warrantees still in force. If the sale is linked to another purchase, he'll need all the details listed above for buyers, plus the date by which you would like the transactions completed. When you're buying and selling, you must pay conveyancing fees on both properties. If you're sharing a mortgage, ask your solicitor to draw up a formal agreement setting out your rights and responsibilities, as this is important when you decide to sell.

Most solicitors will tell you over the telephone what they charge and some may offer a fixed-price deal. Always check what's included in the fees and whether the fee is 'full and binding' or just an estimate. A low basic rate maybe supplemented by more expensive 'extras'. Ask your friends, neighbours and colleagues if they can recommend a solicitor or licensed conveyancer. You can also find a solicitor via the Law Society (☎ 0207-242 1222) or the National Solicitors' Network (☎ 0207-244 6422, Internet: www.tnsn.com) and a licensed conveyancer through the Council for Licensed Conveyancers (☎ 01245-349599). Be careful who you choose as frauds committed by solicitors aren't unknown and have risen in recent years.

It's possible and perfectly legal to do your own conveyancing and there are a number of good DIY books available. You'll need to do at least ten hours work and require a good grasp of details, plus a measure of patience. However, it isn't recommended for most people as it's complex, time-consuming and can be risky. If you miss a mistake in the contract, you could be left with an unsaleable property – if a solicitor or licensed conveyancer is at fault, you can at least sue him. Many people do, however, successfully perform their own conveyancing. If you're short of cash and fancy giving it a try, obtain a copy of the Consumers' Association (see **Appendix A**) action pack, *Do Your Own Conveyancing,* or a good DIY conveyancing book.

PURCHASE CONTRACTS

When buying or selling property in England, Wales or Northern Ireland, prospective buyers make an offer subject to survey and contract. Either side can amend or withdraw from a sale at any time before the exchange of contracts (at which time a sale is legally binding) or a seller can accept a higher offer from another buyer (called gazumping – see page 145). There are no preliminary contracts in England and Wales, where a purchase becomes legal only after the exchange of contracts when a

10 per cent deposit (negotiable) is payable. The exchange of contracts is literally that – a contract with the buyer's signature is sent to the vendor's solicitor, while at the same time a contract bearing the signature o145 the vendor is sent to the buyer's solicitor. Completion (see below) usually takes place around four weeks after the exchange of contracts, although it can be shorter or longer, as agreed between the parties. Note that once you have exchanged contracts (or had an offer accepted in Scotland), you should take out buildings insurance on a property, which is mandatory if you have a mortgage.

Scotland: When you wish to purchase a property in Scotland, your solicitor will usually contact the seller's solicitor and register your interest (the correspondence between solicitors is termed 'missives'). Once the seller's solicitor has had sufficient interest, he'll usually fix a closing date by which time all offers must be submitted in writing. Sometimes property is advertised at a fixed price and the first offer at that price is usually accepted (this is also the normal procedure when buying a new home from a builder or developer). If the seller gives a closing date for offers, all interested parties must make sealed bids, which are opened on that date. The seller normally accepts the highest bid, although he isn't legally bound to do so. Once your offer in writing is accepted, it's legally binding and you cannot pull out, therefore it's vital that you have a survey done (and have the necessary finance) before making an offer. Conveyancing takes place after an offer has been accepted and it usually takes four to five weeks from acceptance of an offer to completion.

The main problem with the Scottish system is that each prospective buyer must have his own survey done, which has prompted a proposed change in the law where the seller is responsible for having a survey carried out prior to selling a property – an excellent idea providing the surveyor is legally responsible for any errors to both the vendor and buyer.

COMPLETION

Completion (or closing) is the name for the final act of buying a property when the balance of the price is paid and the title deeds are handed over. The date of completion is specified at the exchange of contracts and is usually around four weeks after the exchange, although it can be shorter or longer as agreed between the parties. Completion usually takes place at midday, often on a Friday at the end of the month. You should, however, try to complete early in the week in case there are any problems, which can usually be sorted out the next day (if you plan to complete on a Friday, you may need to wait until Monday). Note that completion delays are common and should be allowed for. Unlike in other countries, it isn't usual for the vendor or buyer to attend the completion unless they are doing their own conveyancing. Your solicitor will give you a bill for stamp duty and land registry fees prior to completion, which must be paid by completion day.

Final Checks: Property is sold subject to the condition that it's accepted in the state it's in at the time of completion, therefore you should be aware of anything that occurs between the exchange of contracts and completion. Before completion it's important to check that the property hasn't fallen down or been damaged in any way, e.g. by a storm or the previous owners. If you're buying through an estate agent he should accompany you on this visit. You should also do a final inventory immediately prior to completion (the previous owner should have already vacated the property) to ensure that the vendor hasn't absconded with anything that was included in the price.

You should have an inventory of the fixtures and fittings and anything that was included in the contract or purchased separately, e.g. carpets, light fittings, curtains or kitchen appliances, and check that they are present and in good working order. This is particularly important if furniture and furnishings (and major appliances) were included in the price. You should also ensure that expensive items (such as kitchen apparatus) haven't been substituted by inferior (possibly second-hand) items. Any fixtures and fittings (and garden plants and shrubs) present in a property when you viewed it should still be there when you take possession, unless otherwise stated in the contract. If you find anything is missing, damaged or isn't in working order, you should make a note and insist on immediate restitution such as an appropriate reduction in the amount to be paid. You should refuse to go through with the completion if you aren't completely satisfied, as it will be difficult or impossible to obtain redress later. If it isn't possible to complete the sale, you should consult your solicitor about your rights and the return of your deposit.

Payment: The balance of the price (after the deposit and any mortgages are subtracted) must be paid by banker's draft on the day of completion or transferred to your solicitor's bank account prior to completion day (make sure that you allow sufficient time for the transfer to be made). Note, however, that paying by banker's draft allows you to withhold payment if there's a last minute problem (see **Final Checks** above) that cannot be resolved. If you have a mortgage, the money will be paid to your solicitor by your lender prior to completion, and will be sent by him to the vendor's solicitor by bank telegraphic transfer on completion day. When the final payment has been made the deeds to the property are handed over to the buyer's solicitor including the conveyance or transfer of ownership. Your solicitor will also receive the keys.

After Completion: After completion your solicitor has the conveyance stamped and pays the stamp duty on the property purchase to the Inland Revenue; registers the transfer of ownership with the land registry or registers the land if it was previously unregistered (this can take several months); notifies your lender that the sale has been completed and informs the life insurance company (as applicable); sends the title deeds to your mortgage lender who holds them as security until the loan is paid off or the property is sold; notifies the leaseholder of the sale if the property is a leasehold apartment; and sends you a completion statement listing all the transactions that have taken place, along with his final bill.

HOME IMPROVEMENTS & RENOVATION

Each year the British spend £10 billion on home improvements, much of which is money down the drain. Shoddy work, eccentric taste and inappropriate extensions can actually devalue your home. The best improvements are those done for yourself, not for resale value, as the cost of improvements are rarely recovered when you sell, although they may make a house more saleable. Creating a castle in a road of semi-detached houses is a waste of money if you wish to recoup the cost. While certain improvements add value, others are a waste of money when it comes to an investment. Examples of added value are extensions, a conservatory, extra (or new) bathrooms, central heating (which is a must), new kitchen, landscaped gardens (a beautiful garden will sell an indifferent house) and a garage or double garage. Other popular home improvements include new windows (e.g. double-glazing), painting and wallpapering, home security, insulation and loft conversions. Installing bigger windows and letting in more light is a way of improving many old buildings (providing you don't alter the character of a period house).

If you're planning to buy a house requiring extensive renovation, find out exactly what you're letting yourself in for before you buy. Budgets are invariably too low and it always takes longer than envisaged. If you wish to make improvements to a property immediately after you move in, you should check before completing the purchase whether you need planning permission (e.g. for an extension), and if so, whether it's likely to be approved. An architect can advise you about this. You should also mention any planned improvements or repair work to your surveyor. If you're making improvements yourself, you must also check that you won't be contravening building regulations.

Your lender will also want to know of any changes you plan to make and will want to ensure that structural changes are carried out correctly and professionally. Bear in mind that not all changes you wish to make may be considered by others as improvements and some could detract from a property's market value, particularly changes made to period properties. Note that when buying a period house that's listed (preserved), you're restricted in what you can do to them, which is under the control of English Heritage (☎ 0207-973 3434). There are around 350,000 grade I and II listed buildings in England and Wales, plus a further 175,000 in Scotland and Northern Ireland, where the grading system is different.

One of the first decisions you need to make regarding renovation or modernisation is whether to do all or most of the work yourself or have it done by professional builders. When renovating a period property, it's important to have a sensitive approach to restoration and you shouldn't tackle jobs by yourself or with friends unless you're sure you're doing it right. In general you should aim to retain as many of a property's original features as possible and stick to local building materials such as wood and stone reflecting the style of the property. When renovations and 'improvements' have been botched, there's often little that can be done except to start again from scratch. It's important not to over-modernise an old property so that too much of its natural rustic charm and attraction is lost. Before starting work and as work is in progress, most people like to keep a photographic record of their accomplishments, if only to justify the expense.

Modernisation of old houses should also be done carefully, as what you decide to do away with may constitute the very features that give a house its character. Replacing period doors or windows (e.g. with aluminium double-glazing), removing old fireplaces and knocking two rooms into one may not be considered improvements. However, installing central heating, modern wiring and plumbing, damp and rot treatment and insulation, are all examples of added value improvements. Extremes of taste should also be avoided in, for example, your choice of decoration and carpets, and in particular the colour of your bathroom suite (not everybody can face a black or red bath in the morning – or indeed at anytime). Removing the bath to install a shower also isn't advisable as most Britons prefer a bath (it's better to combine a shower with a bath). Should you need extra finance for home improvements, discuss this first with your mortgage lender. Providing your scheme is sound and you aren't over-stretching yourself financially, it's usually cheaper to extend your existing mortgage than take out a separate loan. Some local authorities provide home improvements grants, particularly to modernise older houses. Grants are also available from councils to help owners and tenants on low incomes pay for improvements and repairs. Check with your local council or a Citizens Advice Bureau.

Be very (very) careful who you employ to do your home improvements. This applies to all work around the house, whether it's an extension or conversion, new windows (e.g. double-glazing), a new kitchen, plumbing, electrical work, carpets – anything. Britain has an almost totally unregulated building industry and anyone can call themselves a builder without any qualifications, experience or registration, unlike in many other countries. The prices charged by workmen can be astronomical and complaints about shoddy workmanship are widespread. Many building contractors work 'on the black' without paying tax or social security and are unregistered for VAT. A bona fide builder should be a member of a reputable trade association such as the Federation of Master Builders or the Guild of Master Craftsmen (check if someone claims to be a member). If it's a large job it should be covered by an insurance-backed warranty such as the Federation of Master Builders' MasterBond warranty scheme. This is particularly important if you're having timber treatment or damp course work done. The best people or contractors to hire are those who are personally recommended by someone you can trust (and even then you cannot be sure). Ask your neighbours, friends, relatives and colleagues if they can recommend someone. Falling this, ask local builders if they can give you the names of previous customers as a reference (but make sure they aren't relatives or friends!), speak to them and inspect the work that has been done.

Always obtain at least three quotations (not estimates) in writing and when comparing prices make sure that all quotes are for the same quality of materials and workmanship, and that everything is included (the 'cheapest' quote may turn out to be the 'most expensive'). Note that for quotations to be accurate, you must detail exactly the work that's required, e.g. for electrical work this would include the number of lights, points and switches, and the quality of materials to be used. If you have only a vague idea of what you want, you will receive a vague and unreliable quotation. Avoid adding to a job or changing your mind halfway through and if problems arise, discuss and resolve them immediately. Better still, rather than rely on quotations for essential work from a builder who stands to profit, you should have a survey done by a member of the Association of Building Engineers (☎ 01604-404121). An engineer will provide an independent survey for a few hundred pounds, which can save you spending thousands of pounds unnecessarily.

A common ploy by the crooks and 'cowboys', of which there are many in Britain, is to give a rough oral estimate and double the price later. Obtain a written agreement (including dates when work will start and finish) and have your solicitor check the small print. Check whether subcontractors will be used and who's liable if things go wrong. **Don't pay anything in advance (apart from a small deposit), particularly a large sum, as it's quite possible that a builder will disappear with your money (it happens regularly).** For a large job you should agree in writing any staged payments before work starts and should avoid paying cash and be wary of workmen who insist on it (pay by credit card if you can, as it provides added protection). Although there are many reputable and excellent builders and craftsmen in Britain, the building industry is full of cowboys and you simply cannot take too many precautions.

If, in spite of your precautions, things go wrong, obtain advice from your local trading standards (or consumer protection) department, citizens advice bureau or consumer advice centre. The Office of Fair Trading (OFT) publishes a free booklet entitled *Home Improvements* that contains excellent advice for home improvers and a list of national associations, many of which provide warranty schemes. The National Home Improvement Council, 125 Kennington Road, London SE1 6SF (☎ 0207-582 7790) is an umbrella organisation for builders, surveyors and architects, and publishes the *Home Improvement Directory* which lists 'reliable' specialists. There are many books available for those planning home improvements including *Getting Work Done on Your House* and *The Which? Book of Home Maintenance*, published by the Consumers Association (see **Appendix A**). There are also many excellent Internet sites for DIY enthusiasts including the Federation of Master Builders (www.fmb.org.uk) and *Homebuilding and Renovating* magazine (www.ihomes. co.uk), both of which have links to numerous other sites, and the Building Information Warehouse (www.biw.co.uk).

Do-It-Yourself (DIY) & Building Supplies: DIY is extremely popular in Britain (it saves you from cowboy builders!), where there's a wide range of DIY equipment, tools and building supplies, which is the equal or better than found in many other European countries. Ask your neighbours about where to buy fittings and materials, as they usually know the best places locally. There are many DIY hypermarkets and superstores in Britain, which in addition to stocking most DIY requirements also have a wide range of tools and machinery for hire. Most DIY stores stock a large selection of goods (and keep most items in stock), accept credit cards and have helpful staff. Always look out for special promotions and even if nothing appears to be on offer it's worth asking, as offers aren't always advertised. Most towns have a hardware store, handy for tools and small items, and building yards which are good for plumbing parts, porcelain, fireplaces and doors. You can use a architectural salvage dealer (e.g. Salvo – ☎ 01890-820499) to find reclaimed building materials and fixtures and fittings for a period house, including doors, porcelain, fireplaces, porches, ironwork, beams, tiles, bricks, flint, floor boards, skirting boards, window frames and chimney pots. Useful Internet sites include www.originalfeatures.co.uk (who specialise in 19th and early 20th century properties) and www.heritage.co.uk.

See also **Buying an Old Home** on page 172, **Inspections & Surveys** on page 180 and **Heating & Air-Conditioning** on page 203.

MOVING HOUSE

After finding a home in Britain it usually takes just a few weeks to have your belongings shipped from within continental Europe. From anywhere else it varies considerably, e.g. around four weeks from the east coast of America, six weeks from the US west coast and the Far East, and around eight weeks from Australasia. Customs clearance is no longer necessary when shipping your household effects from one European Union (EU) country to another. However, when shipping your effects from a non-EU country to Britain, you should enquire about customs formalities in advance. If you're moving to Britain from a non-EU country you must provide an inventory of the things that you're planning to import. If you fail to follow the correct procedure you can encounter problems and delays and may be charged duty or even fined. The relevant forms to be completed by non-EU citizens depend on whether your British home will be your main residence or a second home. Removal companies usually take care of the paperwork and ensure that the correct documents are provided and properly completed (see **Customs** on page 216).

It's advisable to use a major shipping company with a good reputation. For international moves it's best to use a company that's a member of the International Federation of Furniture Removers (FIDI) or the Overseas Moving Network International (OMNI), with experience in Britain. Members of FIDI and OMNI usually subscribe to an advance payment scheme providing a guarantee. If a member company fails to fulfil its commitments to a client, the removal is completed at the agreed cost by another company or your money is refunded. Some removal companies have subsidiaries or affiliates in Britain, which may be more convenient if you encounter problems or need to make an insurance claim.

You should obtain at least three written quotations before choosing a company, as costs can vary considerably. Moving companies should send a representative to provide a detailed quotation. Most companies will pack your belongings and provide packing cases and special containers, although this is naturally more expensive than packing them yourself. Ask a company how they pack fragile and valuable items, and whether the cost of packing cases, materials and insurance (see below) are included in a quotation. If you're doing your own packing, most shipping companies will provide packing crates and boxes. Shipments are charged by volume, e.g. the square metre in Europe and the square foot in the USA. If you're flexible about the delivery date, shipping companies will quote a lower fee based on a 'part load', where the cost is shared with other deliveries. This can result in savings of 50 per cent or more compared with an individual delivery. Whether you have an individual or shared delivery, obtain the latest delivery date in writing, otherwise you may need to wait months for delivery!

Be sure to fully insure your belongings during removal with a well-established insurance company. Don't insure with a shipping company that carries its own insurance, as they will usually fight every penny of a claim. Insurance premiums are usually 1 to 2 per cent of the declared value of your goods, depending on the type of cover chosen. It's prudent to make a photographic or video record of valuables for insurance purposes. Most insurance policies cover for 'all-risks' on a replacement value basis. Note that china, glass and other breakables are usually only included in an 'all-risks' policy when they're packed by the removal company. Insurance usually covers total loss or loss of a particular crate only, rather than individual items, unless they were packed by the shipping company. If there are any breakages or damaged items, they should be noted and listed before you sign the delivery bill (although it's obviously impractical to check everything on delivery). If you need to make a claim, be sure to read the small print, as some companies require clients to make a claim within a few days, although seven is usual. Send a claim by registered mail. Some insurance companies apply an 'excess' of around 1 per cent of the total shipment value when assessing claims. This means that if your shipment is valued at £25,000, a claim must be over £250.

If you're unable to ship your belongings directly to Britain, most shipping companies will put them into storage and some allow a limited free storage period prior to shipment, e.g. 14 days. **If you need to put your household effects into storage, it's imperative to have them fully insured as warehouses have been known to burn down!** Make a complete list of everything to be moved and give a copy to the removal company. Don't include anything illegal (e.g. guns, bombs, drugs or pornographic videos) with your belongings as customs checks can be rigorous and penalties severe. Provide the shipping company with *detailed* instructions how to find your British home from the nearest motorway or trunk road and a telephone number where you can be contacted.

After considering the shipping costs, you may decide to ship only selected items of furniture and personal effects and buy new furniture in Britain. If you're importing household goods from another European country, it's possible to rent a self-drive van or truck. Note, however, that if you rent a vehicle outside Britain you will need to return it to the country where it was hired. If you plan to transport your belongings to Britain personally, check the customs requirements in the countries you must pass through. Most people find it isn't advisable to do their own move unless it's a simple job, e.g. a few items of furniture and personal effects only. It's no fun heaving beds and wardrobes up stairs and squeezing them into impossible spaces. If you're taking pets with you, you may need to get your vet to tranquillise them, as many pets are frightened (even more than people) by the chaos and stress of moving house.

Bear in mind when moving home that everything that can go wrong often does, therefore you should allow plenty of time and try not to arrange your move from your old home on the same day as the new owner is moving in. That's just asking for fate to intervene! If your British home has poor or impossible access for a large truck you must inform the shipping company (the ground must also be firm enough to support a heavy vehicle). Note also that if furniture needs to be taken in through an upstairs window you will usually need to pay extra. See also **Customs** on page 216 and the **Checklists** on page 220.

MOVING IN

One of the most important tasks to perform after moving into a new home is to make an inventory of the fixtures and fittings and, if applicable, the furniture and furnishings. When you have purchased a property, you should check that the previous owner hasn't absconded with any fixtures and fittings that were included in the price or anything which you specifically paid for, e.g. carpets, light fittings, curtains, furniture, kitchen cupboards and appliances, garden ornaments, plants or doors (see **Completion** on page 186). It's common to do a final check or inventory when buying a new property, which is usually done a few weeks before completion. Note the reading on your utility meters (e.g. electricity, gas and water) and check that you aren't overcharged on your first bill. The meters should be read by utility companies before or soon after you move into a resale property, although you may need to organise it yourself.

It's advisable to obtain written instructions from the previous owner concerning the operation of appliances and heating and air-conditioning systems; maintenance of grounds, gardens and lawns; care of special surfaces such as wooden or tiled floors; and the names of reliable local maintenance men who know a property and are familiar with its quirks. Check with your local town hall regarding local regulations about such things as rubbish collection, recycling and on-road parking.

HOME SECURITY

When moving into a new home it's often wise to replace the locks (or lock barrels) as soon as possible, as you have no idea how many keys are in circulation for the existing locks. This is true even for new homes, as builders often give keys to sub-contractors. In any case it's advisable to change the external locks or lock barrels periodically, particularly if you let a home. If not already fitted, it's best to fit high security (double cylinder or dead bolt) locks. It pays to look at your home through the eyes of a burglar and remedy any weak points. Many modern developments have intercom systems, CCTV, alarms, security gates and 24-hour caretakers. In areas with a high risk of theft (e.g. most major cities and resorts), your insurance company may insist on extra security measures and the policy may specify that all forms of protection must be employed when a property is unoccupied. If security precautions aren't adhered to, a claim can be reduced or even dismissed. It's usually necessary to have a safe for any insured valuables, which must be approved by your insurance company.

You may wish to have a security alarm fitted, which is usually the best way to deter thieves and may also reduce your contents insurance (see page 62). It should include all external doors and windows, internal infra-red security beams (movement detectors), activate external and internal lights, and may also include a coded entry keypad (which can be frequently changed and is useful for clients if you let a home) and 24-hour monitoring (with some systems it's even possible to monitor properties remotely from another country via a computer). New high-tech alarms can be purchased with a personal message, e.g. "there's an intruder in the house at number XX, please call the police". With a monitored system, when a sensor (e.g. smoke or forced entry) detects an emergency or a panic button is pushed, a signal is sent automatically to a 24-hour monitoring station. The duty monitor will telephone to check whether it's a genuine alarm (a password must be given) and if he cannot contact you someone will be sent to investigate. Alarms should be approved by the National Approval Council for Security Systems (NACOSS – ☎ 01628-37512).

You can deter thieves by ensuring that your house is well lit and not conspicuously unoccupied. External security 'motion detector' lights (that switch on automatically when someone approaches); random timed switches for internal lights, radios and televisions; dummy security cameras; and tapes that play barking dogs (etc.) triggered by a light or heat detector may all help deter burglars. In remote areas it's common for owners to fit two or three locks on external doors, alarm systems, grills on doors and windows, window locks, security shutters and a safe for valuables. You can fit UPVC (toughened clear plastic) security windows and doors, which can survive an attack with a sledge-hammer without damage, and external steel security blinds (which can be electrically operated), although these are expensive. A dog can be useful to deter intruders, although he should be kept inside where he cannot be given poisoned food. Irrespective of whether you actually have a dog, a warning sign with a picture of a fierce dog may act as a deterrent. If not already present, you should have the front door of an apartment fitted with a spy-hole and chain so that you can check the identity of visitors before opening the door. Bear in mind that prevention is better than cure, as stolen property is rarely recovered.

Holiday homes are particularly vulnerable to thieves and in some areas they are regularly ransacked. No matter how secure your door and window locks, a thief can usually obtain entry if he's sufficiently determined, often by simply smashing a window or even breaking in through the roof or knocking a hole in a wall! In isolated areas thieves can strip a house bare at their leisure and an unmonitored alarm won't be a deterrent if there's no-one around to hear it. Large country homes may be the target of professional thieves who strip a house bare and take everything including the floorboards, doors and fireplaces, which are recycled and sold for use in other homes. In London (where around 20 per cent of all crime takes place) professional thieves even steal antique paving stones, railings, and antique doors and door casings. If you have a holiday home in Britain, it isn't advisable to leave anything of real value (monetary or sentimental) there.

If you vacate your home for an extended period, it may be obligatory to notify your caretaker, landlord or insurance company, and to leave a key with the caretaker or landlord in case of emergencies. One way to avoid burglaries when you're away is to employ house sitters. Home insurance companies usually offer discounts for owners who employ house sitters – you should, in any case, tell your insurance company if you employ a sitter. There are a number of companies including Home Match (☎ 01962-856631), Home and Pet Care (☎ 01697-478515), Homesitters (☎ 01926-630730) and Housewatch (☎ 01279-777412). Check that housesitters are experienced and have been vetted. Companies charge a daily fee (e.g. £20 or £25) plus travelling expenses, a daily food allowance (e.g. £5 per day), and extras for looking after pets such as dogs and cats.

If you have a robbery you should report it immediately to your local police station, where you must make a statement. You will receive a copy, which is required by your insurance company when you make a claim. When closing up a property for an extended period, e.g. over the winter, you should ensure that everything is switched off and that it's secure (see **closing a property for the winter** on page 208).

Another important aspect of home security is ensuring that you have early warning of a fire, which is easily accomplished by installing smoke detectors. Battery-operated smoke detectors can be purchased for around £5 or less (they should be tested periodically to ensure that the batteries aren't exhausted). You can also fit an electric-powered gas detector that activates an alarm when a gas leak is detected. See also **Crime** on page 86.

UTILITIES

Utilities is the collective name given to electricity, gas and water companies (and usually also includes telephone companies). Britain's utility companies have been privatised in the last decade or so, which was quickly followed by increased prices and worse service. However, in the last few years most people have been able to choose their electricity and gas supplier and the increased competition has led to lower prices, with many companies promising savings of around 10 per cent to switch companies. Many companies now provide both electricity and gas, and offer contracts for the supply of both fuels, often called 'dual fuel', which may result in a discount (although you may be better off buying from separate companies). You can find the cheapest supplier of electricity and gas via the Internet (www.buy.co.uk), although you should carefully compare rates, standing charge and services before choosing or changing your supplier.

Electricity

The electricity supply in Britain is 240 volts AC, with a frequency of 50 hertz (cycles). This is suitable for all electrical equipment with a rated power consumption of up to 3,000 watts. For equipment with a higher power consumption, a single 240V or 3-phase, 380 volts AC, 20 amp supply must be used (in Britain, this is installed only in large houses with six to eight bedrooms or industrial premises). Power cuts are rare in most parts of Britain, although some areas experience many a year. Electricity companies pay compensation for a power cut lasting longer than 24 hours, but nothing for cuts of less than 24 hours (which includes 99.9 per cent of cuts).

If you move into an old home the electricity supply may have been disconnected by the previous electricity company and in a brand new home you will also need to get the electricity connected. In the last few years, householders have been able to choose their electricity company from among British Gas, Eastern Energy, Eastern Electricity, East Midlands Electricity, Independent Energy, London Electricity, Manweb, MEB, Northern Electric & Gas, Norweb, Scottish Hydro-Electric, Scottish Power, SEEBOARD, Southern Electric, SWALEC, South Western Electricity and Yorkshire Electricity. Most companies cover the whole country, while a few cover certain regions only. To have the electricity reconnected and the meter read, for which you should allow at least two days, you must choose an electricity company and complete a form. There's usually a charge for connection. You must contact your electricity company to get a final reading when you vacate your home.

Power Rating: Electrical equipment rated at 110 volts AC (for example from the USA) requires a converter or a step-down transformer to convert it to 240 volts AC, although some electrical appliances (e.g. electric razors and hair dryers) are fitted with a 110/240 volt switch. Check for the switch, which may be located inside the casing, and make sure it's switched to 240 volts *before* connecting it to the power supply. Converters can be used for heating appliances but transformers, which are available from most electrical retailers, are required for motorised appliances (they can also be purchased second-hand). Total the wattage of the devices you intend to connect to a transformer and make sure its power rating *exceeds* this sum.

Generally all small, high-wattage, electrical appliances, such as kettles, toasters, heaters and irons, need large transformers. Motors in large appliances such as cookers, refrigerators, washing machines, dryers and dishwashers, will need replacing or fitting with a large transformer. In most cases it's simpler to buy new appliances in Britain, which are of good quality and reasonably priced, and sell them when you leave if you cannot take them with you. Note also that the dimensions of British cookers, microwave ovens, refrigerators, washing machines, dryers and dishwashers may differ from those in most other countries. All electrical goods purchased in Britain must conform to British safety standards. If you wish to buy electrical appliances, such as a cooker or refrigerator, you should shop around as prices vary considerably (see **Household Appliances** on page 72). The British Electrotechnical Approvals Board (BEAB) label indicates that an electrical appliance has been tested for compliance with the appropriate safety standards by an independent approval organisation.

Frequency Rating: A problem with some electrical equipment is the frequency rating, which in some countries, e.g. the USA, is designed to run at 60 Hertz and not Britain's 50 Hertz. Electrical equipment *without* a motor is generally unaffected by the drop in frequency to 50 Hz (except TVs). Equipment with a motor may run okay with a 20 per cent drop in speed, however, automatic washing machines, cookers, electric clocks, record players and tape recorders are unusable in Britain, if they aren't designed for 50 cycle operation. To find out, look at the label on the back of the equipment. If it says 50/60 Hertz, it should be okay. If it says 60 Hz, you may try it anyway, **but first ensure that the voltage is correct as outlined above.** If the equipment runs too slowly, seek advice from the manufacturer or the retailer. For example, you may be able to obtain a special pulley for a tape deck or turntable to compensate for the drop in speed. Bear in mind that the transformers and motors of electrical devices designed to run at 60 Hz will run hotter at 50 Hz, so make sure that equipment has sufficient space around it for cooling.

Fuses: Most apartments and all houses have their own fuse boxes. Fuses may be of three types: wire, cartridge fuses or circuit breakers. Older houses may have rewireable fuses, although these are rare nowadays. Cartridge fuses are found in few houses these days and are colour coded to signify their rating. Circuit breakers are usually fitted to modern houses (and houses that have been modernised) and consist of circuit breakers, which, when a circuit is overloaded, trip to the 'off' position. When replacing or repairing fuses of any kind, if the same fuse continues to blow, contact an electrician – **never attempt to use fuse wire or fit a fuse of a higher rating than specified, even as a temporary measure.** When replacing fuses, don't rely on the blown fuse wire or fuse as a guide, as it may have been wrong. If you use an electric lawn-mower or power tools outside your home or in your garage, you should have a Residual Current Device (RCD) installed. This can detect current changes of as little as a thousandth of an amp and in the event of a fault (or the cable being cut), will disconnect the power in around 0.04 of a second.

Plugs: Regardless of the country you have come from, all your plugs will require changing or a lot of expensive adapters will be required. Modern British plugs have three rectangular pins (which are of course unique to Britain) and are fitted with fuses as follows:

Fuse Rating (amps)	Colour	Watts
1 (or 2)	green	shaver adapters (2-pin) only
2	white	standard lamp
3	red	maximum 750
5	grey	750 to 1,250
13	brown	1,250 to 3,000

All plugs in Britain are 'approved', e.g. shown by an ASTA or BSI symbol on them, which means they have passed an independent test before being offered for sale. Moulded plugs must be fitted to electrical appliances sold in Britain. Items such as audio and hi-fi equipment, electric blankets, radios, table lamps, soldering irons, TVs (some manufacturers recommend a 5-amp fuse) and slow cookers up to 720 watts, should be fitted with a three-amp fuse. Most other heavier domestic items (e.g. iron, kettle, toaster, vacuum cleaner, washing machine, electric fire, refrigerator, freezer, tumble or spin drier, dishwasher, lawn mower) between 1,250 and 3,000 watts need a 13-amp fuse. If you aren't sure what sort of fuse to use, consult the instructions provided with the apparatus. The fuse rating (amps) is calculated by dividing the wattage by the voltage (240). Note that for maximum safety, electrical appliances should be turned off at the main wall point when they aren't in use (in Britain the down position is on and the up position is off).

Wiring: Some electrical appliances are earthed and have a three-core wire. Britain conforms to the standard European colour coding for wiring. The blue lead is neutral and connects to the left pin of the plug marked 'N'; the brown (or red) lead is the live lead and connects to the right (fused side) pin of the plug marked 'L'; if present, the green and yellow lead is the earth and connects to the centre (top) pin of the plug marked 'E'. **Always make sure that a plug is correctly and securely wired, as bad wiring can prove fatal.** Never use a two-pin plug with a three-core flex. If you have old wiring or sockets that accept round pin plugs, ask an electrician about the correct plugs and wiring to use. Leaflets about safety, plugs, fuses, and wiring are available from electricity companies.

Bulbs: Electric light bulbs were traditionally of the Edison type with a bayonet fitting, which is unique to Britain (the British pride themselves on being different). To insert a bulb you push it in and turn it clockwise around 5mm. However, nowadays bulbs (and lamps) with a screw fitting are also widely available. **Note that bulbs manufactured for 110 volts must never be used in Britain, as they will explode.** Low-energy light bulbs are also available and are more expensive than ordinary bulbs, although they save money by their longer life and reduced energy consumption. Bulbs for non-standard electrical appliances (i.e. appliances not made for the British market) such as refrigerators, freezers and sewing machines, may not be available in Britain (so bring extras with you). Plug adapters for imported lamps and other electrical items may be difficult to find in Britain, so it's advisable to bring a number of adapters and extension cords with you, which can be fitted with British plugs.

Safety: Only a qualified electrician should install electrical wiring and fittings, particularly in connection with fuse boxes. You should use an electrical contractor who's approved by the National Inspection Council for Electrical Installation Contracting, Vintage House, 36-37 Albert Embankment, London SE1 7UJ (☎ 0207-564 2323), a list of whom is available from your local electricity company's showroom. Always ask for a quotation for any work in advance and check the identity of anyone claiming to be an electricity employee (or any kind of 'serviceman') by asking to see an identity card and checking with his office. Most electricity companies carry out free visual checks of domestic installations. Special controls can be fitted to many appliances to make their use easier for the disabled, the blind and partially sighted (e.g. studded or Braille controls).

Electricity is the most expensive method of central heating and is up to 50 per cent dearer than other forms of central heating and hot water systems, particularly gas. To reduce bills and obtain the maximum benefit from your heating system, your home should be well insulated (see **Heating** on page 203). Cooking with electricity costs the average family up to three times as much as with gas. For further information and a wide range of electricity brochures, contact your local electricity company's showroom.

Complaints: If you have any complaints about your electricity bill or service, contact your local electricity company. If you don't receive satisfaction you should contact the Office of Electricity Regulation (Offer), Hagley House, Hagley Road, Edgbaston, Birmingham B16 8QG (☎ freefone 0800-451451 or 0121-456 2100) or the Electricity Consumer Council, 5th Floor, 11 Belgrave Road, London SW1V 1RB

(☎ 0207-233 6366). There are also regional offices. For information about bills, see **Electricity & Gas Bills** on page 199.

Gas

Mains gas is available in all but the remotest areas of Britain. However, you may find that some modern houses aren't connected to the mains gas supply. If you're looking for a house and want to cook by gas, make sure it already has a gas supply (some houses have an unused gas service pipe). If you move into a brand new home you must have a meter installed in order to be connected to mains gas (there may be a charge for this depending on the gas company). In some remote areas without piped gas, homes may have a 'bottled gas' (e.g. Calor Gas) cooker. If you buy a house without a gas supply, you can usually arrange to have a gas pipeline installed from a nearby gas main. You're usually connected free if your home is within 25 metres of a gas main, otherwise a quotation is provided for the cost of the work involved. A higher standing charge is made for properties in remote areas.

Gas was previously supplied by British Gas throughout Britain, which was the monopoly supplier to some 19 million homes. However, since May 1998 everyone in England, Scotland and Wales has been able to choose from up to 26 gas supply companies. Depending on where you live, up to 17 companies may compete for your business including Amerada, Beacon Gas, British Fuels, British Gas, Calortex, Eastern Natural Gas, Energi from Norweb, London Electricity, Midlands Gas, North Wales Gas, Northern Electric & Gas, ScottishPower, Southern Electric Gas, SWALEC Gas, York Gas and Yorkshire Electricity. In 1998 almost all the new companies were cheaper than British Gas and some three million households had left British Gas for one of its competitors. If your new home already has a gas supply, simply contact the company of your choice to have the gas supply reconnected or transferred to your name (there's a connection fee) and the meter read. You must contact your gas company to get a final meter reading when you vacate a property.

Gas is the cheapest method of central heating and is estimated to be up to 50 per cent cheaper than other forms of central heating and hot water systems, particularly if you have a high efficiency condensing boiler. Gas companies may install gas central heating and delay payments for a period, e.g. six months. Note, however, that to reduce bills and obtain the maximum benefit from your heating system, your home must be well insulated (see **Heating** on page 203). Cooking with gas costs the average family around two-thirds less than with electricity. There are also a range of other gas appliances, including gas tumble dryers, which are cheaper to run than electric dryers. If you wish to purchase gas appliances, such as a gas cooker or a gas fire, you should shop around as prices vary considerably (see **Household Appliances** on page 72).

Gas appliances can be fitted by independent gas fitters (who offer the fastest service) or your gas company. If you use an independent gas fitter, choose one who's registered with the Council for Registered Gas Installers (CORGI), 1 Elmwood, Chineham Business Park, Crockford Lane, Basingstoke, Hants. RG24 8WG (☎ 01256-372300). Contact CORGI for the names of members in your area or ask your regional Gas Consumers Council office. Special controls can be fitted to many appliances to make them easier to use by the disabled and the blind or partially sighted (studded or Braille controls).

Gas central heating boilers, water heaters and fires should be checked annually, particularly open-flued water heaters, which are illegal in bathrooms (faulty gas appliances kill around 30 people a year). Free gas safety checks are carried out for those over 60, the disabled and those living alone who receive a state disability benefit. You can take out a service contract with your gas company, which includes an annual check of your gas central heating system, boiler and appliances. Without a service contract a repair or routine service could take anything from a few days to a few weeks. Private companies and engineers also maintain gas appliances and may be cheaper than gas companies. Always ask for a quotation for any work in advance and check the identity of anyone claiming to be a gas company employee (or any kind of 'serviceman') by asking to see an identity card and checking with his office.

Note that gas installations and appliances can leak and cause explosions or kill you while you sleep. If you suspect a gas leak, first check to see if a gas tap has been left on or a pilot light has gone out. If not, then there's probably a leak, either in your home or in a nearby gas pipeline. Ring your local gas service centre (listed under 'Gas' in the phone book) immediately and vacate the house as quickly as possible. Gas leaks are extremely rare and explosions caused by leaks even rarer (although often spectacular and therefore widely reported). Nevertheless, it pays to be careful. British natural gas has no natural smell (which is added as a safety precaution) and is non-poisonous. You can buy an electric-powered gas detector which activates an alarm when a gas leak is detected.

For further information and a wide range of gas brochures, contact your local gas company. If you have a complaints about your gas bill or service and you don't receive satisfaction from your gas company, you can contact the Office of Gas Supply (Ofgas), Stockley House, 130 Wilton Road, London SW1V 1LQ (☎ 0207-828 0898) or the Gas Consumers Council, Abford House, 15 Wilton Road, London SW1V 1LT (☎ 0207-931 0977). See also **Heating** on page 203.

Electricity & Gas Bills

Electricity and gas companies usually levy a standing quarterly charge for supplying the service, reading meters and billing, which is added to your actual or estimated consumption and billed as described below. Some companies guarantee prices for a number of years when you buy gas and electricity from them. Value added tax at 5 per cent is applicable to domestic electricity and gas bills.

Electricity: Electricity consumption is charged in units (when bills are paid by direct debit), one unit being equal to one kilowatt (1,000 watts) of electricity. Electricity companies offer a range of tariffs, some of which apply only to homes with night storage heaters and overnight immersion water heaters, when electricity is charged at a lower night tariff (for which a special meter may need to be installed). In addition to night storage and hot water heaters, economy periods can also be used to run washing machines, tumble dryers and dishwashers, e.g. with a timer.

Gas: Most electricity and gas consumers use a credit meter, where you're billed quarterly in arrears for the gas used and pay by direct debit. British Gas levies a standing charge of 7p per day for customers on the standard credit tariff and 1.295p per kWh. Rates are around 15 per cent higher if you pay by cash or a cheque more than ten days after the bill date (rather than by direct debit). Gas bills have fallen by around 20 per cent since competition was introduced in 1996 and in 1998 the average household could save up to £60 a year by switching from British Gas to another supplier. The Gas Bills Hotline (☎ 0845-600 4050) of *Which?* magazine provides an analysis of your gas costs from new companies for £6.95.

Meter Reading: At least every second electricity or gas bill is an estimate (shown by an 'E' or 'A' by the 'Present' meter reading), as meters are read every six months only. If nobody is at home when the meter-reader calls, you can give the electricity or gas company the meter reading on the card provided or on the back of your bill, otherwise you will receive an estimated bill until the next time the meter is read. Some houses have an outside meter box which can be read at any time by the meter reader. Electricity and gas companies are supposed to demand a meter reading if the meter hasn't been read for one year.

You should insist on actual rather than estimated meter readings in order to avoid overpaying or receiving unexpected 'catching-up' bills. In some cases you may receive an actual bill after an estimated bill has been sent out. Always check bills, e.g. by checking against your meter reading, and question bills that are too high. If a bill is in dispute, pay the part that isn't in dispute, i.e. what you normally pay, and question the rest. If you receive an unusually large bill or aren't happy with the size of your bills (who is?), you can ask the electricity or gas board to check your meter. When moving house, you should give notice in writing to have a final meter reading or to empty a coin box.

Payment: Bills can be paid in a variety of ways, including post (e.g. by cheque); in cash or cheque at electricity shops and offices; via a bank or building society credit transfer or by direct debit mandate; or at a post office. Customers who pay by direct debit receive a discount of up to 15 per cent. Note that if you're a new customer without a previous payment record, you may be required to pay a deposit (e.g. £100) if you don't pay your bill by direct debit. If you pay your electricity or gas bill via a budget payment scheme, payments are estimated on your previous year's consumption. At the end of the year, what you have paid is compared to your actual consumption and you receive either a rebate or a bill for the difference. Keep a record of all bills paid for future reference.

Pre-Payment Meter: If you don't have a credit meter, you will have a pre-payment meter, where electricity and gas is paid for in advance, usually by inserting £1 coins in a meter (meters may also be key or token operated). Electricity Key Budget Meters are operated by an electronic key, with which you can purchase 'electricity' for £1 to £50 (in £1 units) from vending machines in (or outside) electricity company shops. There's an emergency credit facility that allows you to use up to £5 of electricity when there's no credit on your key. There's an additional quarterly charge for customers with a pre-payment meter. If you move into a house with a pre-payment meter, you can have it changed to a credit meter free of charge. Those who have difficulty paying fuel bills are often offered pre-payment meters, although a monthly payment plan is a better choice, providing of course you can meet the payments.

Disconnection: If you don't pay your bill a warrant may be obtained from a judge or magistrate to cut off your supply. The electricity and gas industries publish a leaflet entitled *Paying Electricity and Gas bills*, which tells you how to obtain help if you cannot pay a bill. All electricity and gas companies publish a *Code of Practice* on the payment of bills by domestic customers. Most pensioners are protected from disconnection during the winter months. Anyone who's in financial difficulty should contact their local electricity or gas company as soon as possible, who will try to come to an arrangement over any outstanding bills and may recommend a direct payment or pre-payment scheme.

If you're threatened with disconnection and cannot pay your bill, you should obtain immediate advice, e.g. from a Citizens Advice Bureau. If you're disconnected, you must wait two to three days to be reconnected after paying your bill, pay a reconnection charge and may be asked to pay a security deposit. Note that an electricity or gas company cannot disconnect you for non-payment of a bill that isn't for the supply of electricity or gas, e.g. a bill for a repair or other work.

Water

The water industry in England and Wales was privatised in 1989, when ten regional water companies were created to provide water and sewerage services (there are also a further 18 local water-only companies). You're unable to choose your water company (as you are your electricity and gas companies), which have a monopoly in their area. Less than 10 per cent of households in England and Wales have water meters, where you're billed for the actual water used (plus a standing charge). For all other households, water and sewerage rates are based on the rateable value of a property (although rates were abolished in April 1990 and have been replaced by the council tax). In Scotland, fresh water is charged as an addition to the council tax (which includes sewerage) and in Northern Ireland, water and sewerage are paid as part of the domestic rates (there's no council tax).

Supply: Britain's climate has fluctuated from one extreme to another in recent years with floods in winter and droughts in summer. Due to a shortage of reservoirs, many areas of Britain (particularly the south-east) experience an acute water shortage during prolonged periods without rain (e.g. around a week), resulting in water having to be rationed and the use of hose-pipes, sprinklers and car washing banned. (It seems inconceivable there can be a water shortage in a country where it never seems to stops raining!) The ever-spiralling demand for water, which is expected to rise by 20 per cent by the year 2020, has also had an alarming affect on Britain's waterways and wildlife in the last decade.

Wastage & Conservation: The British are notoriously wasteful of water and there's very little conservation and few homes have water meters. The average garden sprinkler uses 200 gallons of water an hour, which is enough to last a family of four for two days. Many people believe that the quickest way to reduce water shortages is to encourage people to conserve water and reduce wastage, e.g. by making water meters compulsory in all homes and charging consumers for the actual water used (although the bulk of the charges for water are for maintaining the infrastructure and have nothing to do with the cost of the actual water). Water companies could also reduce wastage through leaks, estimated to amount to some 25 per cent of the total supply, and build more dams and reservoirs. In recent years profits have been diverted into salary increases for water bosses and shareholders' pockets, rather than invested in infrastructure improvements (water companies have also invested billion of pounds in unrelated businesses).

Water Meters: Water companies in England and Wales will in future be able to decide whether they charge a flat (licence fee) rate for all customers, or charge for the actual amount of water used, calculated by a water meter. Presently you can have a water meter fitted voluntarily in England and Wales, although this isn't possible in Scotland and Northern Ireland. Most industrial customers have water meters. The cost of having a water meter installed varies considerably, depending on your water company (the industry watchdog, Ofwat, gives a benchmark figure of £150). If you have a property with a high rateable value and low water consumption, you would probably benefit from having a meter installed (some people recoup the cost of the meter in a single year). However, for most customers there's no incentive to install a meter as it would result in higher bills. Most new houses are fitted with water meters.

Bills: Water companies include an annual standing charge of from £25 to £40 (for both water and sewerage), which is the same for all properties, plus a variable charge based on the rateable value of your property if you don't have a water meter. If you have a water meter installed, water is charged by the cubic metre. Bills, which usually include sewerage (except in Scotland), are sent out annually and can usually be paid in full, in two six-monthly payments or in ten instalments. In some areas water and sewage are handled by separate companies and homeowners receive bills from each company. Since water privatisation in 1989, water bills have increased by some 40 per cent in real terms. The cost of water varies depending on the local water authority, with the most expensive water companies charging almost double the cheapest. The average unmetered annual water and sewerage bill in 1998-99 was around £250.

Payment: Water bills can be paid by direct debit from a bank account (for which there's usually a rebate), which means that you aren't required to remember when they are due. If you don't pay your water bill, you will receive a reminder ('Final Notice') and if this isn't paid immediately, the full annual amount usually becomes due. If you persistently failed to pay your bill, water companies could previously apply to a county court for permission to disconnect your supply, which happened to tens of thousands of households each year. However, it's now illegal to cut off the water supply to a home.

Quality: The quality of tap water in Britain varies depending on the region. Although drinking water is among the cleanest and safest in the world, it doesn't measure up to European Union standards in all areas. Water bills are expected to rise even further to fund improvements in drinking water quality. In recent years there have been a number of scares about the poor quality of drinking water in some areas, some of which were a result of accidental contamination of the water supply. There are also concerns about the number and level of chemicals contained in water, particularly aluminium, lead (usually from old lead water pipes) and nitrates, although some (like chlorine) are added as part of the water treatment process.

In some areas, homeowners have reported tap water infestations, such as freshwater shrimps or water fleas (the water companies don't charge extra for the 'on tap' food supply). Water companies are loath to admit liability for illness caused by the water supply, as the cost of compensation and clean-up can run into millions of pounds. If you have a tap connected to a garden hose, a washing machine or a dishwasher, or a shower with a flexible pipe over the bath, you must fit a non-return valve that stops pollution from dirty water siphoning back into the mains supply. A non-return valve can be plumbed in or you can buy one that screws directly onto a tap. If you're concerned about the quality of your tap water, contact your local water company or the Drinking Water Inspectorate, Floor 2/a2 Ashdown House, 123 Victoria Street, London SW1E 6OE (☎ 0207-890 5956).

Water in Britain is usually hard, particularly in the south-east, due to a natural excess of magnesium and calcium compounds. Although hard water is generally good to drink, you need a copious supply of decalcification liquid to keep your kettle, iron and other apparatus and utensils clean. Note that water from some taps may be unsafe to drink as it comes from storage tanks. Stainless steel pots and pans will stain quickly when used to boil water, unless they are cleaned soon after use. Distilled water or water melted from ice from your refrigerator or freezer should be used in some electric steam irons. Tap and shower filters must be decalcified regularly.

Before moving into a new home you should enquire where the main stop-valve or stopcock is, so that you can turn off the water supply in an emergency. If the water stops running for any reason, you should turn off the supply to prevent flooding from an open tap when the supply starts again. Contact your local water company if you have a problem with your water supply, as it could have been turned off by them.

If you need a plumber, e.g. as a result of a burst pipe, you may be able to get a recommendation or a list of names from your local water company, which may help prevent you being ripped off. When employing a plumber ask what the minimum call out charge is (it's usually around £1 million plus £500,000 an hour for labour). Britain is famous for the eccentricity of its plumbing, although many burst pipes could be avoided by lagging. If you have a complaint which you cannot resolve with your water company, you should contact you local Customer Service Committee or the Office of Water Services (OFWAT), Centre City Tower, 7 Hill Street, Birmingham B5 4UA (☎ 0121-625 1300).

HEATING & AIR-CONDITIONING

Central heating, double or triple-glazing and good insulation are standard in new houses and are essential in Britain's climate. Around 80 per cent of British homes have central heating (including all new homes) or storage heater systems, most of which also provide hot water. Central heating systems may be powered by oil, gas (the most common), electricity (night-storage heaters) or solid fuel (e.g. coal or wood). Whatever form of heating you use, you should ensure that your home has good insulation including double glazing, cavity-wall insulation, external-wall insulation, floor insulation, draught-proofing, pipe lagging, and loft and hot water tank insulation, without which up to 60 per cent of heat goes straight through the walls and roof. Many companies advise and carry out home insulation, including gas and electricity companies, who produce a range of leaflets designed to help you reduce your heating and other energy bills.

The cost of heating your home varies depending on a number of factors, not least the fuel used, its size and the length of time your heating is switched on. Most people in Britain switch their heating on for limited periods only (using timer controls), e.g. for a few hours in the morning before the occupants go to work or school, and from around 1600 or 1700 when children or parents come home until the family goes to bed. During the day and at night, many people turn the heating off, which is why many British houses are often so cold during the daytime in winter. In order to reduce heating bills, many people selectively heat certain rooms or parts of a house only.

The cheapest method of central heating is gas, which is estimated to be up to 50 per cent cheaper than other forms of central heating and hot water systems, particularly if you have a high-efficiency condensing boiler. Many homes have storage heaters that store heat from electricity supplied at the cheaper off-peak rate overnight and release it to heat your home during the day. In an apartment block is heated from a central system, radiators may be individually metered so you pay only for the heating used, or the cost of heating (and hot water) may be included in your service charges. If you wish to install heating in your home, you should use a company that's a member of the Heating and Ventilating Contractor's Association, 34 Palace Court, London W2 4JG (☎ 0345-581158 or 0207-229 2488), who operate a guarantee scheme for domestic heating.

You can reduce your heating and other energy bills by saving energy. For information contact your gas or electricity company, local Energy Advice Centre (☎ freefone 0800-512012). Wasting Energy Costs the Earth (PO Box 200, Stratford-upon-Avon CV37 9ZZ, ☎ 01908-672787) can provide details of energy surveyors in your area who will perform an energy survey for £50 to £100 depending on the size of your property. Information about energy efficiency is also available from the National Energy Foundation, 3 Benbow Court, Shenley Church End, Milton Keynes MK5 6JG (☎ 01908-501908, e-mail: nef@natenerg.demon.co.uk).

Note that central heating dries the air and may cause your family to develop coughs. Those who find the dry air unpleasant can purchase a humidifier to add moisture to the air. Humidifiers that don't generate steam should be disinfected occasionally (to prevent nasty diseases) with a special liquid available from chemists.

Air-Conditioning: Although summer temperatures can be above 30°C (86°F), British homes rarely have air-conditioning and aren't usually built to withstand the heat. However, in recent years many luxury apartments and houses have been built with cooling systems such as comfort cooling, air cooling or a climate controlled refrigerated air system. If you want to install air-conditioning you can choose between a huge variety of systems including fixed or moveable units, indoor or outdoor installation, and high or low power. An air-conditioning system with a heat pump provides cooling in summer and economical heating in winter. Note, however, that there can be negative effects if you suffer from asthma or respiratory problems.

PROPERTY INCOME

Many people planning to buy a second home in Britain are interested in owning a property that will provide them with an income to cover the running costs and help with mortgage payments. The most common examples are long-term lets, holiday letting and bed and breakfast accommodation. Note, however, that with holiday and short-term letting you're highly unlikely to meet your mortgage payments and running costs from rental income. Buyers who over stretch their financial resources often find themselves on the rental treadmill, constantly struggling to find sufficient income to cover their running costs and mortgage payments.

It's difficult to make a living providing self-catering holiday accommodation or bed & breakfast in most areas, as the season is too short. If you're planning on holiday lets, don't overestimate the length of the season, which varies depending on the region. In some areas it's as long as 16 weeks, while in others it's just ten weeks or less. The letting season is longest in south-west England and the major cities, where properties have year-round letting potential. Bear in mind that income tax must be paid on rental income earned in Britain (see **Taxation of Property Income** on page 118). In the early '90s, many people lost their second homes after they defaulted on their mortgage payments, often because rental income failed to meet expectations. Most experts recommend that you don't purchase a home in Britain if you need to rely entirely on rental income to pay the mortgage.

Location: If an income from your British property has a high priority, you should buy a property with this in mind. To maximise rental income, a property should be located as close as possible to the main attractions, a major city and/or a beach, be suitably furnished and professionally managed. If there are important local events such as international sports events (e.g. Wimbledon), you can earn a small fortune for a few weeks of the year. A swimming pool is a big advantage in summer, when properties with pools are much easier to let, and you can charge a higher rent for a property with a pool (you may also be able to extend the letting season by installing a heated or indoor pool).

Rents: Rental rates vary considerably depending on the time of year, area, size and quality of a property. A modest house sleeping four to six people in an average area can be let for around £500 or £600 per week in the high season. At the other extreme, a luxury property in a popular area with a pool and accommodation for 8 to 12 can be let for £2,000 or more a week in the high season, which generally includes the months of July and August. The mid season usually comprises May, June and September (and possibly Easter), when rents are around 25 to 30 per cent lower than the high season; the rest of the year is the low season. If you're a non-resident and have a UK letting agent you can apply to have your rental income paid gross of tax and pay income tax annually in arrears under the Non-Resident Landlord scheme (see page). See also **Renting** on page 155.

Insurance: If you let a property either long or short-term, you need rent and legal indemnity insurance (premiums are around 3 per cent of the monthly rental). There are a number of specialist insurers such as LetSure, whose policies are sold through letting agents. Europea-IMG (☎ 01403-263860) and Winter Richmond (☎ 01628-470470) offer policies for homes that are either left empty for long periods or let, and both cover accidental damage caused by tenants.

Furnishings & Keys: If you let a property, don't fill it with expensive furnishings or valuable personal belongings. While theft is rare, items will certainly get damaged or broken over a period of time. When furnishing a property for letting, you should choose hard wearing, dark coloured carpets (which won't show the stains), and buy durable furniture and furnishings. Simple inexpensive furniture is best in a modest home, as it will need to stand up to hard wear. Small one or two-bedroom properties usually have a settee in the living room which converts into a double bed. Properties should be well equipped with cooking utensils, crockery and cutlery, and it's also advisable to provide bed linen and towels. You may also need a cot or high chair for young children. Depending on the price and quality of a property, your guests may also expect central heating, a washing machine, dishwasher, microwave, covered parking, a barbecue and garden furniture. Some owners provide bicycles, and badminton and table tennis equipment. It isn't usual to have a telephone in rental homes, although you could install a credit card telephone or a phone that will receive incoming calls only.

You will need several sets of spare keys, which will inevitably get lost at some time. If you employ a management company, their address should be on the key fob and not the address of the house. If you let a home yourself, you can use a 'keyfinder' service, whereby lost keys can be returned to the keyfinder company by anyone finding them. You should ensure that you get 'lost' keys returned, otherwise you may have to change the locks (in any case it's advisable to change the external locks periodically if you let a home). You don't need to provide clients with keys to all external doors, only the front door (the others can be left in your home). If you arrange your own lets, you can mail keys to clients in your home country, otherwise they can be collected from a caretaker in Britain. It's also possible to install a security key-pad entry system.

Landlords must conform to the Furniture and Furnishings (Fire) Safety Regulations 1988 (you can obtain a copy from DTI Consumer Safety Publications – ☎ 0870-150 2500). Furniture mustn't contain flammable substances and gas appliances must be checked annually for leaks. There are large fines (up to £5,000) and even prison sentences for offenders.

Letting & Management Agents: If you're letting a second home, the most important decision is whether to let it yourself or use a letting agent (or agents). If you don't have much spare time you're better off using an agent, who will take care of everything and save you the time and expense of advertising and finding clients. Letting agents charge around 10 per cent for letting only and between 15 and 20 per cent for full management (some specialist companies may charge more, some of which can usually be recouped through higher rents). Most agents charge extra for drawing up a tenancy agreement, inventories and looking after a property between lets. If you want your property to appear in an agent's catalogue, you must contact him the summer before you wish to let it (the deadline is usually September). Note that although self-catering holiday companies may fall over themselves to take on luxury properties in the most popular areas, top letting agents turn down as many as nine out of every ten properties they're offered.

Most agents don't permit owners to use a property during the peak letting season (July and August) and may also restrict their use at other times. There are numerous self-catering holiday companies in Britain, most of whom have agents in many countries (try your local travel agent). Some estate agents in resort areas and cities also act as agents for holiday lets and some specialise in long-term lets. You usually need to notify your insurance company if a property is to be let (see above).

Take care when selecting a letting agent, as a number have gone bust in recent years owing customers thousands of pounds. Make sure that your income is kept in an escrow account and paid regularly, or even better, choose an agent with a bonding scheme who pays you the rent *before* the arrival of guests (some do). It's essential to employ an efficient, reliable and honest company, preferably long-established. Note that anyone can set up a holiday letting agency and there are a number of 'cowboy' operators. Always ask a management company to substantiate rental income claims and occupancy rates by showing you examples of actual income received from other properties. Ask for the names of satisfied customers and check with them. You should choose an agent who's a member of the Association of Residential Letting Agents (ARLA – ☎ 01923-896555).

Other things to ask a letting agent include who they let to; where they advertise; whether they have contracts with holiday and travel companies; whether you're expected to contribute towards marketing costs; and whether you're free to let the property yourself and use it when you wish. The larger companies market homes via newspapers, magazines, overseas agents and colour brochures, and have representatives in many countries. Management contracts usually run for a year. A management company's services should include arranging routine and emergency repairs; reading meters (if electricity is charged as an extra); routine maintenance of house and garden, including lawn cutting and pool cleaning; arranging cleaning and linen changes between lets; advising guests on the use of equipment; and providing guest information and advice (24-hours in the case of emergencies). For short-term lets, agents may also provide someone to meet and greet clients, hand over the keys and check that everything is in order. The actual services provided usually depend on whether a property is a basic cottage or apartment or a luxury mansion costing thousands of pounds a week. A letting agent's representative should also make periodic checks when a property is empty to ensure that it's secure and that everything is in order.

Doing Your Own Letting: Some owners prefer to let a property to family, friends, colleagues and acquaintances, which allows them more control (and hopefully the property will be better looked after). In fact, the best way to get a high volume of lets is usually to do it yourself, although many owners use a letting agency in addition to doing their own marketing. If you wish to let a property yourself, there's a wide range of British and foreign newspapers and magazines in which you can advertise, e.g. *Dalton's Weekly* and newspapers such as the *Sunday Times* and *Sunday Telegraph* in Britain. The English-language newspapers and magazines listed in **Appendix A** also accept advertisements from property owners. You will need to experiment to find the best publications and days of the week or months to advertise.

There are also companies that produce directories of properties let directly by owners. You pay for the advertisement but handle bookings yourself. Local tourist offices can put you in touch with letting agents. You can also advertise among friends and colleagues, in company and club magazines (which may even be free), and on notice boards in company offices, stores and shopping centres. The more marketing you do, the more income you're likely to earn. It also pays to work with other local people in the same business and send surplus guests to competitors (they will usually reciprocate). It isn't necessary to just advertise locally or stick to your home country and you can also extend your marketing abroad (you can also advertise via the Internet). It's necessary to have a telephone answering machine and a fax machine.

What to Charge?: To get an idea of the rent you should charge, simply ring a few letting agencies and ask them what it would cost to rent a property such as yours at the time of year you plan to let. They are likely to quote the highest possible rent you can charge. You should also check the advertisements in newspapers and magazines. Set a realistic rent as there's a lot of competition. Add a returnable deposit (£100 or £200) as security against loss of keys and breakages. A deposit should be refundable up to six weeks before a booking. It's normal to have a minimum two-week rental period in July and August. You will need a simple agreement form that includes the dates of arrival and departure and approximate times. If you plan to let to non-English speaking clients you must have a letting agreement in other languages.

If you plan to let a home yourself, you will need to decide how to handle enquiries about flights and car rentals. It's easier to let clients do it themselves, but you should be able to offer advice and put them in touch with airlines, ferry companies, travel agents and car rental companies (see page 48). You will also need to decide whether you want to let to smokers or accept pets or young children (some people don't let to families with children under five years of age due to the risks of bed-wetting). It's usual to provide linen, which is usually expected, although electricity may not be included in the rental fee.

It's advisable to produce a colour brochure containing external/internal pictures (or a single-colour brochure with coloured photographs affixed to it, although this doesn't look so professional), important details, the exact location, local attractions, details of how to get there (with a map), and the name, address and telephone number of your local caretaker or letting agent. You should enclose a stamped, addressed envelope when sending out leaflets. It's necessary to make a home look as attractive as possible in a brochure without distorting the facts or misrepresentation. Advertise honestly and don't over-sell your property.

Local Information: You should also provide an information pack for clients explaining how things work (such as heating and appliance); what not to do; where to shop; recommended restaurants; local emergency numbers and health services such as doctors, hospitals and dentists; and assistance such as a general repairman, plumber, electrician and pool maintenance (although if you have an agent or local caretaker, he should take care of these). If you allow young children and pets, you should make a point of emphasising any dangers, such as falling into the pool. It's also beneficial to have a visitor's book where your clients can write their comments and recommendations. If you want to impress your guests, you may wish to arrange for fresh flowers, fruit, a bottle of wine and a grocery pack to greet them on their arrival. It's little touches like this that ensure repeat business and recommendations. If you go 'the extra mile' it will pay off in recommendations and you may find that you rarely need to advertise after your first year or two in business. Many people return to the same property each year and you should do an annual mail-shot to previous clients and send them some brochures. Word-of-mouth advertising is the cheapest and always the best.

Caretaker: It's generally advisable to let a property yourself only if you live close by or you have someone (e.g. a friend or family member) who can look after it for you. Otherwise you will find it beneficial or even essential to employ a local caretaker and you may also need to employ a gardener. You can have your caretaker prepare the house for your family and guests, in addition to looking after it when it isn't in use. It's advisable to have your caretaker check it periodically (e.g. weekly) and to give him authority to authorise minor repairs. If you let a property yourself, your caretaker can arrange (or carry out) cleaning, linen changes, maintenance and repairs, gardening and the payment of bills.

Increasing Rental Income: It's possible to increase rental income outside the high season by offering special interest or package holidays, which can be organised in conjunction with other local businesses in order to broaden the appeal and cater for larger parties. These may include activity holidays such as golf, tennis, cycling or hiking; cooking and local gastronomy; and arts and crafts such as painting, sculpture, photography and writing courses. You don't need to be an expert or conduct courses yourself, but can employ someone to do it for you.

Long-term lets: Long-term lets can be anything from one to six months and usually exclude the high season. Most people who let year round have low, medium and high season rates. For long-term lets in the low season, a two to three-bedroom house usually rents for around £600 a month in most rural areas, with the tenant paying for utilities. Note that central heating is essential if you want to let long-term. If you let a property long-term, you should be aware that there are separate laws governing short and long-term rentals.

Closing a property for the winter: Before closing up a property for the winter, you should turn off the water at the mains and drain all pipes, remove all the fuses (except the one for a dehumidifier if you leave it on while you're away), empty the food cupboards, refrigerator/freezer and dustbins. You should also leave the interior doors and a few small windows with grills or secure shutters open to provide ventilation. Many people keep their central heating on a low setting during the winter (which can be controlled via a master thermostat) during absences to prevent freezing. Lock all the doors and shutters and secure anything of value against theft or leave it with a neighbour. Check whether any essential work is necessary before you leave and arrange for it to be done in your absence. Most importantly, leave a set of keys with a neighbour and have a caretaker check your home periodically.

See also **Renting** on page 155 and **Buying for Investment** on page 160.

SELLING A HOME

Although this book is about buying a home in Britain, you may wish to sell your British home at some time in the future. Before offering your home for sale, it's advisable to investigate the state of the property market. For example, unless you're forced to sell, it definitely isn't advisable during a property slump when prices are depressed. It may be wiser to let your home long-term and wait until the market has recovered. You could even take out a mortgage based on the value of your existing home and the one you plan to buy – which in effect is the same as buying-to-let (see page 160). It's also unwise to sell in the early years after purchase, when you may make a loss unless it was a bargain.

In 1999 one in ten homes sold within a week (some sold within as little as 24 hours!), a third within three weeks, and three in five within ten weeks or less. If you home doesn't sell within three months, it's either in an area that isn't in demand or is over-priced. Between March and June is usually the best time to sell a house, although if the market is buoyant anytime is good. Certain homes will always sell, even in a depressed market, for example a roomy period house with a good location and outlook is almost 'bomb-proof' as far as the general market is concerned. Having decided to sell, your first decision will be whether to try to sell it yourself or use the services of an estate agent. Although the majority of properties in Britain are sold through estate agents, a large number of owners successfully sell their own homes.

To speed up the home buying process (to around four weeks), the government has proposed a new law requiring vendors to produce a 'seller's pack' (at a cost of between £350 and £500), which includes commissioning a survey, collecting the title deeds and conducting local council searches, before putting a home on the market. This is mainly intended to reduce the risk of gazumping. However, many buyers wouldn't trust a survey commissioned by the vendor, who could bribe a surveyor to overlook certain matters (of course no surveyor would ever accept a bribe!), and most people would still commission their own report. Another problem is that surveyor's are responsible to the person who commissions a survey only and the buyer would have no come back if a major fault was discovered, which would be disastrous.

Price: It's important to bear in mind that (like everything) property has a market price and the best way of ensuring a sale is to ask a realistic price (a property doesn't actually have a market value and is 'worth' precisely what someone is willing to pay for it). During the recession in the early '90s many properties remained on the market for years because owners asked absurd prices and refused to acknowledge that their homes were no longer worth what they had been in the late '80s before the bottom fell out of the market. **However, don't undervalue your home.** In a seller's market when prices are soaring and houses are in demand, you should test the market first before accepting an offer. If you have an unusual property that's in high demand, such as a converted mill or barn or an outstanding period property, it may pay you to set a closing date and invite sealed bids or to sell it at auction (see page 159).

If your home's fairly standard for the area you can find out its value by comparing the prices of other homes on the market or those which have recently been sold. Most agents provide a free appraisal of a home's value in the hope that you will sell it through them. However, don't believe everything they tell you as they often over-value properties simply to encourage you, and bear in mind that valuations made by different agents can vary by tens of thousands of pounds. You can also hire a professional appraiser to determine the market value.

Depending on where a property is situated and the state of the local property market, you should be prepared to drop the price slightly (e.g. 5 or 10 per cent) and should set it accordingly, but you shouldn't grossly over-price it as this will deter buyers. Don't reject an offer out of hand unless it's ridiculously low, as you may be able to get a prospective buyer to raise his offer. When selling a home in Britain, you may wish to include some appliances and furnishings (such as carpets and curtains) in the sale, particularly when selling a relatively inexpensive property with modest furnishings. You should add an appropriate amount to the price to cover the value of any extras or alternatively you can use them as an inducement to a prospective buyer.

Presentation: The secret to selling a home quickly lies in its presentation, assuming that it's competitively priced. First impressions (both exteriors and interiors) are vital when marketing your home and it's important to make every effort to present it in its best light and make it as attractive as possible to potential buyers. After location the next most important selling point is light, which can be increased by putting in stronger light bulbs, cleaning the windows and painting your home white (if it's really dark you may need to install some new windows). Simple things that may help seduce prospective buyers include fresh flowers, house plants, furniture polish, aerosol spray and the smell of fresh brewed coffee (you can place a few coffee beans under the grill just before viewers arrive!). You should reduce the clutter and furniture to create more space, and keep the décor and soft furnishings light and neutral (check how developers present their show homes and copy them).

It may pay to invest in new interior decoration, carpets, exterior paint and landscaping. Note that when decorating a home for resale, it's important to be conservative and not to do anything radical (such as install a red or black bathroom suite). Bear in mind, however, that a complete decoration may arouse suspicions. It may also pay you to do some modernisation such as installing a new kitchen or bathroom, as these are of vital importance when selling a home. A good kitchen often sells a house and an attractive garden will help sell an indifferent home, but you don't need to spend a fortune. Although modernisation may be necessary to sell an old home, you shouldn't overdo it as it's easy to spend more than you could ever hope to recoup on its sale. If you're using an agent, you can ask him what you should do (or need to do) to help sell your home. If it's in poor repair this should be reflected in the asking price and if major work is needed that you cannot afford, you should obtain a quotation (or two) and offer to knock this off the asking price.

Selling Your Home Yourself: While certainly not for everyone, selling your own home is a viable option for many people and is particularly recommended when you're selling an attractive home at a *realistic* price in a favourable market (or any home in a booming market). It may allow you to offer it at a more appealing price, which could be an important factor if you're seeking a quick sale. How you market your home will depend on the type of home, the price, and the country or area from where you expect your buyer to come.

Marketing is the key to selling your home. The first step is to get a professional looking 'For Sale' sign made showing your telephone number and display it in the garden or a window. Do some market research into the best newspapers and magazines for advertising your property, and place an advertisement in those that look most promising. In recent years an increasing number of people have been selling their homes via daily and local newspapers and specialist newspapers such as *Dalton's Weekly*, *Exchange & Mart* (weekly) and *Loot* (Internet: www.loot.com). *Loot* is a daily newspaper for buying/selling properties privately (and just about anything else) that publishes separate editions for the south-east, east midlands, west midlands, north-west and Northern Ireland. It offers a special service (☎ 0207-372 7262) for property sellers costing £59.95 that includes a 'For Sale' sign, a 'seller's pack' and ads. for nine weeks. *Loot* claims that most of the properties it advertises are sold within three weeks – it's hassle free and almost as simple as selling a car! You can also advertise a home for sale (including a picture) on the Internet via the Property Market website (www.propertymarket.co.uk) and the Private Home Sales Network (Internet: www.privatehomesales.co.uk).

You could also have a leaflet printed (with pictures) extolling the virtues of your property, which you could drop into local letter boxes or have distributed with a local newspaper (many people buy a new home in the immediate vicinity of their present home). You may also need a 'fact sheet' printed if your home's vital statistics aren't included in the leaflet mentioned above and could offer a finder's fee (e.g. £500) to anyone finding you a buyer. Don't omit to market your home around local companies, schools and organisations, particularly if they have many itinerant or foreign employees. It may also be worthwhile holding an open house for prospective buyers.

You should have all the papers and receipts to hand such as a copy of the deeds, warranties for any work carried out, inspections or survey reports, warranties for major appliances such as central heating, planning permission certificates (e.g. for extensions), bills for any work carried out and utility, insurance and council tax bills. You may also wish to make a list of all fixtures and fittings plus anything else (appliances, furniture, garden ornaments, etc.) that will be included in the sale. You may benefit from having a survey done on your home, which may soon be law (see above), although there's a possibility that prospective buyers won't believe it's impartial. You need to find out as much as possible about a prospective buyer, particularly their finance (do they have cash or a mortgage approval) and whether they need to sell first (and if so whether they have a buyer). Be careful not to sell to someone who was introduced to you by an estate agent. When selling a home yourself you will need to engage a solicitor or licensed conveyancer to complete the sale.

With a bit of effort and practice you may even make a better job of marketing your home than an agent! Unless you're in a hurry to sell, set yourself a realistic time limit for success, after which you can try an agent.

Using An Agent: Most vendors prefer to use the services of an agent, either in Britain or in their home country, particularly when selling a second home. If you purchased the property through an agent, it's often advisable to use the same agent when selling, as he will already be familiar with it and may still have the details on file. You should take particular care when selecting an agent as they vary considerably in their professionalism, expertise, experience and honesty (the best way to investigate agents is by posing as a buyer). Note that most agents cover a relatively small area, so you should take care to choose one who regularly sells properties in your area and price range.

Agents' Contracts: Before offering a property for sale, an agent must have a signed authorisation from the owner or his representative. Agents fees vary from 1 to 5 per cent, depending on the agent, the area, the price of the property, the state of the local property market and the type of agreement. Fees are negotiable and you should try to negotiate a lower fee. There are generally three types of agreement, which are described below:

Sole Agency: All agents offer this option, although it isn't always the best deal from the seller's point of view, as you must still pay the estate agent's commission if you sell the house yourself without his help (although you may be able to reserve the right to find a private buyer). Agents will try to get you to sign a contract for three to six months, which you should avoid, as you may wish to change agents if he turns out to be useless. Some agents offer cash inducements in order to obtain 'sole agency' rights to sell a property. You must take care not to sign two sole agency agreements. The fee for sole agency is usually 2 to 2.5 per cent.

Joint Sole Agency: With this type of agreement you sign on with two agents only, both of whom agree to the arrangement and decide how they will split the commission between themselves. Generally it's just as expensive as having multiple agency (see below) and therefore a waste of time. The fee for joint sole agency is usually 2.25 to 2.75 per cent.

Multiple Agency: You instruct as many agents as you like and the one who sells your property receives the commission, i.e. no sale, no fee. This is generally the best deal, as it gives you a wider audience, which may mean you receive a better price (and can therefore afford to pay a higher commission). Using a number of agents also helps avoid dirty tricks (see page 178). It's possible to reduce your fees through a flat fee deal, where you pay a fixed fee for a standard package, although few agents offer this choice. The fee for joint sole agency is usually 2.5 to 3 per cent.

You're under no obligation to sign an agreement with an agent and you should take care before signing one. Note that you must still pay an agent's fee if you sell to someone introduced by him within a certain period (e.g. one year) of the expiry of an agreement. **Don't sign a contract that says that fees will be payable for introducing a buyer who's 'ready, willing and able' to buy, otherwise you could be liable to pay commission if you pull out of a sale before contracts are exchanged (which can happen for a variety of reasons).** Check the contract and make sure you understand what you're signing.

Fees in London and the south-east fees are generally higher than other regions, although sole agency usually includes a 'for sale' board, photographs, information leaflets and may also include some advertising other than in the agent's office window. Elsewhere all of these could cost extra, particularly advertising which is usually an extra. With regard to extras, make sure you know exactly what they will cost and what they include, and obtain the agreement in writing. Generally you shouldn't pay any fees unless you require extra services and you should never pay commission before a sale is completed. Don't tell an agent your lowest price as he may pass it on to a buyer in the hope of making a quick sale.

Some 'property shops' charge a flat fee to sell a home, which is non-returnable if they fail to sell your home. There are also computer (Internet) agencies who will circulate your home's details for a flat fee, e.g. £200. However, you shouldn't rely on selling your home via these methods as they may involve little or no marketing and have a poor success rate. See also **Estate Agents** on page 178.

Swapping Your Home: If you're having trouble selling your home, you could try swapping it with another property. If you decide to swap with a more expensive property than your present home, you pay the difference. Before going through with a swap, it's important to have a structural survey carried out on the other property and to engage a conveyancer to carry out the usual checks. There are 'house exchange' agencies in some areas, some of which have a national list of clients. Many developers offer a part exchange deal on your existing home, although you should be wary of such schemes (see page 168).

See also **Avoiding Problems** on page 144, **Capital Gains Tax** on page 122, **Estate Agents** on page 178 and **Home Improvements & Renovation** on page 187.

5.

ARRIVAL & SETTLING IN

On arrival in Britain your first task will be to negotiate immigration and customs, which fortunately for most people present no problems. Non-EEA nationals must complete a **landing card** on arrival, which are distributed on all international flights and available from the information or purser's office on ships and ferries. British customs and immigration officials are usually polite and efficient, although they may occasionally be a 'trifle overzealous' in their attempts to deter smugglers and illegal immigrants (so it pays to be nice to them).

Britain isn't a signatory to the Schengen agreement (named after a Luxembourg village on the Moselle River where the agreement was signed), which came into effect on 1st January 1995 and introduced an open-border policy between certain member countries. These now comprise Austria, Belgium, France, Germany, Greece, Iceland, Italy, Luxembourg, the Netherlands, Portugal, Spain and Sweden. Britain isn't a member and has no plans to join, ostensibly because of fears of increased illegal immigration and cross-border crime such as drug smuggling. Therefore anyone arriving in Britain from a 'Schengen' country must go through the normal passport and immigration controls, both on arrival in the UK and when entering a Schengen country from the UK.

In addition to information about immigration and customs, this chapter contains checklists of tasks to be completed before or soon after arrival in Britain and when moving house, plus suggestions for finding local help and information.

IMMIGRATION

When you arrive in Britain, the first thing you must do is go through **Passport Control**, which is usually divided into two areas: 'EU/EEA Nationals' and 'All Other Passports'. Make sure you join the right queue or you may waste a lot of time. Passport control is staffed by immigration officers, who have the task of deciding whether you're subject to immigration control, and if so, whether or not you're entitled to enter Britain. You must satisfy the immigration officer that you're entitled to enter Britain under whatever category of the rules you're applying to enter.

The immigration officer may also decide to send you for a routine (and random) health check, before allowing you to enter Britain. Britain has strict regulations regarding the entry of foreigners whose reason for seeking entry may be other than those stated. Generally the onus is on anyone visiting Britain to *prove* that he's a genuine visitor and won't infringe the immigration laws. The immigration authorities aren't required to establish that you will violate the immigration laws and can refuse your entry on the grounds of suspicion only.

EU nationals are given a form IS120 by the immigration officer on arrival, which must be produced if they remain in Britain longer than six months. If you're entering Britain from a country other than an EEA member state, you may be required to have immunisation certificates. Check the requirements in advance at a British Diplomatic Post abroad before arriving in Britain.

CUSTOMS

When you enter Britain to take up temporary or permanent residence, you can usually import your personal belongings duty and tax free. Any duty or tax due depends on where you came from, where you purchased the goods, how long you have owned them, and whether duty and tax has already been paid in another country. Note that there are no restrictions on the importation of goods purchased tax and duty paid in another European Union country, although there are limits for certain goods, e.g. beer and wine.

All ports and airports in Britain use a system of red and green 'channels'. Red means you have something to declare and green means that you have nothing to declare (i.e. no more than the customs allowances, no goods to sell and no prohibited or restricted goods). **If you're certain that you have nothing to declare, go through the 'green channel', otherwise go through the red channel.** Customs officers make random checks on people going through the green channel and there are stiff penalties for smuggling. If you're arriving by ferry with a motor vehicle, you can affix a green or red windscreen sticker to your windscreen, which helps customs officers direct you through customs.

A list of all items you're importing is useful, although the customs officer may still want to examine your belongings. If you need to pay duty or tax, it must be paid at the time the goods are brought into the country. Customs accept cash (sterling only); sterling travellers' cheques; personal cheques and eurocheques supported by a cheque guarantee card; Mastercard and Visa; and some ports and airports also accept debit cards. If you're unable to pay on the spot, customs will keep your belongings until you pay the sum due, which must be paid within the period noted on the back of your receipt. Postage or freight charges must be paid if you want the goods sent on to you. Your belongings may be imported up to six months prior to your arrival in Britain, but no more than one year after your arrival, after transferring your residence. They mustn't be sold, lent, hired out or otherwise disposed of in Britain within one year of their importation or of your arrival (whichever is later), without first obtaining customs authorisation.

If you're shipping your personal belongings (which includes anything for your family's personal use such as clothing, cameras, TV and stereo, furniture and other household goods) unaccompanied to Britain, you *must* complete (and sign) customs form C3, available from your shipping agent or HM Customs and Excise (Excise and Inland Customs Advice Centre, Southbank, Dorset House, Stamford Street, London SE1 9PY, ☎ 0207-928 3344). and attach a detailed packing list. If you employ an international removal company, they will handle the customs clearance and associated paperwork for you. Any items obtained in Britain or within the EU can be brought into Britain free of customs and excise duty or VAT, provided:

● any customs duty, excise duty or VAT was paid and not refunded when they were exported from Britain (or the EU in the case of customs duty);

● they were in your private possession and use in Britain before they were exported;

- they haven't been altered abroad, other than necessary repairs.

The personal belongings you're allowed to bring into Britain duty and tax free depend on your status, as shown below.

Visitors or Students Resident Abroad

If you're a **visitor**, you can bring your belongings to Britain free of duty and tax without declaring them to customs providing:

- all belongings are brought in with you and are for your use alone;
- they are kept in Britain for no longer than six months in a 12-month period;
- you don't sell, lend, hire out or otherwise dispose of them in Britain;
- they're exported either when you leave Britain or before they have been in Britain for more than six months, whichever occurs first.

If you're unable to export your belongings when you leave Britain you must apply to the nearest Customs and Excise Advice Centre for an extension.

People Moving or Returning to Britain

If you're moving or returning to Britain (including British subjects) from outside the EU, you can import your belongings free of duty and tax providing you have lived at least 12 months outside the EU. Your possessions must have been used for at least six months outside the EU before being imported. Tax and duty must have been paid on all items being imported (this isn't applicable to diplomats, members of officially recognised international organisations, members of NATO or British forces, and any civilian staff accompanying them). Articles must be for your personal use, must be declared to customs, and you mustn't sell, lend, hire out or otherwise dispose of them in Britain within 12 months, without customs authorisation.

People with Secondary Homes in Britain

If you're setting up a secondary home in Britain, you can bring normal household furnishings and equipment with you free of duty and tax if you usually live in another EU country. If you give up a secondary home outside the EU, there's no special relief from tax and duty for importing belongings from that home. If you have lived outside the EU for at least 12 months you can import household furnishings and equipment for setting up a secondary home free of duty, **but not free of VAT, which is levied at 17.5 per cent.**

To qualify, you must either own or be renting a home in Britain for a minimum of two years, and your household furnishings and equipment must have been owned and used for at least six months. Articles must be for your personal use, must be declared to customs, and you mustn't sell, lend, hire out or otherwise dispose of them in Britain within 24 months without customs authorisation. If goods are imported separately a customs form C33 must be completed.

POLICE REGISTRATION

Foreigners over 16 may be required to register at their local police station within seven days of arrival if they:

- are non-EEA and non-Commonwealth nationals;
- have limited permission to enter Britain;
- have been granted an extension of stay by the Home Office;
- have been allowed to work in Britain for more than three months;
- have been given leave to remain in Britain for longer than six months.

Registration also applies to the dependants over 16 of anyone required to register, including those who turn 16 while living in Britain. **When required, registration is indicated by the immigration stamp in your passport**. You must report to the police station nearest to where you're staying within seven days, even when you're staying in temporary accommodation. You will require your passport, two passport-size photographs (black and white or colour) and the fee.

You're required to carry your police registration certificate with you at all times, but not your passport. It's advisable to take your police registration certificate with you when travelling abroad, as this will make re-entry into Britain easier. It should be surrendered to the Immigration Officer if you're travelling abroad for longer than two months. Note that unlike many other Europeans, Britons aren't legally required to prove their identity on demand by a policeman or other official.

COUNCIL TAX REGISTRATION

All residents or temporary residents of Britain are required to register with their local authority or council for council tax purposes soon after arrival in Britain or after moving to a new home, either in the same council area or a new area. For information see page 121.

FINDING HELP

One of the biggest difficulties facing new arrivals in Britain is how and where to obtain help with essential everyday tasks such as buying a car, obtaining medical help and insurance requirements. How successful you are at finding help will depend on your employer (if applicable), the town or area where you live (e.g. those who live and work in the London area are much better served than those living in a rural village), your nationality and your English proficiency. Obtaining information isn't a problem, as there's a wealth of data available in Britain on every conceivable subject. The problem is sorting the truth from the half-truths, comparing the options available and making the right decisions. Much information naturally isn't intended for foreigners and their particular needs. You may find that your friends, colleagues and acquaintances can help, as they are often able to proffer advice based on their own experiences and mistakes. **But beware!** Although they mean well, you're likely to receive as much false and conflicting information as you are accurate (not always wrong, but possibly invalid for your particular area or situation).

Your local council offices, library, tourist information centre and Citizens Advice Bureau are excellent sources of reliable information on almost any subject. There are expatriate clubs and organisations in most areas, many of which provide detailed local information regarding all aspects of living in Britain, including housing costs, schools, names of doctors and dentists, shopping and much more. Clubs often produce data sheets, booklets and newsletters, and organise a variety of social events which may include day and evening classes ranging from cooking to English-language classes. One of the best ways to get to know local people is to join a social club, of which there are hundreds in all areas of Britain (look under 'Clubs and Associations' in your local Yellow Pages).

Embassies and consulates usually provide information bulletin boards (jobs, accommodation, travel) and keep lists of social clubs for their nationals, and many businesses (e.g. banks and building societies) produce books and leaflets containing valuable information for newcomers. Local libraries and bookshops usually have books about the local area.

CHECKLISTS

Before Arrival

The checklists on the following pages list tasks which you need (or may need) to complete before and after arrival in Britain, and when moving your home permanently to Britain.

- Check that your and your family's passports are valid!

- Obtain a visa, if necessary, for all your family members (see page 18). Obviously this *must* be done before arrival in Britain.

- Arrange health and travel insurance for yourself and your family (see pages 57 and 66 respectively). This is essential if you aren't covered by an international health insurance policy and won't be covered by the National Health Service (NHS).

- If you don't already have one, it's advisable to obtain an international credit or charge card, which may prove invaluable in Britain.

- If necessary, obtain an international driver's licence (see page 40).

- Open a bank account in Britain (see page 95) and transfer funds. You can open an account with many British banks while abroad, although it's best done in person in Britain.

- It's advisable to obtain some pounds sterling before arriving in Britain, which will save you having to queue to change money on arrival (and you will probably receive a better exchange rate).

- If you plan to become a permanent resident you may also need to do the following:

  - Arrange schooling for your children.

  - Organise the shipment of your personal and household effects.

  - Obtain as many credit references as possible, for example from banks, mortgage companies, credit card companies, credit agencies, companies with which you have had accounts, and references from professionals such as lawyers and accountants. These will help you establish a credit rating in Britain.

If you're planning to become a permanent resident, you should take all your family's official documents with you. These may include birth certificates; driving licences; marriage certificate, divorce papers or death certificate (if a widow or widower); educational diplomas and professional certificates; employment references and curriculum vitaes; school records and student ID cards; medical and dental records; bank account and credit card details; insurance policies (plus records of no-claims' allowances); and receipts for any valuables. You also need the documents necessary to obtain a residence permit plus certified copies, official translations and numerous passport-size photographs (students should take at least a dozen).

After Arrival

The following checklist contains a summary of the tasks to be completed after arrival in Britain (if not done before arrival):

- On arrival at a British airport, port or border post, have your visa cancelled and your passport stamped, as applicable.

- If you aren't taking a car with you, you may wish to rent (see page 48) or buy one locally. Note that it's practically impossible to get around in rural areas without a car.

- Open a bank account (see page 95) at a local bank and give the details to any companies that you plan to pay by direct debit or standing order (such as utility and property management companies).

- Arrange whatever insurance is necessary such as health, car and home.

- Contact offices and organisations to obtain local information (see page 219).

- It's worthwhile making courtesy calls on your neighbours within a few weeks of your arrival. This is particularly important in villages and rural areas if you want to be accepted and become part of the local community.

- If you plan to become a permanent resident in Britain, you may need to do the following within the next few weeks (if not done before your arrival):
  - apply for a residence permit;
  - apply for a National Health Service card from your local health authority;
  - apply for a British driving licence (see page 40);
  - register with a local doctor and dentist;
  - arrange schooling for your children.

Moving House

When moving permanently to Britain there are many things to be considered and a 'million' people to be informed. Even if you plan to spend only a few months a year in Britain, it may still be necessary to inform a number of people and companies in your home country. The checklists below are designed to make the task easier and help prevent an ulcer or a nervous breakdown (providing of course you don't leave everything to the last minute). See also **Moving House** on page 190 and **Moving In** on page 192.

- If you live in rented accommodation you will need to give your landlord notice (check your contract).

- If you own your home, arrange to sell or rent it (if applicable) well in advance of your move to Britain.

- Inform the following:

  - Your employer, e.g. give notice or arrange leave of absence.

  - Your local town hall or municipality. You may be entitled to a refund of your local taxes.

  - If it was necessary to register with the police in your home country, you should inform them that you're moving abroad.

  - Your electricity, gas, water and telephone companies. Contact companies well in advance, particularly if you need to get a deposit refunded.

  - Your insurance companies (for example health, car, home contents and private pension); banks, post office (if you have a post office account), stockbroker and other financial institutions; credit card, charge card and hire purchase companies; lawyer and accountant; and local businesses where you have accounts.

  - Your family doctor, dentist and other health practitioners. Health records should be transferred to your new doctor and dentist in Britain.

  - Your children's schools. Try to give a term's notice and obtain a copy of any relevant school reports or records from your children's schools.

  - All regular correspondents, subscriptions, social and sports clubs, professional and trade journals, and friends and relatives. Give them your new address and telephone number and arrange to have your mail redirected by the post office or a friend.

  - If you have a driving licence or car that you're taking to Britain, you will need to give the local vehicle registration office your new address abroad and, in some countries, return your car's registration plates.

- Return any library books or anything borrowed.

- Arrange shipment of your furniture and belongings by booking a shipping company well in advance (see page 190). International shipping companies usually provide a wealth of information and can advise on a wide range of matters concerning an international relocation. Find out the exact procedure for shipping your belongings to Britain from a British embassy or consulate.

- Arrange to sell anything you aren't taking with you (e.g. house, car and furniture). If you're selling a home or business, you should obtain expert legal advice as you may be able to save tax by establishing a trust or other legal vehicle. Note that if you own more than one property, you may need to pay capital gains tax on any profits from the sale of second and subsequent homes.

- If you have a car that you're exporting to Britain, you will need to complete the relevant paperwork in your home country and re-register it in Britain after your arrival. Contact a British embassy or consulate for information.

- Arrange inoculations, shipment and quarantine (if applicable) for any pets that you're taking with you (see page 75).

- You may qualify for a rebate on your tax and social security contributions. If you're leaving a country permanently and have been a member of a company or state pension scheme, you may be entitled to a refund or may be able to continue payments to qualify for a full (or larger) pension when you retire. Contact your company personnel office, local tax office or pension company for information.

- It's advisable to arrange health, dental and optical check-ups for your family before leaving your home country. Obtain a copy of all health records and a statement from your private health insurance company stating your present level of cover.

- Terminate any outstanding loan, lease or hire purchase contracts and pay all bills (allow plenty of time as some companies may be slow to respond).

- Check whether you're entitled to a rebate on your road tax, car and other insurance. Obtain a letter from your motor insurance company stating your no-claims' discount.

- Check whether you need an international driving licence or a translation of your foreign driving licence(s) for Britain. Note that some foreign residents are required to take a driving test in order to drive in Britain (see page 40).

- Give friends and business associates an address and telephone number where you can be contacted in Britain.

- If you will be living in Britain for an extended period (but not permanently), you may wish to give someone 'power of attorney' over your financial affairs in your home country so that they can act for you in your absence. This can be for a fixed period or open-ended and can be for a specific purpose only. **Note, however, that you should take expert legal advice before doing this!**

- Allow plenty of time to get to the airport, register your luggage, and clear security and immigration.

Have a nice journey!

APPENDICES

APPENDIX A: USEFUL ADDRESSES

London Embassies and Consulates

A selection of foreign embassies and High Commissions (Commonwealth countries) in London are listed below. Many countries also have consulates in other cities e.g. Belfast, Birmingham, Cardiff, Edinburgh, Glasgow and Manchester), which are listed in phone books. All London embassies are listed in *The London Diplomatic List* (The Stationery Office).

Argentina: 65 Brook Street, London W1M 5LD (☎ 0207-486 7073).
Australia: Australia House, Strand, London WC2B 4LA (☎ 0207-379 4334).
Austria: 18 Belgrave Mews West, London SW1X 8HU (☎ 0207-235 3731).
Bangladesh: 28 Queen's Gate, London SW7 5JA (☎ 0207-584 0081).
Belgium: 103-105 Eaton Square, London SW1W 9AB (☎ 0207-470 3700).
Brazil: 32 Green Street, Mayfair, London W1Y 4AT (☎ 0207-499 0877).
Brunei: 19/20 Belgrave Square, London SW1X 8PG (☎ 0207-581 0521).
Canada: Macdonald House, 1 Grosvenor Square, London W1X 0AB (☎ 0207-258 6600).
China: 49-51 Portland Place, London W1N 4JL (☎ 0207-636 9375).
Cyprus: 93 Park Street, London W1Y 4ET (☎ 0207-499 8272).
Czech Republic: 26-30 Kensington Palace Gardens, London W8 4QY (☎ 0207-243-1115).
Denmark: 55 Sloane Street, London SW1X 9SR (☎ 0207-333 0200).
Egypt: 12 Curzon Street, London W1Y 7FJ (☎ 0207-499 2401).
Finland: 32 Chesham Place, London SW1X 8HW (☎ 0207-838 6200).
France: 58 Knightsbridge, London SW1X 7JT (☎ 0207-201 1000).
Germany: 23 Belgrave Square, 1 Chesham Place, London SW1X 8PZ (☎ 0207-824 1300).
Greece: 1A Holland Park, London W11 3TP (☎ 0207-229 3850).
Hungary: 35 Eaton Place, London SW1X 8BY (☎ 0207-235 5218).
Iceland: 1 Eaton Terrace, London SW1W 8EY (☎ 0207-590 1100).
India: India House, Aldwych, London WC2B 4NA (☎ 0207-836 8484).
Iran: 16 Prince's Gate, London SW7 1PT (☎ 0207-225 3000).
Ireland: 17 Grosvenor Place, London SW1X 7HR (☎ 0207-235 2171).
Israel: 2 Palace Green, Kensington, London W8 4QB (☎ 0207-957 9500).
Italy: 14 Three Kings Yard, Davies Street, London W1Y 2EH (☎ 0207-312 2200).
Japan: 101-104 Piccadilly, London W1V 9FN (☎ 0207-465 6500).
Jordan: 6 Upper Phillimore Gardens, Kensington, London W8 7HB (☎ 0207-937 3685).
Korea: 60 Buckingham Gate, London SW1E 6AJ (☎ 0207-227 5500).
Kuwait: 2 Albert Gate, London SW1X 7JU (☎ 0207-590 3400).
Lebanon: 21 Kensington Palace Gardens, London W8 4QM (☎ 0207-229 7265).
Luxembourg: 27 Wilton Crescent, London SW1X 8SD (☎ 0207-235 6961).

Malaysia: 45 Belgrave Square, London SW1X 8QT (☎ 0207-235 8033).
Mexico: 42 Hertford Street, Mayfair, London W1Y 7TF (☎ 0207-499 8586).
Netherlands: 38 Hyde Park Gate, London SW7 5DP (☎ 0207-590 3200).
New Zealand: New Zealand House, Haymarket, London SW1Y 4TQ (☎ 0207-930 8422).
Norway: 25 Belgrave Square, London SW1X 8QD (☎ 0207-591 5500).
Oman: 167 Queen's Gate, London SW7 5HE (☎ 0207-225 0001).
Pakistan: 35-36 Lowndes Square, London SW1X 9JN (☎ 0207-664 9200).
Poland: 47 Portland Place, London W1N 3AG (☎ 0207-580 4324).
Portugal: 11 Belgrave Square, London SW1X 8PP (☎ 0207-235 5331).
Qatar: 1 South Audley Street, London W1Y 5DQ (☎ 0207-493 2200).
Romania: Arundel House, 4 Palace Green, London W8 4QD (☎ 0207-937 9666).
Russia: 13 Kensington Palace Gardens, London W8 4QX (☎ 0207-229 2666).
Saudi Arabia: 30 Charles Street, Mayfair, London W1X 7PM (☎ 0207-917 3000).
Singapore: 9 Wilton Crescent, London SW1X 8RW (☎ 0207-235 8315).
Slovak Republic: 25 Kensington Palace Gardens, London W8 4QY (☎ 0207-243 0803).
South Africa: South Africa House, Trafalgar Square, London WC2N 5DP (☎ 0207-451 7299).
Spain: 39 Chesham Place, London SW1X 8SB (☎ 0207-235 5555).
Sri Lanka: 13 Hyde Park Gardens, London W2 2LU (☎ 0207-262 1841).
Sweden: 11 Montagu Place, London W1H 2AL (☎ 0207-917 6400).
Switzerland: 16-18 Montagu Place, London W1H 2BQ (☎ 0207-616 6000).
Syria: 8 Belgrave Square, London SW1X 8PH (☎ 0207-245 9012).
Thailand: 29-30 Queen's Gate, London SW7 5JB (☎ 0207-589 2944).
Turkey: 43 Belgrave Square, London SW1X 8PA (☎ 0207-393 0202).
United Arab Emirates: 30 Prince's Gate, London SW7 1PT (☎ 0207-581 1281).
United States of America: 24 Grosvenor Square, London W1A 1AE (☎ 0207-499 9000).
Zimbabwe: Zimbabwe House, 429 Strand, London WC2R 0SA (☎ 0207-836 7755).

Publications

BBC Good Homes, Woodlands, 80 Wood Lane, London W12 0TT (☎ 0208-576 2391, Internet: www.goodhomes.beeb.com). Monthly magazine.
Build It, 2nd Floor, Tubs Hill House, London Road, Sevenoaks, Kent TN13 1BL (☎ 01732-452020). Monthly magazine for self-builders.
Country Homes & Interiors, IPC Magazines, King's Reach Tower, Stamford Street, London SE1 9LS (☎ 01622-778778, Internet: www.ipc.co.uk/pubs/counthom.htm). Monthly magazine.
Country Life, 21st Floor, Kings Reach Tower, Stamford Street, London SE1 9LS (☎ 01444-445555, Internet: www.countrylife.co.uk). Monthly magazine.
Country Living, 72 Broadwick Street, London W1V 2BP (☎ 0207-439 5000). Monthly magazine.

Home, SPL, Berwick House, 8-10 Knoll Rise, Orpington, Kent BT6 0PS (☎ 01689-887200). Monthly magazine.

Homebuilding & Renovating, Ascent Publishing Ltd., Freepost BM2127, Sugar Brook Court, Aston Road, Bromsgrove, Worcester B60 3BR (☎ 01527-834400, Internet: www.ihomes.co.uk). Monthly magazine.

HomeStyle, Essential Publishing Ltd., 1-4 Eaglegate, East Hill, Colchester, Essex CO1 2PR (☎ 01206-796911). Monthly magazine.

House Beautiful, 72 Broadwick Street, London W1V 2BP (☎ 0207-439 5000).

House & Garden, Vogue House, 1 Hanover Square, London W1R 0AD (☎ 0207-499 9080). Monthly magazine.

Hot Property, Loot House, 24/32 Kilburn High Road, London NW6 5TF (☎ 0207-372 7722). Weekly newspaper.

Ideal Home, Freepost CY1061, Haywards Heath, West Sussex RH16 3ZA (☎ 01622-778778). Monthly magazine.

International Homes, 3 St Johns Court, Moulsham Street, Chelmsford, Essex CM2 0JD (☎ 01245-358877, Internet: www.international-property.co.uk). Bi-monthly magazine for British and overseas property.

Livingetc, IPC Magazines, King's Reach Tower, Stamford Street, London SE1 9LS (☎ 01444-445555, Internet: www.livingetc.co.uk).

Loot, Loot House, 24/32 Kilburn High Road, London NW6 5TF (☎ 0207-328 1771, Internet: www.loot.com). Daily newspaper for buying/selling properties privately (and just about everything else) and property rentals. Loot publishes separate editions for the south-east, east midlands, west midlands, north-west and Northern Ireland.

Mortgage Matters, The Essential Guides Ltd., Devonshire House, Devonshire Road, Bexleyheath, Kent DA6 8DS (☎ 0208-301 6666). Monthly magazine.

Plotfinder, Freepost BM2127, 91-93 High Street, Bromsgrove, Hereford & Worcs. B61 7BR, ☎ 01527-834439). Magazine for self-builders seeking a building plot.

What House & Homefinder, 46 Oxford Street, London W1N 9FJ (☎ 0207-636 6050). Monthly magazine.

What Mortgage, Charterhouse Communications Group Ltd., Arnold House, 36-41 Holywell lane, London EC2A 3SF (☎ 0207-827 5451). Monthly magazine.

Which? magazine, Castlemead, Gascoyne Way, Hertford SG14 1LH (☎ 01992-822800, Internet: www.which.net). Monthly consumer magazine, available on subscription only.

Your Mortgage, Matching Hat Limited, 143 Charing Cross Road, London WC2H 0EE (☎ 0207-478 4600, Internet: www.yourmortgage.co.uk). Monthly magazine.

Your New Home & Mortgage Matters, The Essential Guides Ltd., Devonshire House, Devonshire Road, Bexleyheath, Kent DA6 8DS (☎ 0208-301 6666, Internet: www.yournewhome.co.uk). Quarterly magazine.

Propert Related Organisations

Architects and Surveyors Institute (ASI), St Mary House, 15 St Mary Street, Chppenham, Wilts. SN15 3WD (☎ 01249-444505).

Association of Building Engineers, Jubilee House, Billing Brook Road, Weston Favell, Northants. NN3 8NW (☎ 01604-404121, Internet: www.abe.org.uk).

Association of Plumbing and Heating Contractors (APHC), 14/15 Ensign House, Ensign Business Centre, Westwood Way, Coventry CV4 8JA (☎ 01203-470626).

Association of Relocation Agents (ARA), PO Box 189, Diss, Norfolk IP22 1PE (☎ 01359-251800, Internet: www.relocationagents.com).

Association of Residential Letting Agents (ARLA), 53-55 Woodside Road, Amersham, Bucks. HP6 6AA (☎ 01923-896555).

Auctioninfo Ltd., PO Box 62, Daventry NN11 3ZY (☎ 01327-361732, Internet: www.auctioninfo.co.uk).

British Association of Removers (BAR), 3 Churchill Court, 58 Station Road, North Harrow, Middx. HA2 7SA (☎ 0208-861 3331).

British Holiday and Homes Parks Association (BHHPA), Chichester House, 6 Pullman Court, Great Western Road, Gloucester GL1 3ND (☎ 01452-526911, Internet: www.parkhome.co.uk).

British Wood Preserving and Damp-Proofing Association, 6 The Office Village, 4 Romford Road, London E15 4EA (☎ 0208-519 2588).

Building Centre, 26 Store Street, London WC1E 7BT (☎ 0207-692 4000).

Building Societies Association/Council of Mortgage Lenders, 3 Saville Row, London W1X 1AF (☎ 071-437 0655/0075).

Building Societies Ombudsman, Grosvenor Gardens House, 35-37 Grosvenor Gardens, London SW1X 7AW (☎ 0207-931 0044).

The Construction Federation, 82 New Cavendish Street, London W1M 8AD (☎ 0207-580 5588).

Council for Licensed Conveyancers, 16 Glebe Road, Chelmsford, Essex CM1 1QG (☎ 01245-349599).

Electrical Contractors' Association (ECA), ECA House, 34 Palace Court, London W2 4HY (☎ 0207-229 1266, Internet: www.eca.co.uk).

English Heritage, 23 Saville Row, London W1X 1AB (☎ 0207-973 3000, Internet: www.english-heritage.org.uk).

Federation of Master Builders (FMB), Gordon Fisher House, 14/15 Great James Street, London WC1N 3DP (☎ 0207-242 7583, Internet: www.fmb.org.uk).

Guild of Master Craftsmen, 166 High Street, Lewes, East Sussex BN7 1XU (☎ 01273-478449).

Heating and Ventilation Contractors Association (HVCA), 34 Palace Court, London W2 4JG (☎ 0207-229 2488, Internet: www.hvca.org.uk).

HM Land Registry, Lincoln Inn Fields, London WC2A 3PH (☎ 0207-917 8888).

Homebuyer Events Limited, Mantle House, Broomhill Road, London SW18 4JQ (☎ 0208-877 3636, Internet: http://eu-net.com/homebuyer). Property exhibitions in Britain and abroad.

Homelands of England, 3 Bear Yard, Orange Street, Uppingham, Rutland LE15 9RB (☎ 01572-822111).

House Builders Federation, 56-64 Leonard Street, London EC2A 4JX (☎ 0207-608 5000, www.new-homes.co.uk/hbf).

Incorporated Society of Valuers and Auctioneers (ISVA), 3 Cadogan Gate, London SW1X 0AS (☎ 0207-235 2282, Internet: www.isva.co.uk).

Institute of Plumbing, 64 Station Lane, Hornchurch, Essex RM12 6NB (☎ 01708-472791, Internet: www.plumbers.org.uk).

Leasehold Enfranchisement Advisory Service, 6-8 Maddox Street, London W1R 9PN (☎ 0207-493 3116).

National Approval Council for Security Systems (NACOSS), Queensgate House, 14 Cookham Road, Maidenhead, Berks. SL6 8AJ (☎ 01628-37512, Internet: www.nacoss.org.uk).

National Association of Estate Agents (NAEA), Arbon House, 21 Jury Street, Warwick, Warks. CV34 4FH (☎ 01926-496800, Internet: www.naea.co.uk).

The National Home Improvement Council, 125 Kennington Road, London SE1 6SF (☎ 0207-582 7790).

National House Building Council (NHBC), Buildmark House, Chiltern Avenue, Amersham, Bucks. HP6 5AP (☎ 0800-688 788 or 01494-434477, Internet: www.nhbc.co.uk).

National Land Finding Agency, 10 Rood End House, Stortford Road, Great Dunmow, Essex CM6 1DA (☎ 01371-876875).

New Homes Marketing Board (NHMB), 82 New Cavendish Street, London W1M 8AD (☎ 0207-580 5588).

Ombudsman Scheme for Estate Agents (OEA), Beckett House, 4 Bridge Street, Salisbury, Wilts. SP1 2LX (☎ 01722-333306).

Royal Institute of British Architects (RIBA), Client's Advisory Service, 66 Portland Place, London W1N 4AD (☎ 0207-580 5533, Internet: www.riba.org.uk).

Royal Institute of Chartered Surveyors (RICS), 12 Great George Street, London SW1P 3AD (☎ 0207-222 7000, Internet: www.rics.org.uk).

Royal Town Planning Institute, 26 Portland Place, London W1N 4BE (☎ 0207-636 9107, Internet: rtpi.org.uk).

Timber & Brick Homes Information Council (TBHIC), Gable House, 40 High Street, Rickmansworth, Herts. WD3 1ES (☎ 01923-778136).

Worldwide Property Exhibitions Ltd., Unit 2, Mortlake High Street, London SW14 8SN (☎ 0208-876 1979, Internet: www.propertyshows.com).

Zurich Municipal, Galaxy House, 6 Southwood Crescent, Farnborough, Hants. GU14 0NJ (☎ 01252-522000).

Miscellaneous

The Association of British Insurers (ABI), 51 Gresham Street, London EC2V 7HQ (☎ 0207-600 3333).

British Tourist Authority (BTA), Thames Tower, Black's Road, Hammersmith, London W6 9EL (☎ 0208-846 9000, Internet: www.visitbritain.com).

Central Office of Information, Hercules Road, London SE1 7DU (☎ 0207-928 2345).

Confederation of British Industry (CBI), Centre Point, 103 New Oxford Street, London WC1A 1DU (☎ 0207-379 7400).

Consumers' Association, Castlemead, Gascoyne Way, Hertford SG14 1LH (☎ 01992-587773).

Good Housekeeping Institute, National Magazine House, 72 Broadwick Street, London W1V 2BP (☎ 0207-439 5000).

HM Customs and Excise, New King's Beam House, 22 Upper Ground, London SE1 9PJ (☎ 0207-620 1313).

Inland Revenue, Somerset House, Strand, London WC2R 1LB (☎ 0207-438 6622).

The Insurance Ombudsman Bureau (IOB), Citygate One, 135 Park Street, London SE1 9EA (☎ 0207-928 7600 or 0845-600 6666).

Law Society, 113 Chancery Lane, London WC2A 1PL (☎ 0207-242 1222).

Law Society of Scotland, 26 Drumsheugh Gardens, Edinburgh EH3 7YR (☎ 0132-226 7411, Internet: www.lawscot.org.uk).

Legal Services Ombudsman, 22 Oxford Court, Oxford Street, Manchester M2 2WQ (☎ 0161-236 9532).

National Association of Citizens Advice Bureaux, Myddelton House, 115-123 Pentonville Road, London N1 9LZ (☎ 0207-833 2181).

National Consumer Council, 20 Grosvenor Gardens, London SW1 0DH (☎ 0207-730 3469).

National Solicitors' Network, 156 Cromwell Road, London SW7 4EF (☎ 0207-244 6422, Internet: www.tnsn.com).

Office of Fair Trading, Field House, 15-25 Bream's Building, London EC4A 1PR (☎ 0207-242 2858).

APPENDIX B: FURTHER READING

The books listed below are just a small selection of the many books written for those planning to buy a home or live in Britain. Some titles may be out of print, but you may still be able to find a copy in a bookshop or library. Books prefixed with an asterisk (*) are recommended by the author.

Buying & Selling Property

Affordable Housing in London, C.M.E. Whitehead & D.T. Cross (Pergamon)

*The Best of British Architecture 1980-2000, Dennis Sharp & Noel Moffett (E&FN Spon)

*The Book of Lofts, Suzanne Rozensztroch & Daniel Stafford (Thames & Hudson)

'Build It' Guide to Building Your Own Timber Frame Home, Rosalind Renshaw (Dent)

*Building Services Thesaurus, G. A. Beale (BSRIA)

*Building Surveys of Residential Property (RICS Books)

Building Your Home, Susan Heal (HarperCollins)

*Building Your Own Home, Murray Armor & David Snell (Ebury Press)

Buying Bargains at Property Auctions, Howard Gooddie (Wyvern Crest)

*Buying a Home When Your Single, Donna G. Albrecht (John Wiley)

Buying a Home on the Internet, Robert Irwin (McGraw-Hill)

Buying a Manufactured Home, Kevin Burnside (Van der Plas)

Buying & Selling Your Home, Richard Newell (Longman Law)

*Buying Your Home with Other People, Dave Treanor (Shelter)

*Daily Mail Guide to Buying or Selling a House or Flat, Margaret Stone (Kogan Page)

*Essential Guide to Buy & Sell Your Home, Keith Carlton (Prentice Hall)

A Fine Restoration, Kitty Ray (Little, Brown)

*'Good Housekeeping' Consumer Guide: Buying and Selling Your Home (Ebury Press)

*Home Ownership: Buying and Maintaining, Nicholas Snelling LLB (Guild of Master Craftsmen)

*The Home Plans Book, Murray Armor & David Snell (Ebury Press)

Homes and Property on the Internet, Philip Harrison (International Briefings)

*Illustrated Dictionary of Building Terms, Tom Philbin (McGraw)

*Lofts, Marcus Field & Mark Irving (Laurence King)

The Mirror Guide to Buying a House, Diane Boliver (Prentice Hall)

New British Architecture (Architecture Foundation)

New London Property Guide: The Only Guide to Buying, Selling, Renting and Letting Homes in London, Carrie Seagrave (Mitchell Beazley)

*The New Natural House Book, David Pearson (Conran Octopus)

*Penguin Dictionary of Building, John S. Scott & James Maclean (Penguin)

Renovating Your Own Home: A Step-by-Step Guide, David Caldwell (Stoddart)

*Save Money Buying and Selling Your Home, David Orange (Foulsham)

A Straighforward Guide to Buying and Selling Your Own Home, Frances James (Straightforward Publishing)

A Straighforward Guide to Letting Property for Profit, G. J. Hardwick (Straightforward Publishing)

*The Sunday Times Personal Finance Guide to Your Home, Diana Wright (HarperCollins)

*Which? Way to Buy, Sell and Move House, Alison & Richard Barr (Which? Books)

*Your First Home: Buying, Renting, Selling and Decorating, Niki Chesworth (Kogan Page)

General

ABC of Gardening, Sally Maltby (Kyle Cathie)

*Collins Care & Repair of Period Houses, Albert Jackson & David Day (HarperCollins)

*Collins Complete Home Restoration Manual, Albert Jackson & David Day (HarperCollins)

Concise Dictionary of Interior Design, Frederic H. Jones (Crisp)

*Concise Encyclopedia of Interior Design, A. Allen Dizik (John Willey)

Creating Space, Elizabeth Wilhide (Pavillion)

Creative Interiors: A Complete Practical Course in Interior Design, Wren Loasby (David & Charles)

*Easy Living, Terence Conran (Conran Octopus)

The Family Home, Joanna Copestick (Conran Octopus)

*'Gardener's World' Practical Gardening Course, Geoff Hamilton (BBC)

*'Good Housekeeping' Traditional Garden Hints (Ebury Press)

Guide to Good Living in London (Francis Chichester)

*Home Extensions, Paul Hymers (New Holland)

*The Home Front Directory, Alison Reynolds & Sarah Childs-Carlile (BBC)

*Interior Design, Philip Graham (Prentice Hall)

Interior Design Ideas, Norman Sullivan (Lock Ward)

**Living and Working in London, Clare O'Brien (Survival Books)

**Living and Working in Britain, David Hampshire (Survival Books)

*London Living, Lisa Lovett Smith & Paul Duncan (Phoenix)

*One Space Living, Cynthia Inions (Ryland)

Rooms to Remember, Barbara & Rene Stoeltie (Francis Lincoln)

*Top Towns (Guiness Publishing)

APPENDIX C: WEIGHTS & MEASURES

Officially Britain converted to the international metric system of measurement on 1st October 1995, although many goods have been sold in metric sizes for many years. The use of imperial measures was officially due to finish at the end of 1999 but has been given a reprieve until end of 2009. Therefore you can expect to find goods sold in imperial (and other old British measures), metric or marked in both metric and British measures. Many foreigners will find the tables on the following pages useful. Some comparisons shown are approximate only, but are close enough for most everyday uses.

In addition to the variety of measurement systems used, clothes sizes often vary considerably depending on the manufacturer – as we all know only too well! Try all clothes on before buying and don't be afraid to return something if, when you try it on at home, you decide it doesn't fit or it's a different colour from what you imagined. The vast majority of British shops will exchange most goods or give a refund, unless they were purchased at a reduced price during a sale.

Women's clothes:

Continental	34	36	38	40	42	44	46	48	50	52
UK	8	10	12	14	16	18	20	22	24	26
USA	6	8	10	12	14	16	18	20	22	24

Pullovers: **Women's** **Mens**

	Women's						Mens					
Continental	40	42	44	46	48	50	44	46	48	50	52	54
UK	34	36	38	40	42	44	34	36	38	40	42	44
USA	34	36	38	40	42	44	Sm	Medium		large		exl

Note: sm = small, exl = extra large

Men's Shirts

Continental	36	37	38	39	40	41	42	43	44	46
UK/USA	14	14	15	15	16	16	17	17	18	

Men's Underwear

Continental	5	6	7	8	9	10
UK	34	36	38	40	42	44
USA	small	medium	large	extra large		

Children's Clothes

Continental	92	104	116	128	140	152
UK	16/18	20/22	24/26	28/30	32/34	36/38
USA	2	4	6	8	10	12

Children's Shoes

Continental	18	19	20	21	22	23	24	25	26	27	28
UK/USA	2	3	4	4	5	6	7	7	8	9	10

Continental	29	30	31	32	33	34	35	36	37	38
UK/USA	11	11	12	13	1	2	2	3	4	5

Shoes (Women's and Men's)

Continental	35	35	36	37	37	38	39	39	40	40
UK	2	3	3	4	4	5	5	6	6	7
USA	4	4	5	5	6	6	7	7	8	8

Continental	41	42	42	43	44	44
UK	7	8	8	9	9	10
USA	9	9	10	10	11	11

Weights:

Avoirdupois	Metric	Metric	Avoirdupois
1 oz	28.35 g	1 g	0.035 oz
1 pound	454 g	100 g	3.5 oz
1 cwt	50.8 kg	250 g	9 oz
1 ton	1,016 kg	1 kg	2.2 pounds
1 tonne	2,205 pounds		

Note: g = gramme, kg = kilogramme

Length:

British/US	Metric	Metric	British/US
1 inch =	2.54 cm	1 cm =	0.39 inch
1 foot =	30.48 cm	1 m =	3.28 feet
1 yard =	91.44 cm	1 km =	0.62 mile
1 mile =	1.6 km	8 km =	5 miles

Note: cm = centimetre, m = metre, km = kilometre

Capacity:

Imperial	Metric	Metric	Imperial
1 pint (USA)	0.47 l	1 l	1.76 UK pints
1 pint (UK)	0.568 l	1 l	0.265 US gallons
1 gallon (USA)	3.78 l	1 l	0.22 UK gallons
1 gallon (UK)	4.54 l	1 l	35.211 fluid oz

Note: l = litre

Temperature:

Celsius	Fahrenheit	
0	32	freezing point of water
5	41	
10	50	
15	59	
20	68	
25	77	
30	86	
35	95	
40	104	

The Boiling point of water is 100° Celsius, 212° Fahrenheit.

Oven temperature:

Gas	Electric	
	°F	°C
–	225-250	110-120
1	275	140
2	300	150
3	325	160
4	350	180
5	375	190
6	400	200
7	425	220
8	450	230
9	475	240

For a quick conversion, the Celsius temperature is approximately half the Fahrenheit temperature.

Temperature Conversion:

Celsius to Fahrenheit: multiply by 9, divide by 5 and add 32.
Fahrenheit to Celsius: subtract 32, multiply by 5 and divide by 9.

Body Temperature:

Normal body temperature (if you're alive and well) is 98.4° Fahrenheit, which equals 37° Celsius.

APPENDIX D: GLOSSARY

Acceptance: Agreeing to accept an *offer* on a property, which constitutes a contract.

Acceptance Fee: See *Mortgage Application* Fee.

Advance: The *mortgage* loan. Also called the capital or principal sum.

Amortisation: The gradual process of systematically reducing debt in equal payments (as in a *mortgage*) comprising both *principal* and interest, until the debt is paid in full.

Annuity Mortgage: A *mortgage* in which both the *capital* and the interest are repaid over a fixed or variable *term*. Also called a *Repayment Mortgage*.

APR (Annual Percentage Rate): Everything financed in a loan package (interest, loan fees and other charges), expressed as an annual percentage (APR) of the loan amount. The APR must be quoted when a mortgage rate is advertised.

Arrangement Fee: See *Mortgage Application Fee.*

Assignment: The transfer of ownership of some kinds of property to another person, such as a lease or an insurance policy that's protecting a loan.

Balance Outstanding: The amount of a loan owed at any given time.

BAR: The British Association of Removers.

Base Rate: The interest rate set by the Bank of England which is used as the basis for setting mortgage and savings rates by banks and building societies.

Bedsit: A studio flat with one room for living and sleeping.

Bridging Loan: A short-term loan designed to allow you to buy a new home before you have sold your existing home.

Broker: A more or less independent agency through which you can seek the most appropriate or economical financial service or product (e.g. insurance, *mortgage*).

Buildings insurance: An insurance policy that protects homeowners from damage to their home. Mandatory when a property has a *mortgage*.

Bungalow: A single-storey detached or semi-detached house.

Capped Rate Mortgage: A *variable rate mortgage* with a maximum interest rate, either for a set period of months or years, annually or over the whole *term* of the mortgage.

Capital: The mortgage loan (also *advance* or *principal*).

Capital Gains Tax (CGT): Tax payable on the profits made from the sale of certain assets, including second homes in Britain.

Capital Reducing Mortgage: A *repayment mortgage.*

Capped Rate Mortgage: A *variable rate mortgage* with a *cap*, usually for a fixed number of years or until a specified date.

Cashback: A payment you may receive when you take out a mortgage, which can be a fixed amount or a percentage of the mortgage sum.

CH: Central heating (fitted in all modern homes). GCH is gas central heating.

Charge: Any right or interest, subject to which freehold or leasehold property may be held, especially a *mortgage*.

Cloakroom: A small room or closet with a toilet and hand basin (called a half bathroom in some countries).

Closing: The final procedure in a property transaction when documents are executed and recorded, funds are disbursed and the *title* transferred from the *vendor* to the buyer. Also called *completion* or settlement.

Closing Costs: Costs the buyer must pay at the time of *closing* in addition to the *deposit*, including solicitor's fees, *mortgage indemnity guarantee* fee and *buildings insurance*.

Closing Statement: A statement prepared by a solicitor detailing the closing costs for both the seller and the buyer.

CML: Council of Mortgage Lenders.

Collar: A collar is the term used when a lenders sets a rate below which interest rates won't fall, regardless of how low the base rate falls.

Collateral: Anything that's pledged as *security* against the repayment of a loan, such as the *title deeds* of a property.

Common Elements: The parts of a property (e.g. apartment or flat) that aren't individually owned.

Completion: The final legal transfer of ownership of a property. See also *closing*.

Completion Date: The date on which a transaction is finalised, the money is paid, *deeds* are handed over and the keys are given to the new owner.

Conditions of Sale: The standard terms governing the rights and duties of both parties as laid down in the sales contract.

Contents Insurance: An insurance policy protecting a homeowner from loss or damage to his personal belongings or home contents.

Contract: The agreement to sell and buy a property, which isn't binding in England and Wales until the *exchange of contracts*.

Conveyance: The act of transferring the *title* of a property and also the document (such as a *deed*) used to transfer ownership.

Conveyancer: The person (e.g. a solicitor or licensed conveyancer) who undertakes *conveyance*.

Conveyancing: The legal and administrative process involved in transferring the ownership of land and buildings from one person to another.

Cottage: Traditionally a pretty, quaint house in the country, perhaps with a thatched roof (although the name is often stretched nowadays to encompass almost anything except a flat). May be detached or terraced.

County Development Plan: A plan drawn up by a county council for the use of land over a period of five years. See also *Zoning*.

Covenant: A promise in a *deed* to undertake (if covenant is positive) or abstain from (if covenant is negative) doing specified things.

Current Account Loan: A *mortgage* that's combined with a current account and credit card and offers all or some of the advantages of a *flexible mortgage*.

Deed: A written legal document that conveys *title* to property and provides evidence of ownership. Also called *title deeds*.

Deed of Assignment: A *deed* used to transfer *leasehold unregistered land*.

Deed of Mortgage: A *deed* used to transfer *title* in a property to the *mortgagee*.

Deed of Transfer: A *deed* used to transfer *registered land*.

Deed Restrictions: A clause in a *deed* that restricts the use of land.

Deferred Start Mortgage: A type of *mortgage* whereby no repayments are made for the first one to three months of the *term*. Only available with *repayment mortgage*.

Deposit: The amount that needs to be paid in cash in order to obtain a *mortgage*, e.g. if you have an 80 per cent mortgage, you must make a 20 per cent deposit. It also usual to pay a deposit (e.g. 10 per cent) on the *exchange of contracts*.

Detached house: A single-family house that stands alone, usually with its own garden (possibly front and rear) and garage.

Differentials: When a lender operates a 'banding system', under which extra interest is charged on larger loans, the 'bands' are known as differentials.

Disbursements: Costs such as *stamp duty*, *land registry* and *search* fees that are payable to the *conveyancer* when a sale is completed.

Discounted Rate: A guaranteed reduction in the standard variable *mortgage* rate, usually over an agreed term.

Early Redemption: Paying off a loan before the end of the *mortgage term*. There's usually a penalty charge for doing this.

Earnest Money: Funds paid with an offer to show good faith to complete a purchase.

Easement: The interest, privilege or right that a party has in the land of another party, e.g. a right of way.

Encumbrance: Any right or interest in a property that affects its value such as outstanding loans, unpaid taxes, *easements* and *deed* restrictions.

Endowment Insurance: Life insurance policy incorporating investments that pays out a specified sum (or more) on a specified date (or an agreed sum in life insurance if the holder dies before the end of the term).

Endowment Mortgage: A type of *mortgage* loan on which only interest is paid. Repayments are combined with savings through a life assurance policy. By the end of the mortgage *term*, the value of the endowment policy should have grown sufficiently to repay the mortgage and (hopefully) leave the *mortgagor* with a surplus. See also *interest only*.

Equity: The amount of value an owner has in a property after the deductions of any outstanding *liens* such as a *mortgage*, e.g. if a property is valued at £100,000 and the amount outstanding on a mortgage is £50,000, the owner has £50,000 equity.

Equity Loan: A second *mortgage* where the owner borrows against his *equity* in a property.

Escrow: A procedure in which documents of cash and property are put in the care of a third party, other than the buyer or seller, pending completion of agreed conditions and terms in sales contracts.

Estate Agent: A person or company selling property on commission. Called real estate agents, realtors and brokers in some countries (e.g. the USA).

Exchange of Contracts: The process of making an agreement to buy and sell a house legally binding.

Fixed-Rate Mortgage: A *mortgage* with a fixed *interest rate* for an agreed period of months, years or the whole term.

Fixtures & Fittings (F&F): Generally a fixture is something attached to a property as part of it, e.g. the bathroom fittings or the kitchen units. A fitting generally usually refers to something that can be removed, e.g. carpets and curtains.

Flat: An apartment or condominium, usually on one floor. A block of flats is an apartment building, high-rise tower block or possibly a large house that has been converted into flats.

Flexible Month Mortgage: A type of *mortgage* whereby no repayments are made in one or two months of a year.

Flexible Mortgage: A mortgage that offers maximum flexibility by allowing over payments, payment holidays, a cheque book and borrow back facilities. See also *Current Account Loan.*

Foreclosure: Legal proceedings instigated by a lender to deprive a person of ownership rights when *mortgage* payments haven't been maintained. Also called repossession.

Freehold: The highest interest in a property that can be held by an individual. In theory the owner is free to do with the property what he wishes, although in practice various restrictions (e.g. *planning permission*) are placed on this right.

Freeholder: One who owns the *freehold* of a property.

FSBO: An abbreviation for 'For Sale By Owner', when a home is being sold privately without the assistance of an *estate agent.*

Funding Fee: A fee incurred by the *mortgagor* when switching from a *fixed rate* to a *variable rate mortgage* before the end of the fixed rate period.

Gazumping: When a *vendor* accepts a higher offer after a previous offer has already been accepted (but contracts haven't been exchanged). The person who made the previous offer is said to have been gazumped.

Gazundering: The term for when a buyer lowers the price agreed just before the planned exchange of contracts in an attempt to force the vendor to reduce the price.

Ground Rent: An annual fee payable by the *leaseholder* of an apartment to the *freeholder.*

Homebuyer's Report: A survey (inspection) of a property which is more detailed than a *valuation*, but less comprehensive than a *structural survey.*

Individual Savings Account (ISA): A tax-free savings scheme.

Individual Savings Account (ISA) mortgage: An interest-only, investment *mortgage* linked to an *ISA.*

Interest Only: Your monthly payments to your lender comprise interest only and you don't pay off the *mortgage* during the life of the loan. This is accomplished by the proceeds from a savings policy such as an endowment. See also *endowment mortgage.*

Interest Rate: A percentage that when multiplied by the *principal* determines the amount of money that the *principal* earns over a period of time (usually one year).

Investment-linked Mortgage: A *mortgage* linked to an *Individual Savings Account (ISA)* or *Personal Equity Plan (PEP)* or other tax-free savings scheme.

ISVA: The Incorporated Society of Valuers and Auctioneers.

Joint Tenancy: Property ownership by two (e.g. a married couple) or more persons with an undivided interest and the right of survivorship, where if one owner dies the property automatically passes to the joint owner(s).

Land Certificate: A certificate from the *Land Registry* to say that you own a property.

(HM) Land Registry: A government office where the ownership of all property in England and Wales (with registered *titles*) is registered. It has its head office in London and district offices in various other towns.

Lease: Permission to own or rent property for a limited period.

Leasehold: Ownership of property but not the land on which it stands. Leasehold ownership is restricted to a number of years (e.g. 99 to 999) and creates a landlord-tenant relationship between the *lessor* (*freeholder*) and the *lessee*.

Leaseholder: One who owns a *leasehold* property.

Legal Charge: To all intents and purposes, the same as a mortgage.

Lessee: The person to whom a *lease* is granted.

Lessor: The person who grants a *lease*.

Licensed Conveyancer: A person licensed to perform property *conveyancing*.

Lien: A charge against property making it *security* for a debt such as a *mortgage*.

Loan-to-Value (LTV): The size of the *mortgage* as a percentage of the value of the property or the price to be paid. An £80,000 mortgage on a house worth £100,000 is equal to an LTV of 80 per cent.

Local Search: An application made to the local authority for a certificate providing information about a property and the surrounding area.

Lock-In: A *mortgage* with a *fixed*, *discounted* or *capped rate*, where the borrower is locked-in to the standard *variable rate* for a number of years during which a high *redemption penalty* applies,

Low Start Mortgage: A *mortgage* where premiums start low and increase by a certain percentage each year until the full premium level is reached.

Maisonette: Part of a house or apartment block forming separate living accommodation, usually on two floors with its own outside entrance.

Management Company: A company, such as an estate agent, that manages a property that's let. Also a company that manages a leasehold property.

Market Value: The current value of a property compared with similar properties, generally accepted to be the highest price a buyer will pay and the lowest price a vendor will accept.

Mews house: A house that's converted from old stables or servants' lodgings (usually 17th to 19th century) and is the town equivalent of a genuine cottage..

MIG: See *Mortgage Indemnity Guarantee*.

MIRAS: See *Mortgage Interest Relief at Source*.

Missives: In Scotland, the letters that are exchanged between solicitors agreeing acceptance of an offer on a property. Once the missives have been exchanged the deal is legally binding.

Mobile (park) home: A prefabricated timber-framed home that can be moved to a new site, although most are permanently located on a 'home park'.

Mortgage: A loan for which a house is the security or collateral. A written instrument that creates a *lien* against a property as *security* against the repayment of a loan. Gives the lender the right to sell the property if payments aren't made.

Mortgage Application Fee: A fee charged by the lender for evaluating, preparing and submitting a proposed *mortgage* loan. Also called an acceptance or arrangement fee.

Mortgage Deed: The document containing the conditions of a loan secured on a property. Also called a *legal charge*.

Mortgage Indemnity Guarantee (MIG): A compulsory insurance policy that's required by a lender for a loan that's greater than a certain percentage of the value of a property, e.g. 75 or 80 per cent. Also known as mortgage guarantee insurance (MGI).

Mortgage Interest Relief at Source (MIRAS): Tax relief allowed on mortgage interest payments at your highest rate of tax. MIRAS was restricted to 10 per cent on the first £30,000 of a *mortgage* for the 1999-2000 tax year. MIRAS will be abolished on 6th April 2000.

Mortgage Protection Policy: Insurance that pays a *mortgage* and protects against *foreclosure* in the event of job loss, major accident, illness or death.

Mortgagee: The company or organisation that lends the money for a *mortgage*.

Mortgagor: The person taking out a *mortgage*.

Multiple Agency: An agreement whereby a number of *estate agents* attempt to sell a given property.

NAEA: The National Association of Estate Agents.

Negative Equity: The situation when the market value of a property is less than the mortgage outstanding on it.

NHBC: The National Home Building Council which provides warranties for new homes.

Non-Status Mortgage: A loan where the borrower isn't required to provide employment or income references.

Offer: A bid to buy a property at a specified price.

Park Home: See *mobile home*.

Pension Mortgage: A type of *mortgage* in which the repayments cover only the interest on the loan, while separate payments are made into a personal pension plan. They are usually available only to those who are self-employed or whose employer doesn't offer an occupational pension scheme.

Period property: A loosely used term for a property usually built before 1900 and named after the period in which it was built, e.g. Elizabethan, Georgian or Victorian.

Personal Equity Plan (PEP): A tax-free savings scheme.

Planning Permission: Permission granted by a local planning authority to erect or alter a building.

Power of Attorney: Authority to act on behalf of another.

Preliminary Enquiries: The questions asked about a property before *exchange of contracts*.

Premium: Payment in respect of a *mortgage* or insurance policy. Can be a one-off payment or periodical.

Principal: The amount of money borrowed to buy a property and the amount still owed.

Principal and Interest Payment: A periodic (usually monthly) *mortgage* repayment that includes interest charges plus an amount applied to the *amortisation* of the *principal* balance.

Private Treaty Sale: A method of selling a property by agreement between the vendor and the purchaser, either directly or through an *estate agent*.

Provisional Loan Approval: A service offered by lenders whereby they provide provisional approval of a loan (for a maximum sum) thus establishing a buyer's price range, strengthening his buying position and shortening the loan approval period.

Redemption: Full repayment of a *mortgage* loan.

Redemption Fee/Penalty: A fee or penalty incurred by the *mortgagor* when redeeming a loan (or part of it) before the end of the *term*.

Refinance: To replace an old mortgage with a new one, either to reduce the *interest rate*, secure better terms or increase the amount borrowed.

Registration Fee: A fee payable by a purchaser to have *title deeds* registered at the *Land Registry*.

Registered Land: Land, the title to which is recorded at the *Land Registry*.

Remortgage: To take out an additional *mortgage* against a property.

Repayment Mortgage: A loan on which part of the capital plus interest is paid back throughout the loan *term*.

Repossession: See *Foreclosure*.

RIBA: The Royal Institute of British Architects.

RICS: The Royal Institute of Chartered Surveyors.

Sealing Fee: A charge made by lenders when you repay a *mortgage*.

Searches: Enquiries made by or on behalf of a purchaser to ensure proper *title* to a property.

Security: Assets such as house *deeds* pledged in support of a loan.

Semi-detached house: A detached building containing two separate homes joined in the middle by a common wall.

Settlement: See *Closing*.

Settlement Day: In Scotland, the point at which the legal ownership of a property transfers from seller to buyer.

Sole Agency: An agreement giving an *estate agent* the exclusive right to sell a property and to collect a commission if the property is sold by anyone (including the owner) during the term of the agreement.

Solicitor: A legal professional similar to a lawyer who traditionally carried out all property conveyancing (now also done by licensed conveyancers).

Stakeholder: One who holds a deposit as an intermediary between the buyer and seller, pending completion.

Stamp Duty: A tax payable by the buyer when a property is purchased for over £60,000.

Stately home: A grand country mansion or estate, usually a few centuries old, many of which are owned by Britain's oldest titled families and open to the public.

Structural Survey: The most in-depth survey of a property usually encompassing all structures and systems.

'Subject to Contract': The words that should be contained in every letter to a seller (or his agent or *solicitor*) before contracts are exchanged.

Superior: In Scotland, the original owner of feudal tenure who's able to impose conditions on the use of the land or property in perpetuity.

Survey (or *Structural Survey*): A thorough examination of the condition of a property before purchase, performed by a professional surveyor.

Tenants in Common: Two or more people who hold property in such a way that, when one dies, his or her share doesn't pass automatically to the survivor but under his will or intestacy.

Tenancy in Common: A form of ownership in which two or more persons buy a property jointly, but with no right of survivorship. Owners are free to will their share to anyone they choose, which is the main difference between this and *joint tenancy*. Often used by friends or relatives buying together.

Tenure: Or 'feudal tenure'. The ownership of property in Scotland.

Term (of a mortgage): The number of years over which a *mortgage* is to be repaid, which can be either fixed (e.g. 15 or 25 years) or variable according to the rate of repayment.

Terraced house: A houses built in a row of three or more usually two to five storeys high.

Time is of the Essence: A legal term whereby if either party is late for completion, the contract can be enforced only by serving a notice to complete setting a time limit to finalise the transaction. This step has serious legal consequences.

Title: The right of ownership of property.

Title Deeds: The documents that confer ownership of land or property.

Title Number: The unique number allocated to each property by the *land registry*.

Title Search: A professional scrutiny of public records to establish the chain of ownership of a property and record any outstanding *liens*, *mortgage*, *encumbrances* or other factors that may restrict clear *title*.

Top-Up Mortgage: An additional loan from another lender when the first lender doesn't provide sufficient finance to buy a house.

Townhouse: Similar to a terraced house but more modern and larger, often with an integral garage.

Tracker Mortgage: A home loan where the *interest rate* 'tracks' the *base rate* and rises and falls in line with it.

TransAction Period: A procedure drawn up by the Law Society intended to speed up the process of preparing the contract.

Transfer: The *land registry* document transferring the ownership of property from the seller to the buyer.

Under Offer: The term used when an offer on a property has been accepted. This isn't legally binding in England and Wales, where sellers can still accept a higher offer.

Unregistered Land: Land which isn't recorded in the *land registry*.

Upset price: In Scotland, the advertised price for a property. Offers should be made above this advertised price.

Valuation: The professional examination of a property to determine its *market value*.

Variable-Rate Mortgage: A *mortgage* loan whose *interest rate* changes in accordance with prevailing interest rates.

Vendor: The person selling a property.

Zoning: The procedure that classifies land and property according to usage, e.g. residential, commercial or industrial, in accordance with a *county development plan*.

INDEX

K

L

M

N

O

P

Q

SUGGESTIONS

Please write to us with any comments or suggestions you have regarding the contents of this book (preferably complimentary!). We are particularly interested in proposals for improvements that can be included in future editions. For example did you find any important subjects were omitted or weren't covered in sufficient detail? What difficulties or obstacles have you encountered which aren't covered here? What other subjects would you like to see included?

If your suggestions are used in the next edition of *Buying a Home in Britain*, you will receive a free copy of the Survival Book of your choice as a token of our appreciation.

NAME: _____

ADDRESS: _____

_____

_____

Send to: Survival Books, PO Box 146, Wetherby, West Yorks. LS23 6XZ, United Kingdom.

My suggestions are as follows (please use additional pages if necessary):

LIVING AND WORKING IN LONDON

Living and Working in London is essential reading for anyone planning to spend some time there including retirees, visitors, business people, migrants, students and even extraterrestrials! It's packed with over 300 pages of important and useful information designed to help you **avoid costly mistakes and save both time and money.** Topics covered include how to:

- get acquainted with London
- avoid and overcome problems on arrival
- choose the best area in which to live
- find a job with a good salary
- find a home to rent or buy
- obtain the best health treatment
- stretch your pounds further
- find the best education and schools
- make the best use of public transport
- survive motoring in London
- find the best shopping bargains
- make the most of your leisure time
- do numerous other things not listed above

Living and Working in London is the most comprehensive and up-to-date source of practical information available about everyday life in London. It isn't, however, a boring text book, but an interesting and entertaining guide written in a highly readable style.

Buy this book and discover what it's <u>really</u> like to live and work in London.

Order your copies today by phone, fax, mail or e-mail from: Survival Books, PO Box 146, Wetherby, West Yorks. LS23 6XZ, United Kingdom (☎/fax: +44-1937-843523, e-mail: orders@survivalbooks. net, Internet: survivalbooks.net).

LIVING AND WORKING IN BRITAIN

Living and Working in Britain is essential reading for anyone planning to spend some time there including holiday-home owners, retirees, visitors, business people, migrants, students and even extraterrestrials! It's packed with over 500 pages of important and useful information designed to help you **avoid costly mistakes and save both time and money.** Topics covered include how to:

- find a job with a good salary & conditions
- obtain a residence permit
- avoid and overcome problems
- find your dream home
- get the best education for your family
- make the best use of public transport
- endure motoring in Britain
- obtain the best health treatment
- stretch your pounds further
- make the most of your leisure time
- enjoy the British sporting life
- find the best shopping bargains
- insure yourself against most eventualities
- use post office and telephone services
- do numerous other things not listed above

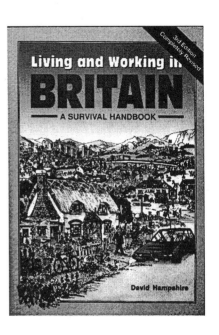

Living and Working in Britain is the most comprehensive and up-to-date source of practical information available about everyday life in Britain. It isn't, however, a boring text book, but an interesting and entertaining guide written in a highly readable style.

Buy this book and discover what it's <u>really</u> like to live and work in Britain.

Order your copies today by phone, fax, mail or e-mail from: Survival Books, PO Box 146, Wetherby, West Yorks. LS23 6XZ, United Kingdom (☎/fax: +44-1937-843523, e-mail: orders@survivalbooks. net, Internet: survivalbooks.net).

ORDER FORM – ALIEN'S/BUYING A HOME SERIES

Qty.	Title	Price (incl. p&p)*			Total
		UK	Europe	World	
	The Alien's Guide to America	Winter 2000-01			
	The Alien's Guide to Britain	Spring 2000			
	The Alien's Guide to France	£5.95	£6.95	£8.45	
	Buying a Home in Abroad	£11.45	£12.95	£14.95	
	Buying a Home in Britain	£11.45	£12.95	£14.95	
	Buying a Home in Florida	£11.45	£12.95	£14.95	
	Buying a Home in France	£11.45	£12.95	£14.95	
	Buying a Home in Greece/Cyprus	Spring 2000			
	Buying a Home in Ireland	£11.45	£12.95	£14.95	
	Buying a Home in Italy	£11.45	£12.95	£14.95	
	Buying a Home in Portugal	£11.45	£12.95	£14.95	
	Buying a Home in Spain	£11.45	£12.95	£14.95	
	Rioja and its Wines	Spring 2000			
				Total	

Order your copies today by phone, fax, mail or e-mail from: Survival Books, PO Box 146, Wetherby, West Yorks. LS23 6XZ, United Kingdom (tel./fax: +44-1937-843523, e-mail: orders@survivalbooks.net, Internet: survivalbooks.net). If you aren't entirely satisfied, simply return them to us within 14 days for a full and unconditional refund.

Cheque enclosed/please charge my Delta/Mastercard/Switch/Visa* card

Card No. __ __ __ __   __ __ __ __   __ __ __ __   __ __ __ __

Expiry date _____   **Issue number (Switch only)** _____

Signature _____   **Tel. No.** _____

NAME _____

ADDRESS _____

_____

* Delete as applicable (prices include postage – airmail for Europe/World)

ORDER FORM – LIVING AND WORKING SERIES

Qty.	Title	Price (incl. p&p)*			Total
		UK	Europe	World	
	Living & Working in Abroad	Winter 2000-01			
	Living & Working in America	£14.95	£16.95	£20.45	
	Living & Working in Australia	£14.95	£16.95	£20.45	
	Living & Working in Britain	£14.95	£16.95	£20.45	
	Living & Working in Canada	£14.95	£16.95	£20.45	
	Living & Working in France	£14.95	£16.95	£20.45	
	Living & Working in Germany	Summer 2000			
	Living & Working in Italy	Autumn 2000			
	Living & Working in London	£11.45	£12.95	£14.95	
	Living & Working in N. Zealand	£14.95	£16.95	£20.45	
	Living & Working in Spain	£14.95	£16.95	£20.45	
	Living & Working in Switzerland	£14.95	£16.95	£20.45	

Order your copies today by phone, fax, mail or e-mail from: Survival Books, PO Box 146, Wetherby, West Yorks. LS23 6XZ, United Kingdom (tel./fax: +44-1937-843523, e-mail: orders@survivalbooks.net, Internet: survivalbooks.net). If you aren't entirely satisfied, simply return them to us within 14 days for a full and unconditional refund.

Cheque enclosed/please charge my Delta/Mastercard/Switch/Visa* card

Card No. _ _ _ _   _ _ _ _   _ _ _ _   _ _ _ _

Expiry date _____ **Issue number (Switch only)** _____

Signature _____ **Tel. No.** _____

NAME _____

ADDRESS _____

_____

* Delete as applicable (prices include postage – airmail for Europe/World)